The 100
Greatest Athletes
of All Time

The 100 Greatest Athletes of All Time

A Sports Editor's Personal Ranking

Bert Randolph Sugar

A Citadel Press Book

Published by Carol Publishing Group

Carol Publishing Group Edition, 1996

A Citadel Press Book
Published by Carol Publishing Group
Citadel Press is a registered trademark of Carol Communications, Inc.

Editorial Offices: 600 Madison Avenue, New York, N.Y. 10022
Sales and Distribution Offices: 120 Enterprise Avenue, Secaucus,
    N.J. 07094
In Canada: Canadian Manda Group, One Atlantic Avenue, Suite 105,
    Toronto, Ontario M6K 3E7

Queries regarding rights and permissions should be addressed to:
Carol Publishing Group, 600 Madison Avenue, New York, N.Y. 10022

Carol Publishing Group books are available at special discounts
for bulk purchases, sales promotions, fund-raising, or
educational purposes. Special editions can also be created to
specifications. For details contact: Special Sales Department,
Carol Publishing Group, 120 Enterprise Avenue, Secaucus, N.J. 07094

Design by Ardashes Hamparian

Manufactured in the United States of America
10 9 8 7 6 5 4 3 2

Library of Congress Cataloging-in-Publication Data

Sugar, Bert Randolph.
    The 100 greatest athletes of all time : a sports editor's
personal ranking / by Bert Randolph Sugar.
        p.   cm.
    "A Citadel Press Book."
    ISBN 0-8065-1614-3
    1. Athletes—Biography. I. Title. II. Title : One hundred
greatest athletes of all time.
GV697.A 1S814   1995
796'.092'2—dc20
    [B]   94–44303
                                                      CIP

To the 100 greats included here—and the thousands more I couldn't "people-horn" in—who over the years, were our real heroes. And to *my* real hero, my bride, Suzy, who blocked out all distractions and passed off my two years of total immersion in this project as normal behavior.

CONTENTS

INTRODUCTION

On the face of it, the assignment sounded simple enough. Put together a book on that sparsely populated island known as the greatest athletes of all time. On one hundred of its inhabitants, in order. My order.

Despite the fact that the amount of money that went with the assignment was somewhat akin to what an ant with a double hernia could pick up and make off with, it sounded tailor-made for me. After all, I reasoned, hadn't I already written two books incorporating that testy adjective *greatest* in their titles, as in *Baseball's Fifty Greatest Games* and *The 100 Greatest Boxers of All Time?* And hadn't one writer, Ken Picking of *USA Today,* once written that I had "probably thought about numbering the greatest pastrami sandwiches ever eaten, number one through fifty"?

And because publisher Steve Schragis had proposed it at Runyon's, an East Side saloon, the idea appealed to me. And to my inner sense of irony. After all, what was the book but a glorified bar bet?

For just as in days of olde, when religious contemplatives were wont to argue over esoterica, like the number of angels on the heads of pins and other such wonders, today's version of same, scholars of the religion known as sports, tend to gather at their favorite watering hole to go through the same exercises. Only instead of angels and such, they argue over who was the "greatest" this and the "greatest" that. And no tonic, however, popular and widely advertised, can have the reviving effect of a barroom argument.

And so it was that I began my travels from watering hole to

watering hole in search of guidance, both liquid and literary. And found myself in the company of several caretakers of sports' eternal flame and other devotees of the life nonstrenuous, descendants of old-time cracker-barrel huggers, each one eager to provide me with long lists of names.

One such night, in search of the similarly sick and afflicted, I found myself with one foot up on the bar railing at just such a sports hangout, crooking my elbow in the companionship of several new acquaintances of the first water. And scotch as well.

I introduced the subject at hand, the compilation of my list of "All-Time Sports Greats" and in no time at all was surfeited with names, far over the union scale of one hundred called for. One of the group, sporting a tie with enough mustard to coat his sandwich, began running down his list of names, which seemed to be nothing more or less than the names of baseball and football greats. Another, who shall go nameless since I never quite got his name despite the fact that he kept handing out cards with a shortened name and cigars with an elongated shape, ventured forward with the names of basketball greats. And a third, snorting something to the effect that he didn't consider certain activities to be legitimate sports—saying what sounded like "How can auto racing be a sport when all they do is turn left?"—went to great lengths to push the names of several track and field greats.

And so it went, far into the night, most of those at the bar nursing their drinks more than their opinions. Many of the names they continued to pour out were names from their youth as they applauded their childhood memories, much as an audience at a concert will applaud a song they recognize more than the performer rendering it.

Now normally, when I hear someone utter those deathless words "I remember," I reach for my coat. This time, however, I reached for my pen to scribble down the nominees, writing them all on official bar stationery—read "napkins." Using more napkins than Rosie had used Bounty during her career as a commercial presenter, I continually added, deleted, and refined the selections as they tumbled out.

Finally, finding that the whole discussion had become a runaway train of thought that would never reach its destination, I took my stack of napkins in hand and asked permission to be excused from the goings-on, not that I would be missed anyway. Permission granted!

As I began to wend my weary way home, I let their thoughts, along with everything else, slowly marinate. What exactly, I asked myself, was "great" athlete? One of the one hundred "greatest"? And how far back should I go to place a laurel wreath marked "greatest" on a perspiring brow? Should I include only those names known to members of the MTV generation or go all the way back to those included in the while-you-get-your-hair-cut weeklies? The simple idea had become woefully complicated.

What exactly, I asked myself, went into the making of a so-called greatest athlete? It seemed that the very word took on an undefined meaning, almost like water assuming the shape of its carrier.

For starters, an athlete's greatness could not be deciphered by statistics. No amount of athletic bookkeeping can account for greatness, no mere won-lost records or championship rings of a quantitative rather than qualitative measure. After all, Yogi Berra won more World Series rings than Babe Ruth; does that make him a *greater* player?

No, we had to look elsewhere for our definition. It was a combination of things, an equation that included dominance, perceived greatness, consistent performance, accomplishments transcending time, and overall excellence that illumined an athlete's greatness, almost as smoke defined light in the movie houses of my youth.

Now it became a chore to wrestle with the problem of ascribing varying degrees of greatness to those I had already identified as belonging to the specie *greatest*. It was a time-honored problem, one best stated by the late Al Buck, who asked, "If you grow a near-perfect peach, then produce a similar fruit, can you honestly say one is better than the other?"

Already drunk on research after reading and rereading the moldering yellowed newspapers and clips of bygone eras, I decided to stir up the research, mix in a liberal serving of advice, and garnish it with my own gauge to come up with my list of *The 100 Greatest Athletes of All Time*.

But even then there is no such thing as objective truth. For one man's objectivity is another's subjectivity. Others have tried compiling such a list before. And so it was than, like someone touching the paint to see if it is dry, I referred to their lists to see if my selections were on target.

Realizing there are almost as many lists as their are so-called experts, I hereby provide you with some that have been served up over the years. They are proof-positive that no two experts see eye-to-eye:

The Associated Press Greatest Male Athlete of the Half-Century (1950)

1. Jim Thorpe
2. Babe Ruth
3. Jack Dempsey
4. Ty Cobb
5. Bobby Jones
6. Joe Louis
7. Red Grange
8. Jesse Owens
9. Lou Gehrig
10. Bronko Nagurski
11. Jackie Robinson
12. Bob Mathias
13. Walter Johnson
14. Glenn Davis
15. Bill Tilden
16. Glenn Cunningham
17. Glenn Morris
18. Cornelius Warmerdam

Greatest Female Athletes

1. Babe Didrickson Zaharias
2. Helen Wills-Moody
3. Stella Walsh
4. Fanny Blanklers-Koen

Greatest Male Athlete, Twentieth Century (Argosy, 1975)

1. Jim Thorpe
2. Babe Ruth
3. Jackie Robinson
4. Muhammad Ali
5. Bill Russell
6. Glenn Davis
7. Ernie Nevers
8. Gordie Howe
9. Jack Dempsey

Greatest Female Athletes

1. Babe Didrickson Zaharias
2. Billie Jean King
3. Sonja Henie
4. Fanny Blankers-Koen
5. Maureen Connolly
6. Alice Marble
7. Stella Walsh
8. Vera Caslavaka
9. Helen Wills-Moody

Bob Oates in the Los Angeles Times (1976)

1. Babe Ruth
2. Muhammad Ali
3. O. J. Simpson
4. Jackie Robinson
5. Ty Cobb
6. John Unitas
7. Jesse Owens
8. Jim Thorpe
9. Jim Brown
10. Bobby Orr

Bill Gallo, New York Daily News, 1995

1. Michael Jordan
2. Joe DiMaggio
3. Sugar Ray Robinson
4. Jim Brown
5. Wayne Gretzky

Before I release you to start your arguments with the person standing next to you at the bar, I want to express my thanks to those who helped me in my research, in no particular order: Jim Murray, Bud Greenspan, Marty Glickman, Harold Rosenthal, Steve Nicholaisen, George Kimball, Carol Davis, Roger Kahn, Bob Costas, Jim Charleton, Don Honig, and Chuck Singer, plus others who unknowingly provided me with biographical background, like Grantland Rice, Stanley Woodward, Red Smith, Damon Runyon, and Ring Lardner. Also to Donald J. Davidson at Carol Publishing, who helped make a chef's salad out of my minced metaphors. And finally, those with cauliflower tongues at sports gathering places where sports is spoken fluently even if some of the patrons can't understand a word of it: Gallagher's, Crocodile Tears, O'Lunney's, the Cafe at Grand Central, Mike Ditka's, O'Riley's, Elaine's, and Runyon's (where it all started), plus all such watering holes, north, east, west and south.

Two caveats: First of all, I don't seek to convince you, that would only weaken you. I just want to stimulate you, for that's the nature of a bar argument. And this book. Second, remember the line uttered by James Stewart at the end of the movie *The Man Who Shot Liberty Valance:* "When the legend becomes more beloved than the facts,print the legend." That we've done in our Rubáiyát of the scotch and soda.

Gentlemen, and Ladies, start your arguments!

BERT RANDOLPH SUGAR
Chappaqua, New York
June 15, 1995

The 100
Greatest Athletes
of All Time

1

Jim Brown

b. 1936

The word *great* is one of those *Rashomon*-like words, much like an empty glass, waiting to be filled with whatever definition one pours into it. Wordsmithies worthy of their calling will call on Mr. Webster's trusty tome to forge meanings for the word, while others, less scholarly, will simply use it as an adjective to describe other words—say, the Great Wall of China, or some such—and let it go at that. But for a quicker, surer definition, we give you the name of Jim Brown.

Using the word in one of its forms, we can describe Jim Brown as the greatest running back in pro football history. But that would be somewhat akin to describing Babe Ruth as the greatest left-handed long-ball hitter in baseball history. Both were more. Much more. And Brown had so many talents they were available at a discount.

This modern Superman got his first toehold on that sparsely populated island of greatness at Long Island's Manhasset High School, where his sports curriculum was a wide one, covering baseball, football, basketball, track, and lacrosse. Winning thirteen letters in the five sports, he was selected an all-state in football, basketball, and track. Not only did Brown average 14.9 yards per carry in football and 38 points per game in basketball, but one of those stories that seem to keep growing like Pinocchio's nose also had Casey Stengel trying to persuade Brown to play baseball in the Yankee farm system.

But despite his many talents the sole petitioner for his services was Syracuse University—and then only on a partial lacrosse scholarship. But before he would leave Syracuse, his achievements would form an institution almost as large as the school itself.

For "all" Brown did at Syracuse was average 13.1 points per game in basketball; become one of the greatest players in the history of lacrosse—if not, to hear old-timers tell it, the greatest; average 5.7 yards per carry, running for 2,091 yards and 187 points—37 of which were points after touchdowns—on the gridiron; and shoehorn in track, where he excelled in the high jump.

Those who remember him from his Syracuse days can still see a 220-pound, finely chiseled Grecian sculpture with a well-knit, heavily muscled body that repaid close inspection, from his wide-as-a-door shoulders that spanned at least two time zones down to his thirty-two-inch waist, hardly big enough to hold his pants up. On the field he set those heavy muscles and big shoulders to the task of becoming, in effect, a one-man strong-arm crew as he carried the ball or lacrosse stick in his left hand, cradling it like a newborn, and used his right forearm and other adjuncts of power with all the force of a wrecking ball to run his own interference, bowling over would-be defenders like tenpins.

At Syracuse they still talk about the one game that defined his greatness on the collegiate level: the 1957 Cotton Bowl game. With selection committees leery of inviting Syracuse to a bowl after several blowouts—the most recent one a 61–6 rout by Alabama in the '53 Orange Bowl—Brown took things into his own hands, and feet, scoring 43 points in the season finale against Colgate on six touchdowns and seven extra points as the Orangemen won 67–6 and captured a bid to play in the Cotton Bowl against the Southwestern Conference representative, Texas Christian University.

It was widely anticipated that the game would turn into a duel between Brown and TCU's great breakaway runner, Jim Swink. But in reality, the matchup turned out to be TCU versus Brown. Script? There was no script, just Brown running, throwing, returning kicks, kicking, and scoring. He scored 21 of Syracuse's 27 points in a one-point loss, 28–27. After the game, TCU's coach Abe Martin put everyone's thoughts into words: "Any man who wouldn't call Jim Brown a great player would have to be ignorant or blind."

That spring, in the annual meat market known as the National Football League draft, Paul Brown, of the Cleveland team of the same name, went shopping for a quarterback who could replace Otto Graham and bring the Browns back to their former preeminence. But when the Steelers picked Len Dawson with the first pick of the '57 draft and two other teams also opted for quarterbacks, Brown was forced to go back to the drawing board and take Jim Brown.

And when, in his very first exhibition game, J. Brown broke away for a long touchdown run on a draw play, P. Brown drew his new recruit aside and anointed him on his padded shoulders: "You're my fullback." And proceeded to place Cleveland's entire offense on his massive shoulders as well. P. Brown had J. Brown going both up the middle and around end, a sort of one-man "Mr. Inside" and "Mr. Outside." And he even, on occasion, used J. Brown as a receiver—which was like getting money from home without writing for it. "When you have a thoroughbred," said P. Brown, giving some rhyme to his reason, "you run him."

It was an alchemy that paid immediate dividends as the Cleveland Browns once again ascended to the top of the Eastern Conference, just as God and Paul Brown had intended them to. And Jim Brown, with a roar to his thoroughbred's heart, carried the ball a total of 202 times to win the rushing championship—including one game against the Los Angeles Rams in which he rushed for a then-record 237 yards.

Over the next four seasons Jim Brown became the greatest carrier since Typhoid Mary as he established homesteading rights to the rushing championship with an average of 5.1 yards per carry and an average of 1,380 yards per season. His style was, in reality, less of a style than what he called "the use of a number of different abilities." With "no set image as a runner" he would veer, slide, cut back, sidestep, spin, jump, drop a shoulder and hit, use a forearm, run all out, etc. The composite picture was of Brown twisting and dodging and stampeding over frustrated tacklers after using his forearm with a resounding "thwaaack," reducing them to smaller pieces as he fought through the picket line of first defense and then, finding daylight, breaking through with an electric surcharge, whereupon, accelerating with a motion that looked as if he were merely stretching his legs, he would pull away from his pursuers, leaving a trail of tacklers in his wake.

But if there was a singular remembrance of Brown it was of the slow, deliberate way he returned to the huddle after each and every carry. Slowly unfolding his body from the ground and walking gingerly back to the huddle, almost as if his feet hurt, his movements were so langourous, as if to say he needed a fortnight's notice to get ready for the next play—whereas in fact his inertia was partly his wanting to see the defensive alignment, partly to conceal from opponents any hurt, and partly, when he pushed off the ground with his knuckles, not wanting to touch the cold ground with his hands, which, he thought, might induce a fumble. But then, somehow, some way, almost as if Gabriel had blown his horn, Brown would come to at the snap of the ball like a clockwork toy and once again take on the ball and the opposing linemen.

But what players remembered about Number 32 said it all. For some, it was like asking a lamppost how it felt about marauding canines. Chuck Bednarik, the all-everything of the Philadelphia Eagles, called him superhuman. Alex Karras, the great defensive tackle of the Detroit Lions, said, "You had to give each guy in the line an ax." Dick Modzelewski, one of the broadest backs in the broad-back line of the New York Giants, said, "He's the best fullback God ever made. If the NFL exists another two thousand years there won't be a fullback as good as him. To bring down Brown I needed the help of the whole defensive line plus Sam Huff." And Huff himself, who made an entire career out of tackling Brown, said, tongue not far removed from cheek, "The only way to stop Jim Brown is to shoot him coming out of the dressing room."

But in 1962 his run came to an end. Literally. Having injured his left wrist in an early-season game and using his wrecking-ball right forearm now to carry the ball, Brown became, in his eyes at least, mortal; his yardage gained was "only" 996, his yards-per-carry only 4.3, and his rushing championship was lost to Jim Taylor of the Green Bay Packers.

The entire 1962 season had been a disappointment, not only for J. Brown, but for P. Brown and the C. Browns as well. For Paul Brown had traded Bobby Mitchell for the draft rights to Ernie Davis, who was expected to give the Browns a powerful one-two running attack. But leukemia struck down the Heisman Trophy winner from Syracuse before he ever played a professional down, and Jim Brown was left without a fellow running back to divert the enemy from ganging up on him. After a lackluster campaign in which Paul Brown became increasingly more removed from the team—so much so that it was a sure bet the team and the coach would not be exchanging cards at Christmastime—Paul Brown was removed by owner Art Modell after a brief player rebellion.

Freed of the constraints of Paul Brown's constant changing of the guards and calling the signals, J. Brown reverted to form in 1963, freelancing across the greensward for 1,863 yards and another rushing title. The next year he repeated as rushing champion, and the Cleveland Browns won the NFL championship over the Baltimore Colts, with J. Brown handling the ball on thirty plays for a total of 151 yards. And then, after winning his eighth rushing championship in nine years, in 1965, Jim Brown stepped out of the football spotlight at the age of twenty-nine, gone from center stage scarcely before he had finished his piece before the footlights.

Explaining why he quit at the top of his game, Brown said, "I got out before I ever had to be like so many guys I've seen—sitting hunched over on the bench, all scarred and banged up, watching some hot young kid out there in their place."

But even though he was to exchange football's spotlight for Hollywood's klieg lights, no one, but no one, could ever take the place of Jim Brown, the athlete who best defines the word *great*.

2

Jim Thorpe

1888–1953

It would take a forest of felled trees to recount all the athletic feats of Jim Thorpe. For like that bevy of blind men who tried mightily to describe an elephant by researching the different parts of its anatomy, any definition of Thorpe's athletic prowess will possess as many different descriptions, depending upon which yellowing news clips one reads.

The Jim Thorpe story began in 1904, when the great-grandson of a Sac and Fox war chief was recruited by Carlisle, a government-operated school for Indians in Carlisle, Pennsylvania, one of those eastern schools that educated Native Americans in the idioms of football and other sports. Only the year before, Carlisle had graduated Albert "Chief" Bender to the

Major Leagues with a baseball in his right hand, and he would stay there long enough to win 210 games and election to the Baseball Hall of Fame. But the then sixteen-year-old Thorpe, who stood only 58 inches tall and weighed just 115 pounds, harbored no such interest in athletics and instead took up the needle, working in the school's tailor shop as part of his curriculum. But three years, an added foot of growth, and seventy pounds later, his curriculum would expand to include a football. And more, much more.

Storytellers have it that the start of Thorpe's athletic career goes back to a day in the spring of 1907. Thorpe, who the year before had taken his first tentative step into the sports water by playing for the tailors' football team in the intramural shop league, had been assigned to clean up the field after the track team completed its daily practice. As he went about his duties, Thorpe chanced upon the high jump bar, set at five feet eight inches, reflecting the best effort of the day. Studying the height of the bar, Thorpe muttered something to the effect of "That doesn't seem very high." One of his fellow students asked, "Ever high-jump?" "Not over a bar," Thorpe answered. Then, after further surveying the bar in his mind's eye, he added, "But if a horse can do it, I can do it." And with that, in the shake of a proverbial leg, he shed his overalls and shoes and, with an easy motion that looked as if he were merely stretching his legs, cleared the bar.

One witness to this birth of a legend was the track-and-field and football coach, Glenn S. "Pop" Warner, himself a coaching legend-to-be. Appraising the potential of the young jumper with the eye of a recruiting sergeant, Warner determined to take the youngster under his avuncular arm to teach him the rudiments of sports and cure him of any stylistic shortcomings. But if Thorpe suffered from anything, it was an embarrassment of riches, as he not only played football and participated in track and field, but also wrestled, played basketball and lacrosse, and excelled in boxing, swimming, and shooting.

With so many talents available at a discount, Thorpe—after playing halfback for the 1907 and 1908 football teams and participating on the track team for three years—left Carlisle in the spring of 1909 in search of dollars. Most, including Warner, thought he had merely returned to his native Oklahoma. But instead Thorpe had accompanied two Carlisle baseball players to

North Carolina, where they all signed on with Rocky Mount of the Eastern Carolina League, a Class D minor league. Over the next two years Thorpe played in eighty games, hit .248 overall, and won 19 games pitching. But as he would later find out, he had committed a crime—at least in the eyes of the Amateur Athletic Union.

Warner, unaware of his star athlete's whereabouts, wrote him a note in the summer of 1911, telling him that "if you come back to Carlisle, I think you have a chance to make the United States Olympic team next year." Several weeks later Thorpe did return, and in answer to Warner's "Where've you been?" answered airily, "Playing ball." Without realizing Thorpe had compromised his amateur standing, Warner began preparing him for the 1912 Olympic Games.

During Thorpe's senior year at Carlisle, Lafayette played host to the Indians in a track meet. The event had been well publicized, and a welcoming committee headed by Lafayette's coach, Harold Bruce, came to meet the train supposedly bearing the Carlisle team. When only Warner and Thorpe alighted at Easton, Pennsylvania, Bruce demanded of Warner, "What's this? We expected the Carlisle track team." "Here it is," replied Warner, casually pointing to Thorpe. The results, repeated in one of sport's most memorable fictions, saw Thorpe win practically every event in a rout for Carlisle.

Thorpe's exploits on the football field were equally legendary. After returning to Carlisle, Thorpe led the Indians to wins over the football powerhouses of the day, including Harvard, Army, Pennsylvania, Brown, Pittsburgh, Minnesota, and Chicago. Performing as the Indians' plunging halfback, he also doubled and tripled as punter, drop-kicker, punt and kickoff returner, passer, and, when necessary, the blocking interference.

Against Harvard in 1911, he scored on four field goals and a seventy-yard run for all of Carlisle's points in an 18–15 win, prompting Harvard coach Percy Haughton to call him "the super player everyone dreamed of." Against a strong Army in 1912, Thorpe lined up to kick from his own ten-yard line. "They think I'm going to kick, both us and Army," Thorpe muttered to the referee, who had dropped back with him. "But I ain't." And with that, Thorpe faked a kick and ran ninety yards to break open the game, which Carlisle won 27–6. Playing Brown on Thanksgiving Day that year, Thorpe "wrecked the entire team," wrote one observer. "He defeated them 32 to nothing—all by himself. Runs of fifty and sixty yards were nothing...." Thorpe was to be named to Walter Camp's all-America team in both 1911 and 1912, and in 1912 led the country with 198 points and 25 touchdowns. He was, in the words of Grantland Rice, "the greatest football player—*ever.*"

Sandwiched in between his two all-American seasons, Thorpe made a stop in Stockholm to stake out his claim to all-time greatness. On the liner taking the Americans to the 1912 Olympic Games, one writer, Francis Albertanti, spied Thorpe resting in a deck chair, laboring under a torpor worthy of a python after its noonday meal. The rest of the American track squad was hard at work, pounding around a stretch of cork laid down on one of the decks under the coaches' watchful eyes. Albertanti, who knew of Thorpe's reputation for never letting success go to his training, approached the athlete and asked, "What are you doing, Jim—thinking of your uncle, Sitting Bull?" Thorpe, interrupted while his surveyor's mind was approximating distances, opened his eyes slowly and said, "No... I'm practicing the broad jump. I've just jumped twenty-three feet eight inches. I think I can win it." And with that he closed his eyes to continue his mental workout.

Mike Murphy, one of the trainers of the 1912 team and an ancient who was committed to the romantic notion that athletes should train, once found Thorpe asleep in a hammock, musing on the mutability of temporal affairs, when he was scheduled to be at practice. Murphy registered a complaint to Thorpe's constant chaperon, Pop Warner, who replied, "Mike, don't worry. All those two-for-a-nickel events you've got lined up for Thorpe won't bother him. He's in shape.... What with football, lacrosse, baseball, and track back at school, how could he be out of shape? This sleeping is the best training ever—for Jim." Other times Thorpe would appear at workouts merely to study the broad jump takeoff or the high-jump pit, place a handkerchief well past twenty-three feet for the first event or at something higher than six feet for the latter, and then sit under a tree and, letting his imagination take over, study his marks with his eyes closed.

No matter what Thorpe did or how he trained, it worked. For when he marched out to compete, he was almost unbeatable. First he captured the grueling five-event pentathlon by winning four of the five events, including the long jump, and then, while the other pentathletes were recuperating from their ordeal, he went back out on the field to take fourth place in the individual high jump. Later he finished seventh in the long jump. Then came the decathlon, an event he had never competed in before; in fact, he had never thrown a javelin until two months earlier. Still, he captured four of the ten firsts and won easily. When King Gustav presented the gold medal to Thorpe, along with a bust of himself, he paid tribute to Thorpe's unprecedented victories in both the pentathlon and decathlon by saying, "Sir, you are the greatest athlete in the world." To which Thorpe is reported to have replied, "Thanks, King."

But such gifts normally come encumbered with strings attached and bills to pay. And before long Thorpe had to pay for them. Almost before the year was out, a reporter for one of those while-you-get-your-hair-cut weeklies in Worcester, Massachusetts, had picked up a copy of *The Reach Baseball Guide* for the year 1910 and found a reference to "J. Thorpe, Rocky Mount" contained therein. He reported his findings to the officials of the Amateur Athletic Union, who, citing his play-for-pay and preaching other pious twaddle, stripped him of his Olympic gold medals and expunged his name from the record books, despite his application for mercy, in which Thorpe pleaded he had only played "because I like to play ball."

Jim Thorpe would go on to play the games he liked for the next twelve years, including six in the Major Leagues with the New York Giants, the Cincinnati Reds, and the Boston Braves—although, truth to tell, he never got the hang of the curveball—and eight in the newly minted National Football League, where he was trotted out, as if he were the queen's jewels, for ceremonial occasions as the league's first president.

But he would remain a bitter man to the end of his life. In his later years, his gold medals still unreturned, Thorpe could only reflect: "At least they couldn't strip me of the king's words." They couldn't. And for many, medals or no, he remains the greatest of them all.

3

Babe Didrikson Zaharias

1914–1956

Before 1932, women athletes, to mix both gender and metaphor, were as overlooked as Whistler's Father. But that was the year when a little, hard-bitten girl out of Texas with a Turkish bazaar of talents, named Babe Didrikson, remade herself from a curio piece into a piece of Americana—and by virtue of her efforts also recast the place of women in the field of athletics.

Mildred Didrikson came out of Beaumont, Texas, a tomboy who was better at sports than any of the other Toms in her neighborhood. This tall and slim youngster, with powerful hands, long-muscled arms, slender but powerful legs, and nearly perfect reflexes and coordination, could do everything. She ran, she threw, she jumped, she swam, she bowled, she cycled, she played baseball, basketball, football, tennis, handball, billiards, and lacrosse—and played them better than most young men her age. Or any age for that matter. The word the most punctilious wordsmith might have used to describe her abundance of talents was *unbelievable*.

The young Didrikson—by now nicknamed Babe, after the other outstanding "Babe" of the era, Babe Ruth, for her ability to hit a baseball a proverbial country mile—started her fantastic career as a basketball star at Beaumont High, averaging 30 points a game. It was while at Beaumont, performing the voodoo she did so well, that she was first spotted by Colonel McCombs, who petitioned her to become a member of his Golden Cyclones, a company basketball team in Dallas sponsored by the Employers Casualty Insurance Company. Babe packed up her enormous bag of talents and moved to Dallas, where she also moved the Cyclones into the AAU Finals three years in a row. An AAU all-American each of those years, Babe finally powered her team to the national championship in 1931, scoring 195 points in six tournament games.

Looking for other fields to conquer, Babe prevailed upon the company powers-that-be to start a women's track team. Entering almost every event known to womankind, she won AAU national track-and-field titles in the long jump, low hurdles, javelin throw, and baseball throw in 1930 and '31. Then came the 1932 AAU championships, where Babe Didrikson may well have written the greatest sports story of all time.

Script? There was no script, only an utterly improbable scenario, for what happened that afternoon. In just three hours, entering eight of the ten events, Didrikson won five of them outright—including the shot put, which she had never tried before—tied for first in another, the high jump, and finished fourth in yet another, the discus, another all-new event for her. And, in the course of so doing, she set four new world records. The Dallas insurance company she was representing won the women's team championship with a total of 30 points; the Illinois Women's Athletic Club finished second with 22. To put her performance in perspective, the Illinois Women's A.C. team was made up of a total of twenty-two contestants; the Employers Casualty company "team" of just one—Babe Didrikson. Of such things are legends made.

Not incidentally, the AAU national championships were also the tryouts for the upcoming Los Angeles Olympics. And Babe Didrikson had already become "the story." Her genius was to be served, not argued with, and one writer ended an essay with: "Miss Mildred Didrikson of Dallas, Texas, who prefers to be called 'Babe,' will lead the American women's Olympic track-and-field team. Such assistance as she may need against the foreign invasion will be provided by fifteen other young ladies."

Two weeks later she hit Los Angeles. And the papers as well. The confident Babe, not content to hide her intentions in either lavender or mothballs, told the press outright: "I came out here to beat everybody in sight. And that's just what I'm going to do. Sure, I can do anything." It was a statement so brazen it reminded everyone of Jesse James, except that James had worn a mask so that people could only guess at his identity. Everyone knew Babe Didrikson. And everyone knew that the five-foot-six phenomenon with the straight black hair could do anything—and everything—she set her mind to do.

But while Babe had set her sights on that "everything," qualifying for five of the six women's events, the Olympic committee, for reasons hard to explain, ruled that women were permitted to enter just three of the six scheduled events. And so Babe, allowed to enter three events, selected the javelin throw, the 80-meter hurdles, and the high jump. Then, on opening day, she went out to make good her boast, winning the javelin throw with an Olympic-record toss on her very first heave—even though the javelin had slipped out of her hand!

Four days later she won her second event—and set her second record, this time a world mark—winning the 80-meter hurdles in 11.7 seconds for the gold. Now, with two events and two records in hand, the Babe had only one more event to look forward to—the high jump, where she could once again live up to her press notices. And set another record. In a brag coated with more than a little mustard and tinged with a soupçon of chagrin at being limited to three events, she told the writers, "I'd break all the records if they'd let me."

And while Babe jumped 5′ 5¼″ to once again tie the same Jean Shiley she had tied in the high jump just a few weeks before in the U.S. trials, setting a new world record, she was nevertheless deprived of her third gold. For the Olympic committee, in one of those curious rulings that pay full faith and credit to track and field's murky traditions, ruled that Didrikson's western-roll style, which saw her head clear the bar before her body, was illegal— even though the committee had allowed her so-called diving in all her previous jumps—and awarded her a silver medal instead of a gold.

Two golds or three, Babe Didrikson was still the darling of the press. "Whatta gal!" they wrote. One of them, Grantland Rice, then the dean of all sportswriters, rhapsodized: "She is beyond all belief until you see her perform. Then you finally understand that you are looking at the most flawless section of muscle harmony, of complete mental and physical coordination, the world of sport has ever seen." Male or female!

"Granny," as he was called by his fellow dandruff scratchers, then decided, "We might be looking at the greatest future woman golfer of all time." So, during the Olympics, he lured her out for a round of golf. He also invited a few fellow sportswriters along to join him and the Babe on her first round. What they witnessed made their eyeballs rotate in their parent sockets, as Babe fed off the golf balls like they were T-bones at a vegetarian's outing. Former Open winner Ollie Dutra, watching one of Babe's 250-yard drives, could only say, "I saw it, but I still don't believe it."

After the Olympics, between barnstorming with the House of David baseball team, pitching exhibition games with the St. Louis Cardinals and Brooklyn Dodgers—and in one striking out Joe DiMaggio—playing professional basketball and billiards, and working out with the football team of Southern Methodist University, Babe, now billed as "The Athlete Who Could Do Anything," took up golf. Seriously. With first Gene Sarazen and Walter Hagen and then Tommy Armour giving her lessons, she went on the amateur tour, winning the second tournament she entered, the 1935 Texas Women's Invitational.

In short order, she married wrestler George Zaharias, changed her name to Babe Didrikson Zaharias, won seventeen straight golf tournaments—including the U.S. Amateur and the British Ladies' Championship (becoming the first American to win it), three National Opens, and four "World" championships— and founded, along with Patty Berg, the Ladies' Professional Golf Association.

By the 1950s, she had become history's foremost woman golfer and been named the Associated Press's woman athlete of the half-century. Then, in 1953, she contracted cancer and underwent major surgery. Within a year she was back on the tour, winning five events, including the U.S. Open by an unheard-of twelve strokes. For the sixth time the Associated Press named her Woman Athlete of the Year. Two years later, her triumph-filled life came to an end, as Babe Didrikson Zaharias lost to the only thing she couldn't beat: cancer. But it had been a helluva run, jump, and drive while it lasted.

Jackie Robinson

1919–1972

Baseball is a tradition-bound sport, a game which not only pays full faith and credit to its heritage but ofttimes etches it in stone. Bill Veeck, who spent the better part of a half century chipping away at that rock, was once moved to comment that baseball was "the only thing besides the paper clip that hasn't changed."

One of those rock-bound traditions was the so-called gentleman's agreement amongst the Lords of Baseball that served as the sport's chastity belt, drawn tight to keep the National Pastime racially pure.

The agreement dated back to one less-than-bright day in June of 1884 when baseball's Dark Ages and Non–Dark Ages merged. For on that day Adrian "Cap" Anson, the legendary player and manager of the Chicago White Stockings, led his team out onto the field for an exhibition game against the Toledo Mudhens. As Anson cast an eye around the field, what should appear but the form of Fleetwood Walker, the catcher for the Mudhens, who, not incidental to our story, was black. Anson's face suddenly turned another color, red, and he shouted, among other maledictions, "Get that nigger off the field!"

And then he dropped the other cleat: "…or I will not allow my team on the field!" The Toledo manager, casting an eye at the large crowd already on hand, gave in to Anson's demand, telling him that Walker—and his brother, outfielder Welday Walker—would be fired the next day.

The next year Anson again went into his demagogic rain dance of bigotry worthy of a giant pooh-bah of the exalted order of the pillowcase and demanded that the New York Giants, then considering the purchase of black pitcher George Stovey from the minor leagues, cease and desist. They, too, gave in to Anson's temper tantrum.

Anson climaxed his vitriolic campaign with a personal appeal at the 1887 winter meetings, calling on all major league and minor league clubs not only to refrain from ever again signing a contract with a black but also for those minor league clubs with blacks currently on their rosters to fire such unsavories forthwith. And although no formal agreement was adopted, there was a gentleman's agreement, one which blackened baseball's name if not its ranks. For Cap Anson and men of bad faith everywhere, the sun was now in its heaven and all was right with the baseball world—even if they had abrogated the United States Constitution in their zeal to keep baseball lily-white.

Over the next six decades the bigoted legacy of Cap Anson remained part of baseball's tradition, in spite of several attempts to prove that the agreement wasn't worth the paper it wasn't written on. But each time the requests were airbrushed over, with baseball demanding that the petitioners adhere to the "black-listing" position of their patron saint, Cap Anson.

But the times they were a-changing. Sociological bread crumbs had already begun to lead to the moment when baseball would overturn the vestiges of Jim Crow. First Joe Louis had beaten the avatar of Aryan supremacy in 1938. Then many questioned why, if blacks had fought and died in World War II, they couldn't play professional baseball. The new commissioner,

A. B. "Happy" Chandler, was supposed to have said, "If a black boy can make it at Okinawa and to Guadalcanal, he can make it in baseball." The bar was not only off the door, but the door was ajar.

The prime mover in permanently removing that bar to the door marked "Closed to Blacks" was Wesley Branch Rickey, a color-blind man who now was to lead baseball's blind. With a reserve of inherited guile, Rickey resorted to his own wiles and ways rather than baseball's murky traditions. While others meekly accepted the gentleman's agreement as unalterable, Rickey knew that like all other "great truths," it was blasphemous. And he determined to challenge it and put a black in Brooklyn Dodger blue.

Throwing up, a probably apt phrase in this scenario, a smoke screen, Rickey formed something called the United States Baseball League, with the entry from Brooklyn to be called the Brown Dodgers. In August of 1945 he sent head scout Clyde Sukeforth out to Chicago to watch the Kansas City Monarchs, with special instructions to "go up to that fellow Robinson and introduce yourself."

"That fellow Robinson" was Jack Roosevelt Robinson, an exceptional athlete and person. The younger brother of Mack Robinson, who had finished second to Jesse Owens in the 200-meter dash in the 1936 Berlin Olympics, young Jackie had been introduced to sports at an early age. And soon found he could excel in almost any sport he tried. In high school he played every sport offered, including tennis, basketball, and track and field. Enrolling at Pasadena Junior College, Robinson broke the school record in the long jump, set by his brother, and gained such fame as a football star that crowds ranging from thirty thousand to sixty thousand came out to see the wing-footed running back described, in the quaint trappings of the day, as "one of the swiftest perambulators in the nation."

Robinson would go on to even greater stardom at UCLA, where he became the school's first four-letter athlete. Called by a rival coach "the best basketball player in the U.S.," Robinson led the Pacific Coast Conference in scoring as both a junior and senior. On the gridiron, he led the nation in 1939 in average yards gained from scrimmage, with 12 yards a carry, and in punt returns, with 20 a return. Braven Dyer, the leading pencil pusher on the West Coast, was moved to write: "His terrific speed, 25-

foot broad-jumping ability, and baffling change of pace made his every appearance a nightmare for the opposition." To cap his collegiate career, Robinson won swimming championships at UCLA, reached the semifinals of the national Negro tennis tournament, and won the 1940 NCAA long-jump title. Then came World War II.

During the war Robinson applied for admission to officer candidate school at Fort Riley, Kansas, where he won his commission as second lieutenant. He won something else as well: a reputation. A fiercely proud man, Robinson fought against injustice in any form and came away with the reputation of being a troublemaker. And worse—although military buses had recently been desegregated, he was court-martialed for his failure to "move to the back of the bus." Army brass decided they could not control his pride or his iron will, and gave him his honorable discharge in November of 1944, happy to get rid of the man they called an "uppity nigger."

Mustered out, Robinson signed on with the Kansas City Monarchs at shortstop for the 1945 season, at the going rate of $400 a month. At the time Sukeforth went up to "that fellow Robinson," the twenty-six-year-old was hitting .345 in forty-one games. Robinson was skeptical about Rickey's intentions—about the Brown Dodgers—and pressured Sukeforth to repeat Rickey's instructions, word for word. Sukeforth could only say, "Jack, this could be the real thing." And, following the rest of Rickey's orders to "bring him in," Sukeforth booked two berths on the train back to Brooklyn.

As Sukeforth ushered Robinson into Rickey's chambers, he began to make the customary introductions. But it was useless. A monologist by nature who could talk through ten cigars on any subject, Rickey had at once commenced his usual sales patter, patter that could sell anyone a combination watch and pocketknife, with a free bottle of elixir thrown in, for a dollar. Punctuating the air with his ever-present cigar and dropping ashes down his shirt front and bow tie, Rickey said, "Jack, I've been looking for a great colored ballplayer, but I need more than a great player. I need a man who will accept insults, take abuse—in a word, carry the flag for his race."

Without missing a beat, Rickey went on, the wrinkles forming a smile of sorts. "I want a man who has the courage not to fight, not to fight back." With that, he launched into a laundry list of insults. "If a guy slides into you at second base and calls you a black son of a bitch, I wouldn't blame you if you came up swinging. You'd be right. You'd be justified. But"—and here he stopped to make his point with all the solemnity of Moses relaying the tablets from the Mount—"you'd set the cause back twenty years. I want a man with courage enough not to fight back. Can you do that?"

So saying, Rickey leaned back in his big executive's chair, his gnarled hands holding his cigar aloft as he stared at Robinson. Robinson sat silent, his face a closed fist, considering his options. Finally, after a few moments, he said, in his high-pitched voice, "Mr. Rickey, if you want to take this gamble, I promise you there'll be no incidents."

From that moment on, Jackie Robinson became history in the making. And a baseball great in the making as well. In his very first game in professional baseball, playing for the Dodgers' top farm team, the Montreal Royals, he hit a homer and three singles. By the end of 1946 he had led the International League in batting and runs scored and led Montreal to the pennant and a win in the Junior World Series as well. After the last game, jubilant Montreal fans rushed onto the field to congratulate their team, raising the players on their shoulders and carrying them around the field. Finally Robinson was able to break away from the adoring throng and made a headlong dash for the clubhouse, leading one observer to comment, "It's probably the only time in history that a black man ran from a white mob with love instead of lynching on its mind."

Called up by the Dodgers just before the '47 season, Robinson was subjected to imprecations impossible to brook or overlook. There were catcalls from the stands and black cats thrown on the field, beanballs thrown at his head and death threats phoned to his home, threatened boycotts by opposing clubs and under-the-belt bench jockeying in language that would have caused a billingsgate fisherman to turn red. But through it all, his air connoting a quiet but conscious force and dignity, Robinson kept his equanimity. And his promise to Mr. Rickey. And answered the only way he could: with his bat and his feet.

For even though Jackie Robinson was ever-dangerous at the plate, his bat dealing out great gobfuls of line drives, it is on the base paths that he is best remembered. Waging his own brand of aggressive cold war, Robinson dominated the base paths like no player since Ty Cobb, disrupting play and pitchers alike. With that patented pigeon-toed gait of his, he could barrel down the base paths faster than you could say...well, "Jack Robinson." Other times he would try fielders with his wide turns and a will-he-or-won't-he hesitation move, daring them to throw behind him, then taking off for the next base. And then there were the rundowns, when, figuring it was a bad bargain that couldn't run both ways, he would jockey between the rundown men and before you knew it would be sliding safely into the base he had originally set out for. He was, as someone once described him, "a man of many facets—all turned on."

At the end of his first year he was named Rookie of the Year; in his third, he was batting champion and Most Valuable Player. And by his fourth season, he had become the spiritual leader of the Dodgers, leading them to six pennants in ten years—a National League record for success that eclipsed the one set back in the nineteenth century by none other than Cap Anson and his Chicago White Stockings.

Baseball's "noble experiment" had worked. But only because the man who had been chosen to break the gentlemen's agreement had constituted a majority of one who thought he could do it. And that's all it took.

5

Babe Ruth

1895–1948

Babe Ruth. The very name brings back memories to the dwindling number of fans who saw this gargantuan figure on toothpick-thin legs boom parabolic shots into the stands time and again and then mince his way around the bases with catlike steps.

To the older adult, he is a legendary figure who gave color to his age in the same way that John L. Sullivan gave color to his. To members of the younger generation, he is merely a name, spoken in reverential terms by their elders and used as a benchmark for modern ballplayers like Hank Aaron and Roger Maris.

But Babe Ruth was more than a mere name. He was an institution, a deity. One prominent Methodist at the time even suggested, "If St. Paul were living today, he would know Babe Ruth's batting average." Legions of sportswriters formed a cult, with high priests like Runyon, Lardner, Rice, and Broun spreading the Ruthian gospel. They called him the Sultan of Swat, the Wizard of Whack, the King of Clout, the Behemoth of Big, and, of course, the Bambino. He was the idol of American youth, and the symbol of baseball the world over. In short, he held a sacred seat in the exclusive inner circle of celebrity.

As each day brought new accolades and exaggerated stories about the man who had become a legend in his own time—including his Beau Gesture, his so-called Called Shot in the 1932 World Series, a moment which will never be fully explained—Ruth contributed to the lore by writing and then rewriting the record books with every swing of his 42-ounce bat. Fans jammed the parks just to see him, booing their own pitchers when he was given a base on balls, oohing and aahing when he struck out. As he drove ball after ball out of the park and record after record out of the books, Babe Ruth became America's most popular sports celebrity.

For the age known as "the Roaring Twenties" and "the Golden Age of Sports" worshiped celebrity. And nobody made it roar like Ruth, a man who dedicated himself to the national pastime of "makin' whoopee." Back in those days, when the hand of Prohibition lay heavy on the land, the Babe somehow kept slipping through its all-enveloping fingers. And yet, almost as if he had another body hanging in his well-stocked closet, he could show up at the ballpark the day after, doff his camel's hair coat and hat, don his New York Yankee pinstripes—covering a build referred to in catalogs of ready-made clothing as "portly" (but not too portly to steal home ten more times than Lou Brock)—and still tear the cover off the ball, a tribute to the concept of burning the candle at both ends.

Ruth had first burst on the scene as a nineteen-year-old left-handed pitcher for the Boston Red Sox back in 1914. But even as he was setting the baseball world afire with his blazing fastball—a fastball that enabled him to win eighty games by the age of twenty-three, more than all but two pitchers in the Hall of Fame had won at that young age—he was also creating some pyrotechnics with his massive bat, leading the American League in homers with 11 in the war-shortened 1918 season. By 1919 Boston management had seen enough and converted the young star into an outfielder, with a little pitching on the side. Many, like Tris Speaker, thought the conversion was a mistake, Speaker saying: "Ruth made a grave mistake when he gave up pitching. Working once a week, he might have lasted a long time and become a great star."

But Ruth set to work to prove his detractors wrong. And soon those remorseless seekers known as writers noticed that Ruth was running up a record home run total, 29, in one season.

Suddenly the home run, suffocated by the bunt-and-stolen-base game made popular by the Orioles before the turn of the century, broke out of its cocoon with a vengeance, courtesy of one George Herman "Babe" Ruth. And then two owners changed the entire course of the game. On January 3, 1920, Harry Frazee of the Red Sox—out of Tapioca City, gone bust after several Broadway bombs and in need of money to stage *No! No! Nanette*—sold Ruth to Jacob Ruppert and the New York Yankees for $125,000.

Ruth and New York were made for each other—both were bigger than life. To borrow the title of Irving Berlin's paean of praise, "Along Came Ruth," and with him came the long ball. And the crowds. In 1920, the Babe "hit," "clouted," "swatted," or "whacked"—pick one of the above—a record 54 home runs, one every 11.8 times at bat, still the record for home run production. One of his cloud-busters caused a bleacherite to die of excitement as he witnessed one of Ruth's mighty swats land near his section high up in the Polo Grounds. Every day brought new accolades and exaggerated stories about the Babe.

As he continued to hit home run after home run, culminating in his record-setting 60 in 1927, Ruth became a sports-page myth. To quote John Kiernan's famous line: "From 'One Old Cat' to the last 'At Bat,' was there ever a guy like Ruth?" To any who ever saw him, the answer was a resounding *no*.

6

Jesse Owens

1913–1980

The names of most sports figures—and their accomplishments—are recorded in monstrous quicksand, its particles shifting constantly and rapidly to conform to changing times and dictates. But when the stylus of the ages comes to write against the name Jesse Owens, it will make a permanent mark; for his footprints will stand forever in the sands of time, larger than life.

But if Jesse Owens had been carefully chosen by Fate for the role of pacesetter not only in the world of track and field but also in that greater world called societal relations, it was hardly apparent in the beginning. Born James Cleveland Owens, the son of an Alabama sharecropper, young Owens was dubbed J.C., in that grand ole southern tradition of abbreviating the first two names into initials. When his father moved the family to Cleveland, to take a job as a laborer in a steel mill, young J.C. Owens was asked his name by a solicitous grammar school teacher on his very first day in school. "J.C., ma'am," came the answer, bathed in a soft 'Bama drawl. "Jesse?" she asked, trying to verify the handle of her new student. "Yes, ma'am. Jesse," came back the answer from the soft-spoken youth, anxious to oblige. And so "Jesse" it became—as in Jesse Owens.

However, life was no easier for the Owens family in Cleveland than it had been in Alabama, especially in those Depression years when the average family didn't have the proverbial two nickels to rub together. "We couldn't afford any kind of equipment," he would remember years later, "and we had nothing to do but run." With few other outlets for his youthful energies, young Jesse just "ran and ran and ran."

By the time he was thirteen, young Jesse was running in formal races. His very first race was something less than the stuff of which legends are made, a losing effort in a 40-yard dash. "I got left in the holes" was the way he remembered it, referring to the custom, before starting blocks, of sprinters digging their own holes in order to get better traction for their starts.

More determined than ever, young Jesse continued to run and run and run. And to master the mechanics of running, so much so that he now appeared to cut himself loose from his original moorings with his very first step rather than chancing being "left in the holes." But running was only the centerpiece of his talents. He also added the long jump and the high jump to the ever-growing list. By the age of fifteen he was running the 100-yard dash in 9.9 seconds, high-jumping 6' 2½", and long-jumping an even 23 feet. Four years later, by now a slender, 163-pound senior at Cleveland East Technical High School, he ran the 100 in 9.4, tying the scholastic world record, ran the 220 in 20.7 seconds on a straightaway, and long-jumped 24' 11¼".

Back in those antediluvian days, before college scholarships were given away as freely as peanuts at a bar, Jesse received nary a nibble. What he did receive for his talents was an offer from nearby Ohio State University to run a night elevator at the State Office Building in Columbus from 5 P.M. till 12:30 A.M. for $150 a month—a king's ransom in those days, when a Roosevelt nickel could buy you a beer and there *was* such a thing as a free lunch.

Between running and running and running the night elevator, studying in the elevator cab on the move, cramming in six hours of sleep when he could, and getting up for classes that started as early as eight in the morning, Jesse still found time for his first love: track and field. It was there that he found himself under the avuncular arm of a coach named Larry Snyder.

Snyder, knowing full well he had the outstanding track-and-field prospect in the country in his charge, took great pains with Owens. Delivering oral deductions of his own reckoning, Snyder took this package of towering talents and made him more towering. Literally. Figuring that the higher Owens jumped, the farther he'd leap, Snyder made Owens jump as high as he could before Newton's law set in and he fell to gravity. Many's the Big Ten official who watched in amazement as Owens flew past him at eye level. Or higher.

Snyder also worked with Owens on his balance—"not too much weight on the arms, not too much on the legs"—giving him a relaxed approach as he ran. And on his starts for the sprints, hurdles, and middle-distance races, concentrating on Owens's getting the jump on the field with his very first stride. That way, he figured, Owens would make his opponents run *his* race. The overall effect was that of a beautifully tooled machine running like a walker on coals, his feet barely touching the ground as he flew down the lane, almost always on his way to another record.

By his sophomore year Owens had broken several school and conference records, as well as the AAU indoor broad-jump record. But his biggest day was yet to come: the Western Conference (read: Big Ten) meet at Ann Arbor, Michigan, on Saturday, May 25, 1935.

It was a day that almost didn't come. A little over a week before the meet, Owens became involved in some collegiate high jinks with his rooming house buddies. Running from the scene of a water fight, he slipped and fell base over apex down a flight of stairs, landing flat on his back. The next day, in a warm-up meet against Northwestern, Owens hit the second-to-last hurdle right on his instep and felt an excruciating pain shoot "right up through my spine."

With a back now up for adoption, and advised to withdraw lest he run the risk of permanent damage to his spine, Jesse spent the week before the Big Ten meet consigned to the underside of a blanket, chemical heating pads taped to his back and stomach, feeling as weak as day-old ginger ale.

On the day of the meet, Jesse was able, with no little effort, to maneuver his aching body into an ancient Hupmobile for his ride to Ann Arbor's Ferry Field. With the old car hitting every bump along the way, Owens felt pain's forefinger jab into his back, into his thighs, behind his knees, and into almost every other part of his body. Finally, the car reached its destination, and, with considerable effort, Owens unfolded his body and hobbled as best he could to trackside. But the pain was so intense he was unable to warm up, and he questioned not only his ability to get down on his mark, but indeed to compete at all.

But in a classic triumph of mind over matter, Owens was able to shut out the aches and pains to concentrate on the thing that mattered: competing in the meet. "My back hurt when I went into the starting crouch," he was to remember years later, "but when the starter said, 'Get set,' I felt no pain at all." And so he hurdled, dashed, and broad-jumped his way to five world records and tied a sixth in less than an hour.

Perhaps his greatest achievement came in the broad jump. With the pain in his back impossible to ignore, Owens and coach Snyder, in concert assembled, decided that the extremes of the moment made their own rules and determined that Owens would make just one jump—no warm-ups, no preliminaries, no anything, just one jump. And so, eschewing the blindfold, they instead placed it in the pit at the 26-foot mark. Believing if 'twere done, then 'twere well 'twere done quickly, Owens hurtled down the runway, exploded from the takeoff board, and soared as high as he could into the air, almost reaching the cumulus of white hanging in the soft Ann Arbor sky, before descending eight and a half inches beyond the handkerchief. It was a new world record, one that was to stand for a quarter of a century, longer than any track-and-field mark has ever stood.

Owens's heroic struggle against pain and the best athletes of his day made him an overnight sensation, a national hero. He would have to wait just one year, until the 1936 Olympics, to become an international one.

Hate had lost its virginity years before 1936. Yet it would come to its ugliest full flower with the Berlin Olympics that year. Ever since Baron Pierre de Coubertin had conceived the first modern games back in 1896, the Olympics had been a showcase for amateur athletics and the ideas of amateurism. Now it was to be perverted by Adolf Hitler and his strutting Nazi brownshirts and other champions of the overdogs into a showcase to glorify "Aryan supremacy." Blustering about their "Master Race," Hitler gutturalized their claims, alternating them with faint impersonal smiles that seemed to cover something that passed more or less for contempt when they referred to "less endowed" mortals— including condescending references to America's so-called "black auxiliaries."

But in just six days, Jesse Owens was to give the lie to such slanders. First he competed in fourteen preliminary heats— running four heats each in the 100 and 200 meters and jumping six times—and all he did was break Olympic records a total of nine times and equal them twice. And then, in the competition for the Olympic gold, Owens won the 100 meters, the broad jump, and the 200-meter dash, and shared in another gold by running the first leg of the 400-meter relay—dominating the Olympics as only Jim Thorpe and Paavo Nurmi had before him.

The hundred thousand fans jammed into Reich Sportsfeld were at first struck to dumb apoplexy by the performance of one of the supposed inferior races. Then, after a queer sensation of disquietude, they erupted into a full-throated bellow and began hollering something that came out, without subtitles, sounding like "Yes-say, Yes-say, Yes-say...Ov-enns." One of those who didn't participate in the cheering was Adolf Hitler, who, maintaining a polite fiction of the nonexistence of the "black auxiliary," had left his box before the medal ceremonies.

"Hell, I wasn't paying attention to Hitler," said Owens, remembering the moment of a lifetime later. "You're running against the fastest guys in the world. Even after the race, you don't pay attention to the stands. You're just happy to get through another race."

Still, the fans in Berlin and everywhere else now regarded Jesse Owens as the supreme athlete. And he was, having four Olympic mountains from which he could look down on the rest of the sports world.

But even if he had not won his Olympic laurels of bay and myrtle, Jesse Owens was no hero pro tem, but one for the ages, one who transcended the world of sports and left his footprints in the sands of time for all time.

7

Wilt Chamberlain

b. 1936

There was only one Wilt Chamberlain—though truth to tell, he looked like two, resembling more the man Jack met at the top of the beanstalk than the beanstalk-thin giant who tore through opposing teams and record books in one swell foop.

While still knee-high to a basket at just six feet eleven inches, the youngster known as "the Big Dipper" and "Wilt the Stilt"—a nickname he detested almost as much as broccoli—scored 2,250 points over three years playing for Philadelphia's Overbrook

High, a phenomenal 37-points-a-game average. In the process, he became a marked man, both on and off the court.

With some two hundred colleges petitioning for his presence and the Philadelphia Warriors of the National Basketball Association putting in an early territorial claim for services, his future lay before him, a clear road such as only an infant enters upon. But even before the newspapers announcing his selection of the University of Kansas as his college of choice had doubled in duty as fish wrappings, those with Delphic franchises began to install him in the pantheon of all-time greats. And began raining on his one-man parade.

Harry Grayson, the NEA Service sports editor, asked, "Why does a Philadelphia boy have to travel halfway across the country to attend college?" Max Kase, of the *New York Journal-American*, added his five cents' worth: "Isn't the NCAA investigating reports of a special trust fund due to mature on Wilt the Stilt's graduation?" And the acrid torrent of words continued with Leonard Lewin of the *New York Mirror* cracking, "I feel sorry for the Stilt. When he enters the [National Basketball Association] four years from now, he'll have to take a cut in salary." It was like planting a rumor to see who answered. Nobody did.

More than a few observers expected this still-growing Goliath, who looked like he could eat apples off a tree without using his hands, to be more dominant on the college scene than even Bill Russell—who had just led his San Francisco team to two NCAA titles—conceding Kansas the championship for the foreseeable future. One coach, who watched him overwhelm his team in a freshman game, called him "the best I've ever seen." Another, North Carolina coach Frank McGuire, seconded the emotion, telling Jayhawker coach Phog Allen, "You're trying to kill basketball by bringing that kid into school. Chamberlain will score about a hundred and thirty points one night and the other coach will lose his job. There might be somebody in the penitentiary who can handle him, but I guarantee there is nobody in college."

At this point in his career, Chamberlain stood seven feet one-sixteenth of an inch and weighed 231 pounds, most of it concentrated in his well-developed neck, chest, and shoulders; his torso was the size of a normal man's, his legs resembled those of a grasshopper. Standing, he could reach a height of nine feet six inches; leaping, twelve feet six. It was almost as if a basket, standing alone and unprotected at ten feet, didn't stand a chance.

But there were other ways of defending against the gifted giant, and Chamberlain played his two years at Kansas with elbows to the right of him and elbows to the left, earning a black belt in basketball. Double- and triple-teaming became the norm as teams gave up the man-to-man defense when playing Kansas, concentrating instead on blunting this one-man offensive machine. When McGuire's Tar Heels played Kansas in the 1957 championship game of the National Collegiate Athletic Association, they threw away all standard strategies, making it just North Carolina versus Chamberlain. Collapsing three men around him on every play—one in front, one behind, and a third dropping off as soon as the ball was thrown to Wilt—Carolina challenged the rest of the Kansas team to take, and make, shots instead of forcing the ball in to Wilt. They couldn't, and North Carolina defeated Kansas in a game that went three overtimes, far past the normal union scale. And yet, with players hanging all over him, much as a shell to a tortoise, Chamberlain averaged 29.9 points and 18.3 rebounds a game over two years.

While at Kansas he dabbled a little in other sports as well, entering the 1956 Kansas Relays as an unattached contestant and tying for second in the high jump behind the world record holder and participating in the shot put and cross-country racing as well.

By now Chamberlain was looking for other worlds to conquer. And so, after two years at Kansas, he left to join first the Harlem Globetrotters and then the Philadelphia Warriors. Signing the biggest contract then known to the NBA, a reported $65,000, he provided the show the curiosity seekers sought and justified his advance billing—averaging 37.6 points a game in his rookie year, most on deadly accurate fallaway jumpers and his patented "finger-roll," scoring more than 60 points a game six times, and leading the league in minutes played and rebounding.

Basketball had never seen anything like him. And for the next two years he continued to serve up points by the heaping plateful, including so many 50-point games that the sports pages began to yawn at the feat but which made any dues-paying fan sit up and take notice. And then, in his third year, the press, too, sat up and took notice, of a meaningless game between Chamberlain's Warriors and the New York Knicks in Hershey, Pennsylvania. For "all" Wilt did in that little one-act drama on March 2, 1962, was make 36 finger-rolls and fadeaways from the floor and, for him, an incredible 28 of 32 foul shots, for an even 100 points, breaking what had been the record by a mere 29.

All of a sudden Chamberlain was as big news as he was big. How big was he? Well, even though the Warriors' press guide held that he was seven foot one, "the Dipper"—or "the Dip," as he was often called—did just that: dip when he came to a doorway, almost as a conditioned reflex. One newspaperman, measuring the height of a doorway as seven foot three, watched as Wilt ducked under it, folding in three parts like a carpenter's rule.

Still, while his height was open to question, his assault on the record books wasn't. For seven straight years he led the league in scoring as the number of his 50-point games rose.

And yet the press, which now sought to add a mustache to the picture of the goateed great, continued to heap calumny on his head, questioning why, if he was so "great," he had never played on a championship team.

Chamberlain was astonishingly sensitive to the smallest oddment of talk and went into a sulk whenever his failure to win a championship was mentioned. This lonely, sympathetic giant merely ascribed it to the fact that "nobody roots for Goliath." One who was sympathetic to his plight, his on-the-court bête noire, Bill Russell of the ever-winning Boston Celtics, said, "Wilt got tricked. Most fans and writers emphasized points, so he went out and got points. Then they said rebounds, so he went out and got the most rebounds. In his mind he had done everything required of a player, because he had led in all the categories that they had told him about. And he still could not win."

But then, in his eighth season in the league, Wilt finally shed his "loser" label and traded it in for one that read "winner" as he led his new team, the Philadelphia 76ers, to the league championship. Although for the first time he didn't win the scoring championship, he led the NBA in shooting percentage and rebounds and was third in assists. He was now, in the words of one of his teammates, "close to perfection."

Traded once again, this time to the Los Angeles Lakers, Chamberlain once again sacrificed his scoring average for rebounds and assists, and again led his team to the top of the NBA heap. He had finally silenced his critics.

By the end of his fourteen-year pro career, Wilt Chamberlain owned the record books, lock, stock, and basket. He had led the league in scoring seven straight times and in rebounding eleven years. Over his long career, he scored 30,335 points, and 50 points in a game 118 times. The next on that 50-point list is Michael Jordan with less than half that, which is like saying that the next in his class isn't in his class at all.

For Wilt Chamberlain was far and away the best of all time at putting the ball in the basket. And that is what it was all about for the man generally considered the greatest player ever to suit up, his name writ as large in the record books as his size.

8

Pelé

b. 1940

The mere presence of Pelé on a field could fill a stadium, in much the same way a great actor can fill a stage with a gesture. When he traveled to Biafra, the civil war then in progress was suspended as the combatants laid down their arms and flocked to see him. In Algiers and Khartoum, political disputes were discontinued for lack of interest during Pelé's visit. Everywhere he went, the story was the same. For Pelé was, simply stated, the number-one attraction in the world's most popular sport, his very name a calling card.

It wasn't always thus. For the man whose one name came to symbolize soccer the world over was in fact born with three: Edson Arantes do Nasciemento, the "Edson" after inventor Thomas Edison. Young Edson was raised in the small Brazilian village of Tes Corocoes by a family so desperately poor that they counted what few blessings they had—none of which included the ownership of a soccer ball—on the fingers of one hand. And so the youngster was reduced to learning the national game by playing with a grapefruit or a stocking stuffed with rags. The man who would come to be known as Pelé would remember: "I got in trouble with my father because we never could find two matching socks in the house."

When Edson was ten, a family friend gave him his first real ball. And like any kid anywhere in the world, the youngster played with his new toy for untold hours, practicing in the streets, on the beach, in the lots of nearby factories, and even against his own house. It was while he was kicking and rebounding the ball against the wall of his house that his father noticed that Edson used only his right foot to kick the ball. He taught his son how to use his left foot to get the same amount of power in both legs. With the first piece now in place, young Edson continued to add to his growing skills by learning how to use his head as a striking weapon and how to dribble, that unique form of filibustering known only to soccer.

The youngster now took his growing package of talents to the playing fields, playing against, and beating, construction workers three times his age. At the ripe old age of fifteen he took that package and hied himself off to the big-league town of São Paulo, where he tried to persuade the team's powers-that-be to take him on. But after receiving a don't-call-us-we'll-call-you answer from São Paulo, he instead signed on with the Santos Football Team on a trial basis for the munificent amount of $75 a month.

The Santos coach would later remember the man-boy named Edson Arantes do Nasciemento: "At first, he was just an errand boy for the older players. He would buy soda for them, things like that." But soon, the coach said, "they were looking up to him" as he began to play with that unique style that became his trademark—a style that combined more looks than could be seen during Carnival in Rio. Always interpreting both his opponent and the playing field in an interesting manner, the youngster controlled the ball almost as if it were attached to his feet by a string, moving about the greensward with the balletic agility of a Nureyev, his legs a blur as his seeing-eye kicks found open teammates and nets alike with remarkable accuracy.

His metamorphosis from errand boy to eloquent and elegant player continued apace as he embroidered his game with dazzling head shots—catching shoulder-high balls on his thighs and driving the ball into the goal with his opposite foot while soaring aloft—and that centerpiece of his ever-increasing talents, the over-the-head scissors kick. By his second year he had become an embarrassment of riches—and had become Pelé as well, a name given him not by claustrophobic headline writers but by his adoring fans, who gave him the godlike name because he played like one.

Pelé continued to electrify Brazilian fans by leading Santos to league championships in his first six seasons, averaging an incredible goal a game. But it was that quadrennial tournament known as the World Cup that did most to prove his potency, as, in both 1958 and 1962, he led Brazil to championships. And when three Italian teams pooled over $2 million in an effort to buy him from Santos, the president of Brazil stepped in to block the sale, declaring what everyone already knew, that Pelé was "a national treasure."

Pelé would lead Brazil to an unprecedented third World Cup championship in 1970 and then in 1974 announce, to the collective weeping and gnashing of teeth of a mourning nation, his retirement from the game. The Santos trainer, with tears in his eyes, could only shake his head and say, "Now people will tell their babies, 'Too bad, you will not see Pelé play.'"

But millions would again see Pelé, this time on the world's largest sports stage: America. For Warner Communications, hoping that Pelé's presence would serve as the first smooth stone to hit the soccer waters of America, then break in never-ending circles, signed Pelé to a contract worth $4.7 million to play for its team, the Cosmos, for three years and 100 games.

Finally, Pelé did retire, after twenty-one years and 1,281 goals, in front of a roaring crowd at Giants Stadium in the New Jersey Meadowlands in one of the most riotous celebrations since the French Revolution. As he raced around the field, waving his shirt over his head and exhorting the crowd to join him in chanting "Love...Love...Love...," one of those in the crowd of

fifty-thousand-plus, Muhammad Ali, could only look and marvel: "Now I understand…he *is* greater than I am!"

Ali understood, as so many others have, that in a day and
age when heroes come and go with all the suddenness and
completeness of the flame of a candle that has been blown out,
the fame of the man originally named after Thomas Edison will
continue to light up the world forever as one of the greatest
athletes of all time.

9

Ernie Nevers

1903–1976

If, as that chronicler of such niceties, Oscar Wilde, was wont to say, "Three addresses always inspired confidence, even in a tradesman," then only one athlete in the long history of sports ever inspired such confidence: Ernie Nevers. For going all the way back to just after Adam and Eve first heard the rush of the apple stampede, Ernie Nevers is the only athlete to have three sports addresses, playing football, baseball, and basketball on a major-league level—thus seeing Bo Jackson and Deion Sanders and raising them one.

In that long list of athletes whose feats go in one era and out the other, the six-foot-one Nevers stands taller still as a certifiable "superstar" long before the word became the cliché du jour served up by the keepers of the twenty-five-cent journals of record for almost every athlete ever to come down the pike.

Listening to the thinning number of fans with thinning hair tell of the legendary feats of this modern-day Paul Bunyon, you might shake your head in disbelief. But Nevers was the real goods, a strong-jawed 205-pounder with striking features capped by tousled blond locks, who more than resembled a Viking of old. And he played like one as well. With an unquenchable thirst for competition, Nevers earned eleven letters in four sports at Stanford University, captaining the football and basketball teams, pitching and playing right field for the baseball team, and, in his spare time, throwing the discus on the track-and-field team.

But even though the curriculum of college life is a wide one indeed, sometimes this athletic prodigy had difficulty shoehorning in all of his extracurricular activities. One afternoon in April, so the story goes, Nevers was to pitch for the Stanford Cardinals at exactly the same hour the team had scheduled a track meet. Nevers's solution was simply to strike out the side in the first inning and then, in full baseball regalia, sprint over to the track stadium to compete in the discus throw. Arriving just as the judge had shouted, "Last call for the discus!" a breathless Nevers, without a warm-up, in uniform and spikes, picked up the metal plate, whirled and spun out, and hurled it into the air. Then, without waiting to watch its flight, he raced back to the baseball diamond, just in time to take his turn at bat in the bottom of the inning.

His baseball coach gave the two-headed athlete an ultimatum: "Baseball or track, but not both!" Nevers chose baseball, much to the disappointment of his track coach, who had spent the rest of the meet looking for his AWOL star—whose throw had won third place. But the baseball coach, Harry Wolter, who had earned his spikes playing major-league ball, knew his baseball flesh, and by the time Nevers completed three years in uniform, his blazing fastball and .400 average had earned him a place on the all-time Stanford team.

On the basketball court, Nevers combined his strength, agility, and reflexes—along with something else: an innovation he introduced to the game, the overhead hook shot—to become, in the eyes of many, one of the two finest basketball players in Stanford's history. (The other was Hank Luisetti, who owns the original copyright on the one-handed set shot.)

But all of this only served as appetizers to Nevers's main

course, football. For Ernie Nevers was a slashing runner who combined power and acceleration with what his coach, Pop Warner, called "the most amazing reflexes I've ever seen in a man." In short, he was an earlier version of Jim Brown.

The centerpiece of Nevers's fame was the 1925 Rose Bowl game against Notre Dame. On paper, it was an extraordinary council of war, Four Horsemen versus one horse. To further even matters up, Nevers was playing on *two* broken ankles. Still, taped and trussed and with extraterrestrial recuperative powers, this one-man wrecking crew nearly undid Notre Dame and its fabled foursome. Playing the entire sixty minutes, Nevers relentlessly ground out yardage, gaining 114 yards rushing (compared to the Four Horsemen's 127) and punting for a 42-yard average. As Notre Dame coach Knute Rockne walked off the field, savoring his troops' 27–10 victory, thoughts of what was and what could have been merged, and he wondered aloud, "What would that man have done to us with two good ankles?"

In 1926, Nevers emerged from Stanford into the pro ranks, signing contracts with the St. Louis Browns of the American Baseball League, the Duluth Eskimos of the National Football League, and the Chicago Bruins of the American Basketball League, a team owned and coached by none other than the legendary George Halas.

Although Nevers was to achieve distinction in both baseball and basketball, again it was football in which he was to make his highest marks. Playing for Duluth—dubbed the "Nevers Eskimos" in tribute to its star—Nevers played all but twenty-nine minutes in his first year, setting records in running, passing, and kicking, including throwing seventeen consecutive completed passes and kicking five field goals in one game.

For two years, in that age of smash-mouth football, Nevers reduced everything, and everyone, to essentials as he ran through, over, and under opposing defensemen stacked up to stop him.

And then, proving that he was human, he missed 1928 because of a broken neck. But he came back in 1929 as the player-coach of the Chicago Cardinals, the last playing coach in the history of the NFL, and scored all 40 points in a 40–6 rout of the Chicago Bears, still an NFL record. Knute Rockne, who witnessed the game, could only tell his players, "That, gentlemen, is how to play football."

By 1931, Nevers had become pro football's answer to Lou Gehrig, an iron man who stopped at nothing and, conversely, let nothing stop him as he played every minute of all nineteen games. In one of those games, knocked unconscious for two minutes, and with the game held up until he regained consciousness, he recovered to carry the ball sixteen consecutive times, the last one for a touchdown.

No wonder his coach, Pop Warner—who, not incidentally, also coached Jim Thorpe at Carlisle—said of Nevers: "He could do everything Jim Thorpe could do, and he always tried harder than Thorpe ever did."

10

Michael Jordan

b. 1963

Michael Jordan didn't so much test the law of gravity as test its elasticity. This fugitive from gravity looked like a cross between a man who had just stepped out of an eighth-floor window and turned left, changing direction in midflight, and a man who had just taken a four-way cold tablet and run three more ways to catch up with it.

Many have tried to explain Jordan, but none plausibly, because nothing about him is plausible. One who tried to capture him in words was Jim Murray, the poet laureate of modern sportswriters, who wrote, "Michael Jordan, 'Air' to his compatriots, played a game ten feet off the ground. You need the RAF to stop him. He only came down periodically to refuel, then he took off again."

In truth, no one, not even Murray, could give a definitive description of Michael Jordan. But one thing was certain: He was the most exciting player to come down the court between basketball inventor James Naismith and the end of time. All other pretenders can be discharged for lack of evidence.

Jordan began his career at the University of North Carolina, where, as a freshman starter playing with the coolness and composure of someone of much greater age and experience, he led the Tar Heels to the NCAA championship, tossing in a straight-as-an-arrow sixteen-footer to give North Carolina a 63–62 win over Georgetown University in the final game. Two years later he added to his list of accomplishments by leading the U.S. Olympic team to the 1984 gold medal and being named the College Player of the Year by everyone who had a piece of hardware to award—from the U.S. Basketball Writers to the Associated Press, and all local franchisees of trophies in between.

And yet, despite a potential that was as plain as egg on the chin of a hungry trencherman in a boardinghouse, Jordan's incredible scoring ability had been effectively hidden under the bushel basket of Dean Smith's disciplined system of North Carolina basketball. Add to that an NBA scouting report that categorized him as a "drive-all-the-time, only-goes-to-his-right, one-dimensional player," and you might have the reason why he was only the third pick in the 1984 NBA draft. There is no other way to explain why he was chosen behind two talls, seven-foot Akeem Olajuwon and seven-foot-plus Sam Bowie—unless it was that, contrary to popular belief, the best place to hide a needle is not in a haystack, but in among other needles, and taller ones at that.

Whatever, it was worse than a blunder; it was a crime. And Jordan underlined the mistake by imposing his will on every team he faced. Threading a needle's eye with his shots, he scored 37 points in his third game in a Chicago Bulls uniform, 45 in his eighth, and 25 or more in ten of his first fifteen as he averaged 28 points per game and won Rookie of the Year honors.

Nonetheless, the Jordan legend truly took flight not from any of his on-the-court heroics but instead from something that happened off the court that rookie season. For, in the spring of 1985, television audiences were treated to the sight of a slender figure standing on an urban basketball court with a ball in his hands and Technicolor shoes on his feet. Slowly, to the accompaniment of revving jet engines in the background, the player began to move across the blacktop, leaning into his run. Then, just as the engines roared in screaming takeoff fashion, the player, propelled as if by some potent force, became airborne, flying high on a magic carpet ride. There, for a full ten seconds, legs splayed and weightless ball extended as he rose to the highest point above the horizon, was "Air Jordan," floating aloft with no geographic metes or bounds.

The wiles of those modern elixir salesmen known as advertisers had not been spent in vain. Overnight, that one commercial made owning a pair of Nikes Everykid's religion and obsession. And made Michael Jordan "Air Jordan." And the Iconic Man for the new generation, as he waltzed a little reality into Everykid's dreams and a little dreaming into Everykid's reality.

Now a negotiable commodity, smooth of coin—and head as well—Jordan returned to the basketball wars for his second season as the NBA's most celebrated player, courtesy of Nike. However, the one thing that could stop him did: a broken foot, which limited his sophomore season to all of eighteen games. And proved only that he was vincible.

Still, with almost superhuman recuperative powers, he returned to the Bulls' lineup ahead of schedule to lead Chicago into the playoffs, where, playing against the Boston Celtics, the eventual champions, he became an aerial circus, twirling, whirling, and pirouetting like a compass spinning out of control. And stopping just often enough to throw in seeing-eye baskets. In three games against the Celts, Jordan averaged 43.7 points, scoring an incredible 63 points in one contest for a single-game playoff record.

By his third year, fans who had followed the game only cursorily had discovered Air Jordan. And shook their heads with a tic of disbelief, salted with a who-are-you-kidding gasp, as they watched Jordan, playing with the torpedoes-be-damned exuberance of a little kid on the playground—complete with tongue hanging out of the side of his mouth—commit crimes against the senses too numerous to mention.

Jordan mainlined excitement, his every move one of high drama. With what seemed like extraterrestrial powers, he could make midcourse variations on a simple dunk; or deal out passes like a casino dealer, ofttimes keeping an occasional card up his sleeveless shirt; or move his feet constantly, almost as if afraid grass would grow under them, as he cunningly jockeyed for positional advantage and then, in the shake of a leg, or quicker, go skyward and throw up a time-release shot with divining-rod sensitivity in the direction of the basket. His heroics were of the sort that give rise to eyewitness accounts told and retold until one day the person who challenges them is labeled an iconoclast. Or worse.

Guarding this human scoring machine was futile, as he threw in did-you-see-that baskets with startling variety and monotonous regularity. And from just about any spot on the floor. Scorekeepers, trying to keep up with him, soon found themselves up for disability pay as he scored 50 or more points eight times in that third year and led the league with a total of 3,041—becoming, along with Wilt Chamberlain, the only player ever to score more than 3,000 points in a season.

But Jordan's 37.1 scoring average was merely the main course on the platter known as greatness. For this smorgasbord of talent also had 430 rebounds, 236 steals, and 125 blocked shots, and set the table for his teammates with innumerable à la carte assists so that they could sup alongside him.

In the 1987–88 season, Jordan again led the league in scoring and upped his totals in all other departments as well, winning not only the scoring championship and the Most Valuable Player award but also the Defensive Player of the Year award—the first time a scoring champion was ever so named. He was, in the words of all-time great Bob Cousy, "literally the Mona Lisa of basketball. He has no faults."

Jordan was now on an unlimited run, running up point totals high in the paint cards as he took possession of the record books, leading the NBA in scoring seven straight seasons and taking the Bulls to the NBA championship the last three of those.

Anyone who followed basketball knew that the census was wrong: there weren't 324 players in the NBA, there was but one. And that one was Michael Jordan, who was not only the most recognizable and most exciting player in the league, but also the best.

As such, he enjoyed all the shuffles that go with celebrity: brass bands, bright lights, and banners. But there were strings attached and mortgages to be paid with being a celebrity, discordant notes in the brass bands that followed in his wake. His every move was now followed by the press, both on the court and off, his every word and gesture scribbled by a thousand pens. Finally, when the tragic murder of his father pulled back the final scrim to his personal life, Jordan, announcing he "had nothing left to prove," packed his bags, and moved his locker from the game he had helped make the number one sport to the sport of baseball, resurfacing as an outfielder for the Class AA Birmingham Barons.

And then, after one year in organized baseball—where he batted .202, with 51 RBIs, 30 stolen bases and 2 home runs in 127 games—Jordan, almost as if he had a rubber band tied to his umbilicus, returned to the game he had made so fan-tastic to once again electrify the crowds and light up the scoreboards. And to provide more of those flights of fancy and fancy flights that had led Elgin Baylor to say of him, "Twenty years from now, if there's still basketball, people will still be talking about Michael Jordan."

11

Carl Lewis

b. 1962

The Fates being uncommonly partial to comebacks, it is one of the most common themes in dramaturgy. Ditto for sports. And in all the lore written on the subject, few athletes, if any, have ever recycled their greatness like Carl Lewis, who, at an age when most track-and-field stars have jogged off into the sunset, ascended his own personal Everest to take his place at the top of the mountain once again.

But, then again, there was never anything Carl Lewis ever thought he couldn't do, no mountain he considered too high to climb.

Born to two track coaches, like most sons Carl Lewis was

brought up in the "family business." By the age of ten, the Family Lewis began entering their young son in kids' track meets in areas neighboring the Lewis home in Willingboro, New Jersey. In one of those, a meet held in Philadelphia—just a stone's throw and a bridge away—young Carl won the long jump, his "first love." As chance and Fate would have it, awarding the medals that day was Jesse Owens, himself the winner of the long jump at the Berlin Olympics some thirty-six years before. "You're really talented," the Olympic legend told the youngster. "You're a little guy, but you beat all the big guys." And then Owens gave the youngster, who one day would succeed him as a legend, the same advice he himself had once received: "Dedication brings its own rewards."

But while young Carl possessed "dedication" by the heaping plateful, he was shortchanged in the size he had been served, and remained that "little guy" until the age of fifteen. Then, like Jack's beanstalk, he began to sprout, so much so that at one point he had to walk with crutches for almost a month while his body adjusted to his sudden spurt in size. As he approached his mature size of six-foot-two, his skills expanded proportionately, even exponentially, until soon he was beating the "big guys," regularly, jumping 26 feet 8 inches by his senior year in high school.

With so many talents, the youth took his still-growing package of skills to the University of Houston, where they were further developed by coach Tom Tellez. Tellez called his young phenom exactly that, "phenomenal," and Lewis, as a still-callow youth of eighteen, proved it by qualifying for the 1980 Olympics, both in the long jump and the 4×100-meter relay. But the Moscow Olympics were not to be, at least not for America, which boycotted the Games because of the Soviet invasion of Afghanistan.

And so, with no international worlds to conquer, Lewis set his sights on the national one. And by 1981 he had ascended to the number one ranking in both the 100-meter dash and the long jump. In 1983, at the U.S. National Championships, he won the 100, the 200, and the long jump, the first time anyone had pulled off that triple since 1886. And two months later he took his act on the road, winning three gold medals at the Helsinki World Championships. All of which was to serve as a prelude to the 1984 Olympic Games.

The 1984 Los Angeles Games were a celebration of nationalism, complete with pageantry, production, and pomp, all designed to show America at her patriotic best. The show-'em-what-we're-made-of brand of Americanism was pure form, overshadowing the real substance of the games. And Carl Lewis got caught up in its groundswell.

With a chance to equal the four golds won by Jesse Owens in the '36 Berlin Olympics, Lewis began his golden assault on Owens's grand slam in the 100 meters. Trailing in the final to Sam Graddy and Ben Johnson, Lewis accelerated and flew by it at the 80-meter mark, flashing by both as if they were parked there, reaching a speed of 28 miles per hour at the finish line and winning by an amazing eight feet—the widest margin in Olympic history.

His next event was one he had dominated, the long jump. Standing exactly 168 feet from his takeoff point, after fidgeting a little, Lewis suddenly lowered his head and took off, straight up, legs pumping high, arms stiff, chopping through the air, absolutely perpendicular. Hitting the board at 23 mph, he took off at a modest angle and like an Icarus without wings ran through the air with two kicks. Satisfied with his second effort, one of 28 feet ¼ inch into the wind, Lewis sat on the grass, determined now to contemplate the five races in front of him and to finesse the rest of his series of six jumps.

But those in the star-spangled crowd, suffering from a sharp lack of understanding, misinterpreted Lewis's decision to save his energies for his two upcoming events. To them his apparent I-say-it's-spinach-and-the-hell-with-it attitude was as profane as belching in church. After first stirring in their seats waiting impatiently for the story to come to its natural conclusion, as all Hollywood stories are supposed to, their bewilderment at his inaction soon began to make itself heard in boos. ·

For few indeed are the number of people sufficiently schooled in track and field to know how difficult it is to perform at world-class levels in both running and jumping. It is somewhat akin to having twenty-eight balls in the air, two of which are your own, and never dropping the wrong two. And Lewis was adept at juggling his priorities, never letting one get in the way of the other. Or dropping either. And even though he was to be proven correct, as attested to by his winning the long jump by almost a foot and going on to win his third and fourth gold medals after resting instead of jumping, he was viewed as such a boor that

ABC-TV didn't even bother to show him winning his fourth gold on live TV.

But then again, Carl Lewis has always been the eye of the storm, his every action—or nonaction, as the case may be—bringing reactions that sounded like all of Solomon's wives had just caught him out on the town with another woman.

When, in 1983, he quickly mastered the "deuce," or 200 meters, Lewis, who could never be charged with excessive humility, said it was "icing on the cake." And when he began exulting before he crossed the finish line in the U.S. championships, he was denounced for "showing up his rivals." Even Edwin Moses, the patriarch of the sport, spoke out: "I think Carl rubs it in too much. A little humility is in order." Other precincts reported in: He was a poseur, contrived, conceited. He was a hot dog. He won too easily, without drama or even a touch of false modesty. And still others "dissed" him by pointing out additional defects, hinting that he was everything from a drug user to a closet case.

But even these critics had to admit one thing: He was different. He was front-loaded, side-loaded, and back-loaded with opinions, all of them different, from his idea of skintight warmup suits that looked like a Goodwill box had thrown up on him to his otherworldly haircuts. He constantly challenged the Napoleons of the track-and-field world in a manner different from any before, demanding coin for appearance fees before such fees were even a glint in promoters' eyes. And, believing that "success always came so easy for me," he tried different things in such diverse and sundry fields as designing and singing, and even flirted with the idea of playing football. Make no mistake about it: Carl Lewis was certifiably different, one who, like Frank Sinatra, did it his way. But Lewis could be excused his idiosyncrasies for he was human. In fact, he was the fastest human out there.

As the 1988 Seoul Summer Olympics approached, Lewis set out to prove once again that he was the World's Fastest Human as well as the world's longest jumper, setting for himself the goal of an unprecedented repeat in all four events—a feat made all the more improbable by the fact that no one had ever repeated as champion in even one of the four.

His first gold came on the bounce, picked up when Ben Johnson, who had run an incredible 9.79 in the 100-meter final to break the world record, was disqualified for using illegal anabolic steroids, leaving Lewis as the holder of the new American record at 9.92 seconds and holder of his fifth gold. Next came the long jump, an event Lewis had dominated for five years, winning, in the process, fifty-five consecutive competitions. Because of a scheduling "mux-ip," Lewis had to jump first, only an hour after running the second of two 200-meter qualifying heats. And though he led after three jumps, instead of saving himself for the 200-meter final as he had in Los Angeles four years before, he opted to jump a fourth time, this one a booming man-in-flight jump of 28 feet 7¼ inches, his second gold of the games and sixth Olympic gold overall.

However, Lewis's mounting gold medal total stopped there, as protégé and training partner Joe DeLoach outkicked him two yards from the finish to beat Lewis by .04 second in the 200-meter final, and the 4 × 100-meter relay team was disqualified for an illegal handoff.

By now Lewis had been at the top of the international sprinting mountain for almost a decade, twice a normal career. But at the age of thirty, in the 1991 World Track and Field Championships in Tokyo, Lewis was to show he was far from through in what *Runner's World* called "the greatest footrace ever run over any distance."

After winning the quarterfinals and semifinals, Lewis's coach, Tom Tellez, took him aside and told him, anger rising in his voice as he spoke, "You ran your best race in the Rome World Championships in the semis. You ran your best race in the Seoul Olympics in the semis. I will not," Tellez said, banging his fist into his open hand, "have you run your best race in the damn semis here."

Chastened and running as if with a fear of being something less than the best, Lewis, third after 60 meters, moved into second spot after 80, legs pumping high—"turning over," as they say—his open hands flat as knife blades as they pumped eyebrow-high, running with the fire of a man of far fewer years. Coming on like an out-of-control express train, Lewis passed Leroy Burrell at 95 meters—"almost like we were standing still," said Burrell—and, leaning now into the finish line, thrust his arms skyward in exhilaration as he crossed in a world-record time of 9.86. In all, six runners broke 10.0 seconds, twice as many as had ever broken the barrier in any single race before.

"But wait," as the Ginzu knife salesman hollers at us from the TV set, "there's still more...." For even though Carl Lewis's career seemed almost at an end at the 1992 U.S. trials, where he failed to qualify for the 100 or 200 at Barcelona that year, making the team only for the long jump and as an alternate on the 4 × 100 relay team, he was far from through. And he proved it, as the man the Spanish call "El Hijo del Viento," or "The Son of the Wind," came back to beat Mike Powell, the man who had out-Beamonized Bob Beamon's famous record in the long jump, and also to anchor the relay team to a victory in world-record time.

The *wunder*-elder had done it again. Practicing his own form of regentrification, he had captured two more golds at Barcelona to add to his previous medals—giving him a total of six individual golds and two relay golds, one behind Paavo Nurmi's record nine, but equaling Nurmi's six individual.

Maybe, just maybe, the man Mike Powell calls "the best track-and-field athlete ever" had not just come back—maybe he had never gone away. And perhaps we, along with all his critics, simply overlooked the greatness of the man who performed as if propelled by his own divine spark, a spark that may continue to glow in the Atlanta Olympics of '96. And *that* will be one helluva comeback story.

12

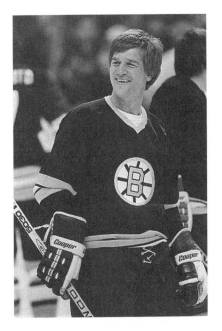

Bobby Orr

b. 1948

The statistics of a hockey rink are large indeed, encompassing as it does an area two hundred feet long and eighty-five feet wide. And in the long apocrypha of ice hockey, no one ever commanded that patch of white so completely as a five-foot-eleven, 185-pound virtuoso named Robert Gordon "Bobby" Orr.

Without putting too fine a point on it, before Orr skated onto the scene those with an honorable and ancient devotion to custom pictured the prototypical National Hockey League defenseman as a member of a paid goon squad whose duty consisted of trying to smash their opponents into smaller, untidier pieces with bone-crushing body checks. Orr was to break that mold with a style that made dust out of conventional wisdom, changing the equation and capturing the imagination.

Orr was only twelve years young when the Boston Bruins

first espied him. But even then they knew that Fate had cut this youngster out of the herd and that he was their future, the man-child who could lead them out of the hockey wilderness and back to the glory years they had once known—years that included the Stanley Cup and the famed "Kraut Line" of Bauer, Schmidt, and Dumart. Employing all the guile at their disposal, the Bruin management somehow inveigled the National Hockey League into granting them rights to this wunderkind.

Signed to a contract at the age of fourteen and assigned by the Bruins to the Oshawa Generals in the Junior A division of the Ontario Hockey Association, the fuzzy-cheeked youngster with the all-Canadian—and all-American—looks showed that, like the hot-walker who already knew how to ride before he was put in the saddle, he knew hockey. And how to play it.

Four years later the eighteen-year-old prodigy reported to the Bruins, signing the most lucrative rookie contract ever. And from the minute his skates met the ice, he began repaying that investment with interest. In his first practice session, one of his new teammates, watching the rookie wonder take the puck from blue line to blue line in less time than it takes to read this, skated over to Orr and said, "Kid, I don't know how much they're paying you, but it isn't enough."

After putting him through the usual baptism of fire and ice—including just-getting-acquainted swipes of the sticks by a welcoming committee including the likes of Gordie Howe and teeth-rattling body checks without so much as a by-your-leave from such as John Ferguson—and finding out that Orr could no more be intimidated than steel melted or ice welded, others looked upon him with envy and a new admiration. "He was," said coach Harry Sinden, "a star from the moment they played the National Anthem in the opening game of his rookie season."

As this marvelously gifted defenseman flashed down the ice, skating rather than flying only because he lacked wings, his opponents were left short of breath, and explanations as well. One player, who had been left opening and closing his mouth like a goldfish, tried to explain the Orr phenomenon by shrugging his shoulder pads and saying, "He has eighteen speeds of fast." But if his lightning was impressive, it was his thunder that made the greatest impact on the game, as Orr, acting like a fourth forward, gave the lie to the slander that defensemen can't play offense.

At the end of his first season, this youngster was named the NHL's Rookie of the Year. His second season saw him awarded the Norris Trophy, acclaiming him the league's outstanding defenseman. And his third season, the 1969–70 campaign, saw this by-now complete player finally, like the contortionist, come into his own. For all Orr did that year was become the first-ever defenseman to win a scoring title. Executing his own hat trick, plus one, he also won the league's MVP award, the Norris Trophy again as the league's outstanding defenseman, and the Conn Smythe Trophy as the most valuable player in the playoffs—playoffs that saw Orr power the Bruins to their first Stanley Cup title since 1941.

Scotty Bowman, who had watched his St. Louis Blues lose the Cup final to the Bruins on an overtime goal by Orr, could only shake his head and comment, "They say the Bruins started rebuilding the year Orr signed. I don't believe that. I think they started rebuilding in 1948—the year Bobby Orr was born."

But the 1969–70 season was only an appetizer for Orr. And for the next six years he fed on his success, scoring 100 points a season each of those seasons; winning two more MVP awards (and becoming the first player in NHL history to win three in a row); winning the Norris Trophy as the best defensive player in the league for the next six seasons (giving him eight years running, or skating, and almost permanent possession of the trophy); and once again leading the Bruins to a Stanley Cup win in 1972 (and, not incidentally, again being named MVP in the playoffs and scoring the cup-winning goal).

By now he was being proclaimed the greatest defensive player in the history of the sport. And more. Milt Schmidt, Boston's general manager and a member of the aforementioned "Kraut Line," called Orr "the greatest player there's ever been, in the past or present." And Ken Dryden, goalie of the Montreal Canadiens, added: "Orr is so clearly the best in hockey. I don't know that there's ever been anybody that so completely dominated a team sport."

Before Bobby Orr finally succumbed to the stabbing forefinger of pain, his knees caving in from the damage caused by too many bone-rattling body checks, he was to leave his mark as the most complete player in the history of hockey. And forever prove that defensive players could play offensive hockey. Orr could, and in the process revolutionized the sport.

13

Paavo Nurmi

1897–1973

Rumor has it that time and man have not always been on the best of terms. For verification we refer you to the works of Virgil, Sophocles, Shakespeare, or any one of a thousand other ancients going back to Day One—and beyond—who cite time as man's worst enemy. But one man didn't buy into those rumors, instead making time his ally, and in so doing becoming the champion distance runner of his time: Paavo Nurmi of Finland.

Nurmi first came upon the sports scene at the 1920 Summer Olympics in Antwerp, a twenty-three-year-old barrel-chested distance runner with incurious eyes, pointy elfin ears, and one of those impassive, stolid faces that looked like it had already been waited on. But it was his style, not his looks, that caught the eye of the international sports community: an unambiguous style that saw him run upright, head erect and in a measured pace, until the instant he hit the final lap—if not instanter—when he would break into a sprint, moving like a greyhound who had just spotted the rabbit.

However, this legend-in-waiting would have to wait for his coronation, as he lost his very first Olympic appearance, the 5,000-meter race, his inexperience allowing France's Joseph Guillemot to dictate the pace and beat him on the final straight-away. Three days later Nurmi got his chance to avenge that loss in the 10,000-meters. Lining up next to Guillemot in his normal stand-up starting position, Nurmi stayed back off the pace, this time set by Scotland's James Wilson, moving with a straight-ahead look of someone who didn't wish to be distracted. But, with two laps to go, Nurmi finally took the lead, and even though Guillemot was to pass him on the backstretch of the final lap, he retook it immediately with a final kick and won going away. It was the first olive out of his Olympic jar, and now they came tumbling out as he added two more golds, in the 10,000-meter cross-country individual and team races, before the 1920 games came to a close.

And yet, Nurmi, a perfectionist forever doomed to be unsatisfied, was tortured by visions of his performance in the 1920 games, especially his loss in the 5,000 meters. Returning to his native Turku, Nurmi laid out a rigid training schedule tailored for the scientific conquest of distances. As part of his regimen, he began to carry a stopwatch, one he continually referred to as he made time, not man, his opponent.

Soon the figure of Nurmi, one arm across his chest, stop-watch in hand, became a familiar sight throughout Europe as the man now called the Flying Finn would glance at his fisted timepiece periodically and then, on the last lap, toss it on the infield and sprint off with an impressive finishing kick to set distance record after record. In all, Nurmi, running with clock-work precision, set world records in an astonishing total of sixteen individual events and ran faster than the then existing world record no fewer than twenty-three times.

As the countdown to the '24 games began, Nurmi intensified his training, unvaryingly beginning with long walks and morning exercises. He also ran 80 to 400 meters several times a morning, always at top speeds. Then he would run a mile at a pace of just under five minutes. Only then would he eat breakfast. As stories of his training grew, rumors had him eating black bread and fish, although he would later say to one writer who asked, "Why should I eat things like that?" Then he would devote the remainder of the morning to running distances of 400 to 500 meters. The afternoon saw him running 10- to 25-minute cross-country distances, followed by a few laps around a 400-meter course at about 60 seconds to the lap. After an evening meal, Nurmi would walk one or two hours, covering a mile in about fifteen minutes. Never again, Nurmi swore, would he rely on guesswork. His fate would now reside in his own hands—or, more specifically, in his hand, in the form of his stopwatch.

It was only such painstaking devotion to duty—and time— that would have enabled Nurmi to accomplish what he did on the morning of July 10, 1924. For when the officials of the Paris Olympics announced the track-and-field schedule, it was discovered that the finals for the 1,500- and 5,000-meter races would be held only a half hour apart. The Finnish Olympic officials protested, feeling that half an hour would hardly give Nurmi an opportunity to recuperate from the rigors of the 1,500. Begrudgingly, the French officials extended the interval to fifty-five minutes, still a seemingly impossible task—even for a Paavo Nurmi.

But much as he had overcome injuries to both legs suffered in a fall on icy roads that Easter, Nurmi set about meeting the scheduling conflict as just another challenge. On June 19, three weeks before the day of the two Olympic finals, Nurmi simulated the two distances in a mirrored performance, first running the 1,500 meters in a world-record time of 3:52.6 and then, after a one-hour rest, running the 5,000 meters and setting another world record, of 14:28.2.

In the first of the two races, the 1,500 meters, Nurmi ran the initial 500 meters at a blistering pace, faster even than Jim Ryun would later when he set his world record in 1967. Then, consulting his stopwatch one last time before tossing it on the greensward, Nurmi sprinted away to a forty-meter lead, all the while conserving his strength for the demanding 5,000-meter run, and coasted to a win in the Olympic-record time of 3:53.6. Then, without indulging in any of the traditional victory exercises, he picked up his sweater and disappeared into the dressing room to rest for his next ordeal, the 5,000 meters.

Scant minutes later Nurmi took his place at the starting line for the 5,000-meter race, lining up next to countryman Willie

Ritola, who had run, and won, the 10,000 meters four days earlier. Nurmi, upset that the Finnish powers-that-be had allowed Ritola to run in his place in the 10,000 meters instead of allowing him to defend his title, determined to "run for myself, not for Finland" and prove to the world that he was indeed the top distance runner in Finland and in the Olympics as well. However, his opponents, trying to take advantage of Nurmi's supposed tired state, set a torrid pace from the start, running the 1,000-meter distance in the same time as future racers would in the 1972 Olympic finals forty-eight years later. Running evenly, almost mechanically, with his efficient and methodical high stride, Nurmi kept pace and took the lead at the halfway mark. Then, for the last eight laps, Nurmi, refusing, as always, to look behind himself, stayed a few yards ahead of the field. As was his custom, Nurmi checked his stopwatch for the last time with 5,000 meters to go, threw it on the infield grass, and, leaving the rest of the field to stare at his heels with dull resignation to their fates, sprinted to the finishing tape in the Olympic-record time of 14:31.2.

Nurmi would go on to win three more golds in the '24 games—the individual cross-country and team cross-country runs and the 3,000-meter team race—plus two more silvers and a gold in the '28 Olympics, including another gold in the 10,000 meters. But the twin hills from which he would forever look down on the rest of the Olympic world would be the two great races he won in Olympic-record time that afternoon in 1924.

Nurmi would have one last hurrah, an appearance at the 1952 Olympic games in Helsinki when, as a fifty-five-year old, Finland's greatest hero was given the honor of carrying the Olympic torch in the final lap around the Olympic stadium. As seventy-three thousand curious and excited fans caught a glimpse of the recognizable flowing stride entering the stadium, a vague roar went up, at first almost subterranean in quality and then erupting into a full-throated bellow. Then the electric scoreboard high atop the stadium flashed one word in giant letters—NURMI—and the stands rocked with the din and roar of patriotism.

It was a fitting appreciation of the man of whom writer Cordner Nelson once wrote, "Nurmi's imprint on the track world was greater than any man's before or since. He, more than any man, raised track to the glory of a major sport."

14

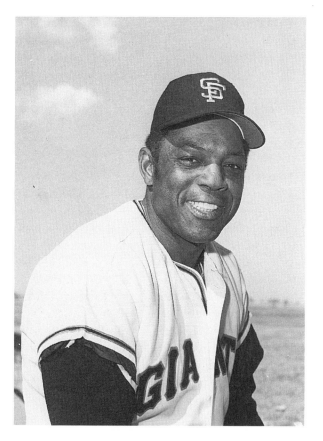

Willie Mays

b. 1931

Those ancients who commit themselves to the notion that athletes are men are herein advised to refer to the words of one of baseball's resident philosophers, Roy Campanella, who gave his opinion on what made Sammy and Roy—and just about everyone else—run and bat when he said: "You gotta be a man to play baseball for a living, but you gotta have a lot of little boy in you, too." For further proof we offer you Willie Howard Mays, who played baseball like a truant schoolboy out on a romp.

The young Mays, just two-plus weeks long of his twentieth birthday, joined the New York Giants on May 25, 1951, bringing with him from Minneapolis a .477 batting average plus a valise of hope that he could somehow get them back into the pennant race. For at that point the Giants were more giants in name than in deed, their record below .500 and their hated rivals, the Brooklyn Dodgers, pulling away from the pack and making the season more of a runaway than a race.

To listen to the rantings of manager Leo Durocher, sounding as giddy about the coming of Mays as Captain John Smith after Pocahontas went his bail, you would have thought Mays should have been granted direct passage to Cooperstown without ever having to play a game. But in his first three games the cupbearer of the Giants' future went hitless. Then, in his fourth game and his thirteenth at-bat, Mays, facing future Hall of Famer Warren Spahn, parked an inside fastball high atop the Polo Grounds roof as Giants announcer Russ Hodges verbally traced the ball's upward arc with a "Bye-bye, baby." However, when Mays followed up that cloud-buster with another 0-for-13 famine, many began to wonder if their confidence in Gibraltar had been misplaced. Still, Durocher carried the torch for Willie, a smile filling his wrinkles as he said to anyone within earshot, "I swear, I'm going to marry him."

Slowly, but surely, Mays began to acquit that affection, as his bat began serving up great platefuls of hits. And the Giants began to creep back into the pennant race.

August 12 was the day when all of New York would fall, like Durocher, in love with Mays. For on that day the Giants stirred the dying embers of hope by beginning a sixteen-game winning streak which, in the words of writer Red Smith, was "the greatest reversal since Serutan." The centerpiece of that streak was a three-game sweep of the Dodgers by the Giants, with Mays now taking center stage as well as center field. In the middle contest of that three-game set the newcomer made what *Time* magazine called "the Throw." With the Giants tied 1–1 and Billy Cox at third with one out in the eighth, Mays, flowing against the current and charted by his unerring instinct, caught Carl Furillo's looping fly ball going to his left and then, instead of stopping to set and throw, spun completely around in a balletic pirouette and "just threw the twine off the ball" on a direct line to catcher Wes Westrum in plenty of time to retire the speedy, and speechless,

Cox. Another who was rendered speechless by Mays's throw was Brooklyn manager Chuck Dressen, whose eye and intelligence rejected the connection, leaving him to mutter: "He'll have to do that again before I believe it!"

From that magic moment on, Mays became the darling of the dues-paying fan, wielding his bat as if it were a toothpick, running the base paths like a soap bubble, and playing the static fields of that old duenna of ballparks, the Polo Grounds, with a devil-Mays-care excitement.

By season's end, as any schoolboy worth his box score will tell you, the Giants had accomplished the impossible, catching the front-running Dodgers at the wire and then beating them in the live-or-die playoffs on Bobby Thomson's home run. But as Durocher himself put it, "The spark was Mays." And everyone knew it.

After two years as a guest of the U.S. Army, Mays came back in 1954 to pick up right where he had left off, leading the league in batting with a .345 average and sparking the Giants to another pennant.

But Mays's eternal fame would rest on one magnificent moment, forever pressed between the pages of time, in the 1954 World Series. The Giants' opponents were the Cleveland Indians, winners of a record 111 games and a heavy favorite to add the Giants to their list of victims. Amongst their number the Indians included the likes of Early Wynn, Bob Lemon, Al Rosen, and Bobby Avila, as well as one of the broadest backs in their big-back attack, Vic Wertz. And so it was that Wertz, already the proud possessor of three hits in three at-bats in Game One of the Series, came to the plate in the eighth inning of a 2–2 ball game with two men on. Durocher replaced his starting pitcher, Sal Maglie, with his left-handed reliever, Don Liddle, all the better, or so Durocher thought, to retire Wertz. Liddle was to throw exactly one pitch, that one right in Wertz's wheelhouse, not to coin a phrase. What happened next was baseball history in the making.

Wertz caught the ball on the meat part of his bat and, getting his full trunk behind his swing, drove a heat-seeking missile which shot abruptly toward the deepest part of center field. Most outfielders wouldn't have been able to strike up even a waving acquaintance with the ball. But, then again, most outfielders weren't Willie Mays, who normally covered enough ground to graze a dozen head of sheep. Mays took off, his back to home plate, with the resounding crack of the bat. The ball, not a parabolic blast which would twist slowly in the wind—especially since there was none that day—cut through the air like a knife through the higher-priced spread, continuing on its unobstructed course.

Commandeering his steed, and heading to that somewhere he commanded it, Mays raced one full furlong in front of the ball, running with resolution and almost out of his hat at the same time. He turned, in midstride, to look over his shoulder for a nanosecond, like an end gauging the flight of a pass, and then turned his attentions back to his breakneck sprint. The ball now began its downward path, heading for the green screen flanking the runway on the right side of center, 480 feet from where it had started. Just as it did, Mays flashed into view, running as if he, and he alone, knew where it would finally come to earth. With his arms beautifully extended and his hands cupped, Mays caught up with the by-now weightless ball hanging in the air just over his shoulder and cradled it, ever so gently, just a few feet shy of the screen.

The fans, at first struck dumb, erupted into cheers, making the stands an Aeolian trombone. But now Mays brought their roar to a strangulated rapture as he added yet another classic move to his once-in-a-lifetime catch. For after cradling the ball like a newborn to insure its safety, Mays, in a move combining grace and genuflection, put out a foot to stop his headlong dash into the screen, pirouetted, and, with every fiber of his being uncoiling like an ancient shot-putter, released rather than threw the ball, losing his hat and his balance in the process. It winged on its way back to the edge of the infield, a mammoth throw equal to Wertz's mammoth hit.

Mays's catch—hereinafter known as "the Catch"—and throw had closed the game, if not the entire Series, like a fist. Forget Dusty Rhodes's pinch-hit home run and the four-game sweep of the Indians by the Giants. For even if the honors belonged to the Giants, the glory then, and forever, would belong to Mays.

And for the next nineteen years Willie Mays's fame was to spread, propped up with reverential anecdotes, cut and restitched to the preferences of the storyteller. Told and retold were stories of "the Catch," "the Throw," his "basket catches," his stolen bases, his booming hits, and, of course, his all-out hustle. All punctuated, of course, by his signature: running out from under his cap, almost as if it had been made one size too small for him, which it was.

Maybe that's why one of the greatest Giant fans of all time, Tallulah Bankhead, once said, "There have been two geniuses in the world—Shakespeare and Willie Mays." For whatever stories people told, and retold, all of their words led to only one conclusion: the phenomenon known as Willie Mays was a thing of beauty. And a boy forever.

15

Muhammad Ali

b. 1942

Part showman, part promoter, and all champion, Muhammad Ali was boxing's—nay, the world's—version of the Pied Piper, always heading up his own parade with a band of admirers in his wake as he rolled through the sixties and the seventies.

Coming upon the scene when the heavyweight championship—if not all of boxing—was just a rumor, this man-boy who answered to the name Cassius Marcellus Clay for the first part of his life proved that charm travels as far as talent, as he became the most celebrated and flamboyant figure in the world of sports in three short years. He strutted with the air of a carnival barker and considered fame his due, so much so that he dubbed himself "the Greatest," a title many of his followers were willing to concede to him after he twice destroyed a supposedly invincible Sonny Liston.

Adding verbal footwork to his amazing agility in the ring, Ali brought a touch of the theatrical to boxing, his jabberwocky making his opponents' heads spin as much as his fast hands.

Muhammad Ali was an amalgam of a strutting fighter cocksure of himself and his skills and of Gorgeous George, the outrageous wrestler. Ali began predicting the outcomes of his bouts "after watching Gorgeous George. I hear this white fellow say, 'I am the World's Greatest Wrestler. I cannot be defeated. I am The Greatest! I am the King! If that sucker whups me, I gonna get the next jet to Russia. I cannot be defeated. I am the prettiest. I am the greatest!' When he was in the ring, everybody boooooed. Oh, everybody just boooooed. And I was mad. I looked around and saw everybody was mad." An idea struck Ali. "I saw fifteen thousand people coming to see this man get beat. And his talking did it. I said, this is a g-o-o-o-o-o-o-d idea!"

And so, the young boxer began talking himself up, forecasting the exact round in which he would dispose of his next opponent: "Archie [Moore] had been living off the fat of the land / I'm here to give him his pension plan / When you come to the fight don't block aisle or door / 'Cause ya all going home after round four."

This braggadocio was too much for the traditional, bottled-in-bond fight fan. They came out in droves to see the braggart beaten. But it was fruitless. In a scenario repeated time after time, he belted out his opponent in the prescribed number of rounds and then strutted around the ring like a conquering hero while the fans fumed.

Everything had a name or a meaning: His opponents were called "the Bear" (Liston), "the Mummy" (George Foreman), "the Washerwoman" (George Chuvalo), and "the Rabbit" (Floyd Patterson); his moves were "the Ali Shuffle," "the Rope-a-Dope," and "the Anchor Punch." And all became part of the language of fistiana.

Ali made great copy with his wonderfully engaging remarks. He called Leon Spinks "so ugly that when a tear runs down his face, it only gets halfway down and then runs back." In answer to whether he was scared of Sonny Liston, he said: "Listen, black guys scare white guys a lot more than black guys scare black guys."

But it was one of those off-the-cuff remarks that came back to haunt him and shortchanged "the Greatest" of almost three years of his career when he was still at the peak of his prowess and glory. For when Ali, aka Selective Service number 15-47-42-127, was reclassified 1-A and asked by the press what he thought of the action of his local Louisville Selective Service Board, he said, "I ain't got no quarrel with them Viet Congs." That, and his decision, based on religious convictions, not to step forward at his induction ceremony during the Vietnam conflict, gave the local Babbitts who controlled the boxing commissions enough ammunition to defrock him and bar him from the ring.

He survived as few others could have survived, by bucking the system. But in the end he was victorious, the United States Supreme Court unanimously ruling in his favor. Ali triumphantly came back in 1970, after three and a half years away, to take up where he had left off—as the undefeated heavyweight champion of the world.

Now Muhammad Ali was bigger than boxing, having transcended the four cornerposts of the ring to become the embodiment of the seventies, a man who had challenged the system and won. And despite his fifteen-round loss to Joe Frazier in what was billed as "the Fight," Ali remained "the People's Champion," a position he elevated to "World Champion" with a stunning eighth-round knockout of George Foreman in the famous "Rumble in the Jungle" in 1974.

Although Ali was to fight on for four more years—with two unfortunate attempts at a comeback—in the eyes of many, he had lived up to his claim of being "the Greatest."

16

Jackie Joyner-Kersee

b. 1962

Forget that moth-eaten quote attributed to Leo Durocher, "Nice guys finish last." First of all, he didn't say it. What he said, in answer to sportswriter Frank Graham after Graham had challenged him to be "a nice guy and admit you're wrong" about something or other, was "I don't want to be a nice guy." Then, Durocher looked out of the Brooklyn Dodgers dugout and saw New York Giants manager Mel Ott. Pointing to Ott, Durocher added, to emphasize his point, "Who ever saw a nicer guy in baseball than Mel Ott? And where is he?" All of which Graham encapsulated into one of the best-known quotes in the annals of sports.

But whatever the quote, it's just plain ol' wrong. And for references, we give you Jackie Joyner-Kersee, who continually disproves Durocher's Law by being, albeit not a "guy," both first and nice.

For if one word describes Joyner-Kersee, it's the four-letter word *nice*. "I don't know a person in this world who has a negative thing to say about Jackie," said Fred Thompson, an assistant coach on the 1988 women's Olympic track-and-field team. Valerie Brisco, a longtime friend of Joyner-Kersee's and a three-time Olympic gold medalist, added, "After the [1984] Olympics, when I was going through phases, Jackie was always sending me cards and letters of encouragement, like, 'Val, you can do it.' She's like that."

That "niceness" was forged in the smithy of her soul at an early age by her mother, who wanted for her daughter what she had never had. Named Jacqueline—after the first lady in the United States—by her grandmother, who knew that "someday this girl will be the first lady of something," young Jackie had her moral compass set upon her mother's exceptional course: one of always being nice to people and understanding that a single mistake can be devastating.

The former was easy; the latter not so. Especially in East St. Louis, Illinois, a place with all the earmarks of an eyesore. With factories idle, houses decaying, and stores boarded up, East St. Louis is a town of no presence and even less future—a place where peer pressure is the pressure to surrender to the streets; where the vicious cycle of children having children is endlessly repeated; and where you have to walk five blocks just to get away from the scene of a crime. At an early age, Jackie, together with her brother, Al, the 1984 Olympic triple-jump champion, determined that "someday we were going to make it—make it out." And they decided to make sports their avenue of escape.

A vivacious youngster reflecting sunshine and clear weather with an electrifying smile that exhibited more teeth than could be found on a dentist's chart and an energetic manner that could light up the whole of East St. Louis, young Jackie first devoted her extracurricular talents to such little-girl activities as modern dancing and cheerleading. Then, at the age of nine, she went out for the track-and-field team at the local recreation center. But even though she made the team as a quarter-miler, her favorite event was the long jump. "When I started in track, no one wanted me to jump," she remembered. "My reputation was as a runner, and my coaches wanted that to be my sole focus. I became a jumper almost by accident. The coach was waiting for one of the girls to jump, and I just ran over and *leapt*. He was amazed at how much distance I covered. And ever since then I've been known as a long jumper." She added, "In a way, I'm still rebelling, wanting to do what I once wasn't allowed to do."

But that rebellious nature came a cropper when rubbed up against the even stronger rules of conduct set down by her mother. "At ten or twelve, I was a hot, fast little cheerleader," she remembered in an interview with *Sports Illustrated*. "But my mother said, with no chance for negotiation, that I was *not* going out with guys until I was [She pauses to express the crushing finality of it]…eighteen! So I threw myself [She pauses to permit guesses: Under a train? Into the river?] into sports and school."

And so, radiating a hard glow of high purpose, Jackie threw herself into sports. Wholeheartedly. In volleyball she was captain of the team and an all-Metro selection. In basketball she averaged 21 points and 14 rebounds a game, was a three-time all-State selection and two-time all-American. And, in her senior year, she led the Lincoln High Tigerettes to a winning margin of 52.8 points a game and the state title.

But it was in track that she raised her performances to unimaginable heights. By thirteen, she was jumping 17 feet. By fourteen, she was competing in Junior Olympic pentathlons, winning four. In her junior spring she long-jumped an Illinois state high school record 20' 7½", a record she later extended to 22' 4¼". And, for good measure, she was the state champion in the 400 meters.

By now hailed by many as the greatest athlete in high school history, it seemed that Jackie had fulfilled the promise of being "the first lady of something." But the best was yet to come.

Upon graduation from Lincoln High, Jackie packed up her bags and her bagful of talent and took them as far away from her mother's absolutisms as she could—to UCLA. Now eighteen, she "didn't care as much anymore about men and clothes and parties. The crisis," she was to say, "had passed."

But now she was to face a real crisis. For even as she played her cards right, Fate stepped in to deal her one from the bottom of the deck. Midway through her freshman year, in January of '81, the ungraspable happened. Her mother, age thirty-eight, had suddenly been stricken by a rare form of meningitis and lay in a coma, brain-dead. Summoned home, Jackie and brother Al took one last look, prayed, and instructed the doctors to remove the life-support system. Two hours later, her mother was dead. As Joy

Duckett Cain wrote in *Essence* magazine: "Her grief-stricken family went into a state of shock. The funeral was harrowing. One daughter fainted, another had seizures, the son could hardly speak. Only the eldest daughter, Jackie, remained calm and dry-eyed through the ceremony and in the days that followed. 'I felt that I was the strong link,' Jackie Joyner-Kersee recalls now. 'If I went back to school and did what I was supposed to do, everyone else would know "Hey—we're not supposed to sit and cry. Jackie's going to get on with her life, and we should, too." I felt that I was the one who was supposed to set the example.'"

And so, carrying her sorrow as excess baggage, Jackie returned to UCLA, there to pick up where she had left off, to resume her studies and to rejoin the basketball and track teams. But with her pillar of strength now gone, her tight rein on her life was shaken. Enter, stage right, an assistant track coach named Bob Kersee to offer her a shoulder.

Kersee had come to UCLA as an assistant women's track coach in 1980, a few months before Jackie's mother died. Kersee, who had also lost his mother at eighteen, volunteered to help Jackie if, as she said, "I had doubts and needed to talk them out."

Kersee also helped Jackie in another way. Then the women's sprint coach, Kersee "saw this talent walking around campus that everyone was blind to." With "no one listening to her requests to do more," Kersee decided to go to the athletic director with a proposition he couldn't refuse. To Kersee, a self-described "hard-ass" who rarely had to do more than cock an eye to get his way, a proposition usually took the form of an ultimatum. His now became: "Either I coached her in the hurdles, long jump, and multievents or I'd quit, because to go on as she had would be an abuse of her talent."

Jackie at first dug in her heels, hesitant to deemphasize basketball and compromise her beloved long jump. But although she resisted, she gradually came around to Kersee's way of thinking and dedicated herself to the pentathlon and the heptathlon. And to becoming the "World's Greatest Woman Athlete."

With Kersee harnessing her speed and spring and grafting on additional skills in the hurdles, the shot, and the javelin, by the following year he could not only see progress but "could see she'd be the world record holder." However, such heady thoughts would have to wait. For a while anyway. For although she qualified for the 1983 World Championships in Helsinki, she was forced to pull out after the first day of competition, fingers of pain stabbing at her leg after she pulled a hamstring. And then, in the 1984 Los Angeles Olympics, she long-jumped poorly and lost the heptathlon gold by a mere five points, 6,390 to 6,385, to Glynis Nunn of Australia.

But 1986 would be Jackie Joyner's year—or, more correctly, Jackie Joyner-Kersee's year, for in January of that year she married Bob Kersee. Their arrangement was a simple one: Off the field, he was her husband; on the field, he was her coach. It was a workable combination, as proved by her performances throughout the rest of that year. On July 7, at the Moscow Goodwill Games, she became the first woman to break the 7,000-point mark in the grueling seven-event heptathlon, with a new world record of 7,148 points. On August 2, just twenty-six days later, she raised that mark by 10 points at the Sports Festival in Houston.

From that moment on she was almost immune to defeat as, in a stop-me-if-you've-heard-this-one-before manner, she won heptathlon after heptathlon, including the gold at the 1988 Seoul Olympics with a new world and Olympic record of 7,291 points. Five days later, she won the long jump with a new Olympic record of 24′ 3½″, the first multievent winner to win an individual gold in sixty-four years. She added a second gold at the '92 Barcelona Olympics, with 7,044 points, and repeated as the gold medal winner in the 1993 World Championships. Add the 400-meter and 60-meter hurdles to her repertoire, and you have someone with more than enough credentials to qualify for the mantle once held by Babe Didrikson Zaharias as "the World's Greatest Woman Athlete."

Her winning efforts were rewarded with enough hardware to open her own trophy shop as she was awarded everything from the Broderick Cup to the Associated Press Athlete of the Year award to the prestigious Sullivan Award. But she won something far more important than mere trophies: She won the admiration and appreciation of everyone in the world of sports for her many off-the-field contributions. Operating under the guiding principle that "I believe it is the responsibility of Olympic champions to give something back to youth, to the public," Jackie Joyner-Kersee devoted untold hours and effort to giving something back to East St. Louis, where she had grown up, donating a portion of all her endorsement money directly to the Jackie Joyner-Kersee

Community Foundation, and, in turn, into the community of East St. Louis.

Bruce Jenner calls this 5′ 10″, 150-pound marvel "the greatest multievent athlete ever, man or woman." Bill Cosby sees Jenner and raises him one, calling Jackie Joyner-Kersee "the best athlete in the world, period." And husband Bob, speaking of his wife's many accomplishments, both on and off the track, says, "There's no period at the end of her sentence yet. Jackie is just 'to be continued.'" And that's a "nice" thing to contemplate.

17

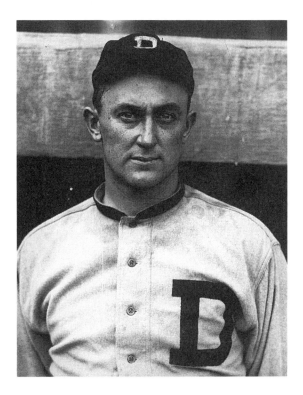

Ty Cobb
1886–1961

Watching Ty Cobb play in his do-or-die manner, one got the impression that he was so unrelenting that after he had been kicked out of the game of life by the Great Umpire in the Sky, he would demand that his ashes be thrown in His face.

For Ty Cobb subscribed to the theory that "baseball is not unlike a war." And he played it that way, with an acid soul, with endless spite and with a burning rage.

Some dime-store psychologist might call it competitive paranoia or even a Napoleonic complex. But it was almost as if Ty Cobb's life were a modern version of a Greek tragedy. For much of what fueled the demons bottled up inside him stemmed from a family tragedy that occurred when young Tyrus's mother, mistaking Ty's father for a burglar, shot and killed the elder Cobb as he tried to enter their house via a bedroom window. Young Ty's scars never healed, and Cobb was to play every one of his 3,033 games with a smoldering fire in his belly, playing each game as if it were his last, brooding and bubbling with inner violence.

With every nerve exposed, Cobb waged a war on the field, and on the record books at the same time. Cobb's long list of accomplishments included twelve batting titles, eight of them consecutive; most games played; highest lifetime batting average (.367); twenty-three consecutive .300 seasons; most runs scored; etc., etc., etc. When he retired from baseball in 1928, he left behind ninety records.

In the batter's box, Cobb, resembling a slight tuning fork, would crouch over the plate in a left-handed stance, his hands a few inches apart on the bat, like a little kid holding up his hands while grandmother winds the wool, all the better to control it— and the path of the batted ball as well. As often as not, Cobb would hit the ball to the opposite field, something he pioneered, moving his back foot when he drove the ball to left, almost backing away from the pitch, and spraying his cluster hits to left, right, or wherever.

Still, even Cobb admitted, he was never more than a natural .300 hitter. It was his speed that allowed him to beat out bunts and scratch hits and add another 50 points or so to his average. Cobb could be outrun in the 100-yard dash by several other ballplayers, but nobody ever ran the 360 feet of a diamond faster than he did.

His speed on the base paths was what set him apart. Harry Hooper, the Hall of Fame outfielder, said that as great as Cobb was as a batter, "he was even greater as a base runner." With nerve and lightning reflexes, Cobb dared to be great, creating havoc on the base paths, marauding more than running. And if someone dared to get in his way, Cobb, announcing he would "cut the heart of my best friend if he ever tried to block the road," would flash his sharpened spikes in that player's direction. He stole so many bases that Cleveland manager Lee Fohl once said, in despair, "He stole everything but our uniforms."

Under all that fire and fight were considerable calculation and cunning. He would pull up entire teams by the roots to study them, his restless brain sometimes figuring out a play—or a weakness—and then waiting a month or a year before the chance came to use it. Studying a pitcher's tics and movements, he would know when to take off, using a quick jump and his reflexes. Or he'd go from first to third on a sacrifice; or score from second on a sacrifice fly; or score from first on a single. Ray Schalk, the Hall of Fame catcher, shaking his head, could only say, in awe, "It was hard to believe the things you actually saw him do."

But Ty Cobb's calling card was intimidation. He would sit in the Detroit Tiger dugout before the game sharpening his spikes. Or participate in that great baseball tradition of bench jockeying, pointing out defects in his opponents' spiritual makeup and liberally adding references to their ancestry.

And so it came as no surprise that Cobb was viewed by opposing fans with the affection European countries lavished on invading Huns. In New York, for instance, he was known as "Terrible Tyrus."

Undeterred, Cobb would challenge his many enemies— fans, umpires, even teammates—to fistfights. Earle Combs of the Yankees said of him: "Cobb had no qualms about baiting, indeed fighting, anyone. And I mean *anyone.*"

Of all of Cobb's many achievements, the one he prided himself on most was the number of runs he scored. As Grantland Rice wrote, "Lord! How he concentrated on runs." And so, one night about a dozen years after he'd retired, he was at the Detroit Athletic Club with Nig Clarke, the old Cleveland catcher. Talk begot more talk, and Clarke mentioned his patented act of rapidly tagging a man and immediately throwing his glove aside, signaling the third out. At that, Clarke laughed, "I missed many a runner who was called out. I missed you at least ten times at the plate, Ty." And that was all he got out, as his boast loosed the Tiger. Cobb, coloring up like an old gobbler and the cords tightening on the back of his neck, lunged at Clarke and began choking him. "You cost me ten runs—runs I earned," screamed Cobb.

There were strings in Cobb's heart that it was better not to vibrate. And very few tried during the twenty-four-year career of the most dominant player ever to play the game.

18

Red Grange

1903–1991

A great athlete is always before his time. Or after it. Red Grange *was* his time.

He was half-man, half-myth. The problem was: Which half was myth? To an age surfeit with heroes Harold "Red" Grange stood taller than most and ran faster than all. In the true tradition of Frank Merriwell, he made the impossible look possible and the possible very probable. The epic grandeur of this man with a football cradled under his arm evoked flavorful nicknames in that quaint way the vital two-cent essay had of describing sports stars of the twenties. He was alternately called "the Galloping Ghost," "the Flying Terror," "the Wheaton Ice-man," and just plain ol' Red, because of his shock of red hair, the color of a smoked meerschaum. In a day and age of one or two nicknames, Grange was so good he had at least four. Grange was to focus the nation's attention on a sport which had, until his arrival, been considered merely newspaper filler between baseball seasons.

At Wheaton High in Illinois, the young Harold Grange blossomed into a five-foot-ten-inch, 172-pound youth whose stylish freedom of movement enabled him to evade oncoming tacklers and amass 75 touchdowns in three years of varsity football. Added to this were 82 points after touchdowns for an incredible 532 points scored. And if that weren't enough, Grange also starred in basketball, baseball, and track, for a total of sixteen high school letters.

In those days before athletic scholarships were handed out with all the abandon of latter-day flyers for a bank opening, this high school phenomenon was without one when it came time to enroll in college. This despite the fact that only the previous spring, while participating in the state interscholastic track meet at Champaign, Illinois, football coach Bob Zuppke had introduced himself to Grange (whom, with a Teutonic accent, he addressed as "Grainch," being unable to pronounce the soft G) and told him, "You may have a chance to make the team here."

And so "Grainch" enrolled in the University of Illinois because "all the kids in the state wanted to play for Zuppke," and also because "it was the cheapest place for me to go." And, in his very first game on the freshman squad, he scored two touchdowns. From that time on, Zuppke paid particular attention to the eighteen-year-old.

At practice the following spring, Grange—now six feet tall and 185 pounds—was given the number that he would carry to fame: 77. It was a number thought by many to be doubly lucky, but when Zuppke was asked how Grange came by it, he replied, "Well, he was in the lineup as a sophomore behind the guy that got 76 and he was ahead of the guy that got 78. That's about it!"

And so Number 77 began, from his very first game, to make his name and number known. Against a strong Nebraska team, he sprinted for a 35-yard touchdown in the first quarter, added a 6-yard scamper in the second, and added still another six points in the third. By the end of his sophomore season, Grange had scored twelve touchdowns, gained 1,296 yards, and been named to Grantland Rice's all-America team.

But the day that would stamp Grange as the greatest open-field runner of all time and make him a living legend occurred the next year, on October 18, 1924. On that day, with Illinois playing host to the previous year's Midwestern Conference co-champions, the University of Michigan, Grange took the opening kickoff on his own 5-yard line, crossed the field like the blades of a scissors coming together and apart, and, leaving would-be Wolverine tacklers strewn over the field, ran the remaining 95 yards unmolested. Two minutes later, Grange burst through the line with his quick start and scampered for another touchdown, this one for 67 yards. Twice more in the first twelve minutes of play he touched the ball, and twice more he swivel-hipped and straight-armed his way to touchdowns, one for 56 yards and the other for 44. He was later to ghost his way to yet another on a 15-yard sprint, and for good measure throw a pass for the team's sixth touchdown in a 39–14 Illini win.

Damon Runyon was to write of his exploits: "He is three or four men rolled into one. He is Jack Dempsey, Babe Ruth, Al Jolson, Paavo Nurmi, and Man o' War." And Laurence Stallings, author of *What Price Glory* and famed World War I correspondent, who had covered many events of earthshaking importance, watching the player they now called "The young Lochinvar come out of the West" play powerhouse Pennsylvania and carry the ball thirty-six times for 363 yards in ankle-deep mud, could only lament, "I just can't write about it. The story's too big for me." Red Grange was *that* big.

A three-time all-American, Grange took on almost mythic proportions, scoring 31 touchdowns and gaining 4,085 total yards in his college career.

Grange's greatest contribution, however, was not to collegiate football but to its poor stepsister, professional football. Up to the time Grange joined the professionals their ranks looked like they had emptied out the missions, with has-beens, never-wases, and names that weren't even household names in their own households playing for pay. But when Grange, under the management of C. C. "Cash and Carry" Pyle, signed with the Chicago Bears on November 22, 1925, it signaled the arrival of the professional game.

From his very first game, played in front of a sellout Cubs Park crowd, through his whirlwind tour, a moveable feast that included eight games in eleven days in every city which had a team or a stadium, Harold "Red" Grange made the game of professional football.

And he distinguished himself in professional football as much as he had in the collegiate ranks. George Halas, his coach and teammate, was to say of Grange, "He was the game's greatest runner until he hurt his knee, and after that the game's best defensive back."

That was Red Grange, half-man, half-myth, and *all* football player.

19

Oscar Robertson

b. 1938

Oscar Robertson did for basketball what Degas did for ballerinas, van Gogh did for sunflowers, and Warhol did for soup cans. The consummate artist with a palette filled with a variety of skills, Robertson was able to lay down layer after layer of his masterpiece, game after game.

The man known as "the Big O"—as in "Offense"—was the most versatile player ever to take his place on the court, a letter-perfect player with a package of skills far exceeding the normal union limit or ever seen in one athlete. Drawing a picture as well as any dictionary will allow, Robertson possessed not only a deadly outside shot but also an ability to create opportunities for both himself and teammates by driving to the basket or threading the proverbial needle with his passes, all with a fluid grace and instinct, coupled with a touch of stylized intelligence. On defense, he could rebound as well as any forward and play the big "D" as well as the big "O." Put them all together and they spelled the complete player.

Red Auerbach, who goes back to the time right after Adam first heard the onrush of the apple salesman, said of Robertson's talents, "He is so great he scares me. No one came close to him." And coaching legend Joe Lapchick once said, "There's never been one like him."

The kid who was to become known as "the Big O" took root at Crispus Attucks High in Indianapolis, an all-black school named after the first American casualty in the Revolutionary War. Robertson led his team to forty-five straight wins, the first undefeated season in the history of the tough Indiana state high school system, and two consecutive state championships—capped by his 39 points in the tournament final in his senior year. Graduating as an all-everything—including the National Honor Society—Robertson had his choice of the choicest basketball factories, all anxious to recruit him on a basketball scholarship. He selected instead the unheralded University of Cincinnati, "because I didn't want to go that far from home and because it had a co-op system of studying and working that I was interested in."

And so, performing as a part-time student, part-time calculator operator at the Cincinnati Gas & Electric Company, and full-time basketball player for the University of Cincinnati Bearcats, Robertson more than acquitted his press notices with his varied talents. A three-time consensus all-American and Player of the Year each of those years, Robertson led the country in scoring three straight years with an average of 33.8 points per game and set fourteen NCAA University Division records, among them the all-time scoring record.

At six-foot-five and 215 pounds, Robertson's package of talents—which included shooting, dribbling, rebounding, and passing—caught the attention of everyone with an eye for basketball delicacies. New York University coach Lou Rossini, whose charges had just been reduced to a state of disability by the one-man team, could only shake his head and say, "The only way to stop him is to put four men on him and have your fifth man guard the other Cincinnati players. Maybe even that won't work!"

Fabled Kansas coach Phog Allen, who had seen them all, was moved to call him "the greatest player of all time for a fellow his size."

Robertson also gained a second reputation, that of being "the Calvin Coolidge of basketball," a reference to his being reserved and quiet in the face of the public glare. After he scored 56 points on his first visit to Madison Square Garden, New York sportswriters crowded into the Cincinnati dressing room, anxious to wear their pencils down to stubs with notes and quotes from the new phenom for their vital essays. One writer asked Robertson what thoughts he had on breaking the all-time Garden scoring record. Hoarding his every word much as a miser does his treasures, Robertson merely answered, "I was glad." Another time, after scoring 62 points against North Texas State, he was asked how he felt. Oscar answered with one word more: "I had fun tonight." And when, in his senior year, he was presented with the ball after having broken the all-time collegiate three-year scoring record, Oscar, making no illiterate request upon the art of conversation, just took the ball and walked off the court without saying a word.

But the Cincinnati Royals were not looking for a public speaker, they were looking for a franchise saver. Over the past three years, while the University of Cincinnati and Robertson were packing them in across town, the city's professional entry in the NBA was drawing only fifty-eight thousand fans to its thirty home games. And so, just one step ahead of the sheriff, the Royals exercised their territorial rights and drafted Robertson in the first round of the 1960 NBA draft.

What the Royals got was an Oscar-of-all-trades, a super-playmaker, a super-scorer, an outstanding rebounder, and a backcourtman unseen since the days of Bob Cousy. And not only did Robertson do everything—leading the NBA in assists with 9.7 a game, finishing third in the league in scoring with an average of 30.5 points per game, and finishing second in team rebounds—but he did it for almost forty-eight minutes a game, every game.

Those trying to stop him found they had about as much chance as a pyromaniac who's just sneezed on his last match. One who tried to defense Robertson was Red Auerbach. When his Celtics finally "held" Robertson to 37 points—along with 11 assists and 22 rebounds—Auerbach confessed to having told his team "to stretch their fingers out wide, with their hands way up, on defense, figuring every little bit helps. You know what Oscar did? He shot through their fingers!" Auerbach wouldn't double-team him because, as he said, "Anytime you leave a man open, Oscar is going to hit him. He controls everything out there, and he wastes the least amount of effort of any player I've ever seen. Every move has a purpose."

Robertson was always trying to expand his space as he fluidly moved, alternately feinting and muscling, changing his gears and moving quickly, but never urgently, as he cunningly jockeyed for position. And controlling both the ball and his defender. One of those who tried to defend him was Dick Barnett, who remembered, all too well, Robertson's modus operandi: "If you give him a twelve-foot shot, Oscar will work on you until he's got a ten-foot shot. Give him ten, he wants eight. Give him eight, he wants six. Give him six, he wants four. Give him four, he wants two. Give him two, you know what he wants? A layup."

Oscar even did the unbelievable, going to the basket against Bill Russell, the man-mountain who liked to stuff the ball back in the shooter's face in what he called a "Wilson Sandwich." But then again, as then-player Art Heyman said in amazement, "None of the other backcourtmen can drive. Except Robertson, and he's so fabulous he can do anything."

Year after year, Robertson would lead the league in assists and average about 30 points a game. And year after year, the Cincinnati Royals would be also-rans, within reach of the promised land, but never quite able to grab the brass ring, through no fault of Robertson's.

And then, in Robertson's tenth year with Cincinnati, the Royals hired a new head coach for the 1969–70 season—Bob Cousy, the player Robertson had so often been compared with. However, what should have been something akin to a match made in basketball heaven between the two great backcourt legends was hardly wrinkle-free, as Cousy determined to change the Royals into his own image and the image of his beloved old Celts by making them into a running team. And, with no room at the team inn for Robertson in the new scheme of things (Cousy confided to newsmen that he "hated the fact that he [Robertson] controlled the ball"), it soon turned corrosive. Cousy, discounting Oscar's talents at less than face value, put him up for adoption.

The Milwaukee Bucks, then on the cusp of an NBA championship after only two years as an expansion club, accommodated Cousy by sending two guards to the Royals for Robertson. Sure enough, the changing of the guards meant a championship for the Bucks, as Robertson, in tandem with Lew Alcindor (later Kareem Abdul-Jabbar), led the team to two long winning streaks of sixteen and twenty games and the NBA championship, which it won by beating the Baltimore Bullets in a 4–0 blowout in the finals. And for Robertson, the trade meant a new life, as, playing with the newfound ardor of a martyr who had just been saved at the stake, he furnished the ballhandling, outside shooting, and backcourt leadership that complemented and increased Alcindor's dominance in the frontcourt.

Three years later "the Big O" would retire. But not before this court artist had posted numbers up in the paint that would be remembered for all time.

20

Bill Tilden

1893–1953

As a rule, great athletes have come from hardscrabble beginnings, fighting their way, rung by rung, up the ladder of success. Bill Tilden was the exception to the rule, born not only with a silver spoon in his mouth but with a silver racket under his arm as well. He was born into the world of shortened names and elongated cigars, the Main Line, "the 400," and silver dinner services—the world of the overdog, opera, Union League Clubs, and their own pastime, tennis.

Known as "the Very Rich," they supported meticulously cultivated turf courts such as the Newport Casino and other fortified art galleries, where initial membership cost $500, but where keeping up appearances might cost a fortune. As the caretakers of tennis's flame, these elitists dreaded allowing the residents of the city directories into their clubby confines, considering the opening up of their game to the masses as much a violation as an after-dinner belch. And so they maintained a polite fiction of the nonexistence of the hoi polloi. Young Bill Tilden was part of this closed world, winning his first tennis tournament at the age of seven at a place called the Onteora Club in upstate New York in front of a gallery containing many of the so-called swells of the era, including the famed actress Maude Adams.

But the world she was a-changin', and the end of "the War to End All Wars" also signaled the end of that era. With the growth of wealth and all the things it bought—most notably leisure time and leisure-time diversions—those things that once were the sole province of the wealthy now became readily available to the masses, including tennis. This once-elitist pastime became a popular sport. Ironically, the man who would establish the game of tennis as a game for those viewed as gibbering and grubbing cave dwellers by those at the Newport Casino and their like was someone with impeccable social credentials: William Tatem Tilden II.

Like tennis itself, Bill Tilden got off to a late start. Having spent the better part of his youth as a struggling fringe player, Tilden was best known for his cannonball serve and his chop shot. Finally, after a period of painstaking dedication to practice, Tilden had honed his skills to the point where he was good enough to advance to the final round of the 1919 National Tennis Championships at Forest Hills. There the man now known as "Big Bill"—in tribute to his long, lanky build and to distinguish him from his 121-pound opponent in the finals, "Little Bill" Johnston—lost, three sets to one, his backhand betraying him.

That would be the last time Johnston—or almost anyone else, for that matter—would beat him. With an obvious disinclination to be anything but the best, Tilden repaired to a friend's house in Rhode Island for the winter. There, practicing as if he were his own guinea pig, he played every day on an indoor clay court, hour after hour, day after day, week after week, until his backhand had become his strength.

Returning to the tennis wars, Tilden not only became a winner, he became the dominant force in the game. Chosen as an alternate for the U.S. Davis Cup team behind the aforementioned Johnston and Norris Williams, Tilden began his victory campaign in England, winning at Wimbledon, returning the Davis Cup to the United States and then, at Forest Hills, handling Johnston's ferocious forehand with his newly minted backhand and playing superbly in the backcourt, winning his first national singles championship.

For the rest of that decade known as the Roaring Twenties, Tilden became the most dependable story in sports, dominating the game as no other athlete ever dominated his or her sport—before or since. He *was* the decade. The stoop-shouldered, vulture winged player with the enormous wingspan won just about everything there was to win, including seven U.S. singles championships, six consecutively; three Wimbledons; and seven straight Davis Cups—during which he won thirteen straight singles matches and four of the six doubles he played. He was virtually unbeatable, so much so that the press began referring to him as "Tilden, the Invincible." And he was now included in that pantheon of greats of the so-called Golden Age of Sports that had been launched on the floodtide of the Dempsey-Willard fight, along with Jack Dempsey, Babe Ruth, Red Grange, and Bobby Jones.

The man Allison Danzig, of the *New York Times*, called "the greatest tennis player the world has ever seen" put that greatness on display several times during the decade. Two of those times came at Forest Hills, where Tilden had staked his homesteading rights to the U.S. singles championship. In the 1922 finals against Little Bill Johnston, Johnston had stroked one of his patented forehands seemingly out of reach of the long-limbed Tilden. But Tilden, reaching out the way a lion in pursuit of his prey might set a lightning-quick paw upon a careless rabbit in its path, threw out his racket and, with a desperate effort, lobbed it high over Johnston's head. As the ball rose to the highest point above the horizon, it looked like it was headed over the back wall. Then it seemingly became weightless and died, dropping just inside the baseline, completing an impossible shot. Just as the ball hit inside, a spectator leaped up and screamed, "He's a liar! He didn't do it. No one could do it!" But Tilden could. And had.

The next year, again with Johnston the party of the second part, and with storm clouds playing hide-and-seek with the sun and swirling overhead, Tilden took one look at the threatening clouds and then, without so much as a by-your-leave, ripped across four straight service aces to close out the match and the title just before the downpour, then ran off the court like the rain that was right behind him.

Bill Tilden was the perfect symbol of the tennis era. With airs enough to attract the fancy and ambitions enough to catch the fancy of the sporting crowd, Tilden, majestically dressed in his all-whites with a bushel of rackets cradled under his arm, looked like tennis. But it was his play that truly captured the imagination of the crowds and transformed tennis into a popular sport.

And Tilden played as if he had been carefully chosen for the role. He could volley an opponent dizzy, come back from the brink of disaster with a last-second rally, cover the court in three long, bounding strides, or explode a sizzling forehand down the line. To him tennis was a game of chess played with a racket.

But it was more. For Tilden possessed all the eccentricities of genius. He was shrill and brilliant and as temperamental as an operatic diva, sometimes indulging himself—and enlivening a match—by giving the gallery a show, or prolonging a game just so he could further his own enjoyment of his sheer wizardry. "He combed his dark hair with an air," wrote John Kiernan. And Paul Metzler called him a flamboyant showman who "dramatized or burlesqued his way through many a match."

But whatever he was, Bill Tilden was what Allison Danzig called "the most complete player of all time." Purple prose, indeed, for someone born to the purple.

21

Jack Nicklaus

b. 1940

Follow the historical bread crumbs back through the mists of time and you'll find men who, having beaten a legend, are destined to walk forever in their shadow. For instance, the name of Hannibal, the conqueror of the Alps, is known to every schoolchild. But the names of *his* conquerors are lost to the ages. And while the name Napoleon is storied, the name of the man who beat him, Wellington, is rarely, if ever, uttered. So too with Alexander the Great and almost every other legend you care to name.

The same thing happens in sports: those who dethrone or surpass legends are forever destined to play second banana in sports history to the men they supplanted at the top of the

mountain. For references see Gene Tunney, who beat Jack Dempsey and was forever in his shadow; Hank Aaron, who surpassed
Babe Ruth's home run record and was relegated to playing
shadow tag with the Bambino's image; and, more to the point of
this biographical sketch, Jack Nicklaus, who seemed forever fated
to remain in Arnold Palmer's shadow.

To prove our point, we now take you to the 1962 U.S. Open,
played at Oakmont, Pennsylvania, Arnie's backyard. At the very
height of his reign and fresh from his third Masters' title, the king
was "coming home" for what his fervent followers, known as
Arnie's Army, thought would merely be a tee party for their hero.

As the Fates would have it, Palmer was paired for the first
two rounds with the new kid on the pro tour block, Jack Nicklaus.

Nicklaus, a collegiate star out of Ohio State and twice
national amateur champion, was a curious-looking piece of
goods. With the body of a large pot roast, his stomach succumbing to gravity and flowing over what little could be seen of his belt
in rather generous potations, and his face that of an artificially
ripened tomato topped by a closely cropped sandy crew cut that
owed as much of its existence to the period as to an overzealous
barber, Nicklaus looked every bit his college nickname, Blob-O.
Or, as he was referred to by his new fraternity brothers on the pro
tour, Ohio Fats. Hardly what could be called a fashion plate,
Nicklaus wore clothing no respectable rag-bag would have stood
sponsor for, possessing, as one writer noted, "all the color of a
hospital ward," his pants bagging at the knees, his shirt coming
out of its anchoring place. All in all, he looked like the personification of the weekend golfer.

But even if he didn't quite cut a figure, he had quite a cut.
Using his club less as a club than a howitzer, Nicklaus got every
ounce of his dense 205-pound pot-roast frame into every shot—
admitting to writer Jim Murray that he derived his power "from
my ass," ample reason indeed for his great power—and driving
the ball prodigious lengths off tee and fairway, straight as an
arrow to the lodestone. When his drives went, on an average, 280
yards, what did it matter that he didn't possess the fluid swing of
a Sam Snead? And not to be confused with Snead, one of the
greatest tee-to-green golfers of all time, Nicklaus could also use
his putter as well, in a surgical nature, almost like a scalpel,
making him the complete golfer—almost a textbook version of
what a great golfer should be.

However, the presence of this new phenomenon was of little or no concern to Palmer's adoring gallery. After all, they reasoned, hadn't Nicklaus, then a twenty-year-old amateur, finished two strokes behind Palmer in the Open two years before? And wasn't their beloved Arnie, as he himself had said, "at home" now? And so the parishioners, all there to worship at the Shrine of St. Arnie, practiced a maltreatment of their lungs, cheering their hero's every shot with "Go get him, Arnie!" and "We're with you, Arnie baby!" and then rushed the greensward, storming their way to the next hole without waiting for Nicklaus to finish holing out.

Even with the sounds of the riotous assemblage ringing in his ears, Nicklaus paid them as much heed as he might have a passing wind, his concentration such that he could divorce himself from everything around him, all the better to focus on the only thing that mattered: his golf game. His detachment, even at this stage in his career, was so complete—and so amazing—that golf great Gene Sarazen, who had seen them all over the past half-century, was moved to comment: "This boy has an iron pipe running through his head from one ear to the other. Everything that's said goes in one ear and out the other."

After thirty-six holes, it looked like the hopes of Arnie's Army would be acquitted. For even though he was putting badly, Palmer led the field, with Nicklaus three strokes back.

After Saturday morning's round, Nicklaus had gained a stroke, reducing Palmer's lead to two. During the afternoon final eighteen, Nicklaus crept closer and closer, finally pulling even. But victory was still within Palmer's grasp. All he had to do was hole a 12-foot birdie putt on the final hole and the title would be his.

He didn't.

With both Palmer and Nicklaus finishing with 283s, a Sunday playoff—with no tomorrows, no more rent to pay, and no use—would decide the winner. And ten thousand of Arnie's faithful flocked out to see their idol beat the young upstart who had dared to even think about beating him. But after the drama of Saturday, Sunday's playoff was anticlimactic, as Palmer's bogey on the first hole ended the competitive phase of the playoff right then and there. Nicklaus, with no outcaving of the knees from the pressures and looking neither to left nor right, played his game and beat Palmer by three strokes for the championship. His first.

In 1963, Nicklaus—by now called "the Golden Bear" after a headline in an Australian paper trumpeted "Golden Bear Arrives From U.S. Today" the previous winter—won both the Masters and the PGA, giving him three major titles in less than two years on the tour. Nicklaus had set his sights high. Simply stated, he wanted to become the greatest golfer in the history of the sport. Recognizing that only the majors count in history, he took direct aim at them. When he won the Masters in 1965, former champion Arnold Palmer helped him on with the green jacket that went with the title. But even though he had taken the green jacket from Palmer, he took little else, adoring galleries continuing to applaud Palmer's every move while jeering the crew-cut kid who challenged their darling's supremacy.

The following year, 1966, Nicklaus and Palmer were even after thirty-six holes of the Masters. In the third round, Nicklaus broke it open with a record 64 and finished with a 271, three strokes better than Ben Hogan's 1953 record. Watching the legend-in-the-making successfully defend his title and set the Masters' record, Bobby Jones could only shake his head and say, "Palmer played superbly, but Nicklaus played a game with which I am not familiar."

By 1967 everyone would be familiar with Nicklaus's game, as he sealed his hold on immortality by winning the Open. But not before Palmer, in one of his famous all-or-nothing cavalry-charge finishes, had made a run at him. Playing with Nicklaus in the final round, Palmer actually led at one point. But not for long. As Nicklaus porpoised as much as strode to the eighteenth tee, he was thinking birdie. Par would give him a three-shot victory, but a birdie would give him a 275 for an Open record. Overanxious, he pushed his drive into the rough on the right, and a bad recovery left him a long way from the pin. Undaunted, he hit a one-iron, straight and long, to the green, leaving it about twenty feet from the cup. Now he was just two putts away from tying the record. As calm as an oyster on the half-shell, he put his first putt into the yawning hole for a birdie, a 65 for the round, and a record-setting 275 for the tournament. He had surpassed Ben Hogan's all-time tournament standard and beaten Palmer by four strokes.

Time, like taffy, stretches out. And, by 1970, Jack Nicklaus had stretched out as well, losing twenty pounds—down to a trim 190—letting his crew cut grow out to golden locks and adopting a whole new wardrobe. Fat Jack had indeed become the Golden

Bear. His new look hardly affected his golf game, with his win in the '70 British Open bringing his major win total up to ten, just three shy of Bobby Jones's all-time record of thirteen. And counting.

But he wasn't just in Jones's shadow—he was still walking in Palmer's shadow, as well, one he could not fit into.

All that would change in 1980. For that was the year the U.S. Open was held at Baltusrol, the site of Nicklaus's 1967 win. The first big story of the tournament was a record 63 posted by Tom Weiskopf. Within minutes, another 63 went up on the leader board, this one belonging to Nicklaus. The Bear was alive and well and rampaging through New Jersey. Before he was through, he would break his own Open mark—set at Baltusrol lo those thirteen years before—with a four-round total of 272. And win his fourth Open.

His victory was like the drawing of a champagne cork. All of a sudden the throng, which had been held back by the tight ropes and light security, gathered momentum and burst from behind the ropes to surround their newfound hero. Not since the giddy days of Arnie's Army had there been such a spontaneous outpouring of affection for a golfer.

Jack Nicklaus had finally stepped out of the shadow in which he'd lived and into the limelight—to suddenly be accepted, as *Sports Illustrated* wrote after his win, as "the greatest golfer ever."

22

Gordie Howe

b. 1928

In any listing of great athletes, the finger of history pauses longer over the name Gordie Howe than any other. For parts of five decades this reject from the law of averages desired only what he could accomplish. And he accomplished much, as attested to by those balanced columns of unassailable sums and straight-angled figures called statistics.

For thirty-two long years, from his youthful days in Detroit to his final hurrah in Hartford as one of old age's credentialed couriers, Howe established the improbability of the calendar.

This hockey great, who weighed 204 pounds when he broke into the NHL in 1946 and 204 when he broke out in 1980, set every record known to hockeykind during those thirty-two years: most points, most assists, most goals, most games—and even most stitches and most serious injuries. His worth was so great that Canada's prime minister called him Mr. Hockey, and Bobby Hull admitted, "I'd like to be half as good as Gordie."

NHL coaches called Howe "the smartest player, the best passer, the best playmaker, and the best puck-carrier" in the game. But the most important component of his genius was his roughness. As a rival once said of Howe, "He was everything you'd expect an ideal hockey player to be. He's soft-spoken and thoughtful. He's also the most vicious, cruel, and meanest man I've ever met in a hockey game."

As hard as a picnic egg when he first skated onto the ice as a Detroit Red Wing, Howe was more dangerous in warfare than the Turks. Finally, his exasperated coach, Jack Adams, watching the Red Wings' opponents lining up on the side of the undertaker, had seen enough and said to his young right wing, "Okay, kid, you've convinced everybody in the league. Now how about showing me you can play hockey."

And so, Howe became more subtle in his aggressiveness, though he still hardly practiced pacifism with his stick—or with his elbows, his newfound subtlety earning him the nickname "Mr. Elbows" from his opponents. One of those who remembered, only too well, was Phil Esposito, who met Howe and his educated appendages the first time he lined up alongside him. "I was with the Chicago Black Hawks, and we were getting ready for a face-off," Espo recalled. "I looked up at him and he said something like, 'Hi, kid.'" Then, after the puck was dropped, Howe, no gentle despoiler he, planted an elbow in the "kid's" jaw that cost the rookie several front teeth.

Word soon got around that there were certain dangers to be as strictly observed as railroad crossings, and that getting too near Howe was one of them. Vic Stasiuk, the onetime coach of the Philadelphia Flyers, claimed that over the years Howe built his own "working area" that allowed him to "skate around in an invisible glass tube. He has let it be known that he does not like people to get within three feet of him," Stasiuk said. "And you know what? Nobody does."

Fully believing genius was to be served rather than argued with, Howe was setting his sights on the goal rather than on the occasional player foolhardy enough to skate too close to him. And when he concentrated on the goal, he was the greatest craftsman hockey has ever known.

With precision in every movement, Howe would always skate briskly but never urgently, guiding his deceptively dense frame down the ice, his sloped shoulders minimizing the size of his treelike body and tree-stump neck. His ice-cold composure was such that his incurious eyes always seemed affixed on a spot, whether that spot was an angle he was seeking to gain on a defenseman, a teammate flashing down ice for a pass, or the goal itself. Then, the only offensive player in NFL history to stickhandle and shoot ambidextrously would, after what seemed only a nanosecond, unload, the sound of stick meeting puck resounding like the slap of surf against shore. It was this package of incredible talents that caused many to call Howe the "greatest player ever to play in the NHL."

But that package came close to never being unwrapped. In his first three years in the NHL Howe scored a grand total of 35 goals, more interested in imposing his will on everyone he faced than in implanting the puck in the net. But then, after being exhorted by his coach to "play hockey," the thunder that had taken so long to erupt finally came during the 1949–50 season, as Howe scored 35 goals and added 33 assists. However, in an unrehearsed, unplanned, and unmitigated disaster, his career almost came to a tragic end in the playoffs after that season.

It happened in the opening game of the playoffs against the Toronto Maple Leafs. As Ted Kennedy of the Maple Leafs drove to the center line, Howe cut toward him, skating fast. Nearing the board and fearing he was about to be boarded by the fast-flying Howe, Kennedy lifted his stick. It caught Howe full in the eye, cutting his eyeball. He fell to the ice and skidded, headfirst, into the boards. Rushed to the hospital with a fractured skull and severe brain damage, Howe was placed on the critical list, his life in danger. "They drilled a hole through the skull to relieve the pressure" is all Howe remembers. The question was not whether he would ever play hockey again, but whether he would live. But Howe, with remarkable recuperative powers, came back to lead the league in scoring the next year. And to this day, as a memento of his injury, he still blinks like a man just awakened from a noonday nap, so much so that some call him Blinky.

It was just the first of many injuries this amazing specimen would suffer throughout his career, a career that saw him demonstrate an infinite capacity for taking hurt as well as dealing it out.

Howe would go on to play for the Red Wings for a glorious twenty-five years, leading the NHL in scoring another five times, being voted the league's Most Valuable Player six times, and being named to the All-Star team a record twenty-one times. After one year of sitting on the sidelines as a vice president for the Red Wings, Howe, whose reflexes were always stimulated by a good challenge, began to salivate like Pavlov's dog at the prospect of coming back to play hockey with his two sons, and signed on to play for the Houston Aeros of the World Hockey Association.

But Howe, now forty-five years old, did not sign with the Aeros to be trotted out for ceremonial occasions, like the queen's jewels. He came to play. And play he did, so well, in fact, that he was named the WHA's most valuable player, scoring 100 points and, by passing off to his sons, piling up his most single-season assists ever. Six years later he was still playing, this time with the Hartford Whalers of the NHL and, at the age of fifty-one, appearing yet again in the All-Star Game.

Gordie Howe, called by none other than Bobby Hull "the greatest hockey player that ever played," also was the longest-running show, not only in hockey, but in sports.

23

Martina Navratilova

b. 1956

The only thing longer than Martina Navratilova's name was her reign as tennis's prevailing tsarina. Longer still was her acceptance by the grandstand gallery. And longest of all was her journey to the top, starting with her trip from her native Czechoslovakia. And therein begins our story of one of the sport's—if not all of sports'—greatest athletes.

Her story starts, as it should, at the beginning, with her birth as Martina Subertova in Prague, Czechoslovakia—a country far easier to pronounce than spell. Marina later moved to Revnice, where, as a youngster, she took up the game of tennis and the name of her stepfather, Miroslav Navratil, adding the feminine ending "ova."

Her first coach was George Parma, a former Czechoslovak Davis Cupper, who told his student: "Work hard, Martina. Compete wherever you have the chance. Get to see the world. Sports is one way you'll be able to travel."

And travel she did, setting out Columbus-like for new worlds and using her tennis racket as her passport. On her first visit to the United States, early in 1973, she faced top-ranked Chris Evert. And although Evert "beat me, 6–3, 7–6...or 7–6, 6–3...5–4 in the tiebreaker, I said to myself, 'If I can do this the first time against the best in the world, maybe next time...'"

Besides discovering something about her potential abilities, the seventeen-year-old also discovered something about America. Her first impression, she was to write in her autobiography, "was how friendly Americans were. You can be honest and be yourself with Americans. I always felt I could be me, the real Martina, from the first time I came to the States."

She also discovered that indigenous American institution for the distribution of indigestion, the fast-food restaurant. And, like any normal teenager, fell in love with Big Macs, french fries, and milk shakes, along with other compounds delightful to the palate of a newcomer to fast foods. Several trips to the new worlds of America and fast foods later, Martina took on the look of someone who had spent too much time leaning against the where-to-dine columns in the many tournament programs, less a tennis figure than a figure of what tennis writer Bud Collins described as "the Great Wide Hope."

But Martina was soon to feed on something other than fast foods: tournament wins. The next year, in a tournament that begot no more than a small lake of print around an islet of illustration, held in Orlando, Florida, she won her first U.S. tourney. The Czech teenager, not knowing a soul at the tournament and with less than a handful of English words at her command, didn't quite know how to express her elation. First she made a little leap of joy; then she uttered a few sounds that made a fair stagger at arranging themselves into language of some sort, punctuated by a shout of exultation; and then, on her way off the court, having no one to share her euphoria with, she threw her arms around a lamppost, looking like a little kid hugging a Christmas tree. It was to be the hors d'oeuvre in what was to become her new diet, a steady diet of tournament wins.

Over the next year she was to add wins in the French Open

mixed doubles and women's doubles, amass more than $119,000 in earnings, and be named *Tennis* magazine's Rookie of the Year. But it was her free-spirited, almost free-thinking, style that brought her the most attention. Almost completely "Westernized" by now, her tastes ranged from American hamburgers to offbeat outfits—including one she wore to the 1975 U.S. Open, a dress especially designed for her by Teddy Tinling, the renowned tennis fashion designer, a brightly colored floral print which Martina described as being "like my personality—wild!"

And so it came as no surprise that the day after she had been eliminated in the semifinals of the 1975 U.S. Open by Evert, she asked for political asylum in the United States. Some thought that the reason for her application was that her homeland, Czechoslovakia, appropriated a large percentage of her earnings and that Martina was on the threshold of becoming the game's dominant player in the next decade and could make as much as $200,000 a year in endorsements. Others, including her good friend Chris Evert, with whom she "talked a lot," believed that the sensitive Martina wanted to stay in America, where the teenager could, as Martina put it, "be me." Whatever, her application was granted, and the bouncing Czech became both: the most dominant player in woman's tennis and herself, an exuberant court figure who could be seen punching the air here with her hand, there berating herself on the court, and most times just smiling that full, endearing, vulnerable smile of hers.

Martina, having first stretched herself out by going on a special diet, began a stretch of wins over the next three years, beginning with the 1978 Wimbledon singles championship—the first of her eight Wimbledon crowns, including an unprecedented six in a row.

Her overwhelming serve-and-volley game was almost an anachronism amongst the many baseline bangers then on the tour. From her booming left-handed serve, delivered with a motion that was eloquent in the energy put behind it and sounded like one of those explosions that caves in half a street, to her play at the net, where, frescoing the ball rather than lacing it gingerly, she soon had her opponent racing back and forth like a hare trying to escape pursuing hounds, she imposed her will on almost everyone she faced.

Well, almost everyone. For the one player she couldn't seem to beat was Chris Evert, who held a commanding lead in their head-to-head battles. A perfectionist, forever doomed to be unsatisfied, Martina exhibited her own insecurity to a fault, exhorting herself on the court with a plaintive "come on" and calling herself an "idiot" or hitting herself with her racket when she did something that didn't meet with her own high standards. After undergoing continual self-examination, she now looked elsewhere for help in attaining that perfection she sought, and hired basketball legend Nancy Lieberman to teach her conditioning and, more important, the use of intimidation on the court.

And so, after a physical training regimen that included lifting weights and learning intimidation, Martina, after two-plus years of subpar performances, returned to the tennis wars. By 1982 Martina had made winning tennis tournaments almost a vocation in and of itself, and she won 90 matches while losing only three. The next year she was nearly invincible, this refugee from the law of averages, winning 86 of 87 matches (the only time she was proven "vincible" was against Kathy Horvath in the fourth round of the French Open).

Beginning with Wimbledon in 1983 and lasting through the '84 Australian Open, Martina became a repeating decimal, winning six consecutive Grand Slam singles titles and 74 consecutive match victories. And from April 1983 through July 1985, teaming with Pam Shriver, she won 8 consecutive women's doubles titles and 109 consecutive doubles matches. No player ever dominated the court, or a sport, as Martina Navratilova did during those years.

And the fans, who had once viewed her as an underachieving hotblood—or even worse, a "hot dog," and taunted her as such—now came back like pigeons to a ship to cheer her every move, won over by her grit, passion for the game, and humanness.

By the nineties, when, in the Indian summer of her career, she came back to play at that fortified art gallery known as Forest Hills, the fans greeted her as they would a diva. Having cheered her at the beginning of her career in faith and midway through in hope, they were now, nearing the end, cheering her in appreciation. Jimmy Connors, who shares the adulation of the galleries, said of Martina, "She has had a career that can be matched by not many...not anybody at all."

It had been a very long trip indeed for Martina Navratilova, but one of the most rewarding journeys in sports history.

24

Walter Payton

b. 1954

Walter Payton belonged to the hard-hat city of Chicago—that "City of Big Shoulders," to cop a line from Carl Sandburg—just like its stockyards. For Payton was a hard-hat athlete, one who rolled up his sleeves, spat on his hands, and went to work, giving an honest laboring man's effort each and every time. And for thirteen years he carried the Bears on his big shoulders, longer than any other Bear hero—longer than Red Grange, longer than Bronko Nagurski, longer than Sid Luckman, longer than Bill Osmanski, longer than George Blanda, longer than Rick Casares, longer than Gale Sayers, and even longer, as a player, than "Papa Bear" himself, George Halas.

But Walter Payton also belonged to the Chicago of fast-paced Rush Street. And therein lies the secret of Walter Payton. For he was, in reality, two backs rolled into one.

One Walter Payton was a slashing, punishing runner who attacked the line of scrimmage, a one-man power surge who challenged tacklers looming as large as the Rockies, giving them a forearm here, a high step there, and, when all else failed, toting one or two 240-pound linemen on his back as he lunged for the first down. The other was one of the most ingenious runners who ever existed, spinning like an out-of-control Water Pik as he shed tacklers the way a snake sheds skin and then, with a change of gears and a few more artful dodges, turning toes to pasture. And goal line. Either way, Payton's style made great demands on tacklers, who, like diners who have to keep one eye on their umbrella and the other on their entree, had no idea which of the two Paytons to protect against.

But the most important component of Payton's genius was none of the above. Instead, it was found in his incredible balance—a balance worthy of the early Flying Wallendas.

That pluperfect sense of balance was first seen not in a Bears uniform, nor even in the uniform of tiny Jackson State College, where he was to first show his potential greatness. It was first showcased on the nationally televised *Soul Train,* where, as a teenager, little Walter Payton, even then known as "Sweetness," danced on his hands to the accompaniment of whatever the top hit song happened to be that day.

Payton would go on to break more records than *Soul Train* ever played, beginning at Jackson State. There, as a five-foot-ten, 202-pound one-man reign of terror who could walk on his hands and fly on his feet, he ran into the NCAA record books with 66 touchdowns and 464 points.

The tatterdemalion Bears, who had been so devoid of talent and promise that one '74 late-season game had drawn all of 18,802 fans to Soldier Field, with another 36,951 "no-shows" disguised as empty seats, pulled up the football landscape by its roots to unearth a building block in their efforts to rebuild. And, by drafting Payton on the first round of the '75 draft, the fourth player chosen overall, they had. Payton's first year was good, by Bear standards, but hardly the stuff of which legends are made, as he gained just 679 yards on 196 carries—and missed one game, the only game he would miss in his thirteen-year professional career.

If anyone thought the Bear was asleep just because they hadn't heard him roar, the 1976 season would give them pause.

For that season the Bears' unimaginative offense consisted of Payton running left, Payton running right, and Payton running right up the center as the man with the sweet style rushed for 1,390 yards, 34 percent of the Bears' total offense and most in the National Football Conference.

But 1976 was merely an indication of things to come. For, by 1977, as *Sport* magazine wrote, "O. J. Simpson was a man who leaped past old ladies in airports while Payton was the premier running back in football."

If there was any doubt that Payton was, as advertised, the NFL's "premier running back," that doubt was put to rest in the tenth game of the 1977 season, when—playing against the Minnesota Vikings and their vaunted "Purple People Eater" defense, and with a touch of flu—Payton battered, rammed, raced, and just plain ol' flew for a single-game record of 275 yards. When, at the end of the game, Viking defensive end Carl Eller finally stopped Payton to shake his hand in congratulations, it was as close as Minnesota's defense had gotten to him all day.

But Eller and the Vikings weren't the only ones who had difficulty stopping Payton. It almost seemed as if opposing teams needed a Geiger counter to find him and a net to hold him. "I don't know if there's a way to stop him," admitted Green Bay coach Bart Starr after watching the movable feast named Payton eat up his Packers. Apparently no one could, as Payton averaged 1,307 yards a season in his first three years in the NFL, the highest average in league history, and then, with 1,000-yard seasons flying by like exit signs on Lake Shore Drive, added 1,395 and 1,610-yard seasons to his growing total, more than enough to be voted to the NFL team of the seventies.

Payton continued to lay waste to the landscape with a style that almost looked like he was just stretching his legs. But Payton's legendary leg strength didn't come naturally; he had worked—and worked hard—to build it up. From a kid, when he ran up and down hills to strengthen his legs, to his daily regimen of working to get his legs and upper body almost equally strong, he knew, as he said, that "I get stronger—and gain more yards—as the game goes on. It's like hitting two hammers together: After a while, one begins to dent." And when push came to shove, the dentee was rarely Payton. Add to that a steely straight-arm that was, as one of his teammates said, "like a recoilless rifle that left a number of defensive backs with fewer neck vertebrae because of it," and the ability to explode into a tackler trying to tackle him, and you have a beautifully tooled running machine.

But, if truth be told, Walter Payton was anything but a machine. For even while he was gobbling up great gobs of real estate, he continued to play with all the exuberance of a child on the playground. And that's what it was to Payton—a game, one he had fun at, leaping to his feet almost before he had fallen to the lap of the earth after being downed to rush back into the huddle with a little kid's enthusiasm. Other times that enthusiasm could be seen in Payton's leading the stadium in cheers during time-outs or in his letting out inhuman screams during team meetings. Or just in his inching the ball forward after he was downed, a move he figured gained him about an extra 100 yards during his career. Or even by emulating his earlier days by walking 50 yards on his hands across a football field.

On his way to the all-time rushing record, Payton would continue to lay down layer after layer of his masterpiece, carrying the ball over, under, and around opposing linemen for 1,000-yard-plus seasons, season after season. And carrying the Bears with him as well. The team he had joined in 1975 that was but 4–10 was, by 1985, a 15–1 team. And Super Bowl champions. But while the spoils belonged to the Bears, the glory belonged to Walter Payton, an athlete who had carried his parents' precept of "Whatever you do, try to be the best" onto the football field. And who, while he was around, turned Chicago, "the Second City," into the first.

25

Sugar Ray Robinson

1920–1989

Any and all descriptions implying greatness can be applied to the man born Walker Smith, but the one appellation that stuck was first uttered by Jack Case, who, while witnessing for the first time a young lanky boxer fighting for the Salem Crescent gym in New York, remarked to the manager of the team, George Gainford, "That's a sweet fighter you've got there." "Sweet as sugar," replied Gainford for posterity. And so it was that "Sugar" Ray Robinson was born.

Robinson came by the other part of his name honestly. Or

somewhat honestly. For back in those days when the bootleg circuit (unlicensed fights held in small clubs) held sway, the youngster who originally went by his given name—or "Smitty" to friends—borrowed the amateur card of a friend named Ray Robinson and became, from that night forward, the man who would go on as Ray Robinson to become "the Greatest Pound-for-Pound Fighter in the History of Boxing."

No single label for Robinson is adequate. He was boxing's version of Rashomon—everyone saw something different. He could deliver a knockout blow going backward; he was seamless, with no fault lines; his left hand, held always at the ready, was purity in motion; his footwork was superior to any that had been seen in boxing up to that time; his hand speed and leverage were unmatchable; and so on and so forth. He was magic in the ring and, in those rare moments when his greatness was challenged—or, worse, his carefully marcelled hair mussed—Hemingway's "grace under pressure."

Robinson went unbeaten, untied, and virtually unscored upon in his first forty fights, and it wasn't until his forty-first, against Jake LaMotta in Detroit, that his express route to greatness was derailed on a 10-round decision loss. It was a decision he would reverse five times. Robinson went on to become both welterweight and middleweight champ, losing only that one fight to LaMotta in his first 123 bouts—in which he managed a total of 78 knockouts.

But while Robinson was the shellac for the rough exterior of the sport, boxing was being run by the International Boxing Commission and a group of characters to whom legitimate business was only a figure of speech. And when Robinson disobeyed their commands and failed to carry LaMotta in their sixth fight—the fight called the St. Valentine's Day Massacre and immortalized in the movie *Raging Bull*—he was banished from the States and forced to ply his trade in Europe. Sugar Ray went first-class, taking with him an entourage worthy of the name and including two of everything, like Noah—as in two hairdressers, two chauffeurs, and pairs of other essential hanger-onners—as he toured the Continent. On one of his stops, he left behind the middleweight championship, in the hands of Britisher Randy Turpin—who lost it back to Sugar Ray three months later. It would be the first of four times he would redeem a title he had "lent" to others.

After losing to the heat, and incidentally to Joey Maxim, in an unprecedented bid to gain the light heavyweight championship on a night that turned him into a wilted head of lettuce, Robinson retired due to lack of opportunities and opponents. But if John Updike was correct when he said, "Retirement is a little like death," Robinson must have died a thousand times, for he came back to reclaim his title from Bobo Olson and stage his classic fights with Gene Fullmer and Carmen Basilio in the twilight of his career—proving that the great ones can come back, and back again.

Sugar Ray Robinson was, indeed, the sweetest practitioner of "the Sweet Science."

26

Joe DiMaggio

b. 1914

Joe DiMaggio was like an artichoke: The more you peeled away, the more you discovered. Afield, he was as light as a cucumber sandwich. With concentration in his every move, he made conscious efforts with unconscious—and uncommon—ease. Nothing fancy, nothing spectacular, mind you, just a graceful glide in long, loping steps over the center field greensward until he made a fly ball disappear into his outstretched glove. At bat, he was, in the words of Bob Feller, "simply the best there ever was," with his feet far apart, his bat slightly off his shoulder, his strong, quick wrists, textbook swing, and flawless follow-through that gave the bat a pure, flowing arc. Casey Stengel, who had seen them all, said, "Joe never threw to a wrong base in his career. And he was thrown out trying to take an extra base only once...and the umpire was wrong on that one." In short, according to Casey, "He made the rest of the players look like plumbers."

However, if all the opinions of DiMaggio's greatness were laid end to end, they still wouldn't reach a conclusion. With one exception: that his 56-game hit streak, which stands as one of baseball's great achievements, also stands as a monument to this great athlete.

It all began back in 1933, when Vince DiMaggio asked the San Francisco Seals to take a look-see at his "kid brother." "The kid brother" hit .340, drove in a league-leading 169 runs, and put together a Pacific Coast League record hit streak of 61 straight games.

Three years later DiMaggio joined a New York Yankee team that had won only one pennant in the last seven years. And instead of just making the team, he made it a *winning* team, leading the Yankees to a World Series in his first year. A year later, in 1937, he hit .346 and led the league in home runs, runs scored, and slugging average. And the Yankees won the World Series again. In 1938, he hit .324, and the Yankees once again won the World Series.

New York is a town in which reputations are built larger than the tallest buildings. Having more than justified his buildup, DiMaggio was now one of those whose deeds had made him much taller than most of the man-made monuments found on the island of Manhattan. By 1939 his popularity had transcended the boundaries of New York. His classic features, with the handsome face and nose inclined to Roman, graced the covers of several national publications, including *Life* magazine; his name was captured in the headlines of the daily newspapers; and his exploits were universally embraced and adopted everywhere by those with an eye for diamond delicacies.

With his record beginning to read almost like a tour map of his achievements, 1939 saw the man the writers had now taken to calling "the Yankee Clipper," "Joltin' Joe," and just plain ol' "Joe D" lead the American League in batting with a .381 average and win the Most Valuable Player award. Not incidentally, for the fourth time since he'd joined them four years earlier, the Yankees won the World Series.

The Yankees finished second in 1940, but not because of DiMaggio, who won the batting title for the second time with a .352 average. But 1940 was to serve as a table setting for Joe

DiMaggio's greatest year, the year of his 56-game hit streak, a year when he would capture the headlines and hypnotize the nation as no athlete had since Babe Ruth had hit 60 home runs fourteen years earlier.

But if 1941 was his year, 1949 was his moment. That year, DiMaggio, tortured by a stabbing pain in his heel, spent the first sixty-five games of the season on the disabled list. And then, one sunny morning in June, after spending the previous two-plus months in seclusion anointing his aches and watching his bones mend, DiMag found that the pain he had experienced in something so simple as placing his heel on the ground had disappeared. The first three games DiMaggio had his name penciled in on the Yankees' batting-order card were against the Boston Red Sox on their home turf, Fenway Park. And all DiMaggio did in the crucible of that three-game series was hit four homers, knock in nine runs, and score five more as he rewrote the legend of Joe DiMaggio with his bat—and sparked the Yankees to a three-game sweep in a tight pennant battle.

In 1950, he had one more DiMaggio-type season, leading the League in slugging average and finishing in the top five in home runs, RBIs, and total bases. But after 1951—when his stats tumbled to the lowest in his thirteen-year career—he packed it in mothballs, saying "I feel that I have reached the stage where I can no longer produce for my ball club, my manager, my teammates, and my fans the sort of baseball their loyalty to me deserves." And so saying, he departed with a quiet dignity.

The game and its fans continued to idolize, even lionize, Joe D.—baseball, in its centennial year, selecting him as its "Greatest Living Player." The DiMaggio mystique still remained, as when, shortly after calling it quits, in a wedding of two national pastimes, he married film legend Marilyn Monroe, saying, with rare humor, "It's got to be better than rooming with Joe Page." The marriage didn't take, just long enough to give us one of baseball's greatest lines: when Marilyn, having returned from entertaining the troops in Korea, gushed, "Joe, you never heard such cheering, and DiMaggio answered, "Yes..."I have...."

And for thirteen years, and for years thereafter, he had indeed. Joe DiMaggio built his monument with neither a boast nor a brag. A team player and a great player, he built it the old-fashioned way—with skill and with honest, if seemingly effortless, labor.

27

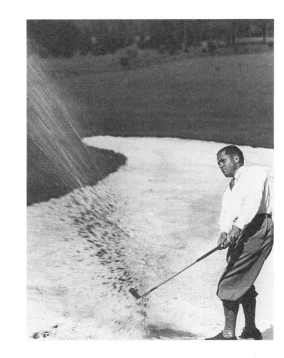

Bobby Jones
1902–1971

Despite his possessing all the paraphernalia of a great, one of the most interesting aspects of Bobby Jones's storied career was the dazzling uncertainty of it for the first seven years, as he flashed his brilliance on and off, like a loose electrical connection. But Jones was to see the Pharaoh's seven lean and seven fat years and raise them one, at least in the fat-years department. And therein lies our story, the story of an overnight sensation, even if it took him seven lean years to get there.

Jones first appeared on the national scene in 1916. The fourteen-year-old was dense of body, with sloping muscular shoulders, powerful thick wrists, and the outsized face of a young southern gentleman—which was only fair, hailing as he did from Atlanta, Georgia.

116

Young Bobby (a name he detested, preferring instead the palindromic "Bob") had been playing the game since the age of five. His family lived just off the thirteenth fairway at Atlanta's East Lake course, and almost before he knew it the youngster had taken to amusing himself by scuffing around the course with an old ball and a cut-down club. By the age of seven he was swinging a midiron, by nine he was the club's junior champion, and by twelve he was driving the ball 240 to 250 yards and registering a score of 70.

Only the year before that first national appearance, Grantland Rice, then the nation's premier sportswriter, stood watching the boy wonder in the company of Alec Smith and Jim Barnes, two former Open champions. As the threesome watched, Jones played his approach, a mashie shot, to some green now lost to the long-ago past. After watching the ball land within ten yards of the cup, they then saw a club, which had been thrown by the youngster in disgust, land against a tree. "It's a shame," Rice remembered Smith as saying, "but he'll never make a golfer...too much temper." Rice was forced to agree: "That one fault could prove his biggest hazard. If he can't learn to control it, he'll never play the kind of golf he'll be capable of shooting." But it would be years before Jones could control his temper as well as his clubs.

When Jones arrived at Philadelphia's Merion Cricket Club, outside Philadelphia, for his first crack at the National Amateur in 1916, he made an immediate hit with the galleries, looking almost Jackie Cooganesque with his blue beret, his blue eyes, and his winning smile. But there was nothing winsome in his manner, his southern manners matched by a southern temper which manifested itself in some championship club throwing. His opponent in the first round was Eben Byers, a former amateur champion in 1906 and himself not averse to wrapping his hickory shafts around the nearest tree. Their match was less a battle of shots than a battle of tempers, won by Jones 3 and 1 because, as he put it, "Byers ran out of clubs first."

The next day, in front of an appreciative gallery, he defeated Frank Dyer, 4 and 2. In the third round, playing against the defending champion, Bob Gardner—and in front of a tremendous gallery which would have done justice to an Armistice Day welcoming crowd—he kept in check both his temper and his shots before losing on the thirty-first hole. The gallery cheered his every miraculous recovery shot with the lapping of applause rising up and dying down quickly. This response would become typical at Jones matches—from that round right through his final round at the same club in 1930, where he capped off his "Grand Slam."

Over the next few years Jones continued to struggle with his temper, seemingly destined forever to be a man by his own acts undone. But the line had to terminate somewhere, and that somewhere was at the 1921 British Open. Playing mediocre golf, at best, he took fifty-eight shots for the first eleven holes and then picked up his ball. In boxing it would have been the equivalent of throwing in the towel; in golf, it was unpardonable. Especially at the British Open, with its reverence for golf's traditions by those who keep their lips stiff and upper. Jones was to learn his lesson and, at nineteen, become a man.

It still remained for him to become a champion. That day finally arrived at the 1923 U.S. Open at the Inwood Country Club on Long Island—but not before a disastrous double-bogey on the seventy-second hole forced him into a playoff against the wee Scot, Bobby Cruickshank. On the eighteenth hole of the playoff, the match was all even. It was Cruickshank's honor, and he hit a half-topped drive that hooked into the rough. Jones's drive was long and hugged the right side, landing in a soft spot at the edge of the rough. Jones was faced with a choice: whether he should lay it up short of a large water hazard before the green or take a chance and hit a one-iron over it onto the edge of the rough. Eschewing the blindfold, cigarette dangling from his lips, he decided to go for it and drilled it up onto the green, some 190 yards away and to within 5 feet of the pin.

That was it! Bobby Jones had won his first championship. And from then on, there was no stopping him as they came tumbling out, tournament after tournament. It became the field against Jones.

Over the next eight years—the "fat years," if you will—Jones set a standard which would never be equaled. He would win at least one major American title each year: four Open victories and five Amateurs. No one ever played better golf for such a sustained period.

As 1930 began, Bobby Cruickshank said of Jones, "He's simply too good. He'll go to Britain and win the Amateur and the Open and then he'll come back over here and win the Open and the Amateur. He's playing too well to be stopped." And then

Cruickshank backed up his prediction with a $500 wager, fortunate to get the 50-to-1 odds set by Lloyd's on Jones to win what people were now calling "the Grand Slam"—and what one sportswriter called "the Impregnable Quadrilateral of Golf."

The 1930 British Amateur was held at the historic Royal and Ancient Club at St. Andrews where, after eight close rounds, Jones won his first British Amateur. And the first part of the Grand Slam. Now it was on to Hoylake for the second part, the British Open. Without exertion, he finished two furlongs ahead of the field. He was halfway home, and Bobby Cruickshank's bet was beginning to look like a lock.

A hero's welcome awaited him upon his return from across the pond. New York City staged one of its patented ticker-tape parades. Asked what the uproar was all about, a bored New York policeman told one of Jones's friends, "It's for some damn golfer."

At the U.S. Open at Interlachen near Minneapolis, the result was never in doubt. Referring the matter to his putter, "Calamity Jane," he rammed in a 40-foot putt on the seventy-second hole, good for a birdie and the Open title. Now it was three down, one to go. And Bobby Cruickshank's bookmaker was hearing footsteps.

The fourth leg of the Grand Slam was a "gimme," as Jones tied a record in the qualifying round and then roared through the field, Gene Homans, his final victim, succumbing 8 and 7. The Grand Slam had been conquered for the first—and last—time.

At the age of twenty-eight, with no more worlds to conquer and his place in history secure, Bobby Jones retired. In a day and age when heroes come and go with all the suddenness and completeness of a candle flame that has been blown out, leaving barely a trace of smoke, Bobby Jones had gone out at the top of his game, leaving a record and a magnificent glow that will never be forgotten.

Elgin Baylor

b. 1934

Many's the name that just tends to lie there, giving neither definition nor direction to the person wearing it. Other names tend to obscure an appreciation of the person they're attached to. But there is one name in the annals of sports that carries the true meaning of its owner: Elgin Baylor.

For Elgin Baylor's father owned a watch. A gold watch. A pocket watch. An Elgin, to be specific. "And that's what he named me after," Baylor would say. Which was only fair, since Elgin Baylor would become a Swiss movement to be watched in the years to come.

But it would take Elgin time before he became a star. Born in

Washington, D.C., into a world that predated integration, young Elgin was overlooked by the eastern basketball fraternity, even though his credentials included being named to the all-city basketball team. It was here that Fate stepped in, albeit in a roundabout way, and offered Elgin a scholarship—for football.

It was one of the strangest cases of association since Professor Rorschach first toppled over his inkwell, but it happened that one of Elgin's friends from back home, Warren Williams, had gone off to the small College of Idaho on a football scholarship. When asked if he knew any more football players back east, Williams replied that he knew a terrific football player named Elgin Baylor and that he was an end, or some such—even though Baylor's entire football experience consisted of some pickup games and a few freelance games at the Northwest Boys Club.

And so, with the College of Idaho the sole petitioner for his services, Elgin entrained to the metropolis of Caldwell, Idaho, becoming one of the college's 485 students. When he finally arrived, two weeks after preseason practice had already begun, he was greeted by rain. After three days, with the rain on a steady run, the team repaired to the gym, where Elgin played basketball with other members of the team. Somewhere around the fourth day Elgin remembers the coach—who, not incidentally, was also the basketball coach—coming over and saying, "I didn't know you could play basketball." Baylor responded, "You never asked." The coach, knowing which side of sports his bread was buttered on, asked Baylor if he would be interested in playing basketball rather than football. "Fine," said Baylor. "I'd rather play basketball." So ended a football career—and began a basketball one.

But Fate wasn't through with Elgin. Not yet, at least. For one night, after the completion of his first season, as Elgin was wandering down the halls of his dorm, what to his wondering ear should he hear but a radio broadcast of the 1955 NCAA finals between San Francisco and LaSalle. Baylor sat down to listen, almost as if he were watching the game on the radio, with its flow of sound and imagery. "I'd read about Tom Gola and Bill Russell in the papers, but just to listen to the game on the radio was like seeing them play," Baylor remembered. "I could see them blocking the shots and rebounding and scoring. It was so exciting it was better than any game I'd ever actually seen. And, as I listened, I said, 'Gee, it would be great playing in an NCAA championship or for an NCAA school.'"

That intellectual balloon ascension gave birth to the thought that he wanted to transfer to a school, preferably one in the Northwest, that played big-time NCAA basketball. He sent out applications, and his wish came true when one of the schools that contacted him was Seattle University. And over the next three years Elgin led the Chieftains to a record of 66 wins and 21 losses, his twisting, driving layups and unbelievable jump shots leaving onlookers bubbly-eyed and with powers barely those of respiration.

In his third year, Elgin got the other part of his wish: to play in an NCAA championship. Making moves within moves, Baylor continued to astound and astonish onlookers as he led Seattle into what had not yet been dubbed "the Final Four." In the semifinal game, against Kansas State, he pulled what his former coach, Al Brightman, called "one of the damnedest things I ever saw him do. Bob Boozer of Kansas State was playing him head-on. Elgin bounced the ball off Boozer's head, then dribbled it right around him and went for the hoop. He did it because it suddenly seemed like the right play. And it was." There were many more "right plays" for Elgin, and although Seattle came up short against Kentucky in the finals, he was named the tournament's Most Valuable Player, having scored 135 points in five games. Added to his all-American honors, it made him the hottest pro prospect in the class of '58.

The Minneapolis Lakers were then the weakest franchise in the NBA, hovering somewhere between bankruptcy and total invisibility. A threadbare and lackluster team, this group of life's losing stuntmen had a less-than-awesome 19–53 record for the 1957–58 season. They needed help, badly, both on the court and at the gate. That help came in the form of Elgin Baylor, who signed with the sickly Lakers for the then-healthy sum of $20,000.

Baylor reported to the Lakers' training camp and remembered thinking: "I never saw so many big people in my life. In college you see a couple of big guys, but they don't always have the physical ability that you have. And then, when I went to training camp and saw these big guys, I wondered if I really could make it. But right after the first practice I could sense that I was as good as they were."

No, make that *better*. Much better. Beginning with his very first game, against the Cincinnati Royals, Elgin made a partial payment, with interest, on the $20,000 investment, scoring 25 points. In another game against the Royals, he scored 55 points, the highest single-game total for the season. Looking part St. Vitus and part St. Paul, he showed more variations on a theme than Mussorgsky ever thought possible—whether it was driving to the basket fasterthanyoucanreadthis, using lightninglike deception to either take his jumper or set up another teammate, or twisting and turning, all done with a head tic, a motion like a turtle pulling his head into his shell, that presaged an act of offensive destruction.

But if Baylor was a scoring machine, he was a rebounding one as well. A six-foot-five forward, even though dense of body, should have no chance of fighting his way through a forest of elbows and bodies to pull down rebound after rebound, especially against men who looked like they had met Jack at the top of the beanstalk. But that's what Baylor did, time and again, with persistence, strength, timing, if-at-first-you-don't-succeed-try-try-again effort, and a specialized intelligence. Teammate Jim Krebs could only marvel, "He'll go up, come down, go up again. I've seen him go up four or five times. And he has great timing. Somebody like myself, I have to rely on blocking out. But 'Elj' can get there right at the right instant."

At the end of his rookie year, Baylor was fourth in the league in scoring, with a 24.9 average; third in rebounding, with a 15.0 average; and ninth in assists, with 4.1 per game. Elgin's time had come.

Baylor moved his scoring average up to 29.6 points per game in 1959–60, and then the Lakers themselves moved, to Los Angeles, for the 1960–61 season. But the second set of scenery suited Baylor, who quickly became one of the brightest stars in the City of Stars with his à la carte moves and all-around playmaking ability. And, of course, his scoring, which included a 71-point effort against the New York Knicks and an overall 34.8 average.

By now his coach, Fred Schaus, was calling him "the greatest cornerman ever to play pro basketball." But even "the greatest cornerman" couldn't bring L.A. a world championship, and in 1961–62, 1962–63, and 1964–65 the Lakers lost in the finals to the Boston Celtics, a team loaded to the gunwales with talent.

It was in the opening game of that 1965 championship series, against the Baltimore Bullets, that Elgin twisted for one of his jump shots and came down like a puppet whose strings had been cut, twisting in pain. Players on the Baltimore bench distinctly heard a "pop." Baylor got up and tried running again, but collapsed, hard, writhing in agony. Running up and down the hardwood for 23,445 pro minutes had taken its toll—he had ripped off the upper eighth of his kneecap.

They removed part of his kneecap, tendons, and ligaments and scraped out sharp flecks of calcium. The doctors looked tombstones, and local papers read "please carry" obits, but Elgin, cemented in a cast from ankle to hip, tried, like Humpty Dumpty, to put the pieces back together. To be, well, Elgin Baylor again.

If, as Thomas Carlyle once said, genius can be defined as an infinite capacity for taking pain, then Elgin's qualifications were more than in order, as he punished himself to get back in playing shape. Shot full of Novocain, the man who called himself the Fabulous Invalid made a small step in the 1965–66 season. To announcer Chick Hearn, "It was like watching Citation run on spavined legs." Still, he pushed himself, regaining the body control if not the moves that had made him singular.

By now the man called Elgin could be likened to a clock that needed a fortnight's winding to insure a year's running. But somehow, someway, he came back the following season and the season after that to average 26 points a game and once again power the Lakers into another losing championship series with the Celts.

After two more seasons, the sands in his hourglass finally began to fill up. The aches and pains could not be assuaged, even by Novocain. And so, true to his pride, Elgin Baylor, after fourteen years, retired, saying, "I do not want to prolong my career when I cannot maintain the standards I established for myself." But those standards will stand the test of time, for all time.

29

Emil Zatopek

b. 1922

Picture, if you will, a man with a look of being eternally put-upon, his face full of scowls and frowns, grimacing as if he had just swallowed something or other, tongue lolling out of his mouth, eyes cast to the heavens in supplicant glances, arms clawing at his abdomen with each agonizing step, and you have that curious piece of goods named Emil Zatopek.

To watch Emil Zatopek run a race was to watch, as one writer put it, "a man who ran as if tortured by internal demons." His style, one peculiarly striking to the optic nerve, made it seem as if he were dying with each and every step. It was almost, as one writer wrote, like watching "a man who has just been stabbed in the heart."

But Zatopek's accomplishments were as striking as his style.

125

Zatopek began his racing—and grimacing—in his native Czechoslovakia at the advanced age of nineteen. In his very first competitive event, a 1,400-meter race, he turned in the unimpressive time of 4 minutes, 24.6 seconds. Within months, hobnailed boots began marching through his beloved homeland, and Zatopek traded in his track shoes for army combat boots, joining the Czech army to defend his country against the invading Nazi hordes. For the duration of the war Zatopek continued to train, running at least ten miles a morning, alternating between jogging and sprinting in his heavy army boots—and sometimes at night, wearing his boots and carrying a flashlight.

With the end of the war in 1945, Zatopek went out to prove he was not just an also-ran who also ran, biking some three-hundred-odd miles from Prague to Berlin and inviting himself into a meet for Allied troops. Despite being told to go away and receiving other such don't-darken-our-towels turnaways, Zatopek stayed around, and won a distance race.

He was to make his bow on the international stage in the 1948 London Olympics, winning the 10,000 meters, only two months after his debut in the event, and finishing just one and a half meters behind the winner in the 5,000 meters on a rain-soaked track. He was to embark on a steady run of wins across the Continent, almost all in record times, in distances from 5,000 to 30,000 meters.

Then came the 1952 Helsinki Olympics and the most amazing performance by any distance runner in the history of the games.

Zatopek began his beguine in the 10,000 meters, breaking the Olympic record for both speed and agony as he wore out his opponents and won by 100 yards.

Three days later Zatopek went out to try for a distance double that had defied every lower-cased Olympic god since Finland's Hannes Kolehmainen won both the 5,000- and 10,000-meter races back in 1912. With enough coolness to branch out and franchise it, Zatopek decided to have a little fun during the qualifying heats. First, he could be seen chatting with the other runners during the final laps, almost as if he were conducting a two-man debating society, and then, after it had become clear who the five qualifiers would be, he would slow down and allow the other four to pass him, directing them to go by much like a traffic cop directing traffic.

But the finals were a far more serious matter, not only for Zatopek, but for the sports world at large. Or so it seemed. One Paris newspaper carried the banner headline: "La Finale du 5,000 Metres? Ce Sera la Bombe Atomique des Jeux! (This will be the atomic bomb of the games!)"

The runners assembled at the starting line harbored enough ambitions, past, present, and future, to make it one of the most talent-laden fields in Olympic history. At the gun, Zatopek— along with the German favorite, Herbert Schade; the French-Algerian, Alain Mimoun; Chris Chataway, who would later gain fame as Roger Bannister's "rabbit"; and England's Gordon Pirie— broke away from the pack, leaving the rest of the field to plod along with a dull resignation to their fates. As the laps wound down, and the lead passed back and forth in a cavalier manner, it appeared that any one of the five could win.

The bell lap sounded like the gun of a rallying army as first Zatopek, looking as if he had been made mad by the gods and fearing that they were now about to destroy him, moved into the lead, followed by Schade. Then in the backstretch, Chataway made his move, taking over the lead, with Mimoun and Schade hard on his heels, leaving Zatopek back in fourth place. Going into the last turn, the tortured vision of Zatopek, weaving, staggering, gyrating, and running, as one observer said, "as if there was a scorpion in each shoe," could be seen swinging wide, his red uniform flashing by the others. He began pulling away, tortured step by tortured step, winning by five yards over Mimoun in the Olympic record-setting time of 14:06.6.

It was Czech and double Czech for Zatopek. Not since the 1912 Olympics had any man captured both the 5,000- and 10,000-meter races. Now that distance double belonged to Emil Zatopek, and in Olympic record-setting times. But he wasn't through yet— not by a long shot.

And it *was* a long shot. The very afternoon that he captured the 5,000 meters, he learned his wife had just won a gold medal in the javelin throw. With a smile crossing his well-worn map, Zatopek said, "At present the score of the contest in the Zatopek family is 2–1. This result is too close. To restore some prestige I will try to improve on it—in the marathon race." But few expected him to win, his never having run a marathon before.

But to Zatopek it was merely a case of higher calculus as he tried for an unprecedented triple. Used to ritual distances,

Zatopek was unconcerned about his audience; his only concern was the possibility of pacing strategies he knew nothing about, since these were unexplored waters. Always interpreting his race, and his rivals', in an interesting manner, Zatopek decided to run with the man he considered the favorite, Jim Peters of Great Britain, who only six weeks before had run the fastest marathon in history. Finding Peters's running number in that morning's newspaper, Zatopek sought him out on the starting line from amongst that rolling stock known as marathoners and introduced himself. And stayed with him, trailing as does a tail a comet, as Peters took off at a record-breaking pace.

After sixteen miles, Zatopek, running elbow to elbow with Peters, turned to his running rival and asked, tongue firmly implanted in cheek, "We go a little faster, yes?" A flustered Peters could only answer, "Pace too slow," and, pretending to be fresh, picked up the pace. Still, there was a grinning Zatopek at his elbow, grinning and asking, "Don't we go faster?" Finally, after twenty miles, Peters, his legs developing cramps, could no longer keep up with Zatopek and dropped out. Running with an unrelieved black scowl on his face, Zatopek kept pulling away from the rest of the field and entered the stadium far ahead of any challengers. As the huge crowd caught sight of him, they greeted him with chants of "Za-to-pek, Za-to-pek," as the "Czech Choo-Choo" completed the final lap of the marathon in record time, before any of the other runners had even entered the stadium. The hero of the 1952 games was already signing autographs when the second-place finisher, Reinaldo Gorno of Argentina, arrived. And when Gorno crossed the finish line, who was there to greet him with a slice of orange? Emil Zatopek, of course.

By winning an unheard-of "triple" in distance races, Emil Zatopek established himself as one of the all-time greats, called by none other than Roger Bannister, the first man to run a mile in less than four minutes, "the greatest athlete of the postwar world"—in either the scowling or non-scowling division.

30

Wayne Gretzky

b. 1961

Just when it seemed that all the technicians in sports had disappeared, save for a few preserved as classroom fossils, along came a little necromancer named Wayne Gretzky who brought with him a science heretofore unknown to hockeykind, playing the game like chess with skates on. In the process, he managed to stake more claims to titles than a Yukon claim jumper, transforming the National Hockey League record book into his own personal diary.

Gretzky's ability to use the ice rink as a chessboard can be traced back to his childhood, where, when he was just a toddling tot growing up in Brantford, Ontario, his father strapped skates on his little feet almost as soon as he had learned to walk on frozen toes. As soon as little Wayne turned those toes to ice, Papa Gretzky began putting him through a series of drills that would make him, in time, the greatest scoring machine in the history of the game—drills that included having him zigzag between tin cans laid out on the ice to circumscribe a Z, hip-hop over sticks as he received passes, and slap-shoot the puck into smaller and smaller targets. But the most important part of his development was his practice of cutting across the ice to intercept a puck as it careened off the boards as he followed his father's guiding principle—"Skate to where the puck is going to be, not to where it has been"—rather than merely following the puck itself.

Practice made more than perfect—it made a prodigy, a prodigy with a puck. One who, by the age of six, was playing in a league with ten-year-olds, and four years later was playing in a novice league against fully developed teenagers. But young Wayne more than made up for the age disadvantage with his hockey I.Q.—his Ice Qualifications—drilled into him by his father, especially the rule, tattoo'd into his subconscious, about cutting off the puck rather than just chasing it. Putting these teachings into practice, young Wayne was able to extend his guesswork, like that of a slide rule, able to go to the third place, knowing where the puck had been, where it was now, and where it was going to be. In doing so, he was also able to score an average of four and a half goals per game against the older youngsters.

With each passing teenage year young Gretzky's fame grew in range and breadth, his scoring prowess and radarlike powers commanding headlines across the length and breadth of Canada. By the age of sixteen this myth-in-the-making had put into port at Sault Sainte Marie, there to finish his hockey education.

It was while he was at Sault Sainte Marie that Fate conspired to add one more piece to the Gretzky legend: his wearing of Number 99. Seems that young Gretzky had wanted to wear Number 9, in tribute to his hockey idol, Gordie Howe. However, as luck and circumstances would have it, the number was already assigned to one of the members of the team, and the Soos' general manager, Muzz MacPherson, would not hear of Gretzky's taking the number from someone who already was sporting it. Not incidental to the story, 1977 was also the year that Phil Esposito and Ken Hodge, only recently traded to the New York Rangers, began to wear Numbers 77 and 88. So MacPherson, wishing to double Gretzky's pleasure, suggested the Number 99 to his young phenomenon. Gretzky originally rejected the idea, but after wearing Numbers 19 and 14, switched over to the number that would later bring him fame—and vice versa—in double tribute to his childhood idol.

But 9 or 99, it made no difference, as young Gretzky continued to thread the goal like the proverbial needle, scoring 182 points in sixty-four games. And caught the eye of the Indianapolis Racers of the upstart World Hockey Association as well, signing a four-year, $875,000 contract. But after only eight games, the Racers, finding themselves skating on financial thin ice, discovered that their smooth-faced rookie was also smooth of coin, negotiable in every way, and sold his contract to the Edmonton Oilers, then of the WHA.

And so it was that Gretzky picked up his sticks and moved to Edmonton, there to begin his one-man assault on the record books. In that first full year of "major" league hockey, still three years shy of voting age, the player they now called the Kid scored 104 points on 43 goals and 61 assists. But then again, sniffed his critics, it was *only* the WHA, a league made up of has-beens and never-wases. In 1979, the WHA went funct, and Edmonton joined the established National Hockey League. And Gretzky, now playing in the "major" majors, took on a stellar brightness and stardom as he continued to impose his will on all, scoring 137 points on 51 goals and 86 assists.

Every year thereafter was like a watering of last year's crops as Gretzky continued filling the bottomless cup of his accomplishments, becoming the first man in NHL history to break the 200-point mark—not once, but four times!—scoring a record 92 goals in a season, etc., etc., etc., and, in all, piling up so many records that the recordkeeper's mind rattled at the thought of posting his continually mounting numbers.

But even as Gretzky's silver skate was being measured and his supporters were left winded trotting out catchall descriptions of him, like "the Great One," he had still failed to win over his detractors. For those caretakers of hockey's flame, a thinning number with thinning hair, viewed the game with a reverence that paid full faith and credit to hockey's traditions, going all the way back to the days of "the Original Six" clubs in the NHL, and viewed expansion and its by-products—like Gretzky and his

Zamboni-sized truckload of records—as abominations. They were so confused by the number of new teams in the NHL that someone suggested were they to watch the Jets battle the Sharks they would be hard pressed to know if they were witnessing a hockey game or *West Side Story*.

And they were equally confused by Gretzky's almost chesslike game, a style with which they were totally unfamiliar. He had, they said, only average speed, underaverage size, and no average defensive abilities. Hell, they scoffed, he didn't body-check, back-check, or even bed-check. And then there were those who hinted that he avoided, rather than took head-on, those lumber-laden goons who, like three-alarmers at a paint factory, cleared the place out—especially of puck-carriers.

But for Gretzky, the door of opportunity never needed to be knocked down—it could be *opened* with the right combination. And Gretzky had that right combination, a combination of instinctive moves that enabled him to avoid running into those big, burly defensemen with bad intentions and still be able to control both the puck and the game. It was, as one teammate once said of Gretzky's Geiger-like sensitivity, "almost as if he had a rearview mirror in the back of his head."

Henri Richard, a center known for his own wonderful moves, was moved himself to say of the wunderkind: "He has the greatest moves I've ever seen." They were moves to be watched, framed, even pressed between the pages of hockey books, now and forever. Here he could be seen doubling back, like a hare escaping the hounds, to get ahead of the puck; there, pointing for the puck like a dog for a pheasant, his eyes always affixed on its flight. And everywhere, skating with a tactical and tacit understanding of where he was and where he had to be.

And once he had engulfed the puck, like a cat lapping up cream, he would use that extrasensory perception of his to maneuver it into position to shoot, or pass, ofttimes needing a space only as large as a napkin—especially behind the net. Harry Sinden, general manager of the Boston Bruins, saw Gretzky and couldn't believe what he was seeing, saying, "Gretzky sees a picture out there that no one else sees. It's difficult to describe, because I've never seen the game he's looking at."

Nor had anyone else, for that matter. For it was difficult, if not impossible, to believe that this reed-thin, almost under-nourished player with a faceful of youth, a headful of blond hair, and a stickful of goals had been able to rewrite the hockey record book using the style of a chess grandmaster. But he had, many times over.

And down through the years, as he made record-setting a vocation unto itself (and set every hockey record imaginable, fifty-nine by last count and still counting, including the "always-thinking" record) Wayne Gretzky would enter his name one more time in that book kept by all of sports—for being the most statistically dominant athlete in the history of team sports.

31

Edwin Moses

b. 1955

For most sports fans, the greatest mythic figure of constancy remains Joe DiMaggio and his incredible 56-game hit streak, a record which stands as a lasting monument to his consistency, persistency, and excellency. But for an even greater achievement, we offer for your consideration the name Edwin Moses, whose streak of 122 consecutive 400-meter hurdle races without a loss stands as an even greater monument to all of the above—2.1785716 times as great, if you're using a computer.

In that fifties tour de farce *Singin' in the Rain*, Gene Kelly and Donald O'Connor do a wonderful riff, chanting as much as singing to their voice teacher, "Moses supposes his toe-ses are roses, but Moses supposes erroneously." However, the Moses named Edwin never supposed anything, erroneous or no. For

Edwin Moses was a master at reducing the art of hurdling to a science heretofore unknown to track and field, connecting the dots between computers, physics, physiology, and biochemicals to develop his own menu, leaving absolutely nothing to à la carte chance.

Despite the fact that "most people think running is just physical," Moses has said, "it takes a lot of technical work." The epitome of calculation, Moses combined the rhythm of hurdling with the algorithm of computer problem-solving in a finite number of steps to determine upon his revolutionary thirteen strides between hurdles instead of the normal fourteen. "It's a lot of work putting all the data points into the computer," the man *Life* magazine called Mr. Wizardry said, as he monitored his heartbeat during his sadistic workouts with painstaking discipline, all the better to plot graphs on his recoveries. But then again, Edwin Moses always researched everything with a down-to-the-eyeteeth precision.

That research began at an early age when young Moses, growing up in Dayton, Ohio, was more given to collecting fossils and dissecting frogs than to running races and breaking records. But if his curiosity killed frogs instead of cats, it also led him to the equally curious world of track and field. Like any normal child who, as an example of nature, abhorred a vacuum, the young Moses filled his by reading. One of the books he chanced to come across was a Boy Scout handbook. And what to his wondering eyes should appear but a chapter on track and field equal to all the correspondence courses in the country. Moses, who would go on to write volumes himself on the subject, found the words fairly leaping off the page at him and was moved to test out his new fascination.

Jump-cut to 1976. Moses is now a skinny, six-foot-two twenty-year-old junior at Morehouse College in Atlanta, Georgia, majoring in physics and minoring in track and field. And although he had never run the 400-meter hurdles in international competition before the March 27 Olympic trials, he decided to enter the event in an attempt to qualify for the '76 Summer Games in Montreal. Moses not only qualified, he would go on to win the gold medal in the world-record time of 47.64 seconds—winning by eight meters, the largest winning margin in the history of the event. Ever the perfectionist doomed to remain unsatisfied, Moses afterward would say that his only regret had been having

his training for the Olympics so interfere with his studies that his
grade-point average had "fallen" to a 3.57.

Edwin Moses's life was always one defined by numbers,
whether they were in his grade-point average, those he crunched
out of his computer, or those represented by his long-running—
and jumping—victory streak, one that started the next year,
1977.

After losing to Harald Schmid of West Germany on August
26 of that year, Moses would go on to outdistance the field a week
later in Düsseldorf to begin the longest winning streak in the
history of track—if not all of sports. Over the next nine years,
nine months, and nine days, a period covering 107 finals—a total
of 122 races, if you include preliminaries—Edwin Moses would
remain immune to defeat.

His wins began passing by with the regularity and monotony
of exits on the Santa Monica Freeway—his nineteenth consecutive win in finals coming in the 1984 Los Angeles Olympics,
along with his second gold medal, and his hundredth straight at
the Budapest Grand Track and Field Meet in '86—as he continued to bound over the hurdles (or 36-inch "sticks," as they're
called) with the greatest of ease, leaving world records, competitors, and under-48-second times in his slipstream.

As the streak of the man they called King of the Sticks
mounted, the man who under normal conditions kept his emotions in a tight fist retreated even further behind his tinted
glasses, into his own sparsely populated island, suffering Promethean agonies under its growing pressure, his privacy compromised, his space invaded. As later rival Danny Harris said,
"Nobody gets into Edwin's world." And Edwin's world had
become less that of a competitor concentrating on running fast
than that of a conservator worrying about winning all the time.

Knowing winning was everything and losing nothing,
Moses, who calibrated every detail down to the smallest nth,
carefully plotted his course—choosing to run, it was rumored,
only in those races where he knew the crowds might be more
responsive and the competition less challenging. His favorite
stomping—and hurdling—grounds were in Europe, where he
was greeted with wild hosannas and accepted as one of the all-
time greats.

But, like good wine, Moses had aged, gracefully, but aged
nevertheless, his performances leveling off with each passing

year. On June 4, 1987, at the age of 31 years and 10 months, an age at which most hurdlers are home collecting social security, Moses found himself in Madrid at the International Meet, there to defend his streak. And to meet Danny Harris, the twenty-one-year-old three-time collegiate champion.

The last time the two had conjoined had been three years before at the '84 Los Angeles Olympics. In those games, like the superman he was, Moses had been faster—like the cartoon Superman—than a speeding bullet, the bullet being Harris, who had won the silver. Now, at Madrid, Moses would have to bite the bullet.

With dusk beginning to settle over Vallehermoso Stadium, the hurdlers took their places in the blocks, all hunkering down, nothing but asses and elbows. All, that is, except Edwin Moses, who was caught up in his own private vision at that very moment, performing a little one-act game of one-upmanship, jogging a prerace "victory" lap around the infield to the warm applause of the twelve thousand fans and giving his opponents an opportunity to show their reverence, as much to his forceful personality as to his talents. Then he slowly came back to take his position and await the starter's call.

Harris got off to a fast start and by the sixth of the ten hurdles was in the lead. But by the eighth hurdle, Moses—who had calculated it took 3.1 seconds between hurdles at the start and 4.8 toward the end—had rallied, even forging a slight lead. The two went over the ninth hurdle, stride for stride. And then, as Agatha Christie was wont to say, there was one.

UCLA sprint coach John Smith had once said of Moses, "The critical thing Edwin has going for him is that he looks like Gregory Hines going over the last hurdle." But this time, as Pat Butcher wrote, "He looked more like Chevy Chase, trying to go through the hurdle rather than over it." Harris would hit the finish line first, winning by the mere billowing of a shirt as, in the words of a *Sports Illustrated* headline, "The Reign Ended in Spain."

The ungraspable had happened: Edwin Moses had lost. It was enough to make adoring Spaniards wonder if their faith in Gibraltar had been misplaced. And enough to cause Moses to momentarily lose his place in his chapter of history as, almost in a conditioned reflex, he began to circle the track in a "victory" lap—prompting one observer to comment, "I suppose he has gotten so used to taking laps of honor that he is still doing so, even though he has not won." At first a queer sensation of disquietude fell over the stands. But then a small rumble that started somewhere in the bowels of the stadium began to make itself heard as twelve thousand voices began chanting his name and twice twelve thousand hands met in rapturous applause. And then, in response to his famous gap-toothed grin, they saluted him with the traditional chant normally reserved for victorious bullfighters: "Torero! Torero! Torero!"

His astounding supremacy had come to an end; Edwin Moses had proven to be vincible. But now Moses, who normally said little, stepped out of character, saying, "I'll be back, because now they've got me mad. And I haven't been mad in years."

Three months later, in the World Title Championships in Rome, he was to keep that promise, as he nipped both Harris and Schmid in a photo finish to reestablish himself as the master of the 400 meters. At least momentarily. Afterward he would take a twelve-minute victory lap, this time well earned, and say, "I've created a monster. It's harder and harder to win."

And it was, as Moses, by now an ancient (at least by track standards) thirty-three, chased his third gold medal at the '88 Seoul Olympics and came up short, winning only a bronze. Time had finally caught up with him (although, ironically, he had run faster for his bronze than he had for either of his golds).

It was, as Moses said, getting "harder and harder." It seemed that the only thing this grandmaster, in all his years of calculation, had been unable to calculate was the formula for an age conversion chart. Otherwise, by any computation, Edwin Moses had proven, by the numbers, that he was the greatest hurdler of all time.

Rod Laver

b. 1938

The world of sports, much like the world of science, is an orderly system, one with a method of double-entry bookkeeping that allows the tying together of almost every event, participant, date, and record to prove something or other. Take the year 1938, for instance, when three seemingly unrelated occurrences helped to form not only the future but the very fabric of the sport of tennis.

For if one were to pull the thread marked "1938," one would find the following: It was the year when Don Budge not only became the first player to win the Grand Slam of tennis but also was to lead the United States to a 3–2 win over Australia in the finals of the Davis Cup, symbolic of world supremacy. It was also the year when a slender, sandy-haired Australian named Harry Hopman would make his first appearance on the world tennis scene as captain of Australia's Davis Cup team, signaling the beginning of Australia's dominance as a world tennis power. And, half a world away, in Queensland, Australia, it also marked the natal year of a bouncing baby redheaded male named Rodney George Laver.

Put all these disparate facts together and you have the beginnings of a story: one of Rod Laver and how he would surpass the original owner of the Grand Slam copyright, Don Budge, by winning two and becoming, in the process, one of tennis's all-time greats.

First, Harry Hopman, the party of the second part. Called the Fox by his countrymen, Hopman had captained the '38 Australian Davis Cup team, which had lost in the finals to the defending champions, the United States, 3–2. The next year Hopman and his Aussie team had reversed the result and carried the Cup off to Australia, where they put it in cold storage due to a bigger battle going on at the time, World War II.

With the advent of the war, Hopman disappeared into the financial world of Melbourne, only to reemerge in 1950 to lead the fortunes of the Down Under continent. And what fortunes they were. Where once tennis in Australia had been the private preserve of the privileged few, a polite garden-party adjunct, by 1950 it was being played by some two hundred fifty thousand registered competitive players in a climate that, like California's, favored outdoor sports.

Harry Hopman moved into this nation of game players with the eye of a recruiting sergeant—and the methods of a drill sergeant. First he cut out of the herd two youngsters, Frank Sedgman and Ken McGregor, both of whom had attainments which already stood out on them like labels on oceangoing steamer trunks, and set sail across the Pacific to challenge the United States for the 1950 Davis Cup. Sedgman and McGregor were successful in their quest, as they were in retaining the silver bowl in '51 and '52.

When Sedgman and McGregor had both hit their amateur peaks and hit the road as well by turning professional, Hopman went, in assembly-line fashion, back to Australia's tennis factories to fill their places with younger stars like Lew Hoad and Ken Rosewall. And then, when Hoad and Rosewall went into the pro ranks, Hopman again replenished his ranks, this time with Malcolm Anderson and Neale Fraser. Indeed, there seemed to be no end to the talent available to Hopman, as the Aussies went on to become repeat winners in Davis Cup competition, winning it fifteen of the eighteen years of Hopman's reign.

If there was one fault to find with Hopman's reign—no, make that regime—it was the fact that he was a stern disciplinarian, almost a drill sergeant. A stickler for conditioning and detail, he kept players on the courts for hours, emphasized weight lifting, and imposed strict curfews. He also controlled the off-court conduct of his players, forbidding them to talk to the press and fining any of them so unrefined as to use the wrong fork at the dinner table. But whatever he did, it seemed to work.

Nothing worked for him as well, however, as something he did in 1959. Stung by the loss of the Cup to the Americans for only the second time in nine years in the '58 Davis Cup finals, Hopman added a newcomer to the '59 team—a flame-haired youngster with an equally flaming backhand and a powerhouse serve: Rod Laver.

At first blush Rod Laver looked like anything but the rightful successor to the mantles of Sedgman, McGregor, Hoad, Rosewall, et al. Standing only five feet eight and a half inches and weighing but 155 pounds, he was a bandy-legged, frecklefaced youth with a small, hawklike nose that looked like it had probably wandered around his pinched face until it found a final resting place. But there were also some hints of potential greatness, most notably a Popeye-like left forearm that was the same size as Rocky Marciano's and whippetlike legs that enabled him to reach anything. Add to that a wristy spin shot he could snap off like an electric switch and the ability to put every fiber of his being into every shot, and you may have the reason why he was the personal favorite of Hopman's, who had recognized his talents when he was playing in junior tournaments and had accompanied his favorite redhead on his first world tour, when Laver was just eighteen.

Now, at the age of twenty-one, Laver led a Davis Cup team that recaptured the hardware it had lent to the United States the year before and took it back to Australia—where God and Harry Hopman had intended it should be in the first place. That same year Laver won the mixed doubles at Wimbledon and the Australian doubles championship. In 1960 he added the Australian singles championship, and in 1961 he rode his howitzerlike serves and topspin drives to the Wimbledon and German singles titles. All of which leads us, as surely as calendar pages turn, to the year 1962 and one of the greatest years any tennis player would ever have, as Laver became the first man since Don Budge to win the historic Grand Slam of tennis—the Australian, French, British (Wimbledon, that is), and United States championships.

Now, following the yellow-brick and clay and grass road that so many others before him had traveled, Laver turned professional, leaving behind him the many tournaments at which he had made his mark and his name. Or so it seemed.

But the winds of change they were a-blowing throughout the tennis world. Beginning with the 1957 Wimbledon tournament—when Lew Hoad turned professional less than twenty-four hours after winning the championship—the powers-that-be had seen more and more of the top tennis players in the world coin their freshly minted trophies by going into the pro ranks, leaving the so-called "amateur" events, like Wimbledon, devoid of the top names in tennis. And the excitement they brought. Tiring of this, and the hypocrisy of "shamateurism"—with its fake expense accounts and under-the-table payoffs and bonuses to amateurs—the all-powerful British Lawn Tennis Association recommended that Wimbledon become an "open" event, open to both amateurs and professionals.

Defying the International Lawn Tennis Federation, the British Association, which had been the first to accord women equal status with men, again made tennis history by voting to stage the 1968 All-England Championships as an "open" event. Among those professionals returning to and refreshing the ranks were Pancho Gonzales, Lew Hoad, Ken Rosewall, Tony Roche, Roy Emerson, John Newcombe, Alex Olmedo, and, of course, the reason for this digression, Rod Laver. The finals pitted two professionals against each other, Laver and Roche. And the winner was—drumroll, please!—Rod Laver.

It is well-nigh impossible to catch lightning in a bottle once, let alone twice. But that's what Laver did in 1969. Now at the top of his game and with all barriers to open competition down, Laver readied his assault on his second Grand Slam.

The Grand Slam is four jewels, each in a separate setting. The 1969 Australian championship was played on tricky resodded Australian grass, the French championship on slow French clay, Wimbledon on a garment of green turf, and Forest Hills on grass.

It would be nice to say that Laver "breezed" through all four, but such was not the case. For his Grand Slam express was almost derailed in his very first tournament, the Australian, played at the Milton Courts in Brisbane under a broiling 105-degree sun. In the semifinal round, playing against Tony Roche, Laver soaked through three sun hats and played the longest set he had ever played, winning, 22–20. But, by the end of the third set, which Roche won 9–11, Laver was as groggy as a Marciano opponent. Allowed to take a shower during intermission, the two came back to pick up where they had left off. And where they had left off was with Roche winning. Down 5–0 and at deuce in the sixth game of the fourth set, Laver added some mental agility to his physical ability by playing that game to win, understanding that even if he were to lose 6–1 on Roche's service, he would serve first in the fifth and final set.

Pancho Gonzales had once said of Laver, "He played every game as if he were behind 5–love…his concentration is so intense." And so it was now. Laver did lose that fourth set, 6–1, but by winning the sixth game he now served first in the final set. And the man who could play his opponent as well as he played the ball was able to apply the pressure he wanted on Roche. "I screwed my mind into working for every point as though it were the last."

And so, wringing out his third, and last, sun hat, and screwing up his mind, Laver now did likewise to his opponent. With Roche serving in the eighth game, behind 3–4 and 15–40, Laver drove one of his patented left-handed backhands with all the wrist snap he could muster, loading the ball with enough topspin to propel a carousel for a week. It was a passing winner and gave Laver a 5–3 lead. Laver went on to hold service and win the set, and the match, 7–5, 22–20, 9–11, 1–6, 6–3.

Laver would then go on to beat Andres Gimeno in the Australian final, Ken Rosewall in the French, John Newcombe at Wimbledon, and Roche again at Forest Hills to complete his second Grand Slam—seeing the original owner of the copyright, Don Budge, and raising him one.

And in so doing the man Gonzalez said "had no weakness at all" would establish his own claim to greatness. One for the ages. Beginning in 1938.

33

Daley Thompson

b. 1958

To paraphrase George Orwell, all athletes are created equal, except some more so than others. In a day of ultraspecialization, athletes can become stars on the basis of one strength—a baseball player can hit home runs or throw a fastball, a football player can be a superb runner or throw the ball with unerring accuracy, a golfer can drive the bejesus out of the ball or putt well, etc., etc., etc. But to be a decathlete, you must be a complete athlete, able to do it all, mastering a wide range of disciplines with the balance of a Renaissance man.

Since time immemorial, and even before, the man known as "the Greatest Athlete in the World"—a title originally bestowed on Jim Thorpe by King Gustav V after the 1912 Olympics—has been the decathlete. And no man deserved that title more than Daley Thompson, the gregarious offspring of a Nigerian father and a Scottish mother with a Turkish bazaar of talents.

Born Francis Morgan Thompson, the youngster was given the African nickname Ayodele (meaning "Joy Enters the House") by his father, Frank Sr., to distinguish him from all the other Franks in the family. The name was later contracted to Dele and then, finally, corrupted to just plain ol' Daley. But, truth to tell, it was not joy which had entered the house so much as constant havoc. "That child was a terror from the minute he was born," his mother later recalled. Hyperactive, strong-willed, and given to street fighting, the young Daley was always on the edge of falling into his own volcano.

Unable to cope with the blithe spirit that ever was, his parents bundled him off at the age of seven to a state-supported boarding school for troubled children. It was there that the unhappy youngster finally found sports—and found himself in the process, discovering his fortes: running and jumping.

After boarding school, the young Thompson enrolled in a small London college, where he devoted himself to becoming England's fastest sprinter. But one of his early coaches quickly saw that the youngster possessed an abundance of talents. Determining that the curriculum of the decathlon was a far better school for Thompson, he began to press the youngster to turn his many talents to the ten-part event. Predictably the headstrong Thompson dug in his heels, and it was only after what one teammate remembered as a "lot of blood and tears" that he finally admitted to himself what his coach had already figured out: that his chances of attaining world-class status were far greater in the decathlon than in the sprints.

Thompson's first taste of competition came in 1975, when, as a sixteen-year-old, standing six-foot-one and weighing 189 pounds, he entered the Welsh Open—but not before he had to obtain a special dispensation because he was underage. With an obvious disinclination to finish second, he won his first de-cathlon, amassing 6,685 points, exceeding the British junior record by some 2,000 points. He would go on to win the '75 AAA junior championships with 7,000 points, more than the senior winner, and close out the season by setting another British junior record with 7,100 points. Daley was now convinced that the decathlon was to be his calling.

But if Daley had determined on the decathlon as his calling, his mother had not. His decision to undertake a full-time commitment was not welcomed at home, and his mother, wanting her son to go to work, told him either to get a job or get out of the house. And so, Daley got out, all the better to concentrate on the great demands made on him. "The streets were full of athletes like him," she was to say later. "I had no idea what his potential was, or where it would lead."

But Daley, in his usual cocksure manner, was sure what his potential was. And was determined to reach it. To further his ambitions, he moved in with coach Bruce Longden in late '75, where, Daley recalled, "We talked athletics twenty-five hours a day—about everybody's technique and style, about races. Then we'd watch films of the races."

Divorcing himself from all around him, almost as if wearing permanent blinders, Daley toiled untold hours to perfect the ten disciplines that make up the decathlon—in order: the 100 meters, long jump, shot, high jump, 400 meters, 110-meter hurdles, discus, pole vault, javelin, and 1500 meters. For, in the final analysis, the decathlon is all about balance and compromise. The athlete must be able to compete in the 1500 meters, but he must also be able to develop the talents of a sprinter; he must be able to find the power and strength to throw the shot, discus, and javelin, but still not compromise the spring and lift needed for the jumping and vaulting events. And so Daley, whose strengths included his snap in the explosive sprinting and jumping events as well as the pole vault, set his granite jaw and heavy weight lifter's muscles to the task of conquering all ten physical tests.

Daley's obsessive devotion to training paid dividends when he qualified for the 1976 Olympics, becoming the youngest man to qualify for the Olympic decathlon since Bob Mathias in 1948. At the Montreal Games, he celebrated his eighteenth birthday by finishing, appropriately enough, eighteenth, with 7,905 points, 526 points behind the winner, Bruce Jenner. Thompson spent most of his time studying Jenner, taking note of everything from Jenner's demeanor to his physical strengths. Jenner's poise was what impressed Thompson most. "I saw that, well, he wasn't that talented, physically. He was just a hard worker. I learned from him the necessity of it."

Returning home, Daley put his observations into practice, training with a concentration and intensity to equal that of a monk. He was obsessive, driven to the point where, as he later admitted, "the decathlon meant life or death to me."

Over the next four years Thompson chased Jenner's world-record 8,617 points, topping 8,000 for the first time in 1977 and then, the next season at the Commonwealth Games, amassing the third-highest score in decathlon history—which, because of excessive wind assistance in the long jump, could not be ratified. However, three weeks later, in the European Championships, he fashioned a valid record total of over 8,200 points, although he placed second to Aleksandr Grenbenyuk of Russia.

The defeat was devastating to the man to whom the decathlon was a matter of "life or death." "I've never considered suicide," he told one writer, "but I would think that's how people feel. Nothing matters, because you lost. You knew you were going to win, and you lost."

The defeat further forged a resolve in the smithy of his soul and increased his obsession with training. He worked even harder than before, if that were possible, on his weaker second-day events and on the grafting on of throwing skills, all the while continuing a regimen that saw him begin his day with a three-mile run at 5 A.M. and continue until long after the sun had set on his future decathlon empire.

After taking a year off from the decathlon wars, Daley returned in 1980 to finally stalk Jenner's record to its knees, scoring 8,622 points at the pre-Olympic trials in Gotzis, Austria. He followed that up by winning the Olympic gold at the 1980 Moscow Games, where he was finally proclaimed "the Greatest Athlete in the W."—something he always knew in his heart of hearts he would be. He celebrated his coronation by irreverently whistling "Nearer My God to Thee" from the victors' stand in tandem with the public-address system's rendition of the British National Anthem.

All of a sudden Daley Thompson was an overnight sensation—even if it had taken him five hard years to get there. Fans all over the British Isles fell in like with the beautifully tooled machine who possessed a faceful of boyish pleasantness hiding behind a brush-broom mustache, whose two horizontal slits he used for eyes lit up every time he laughed to himself, the smile filling his face and lifting his mustache.

Everyone took a liking to him, everyone, that is, except those in the writing dodge, who felt his cockiness bordered on arrogance and found his manner to be off-putting and even abrasive. Wearing their pencils down to stubs, they wrote of the time he made jokes about Princess Anne and of his swearing when he received a BBC Sports Personality of the Year Award. And they turned near-apoplectic when he told the seven-year-old daughter of one of Britain's Olympic selectors to "fuck off" when she requested his autograph.

But through it all, Thompson continued his cymbal-clashing, both for himself and for the sport he loved so much—a sport that, when he'd first begun, elicited about as much interest as local bonds. And he continued winning as well, going undefeated for the next six years, one of those wins coming in the 1984 Los Angeles Olympics, when he recycled his greatness by setting a new world record and once again reigned as "the Greatest Athlete in the W."

But as it must to all great athletes, the sand in Thompson's hourglass began to fall to the bottom and, compromised by aggravating injuries and advancing age, he finally called it a career after failing to qualify for his fifth Olympics, the 1992 Barcelona Games, the victim of a torn hamstring.

But it had been a helluva run, jump, and throw while it lasted. One that not only brought him the mythic title, but also "Greatest Athlete," etc. When someone suggested to Thompson, "Jim Thorpe's not here and you're lucky he's not," he responded, "He's lucky he's not!" Words worth stenciling on all the winners' ribbons the world over.

34

Johnny Unitas

b. 1933

The most important telephone call in history came on March 10, 1876, when Alexander Graham Bell—or, as Hollywood would have it, Don Ameche—picked up his newfangled contraption and said into it, "Mr. Watson, come here, I want you." The second most important call may have been the one for just 80 cents made almost eighty years to the day later, when Baltimore Colts general manager Don Kellett called a twenty-two-year-old semipro quarterback named Johnny Unitas and said substantially the same thing.

Kellett would later say he had been moved to make that call because, one day in February of 1956, he had been going over some old league waiver lists and when he came across Unitas's name, "it rang a bell," as in Alexander Graham. However, Weeb

Ewbank, then the Colts' coach, would have none of the waiver story, labeling it pure fiction and part of the blarney that is the coin of the realm for sports' many storytellers. "Unitas was signed," remembered Ewbank, "after we got a letter from a fan telling us that there was a quarterback in the Greater Pittsburgh League who deserved a chance with the Colts." And then Ewbank, with a twinkle in his eye, added, "I always accuse Johnny of writing the letter himself."

But whatever prompted the phone call, whether waiver lists or a letter, was unimportant. What was important was that the phone call was made. It represents just one more example of how that grappling hook known as Fate always has a way, as they say in telephone ads, of "reaching out and touching somebody," that somebody in this case being Johnny Unitas—whose story was a story of breaks, both figuratively and literally.

Unitas's first break came when the starting quarterback at tiny St. Justin's High in Pittsburgh broke his ankle. With fewer than three hundred students—most of them girls—to choose from, the coach merely picked the strongest passing arm on the team and conscripted the owner thereof, young Johnny Unitas, to fill in. Unitas did more than just fill in, as attested to by his selection to the Pittsburgh all-Catholic team for the next two years. In his senior year, Unitas's selection was rewarded with letters of inquiry from several institutions inviting him to come to their campuses for a "look-see."

Seeing, however, was not necessarily believing in. After taking one look at the six-foot-one, 145-pound beanstalk posing as a quarterback prospect, the Notre Dame backfield coach sent him packing with the comment, "The boy is too light. I'm sending him home." Indiana passed on him as well. Next came the University of Pittsburgh, where he received a scholarship offer, but somehow failed his entrance exams. Finally, the University of Louisville offered him a scholarship. And so it was that Unitas took his burgeoning talent and still-unfilled-out frame to join the college of Cardinals.

One game during Unitas's freshman year would showcase all the traits that would come to define the Unitas-on-the-field persona in years to come. Against a heavily favored Houston team, with the score tied at 21 in the fourth quarter and the ball on the Houston 40-yard line on fourth down and two to go, everybody—from Houston to the Louisville players—expected

Unitas to send one of his big backs into the line. One of them, Bill Pence, the Cardinals' biggest back in their broad-back attack, said, "Gimme the ball. I'll get the two yards for you." Unitas, whose face was normally saturated in politeness, affixed prisoner-taking eyes on Pence and in a voice as feisty as that of a Kentucky feudist, gave Pence a verbal wrist-slap: "When I want you to take it, I'll tell you." And then, the youngster crossed up everybody by fading back and throwing to his end for a touchdown.

Later in the same game, with the score now 28–21, Louisville, Unitas found himself lining up behind his own goal line after a Houston quick kick had pinned the Cardinals deep in their own territory. Two times Unitas had done the conventional thing, pounding the ball into the line; two times it had been to no avail. Now, with the coolness and composure of a man of far greater age and experience, Unitas shocked everybody, including the Louisville head coach, by dropping deep into his own end zone and, after dodging a couple of onrushing linemen, firing a perfect pass to end Babe Ray on the Louisville 40. Ray was all by his lonesome when he caught the ball, and all alone when he crossed the Houston goal line some sixty yards later.

In his first two seasons as the Cardinals' quarterback, Unitas filled out his frame, gaining some fifty pounds, and filled out his resumé as well, gaining some 2,000 yards through the air and throwing 21 TD passes. His last two seasons were less impressive as the Louisville team, and Unitas, suffered through a couple of subpar years. Nevertheless, his credentials were such that he came to the attention of the Pittsburgh Steelers, who drafted the by-now 195-pound quarterback on the ninth round of the 1955 NFL draft.

Finding themselves with four quarterbacks in camp— Unitas, Jim Finks, Ted Marchibroda, and Vic Eaton—the Steelers decided that three was enough of a crowd. After determining to the best of their nonwisdom that Unitas had no presence and even less of a future, they gave him his walking papers. But before leaving camp Unitas fired off a wire to Paul Brown, the major domo of the Cleveland Browns, who had shown an interest in him, asking for a tryout. Brown wired back saying that he was set for the season with Otto Graham and George Ratterman but that he would be interested in seeing Unitas the following summer at the Browns' training camp.

Nursing unconquerable hope that he could still make it in the pros, despite the Steelers' assessment of his potential, or lack thereof, Unitas pocketed the $10 bus fare the Steelers had given him and hitchhiked home to Pittsburgh, there to find employment and, more important, to stay ready for another NFL tryout, when—and if—it came. Fed more by the hope than by the $6 a game he made playing for a local semipro team named the Bloomfield Rams, a team of such low estate it played on sandlot fields decorated with stones, debris, and more than a few leftover bodies from the inevitable donnybrooks that broke out, Unitas awaited the phone call he was sure would eventually come. But when it came, it didn't come from Paul Brown; instead it came from Don Kellett.

All of which serves to take us back to the beginning of the story of Johnny Unitas and of how he recycled his career. For Kellett's offer was, in a Mario Puzo sense, an offer Unitas couldn't refuse: If he made the team, he would receive a $7,000 salary.

Raymond Berry, that curious piece of goods who had a slight gimp and wore contact lenses—some say in the back of his helmet—and who would become half of one of the longest-running passing combinations in NFL history, remembers the first time he saw Unitas. "I recall standing with a few other players on the hill overlooking the field where we train in Westminster, Maryland, and watching several rookies working out. 'Who's the other quarterback?' someone asked. 'I don't know,' another fellow said, 'but I hear he's looking good.'"

That "other quarterback" was, of course, Unitas, who had been brought into camp as the backup QB to George Shaw to take the place of Gary Kekorian, who had retired to go to law school. Since Shaw, the Colts' first draft choice in '55, was rated the best young quarterback in the NFL, Unitas didn't figure to get much playing time. But then came another one of those "breaks" that charted Unitas's career, this one a break of Shaw's leg in the fourth game of the '56 season.

Rushed into the game, Unitas's debut was anything but auspicious: His first pass was intercepted by Chicago's J. C. Caroline and returned 59 yards for a TD; his next play was a botched handoff to fullback Alan Ameche that the Bears recovered and took in for a score; and there were to follow still another mix-up in the backfield, another fumble, and another score for the Bears, who ran up their biggest total, 58 points, since their 73–0 title victory over the Redskins in 1940. But in spite of his first-game jitters, Unitas still gave some hint of what was to come when, in the fourth quarter, he threw a 36-yard TD pass to end Jim Mutscheller.

Rather than showing his white feather, Unitas came back as a starter the very next week to lead the Colts to an upset win over the Green Bay Packers, and followed that up with the Colts' first-ever win over the Cleveland Browns. By the end of the season, Unitas had thrown nine touchdown passes—including one in the last game of the season which would be the beginning of the longest consecutive-game TD streak by any quarterback in history: forty-seven straight—and had posted the highest completion average ever recorded by a rookie, 55.6 percent.

Those last eight games of the 1956 campaign were to serve merely as a throat-clearing. For not only had Unitas proven his pro potential, but he had established himself as the Colts'—if not the NFL's—quarterback of the future.

In 1957, his first full year, he led the league in touchdowns and yards gained—2,550, the exact yardage gained by the combined three quarterbacks the Steelers had kept back in '55 instead of Unitas, all of whom had now passed from the scene—and earned the No. 1 quarterback rating.

He had also earned something else: the respect of his peers. Raymond Berry, who was the perfect blend for Unitas's passes, said of his quarterback, "What can I tell you about John Unitas? Well, I can tell you about his uncanny instinct for calling the right play at the right time, his icy composure under fire, his fierce competitiveness, and his utter disregard for his own safety."

It was this last quality, his infinite capacity for taking hurt, that most singled him out from other quarterbacks. Hanging on to the ball until the very last split second allowed him to complete a lot more passes—and also to get tackled a lot more. Sid Gillman, coach of the Los Angeles Rams, who had just seen Unitas pick his team apart, could only marvel, "Unitas doesn't let anything bother him. He just stays in there until he's ready to throw. I don't know what he uses for blood, but whatever it is, I'll guarantee you it isn't warm, it's ice cold."

Jim Parker, who came aboard in '57 to serve as Unitas's personal bodyguard, said of the man he protected, "He's got so much guts. I've seen him bleedin' from his ears and his mouth and his nose. The Bears broke his nose and he was bleedin' like a hawg and he threw the winning touchdown pass."

Add to all of the above his ability to interpret the game and his opponents in an interesting manner—from his changing the signals at the line of scrimmage (in effect abandoning the main text and doodling in the margins); to his taking total control of all twenty-one other players on the field (a control that extended to the huddle, where, as John Mackey, a longtime teammate, said, "Being in a huddle with John Unitas is like being in a huddle with God"); to his double-pumping to fake his opponents out of their socks; to referring the matter to his high-top shoes to run the ball when the going got rough—and you have a complete picture of Johnny Unitas, the complete quarterback. He was so complete that he even, as Raymond Berry said, was "the only quarterback I ever saw who goes downfield to block after he has thrown a pass."

All of these talents merged in 1958, as he led the Colts to the Western Conference championship. But not before Unitas, in the sixth game of the season, a 56–0 rout of the Packers, was tackled, hard, by Green Bay's Johnny Symank, putting him in the hospital with three broken ribs and a punctured lung. He returned four games later to lead the Colts back from a 27–7 halftime deficit to beat the 49ers 35–27 and set up "the Greatest Game Ever Played," the NFL championship game against the New York Giants.

The game itself was one of the most two-sided affairs in the history of pro football, with the Colts jumping off to a 14–3 halftime lead and then the Giants, giants that day in deed as well as name, coming back after a gallant goal-line stand to take a 17–14 lead. With a little under two minutes showing on the Longines scoreboard clock at the cold end of Yankee Stadium, the Colts took over on their own 14 for what would obviously be their last drive toward that clock. As they formed their huddle, Unitas, knowing full well that the deficiencies of the day would not be supplied by the morrow, issued a call to arms, and legs: "We've got some eighty yards to go and two minutes to do it in. Now we find out what stuff we're made of." The "stuff," as he called it, was pure Unitas, as he managed seventy-three of the yards on five throws, the last three for sixty-two yards to Berry, with Lenny Moore keeping the Giants defense busy deep. With but twenty seconds remaining, placekicker Steve Myhra swung his trusty right foot and chip-shot the tying field goal through the crossbars, forcing the game into overtime, the first "Sudden Death" game—as NFL Commissioner Bert Bell, as in Alexander, called it—in professional football history.

The Giant partisans roared presumptuously when one of the striped-shirt boys inspected the coin tossed to start the "Sudden Death" and patted Giant captain Kyle Rote on the helmet to indicate that the Giants had won the toss and the ball. But the Giants came up twenty-four inches short of a first down and had to give the ball back to the Colts. Don Chandler's punt of seventy yards was returned to the Colts' 20.

Now it was Unitas's turn with no time limit. In what *Sports Illustrated* would call "the 13 Plays to Glory," Unitas took the Colts inexorably downfield, alternating runs with passes, the last of his five throws a stunning case of derring-do in typical Unitas manner. With the ball on the 8, within easy range of Myhra, Unitas called for a shaft into the flat to Jim Mutscheller. Mutscheller caught the well-placed bullet and fell over the flag on the 1-yard line. On the next play, at 8:15 of overtime, Alan "the Horse" Ameche cantered the last yard unmolested for the 6 points and the win. In the postmortem afterward, Giant coach Jim Lee Howell paid tribute to Unitas's riverboat gambling, calling the pass to Mutscheller "a great call. You have to do things like that in this game."

And for the next fifteen years Unitas continued to play like a riverboat gambler, playing his cards—and his Redskins and his Giants and his Rams and all the other teams—excellently indeed, imposing his will on them. And on the record books as well. In the process he became, as Sid Luckman, himself a Hall of Fame quarterback, said, "the greatest quarterback ever to play the game. Better than I was, better than Sammy Baugh. Better than anyone."

But, then again, it was only fitting that a man who had been called for just 80 cents would be called again, this time "the greatest." And prove, to phrase a turn, that while many are chosen in the NFL draft, few are called.

35

Bill Russell

b. 1934

The game of basketball was founded by John Naismith back in 1891 when he hung up some recycled peach baskets in a YMCA gym in Springfield, Massachusetts. But it was confounded sixty-five years later some eighty miles down the Mass Turnpike in Boston by Bill Russell.

For before Russell, the game of basketball was just another form of H-O-R-S-E—two-handed set shots, one-handed shots, hook shots, and jump shots—with nary a thought given to D-E-F-E-N-S-E. Russell would change all that—and in so doing become a link in the natural progression of the game.

This dominating influence started as anything but. A

156

skinny six-foot-two, 128-pound teenager who looked like he worked in an olive factory dragging the pimientos through, with no other dimensions except height you could notice, Russell began his basketball career as a third-string center on his high school junior varsity team. "I wasn't really third-string," Russell was to recall years later. "We had fifteen uniforms and sixteen players, so another guy and I split the fifteenth uniform."

Figuring it could only get better, it couldn't get worse, young Bill again went out for the junior varsity in his junior year. But, on the very first day of practice, he was cut. However, his former jayvee coach, who had seen something in the youngster, was by now coaching the varsity squad and invited Russell to join. He wound up as a member in good sitting, spending the entire season polishing the seat of his pants on the bench. "At least," he remembered, "I had my own uniform."

Growing by proverbial leaps, bounds, and inches, Russell made the varsity team in his senior year. As a starter, though hardly as a star. Possessing the reach of the proverbial boarding-house roomer, Russell would block shots, force opposing players to change routes when they entered his line-in-the-sand zone, and sweep the boards with moves that looked like balloon ascensions. But these defensive skills were overlooked by that balanced column of straight-edged figures known as the box score.

And so it seemed that Russell's great defensive skills would go as unnoticed as Whistler's father. That is, until one game in his senior year when he scored his highest number of points ever, 14. That was also the night a member of San Francisco University's 1949 NIT championship team happened to be in the stands. He was there to scout a player on the opposing team. But after watching the spindly-legged youth with the sharp, vulture-winged elbows dominate the game, the USF alumnus decided that Russell would fit right in with San Francisco's possession-style game, and recommended the youngster for a scholarship.

When the Dons' coach, Phil Woolpert, got his first gander at the gangly six-foot-six youth who had been delivered unto him, he wondered whether he had wasted a scholarship on the awkward-looking recruit. However, he didn't wonder long, as Russell turned the game upside down with his defensive skills. "No one had ever played basketball the way I played it," Russell was to say. "They had never seen anyone block shots before. I like to think I originated a whole new style of play."

And he had. With the moves of a startled doe and the wingspan of a prehistoric bird, Russell was to change the basic equation of the game. Here he could be seen setting out a paw, much like a lion in pursuit of its prey, swatting away a ball; there, rising to the highest point above the horizon, blocking shots; and everywhere, controlling the backboards and the action.

By his junior year—and by now a six-foot-seven, 205-pound force to be reckoned with—Russell, together with K. C. Jones, led San Francisco to a 28–1 record, including twenty-six straight wins after an early-season loss to UCLA. Then Russell capped off his championship season by leading the Dons to the 1955 NCAA crown, scoring 118 in five games and being named the tournament's MVP.

All this merely served as a table setting for the 1955–56 season. By now a full-fledged six-foot-nine, Russell's awesome presence in the middle forced opposing players so far outside they needed cab fare to get to the basket. It enabled the Dons, allowing just 52.2 points per game, to lead the nation in defense. But more important, this daddy longlegs in basketball shorts led San Francisco to an undefeated season—twenty-nine straight wins—as it extended its unbeaten streak to a record fifty-five games.

Russell continued to rewrite his growing legend in the postseason NCAA tournament as the Dons, forced to defend their championship without Russell's "go-with," K. C. Jones, won their second straight title, Russell climaxing his collegiate career with a game-high 26-point performance in the final game.

Despite those 26 points, Russell's scoring statistics were still considered relatively modest. After all, those oracles who had committed themselves to the ancient and honorable notion that only the higher calculus of points-per-game really meant something, could count some thirty other college players who had averaged more points than Russell. To them, defensive players were basketball players only in the way raisins were considered fruits—that is, technically, and only in a manner of speaking.

One who viewed such great truths as blasphemous was the Boston Celtics' Red Auerbach. Auerbach, who kept his own counsel, never gave Russell's chances a second thought; the first covered them all, thank you. Refusing to maintain a polite fiction of the nonexistence of defensive B-ball, Auerbach reasoned that even though Russell's scoring figures weren't up there in the high numbers, his opponents' numbers weren't up there either—the Russell-led Dons having led the country in defense over the past two years.

Moreover, over the past five years he had been assembling the building blocks of what would ultimately be called the Celtic "dynasty." In 1951 he had added Bob Cousy; in '52, Bill Sharman; in '55, Frank Ramsey. But even with this fast-breaking group of hot shooters, Auerbach lacked the one necessary ingredient for a championship team: a strong rebounder to get the ball to his run-and-gunners. And, with the new twenty-four-second rule, introduced two seasons before, Auerbach knew that the fast break would equal wins in the new NBA equation. That is, if he could just get the right linchpin. And that right linchpin, he felt, was Bill Russell.

But Auerbach faced two problems in landing the answer to his dreams. One, the Celtics had sixth choice in the upcoming draft, behind two teams that had expressed interest in Russell— Rochester, which had first choice, and Minneapolis, which was seeking a successor to the recently retired George Mikan. The second problem was Russell himself. For Bill Russell was a proud man, a man with his own agenda. And that agenda included not only going to the 1956 Olympics, which were to be held that fall in Melbourne long after the NBA season started, but dealing with the NBA on his terms, not theirs. Besides which, he already had an offer from the Harlem Globetrotters for what was announced as a lucrative contract—although, truth to tell, it was hardly as lush as it was announced to be.

But all the pieces were to fall into place for Auerbach's master plan. First, Rochester, hardly examining the bottle's contents, only the bottle itself, passed on Russell and instead chose Sihugo Green of Duquesne. Then, St. Louis, with the second choice, was about to pass on Russell as well, already having Bob Pettit in the middle and not enough money to bid for Russell's services. Besides, Russell had misgivings about playing in St. Louis, the most southern city in the NBA and hardly a hospitable place for a black athlete in the fifties. And so Auerbach, talking through his hat and his cigar at the same time, offered the Hawks a trade: "Easy" Ed Macauley, the Celtics' center for the past six years and a graduate of St. Louis University, and rookie forward Cliff Hagan for the rights to Russell.

The bread Auerbach cast upon the waters came back pudding. But not before Russell had played in the Olympics. When Russell entered the Celtics' lineup for the first time, on December 22, 1956, Boston had a 16–8 mark. In that first game—ironically, against St. Louis—he played twenty-one minutes, took down 16 rebounds, scored 6 points, and helped the Celts beat the Hawks, 95–93. Over the next forty-eight games Russell would bring a new dimension to pro basketball, not merely setting up the plays, but thinking them out, engineering them, and then fully orchestrating them. With hands so large the Armour Packing Company could have packaged them and leaps so high they could be plotted only by air traffic controllers, Russell dominated the boards—adding yet another "nicety," doing a fandango with his heels on opposing players' toes. And introduced the "Wilson Sandwich," smashing the ball back into astonished shooters' faces with all the force of a wrecking ball, there to pick up their teeth and take bromos at the same time. Not incidentally, he led the NBA in rebounds per game, with 19.6, and the Celts to their first NBA championship—over Easy Ed Macauley, Cliff Hagan, and the St. Louis Hawks.

Russell's second year went to the proving of his potency, as he led the league in rebounds a second straight year, this time with 22.7 per game, and again led the Celts into the finals, against the same St. Louis Hawks. With the series tied at one game apiece, Russell injured his ankle. And hampered his mobility. Without him, the Celtics lost three of the last four games. And the championship.

If you were keeping score, 1958–59 was the official beginning of the Celtics' so-called dynasty. With Russell dominating the inside and making opponents—including the newly arrived Wilt Chamberlain—wilt like snails that had just received a handful of salt between their eyes when they challenged him and Cousy and Sharman fast-breaking in the blood rush of two strides down the parquet floor to take his outlet passes, the Celts ran through the league with the best regular-season record and then raced past the Warriors and the Hawks for the championship.

Over the next seven seasons, Russell and the Celtics "8-peated," dominating the league with consistent defense and persistent defense. The man NBA forward and wit Tom Meschery called the Bearded Eagle played with an elegance and an arrogance, serving as the wheelhorse of those championship teams and quarterbacking them to their unprecedented streak.

And when, as all things must, that streak finally came to an end, the Celtics started another mini-streak—this time with Russell as head coach. The first black coach in all of sportsdom won two more championships, to give him eleven in thirteen years, going out a winner—just as he had come in.

One way to gauge an athlete's greatness is to tote up his personal accomplishments, his records. Another way is to count his championships. And if you were to count the banners hanging in the rafters of the Boston Garden, so many of them attributable to one man, Bill Russell, you would have to conclude that this proud player *deserved* to be proud, as one of the greatest athletes of all time.

36

Sammy Baugh

b. 1914

Suffice it to say that there are more great pictures of athletes than there are pictures of great athletes. But there was one "picture perfect" athlete, one who looked like he was made to play the part of a great athlete: Sammy Baugh.

You could just look at any photo of Baugh, and even if you didn't know his name you could see that the reed-thin, leathery 180-pounder, standing ramrod straight at six-foot-two with his whiplash right arm cocked high over his head, cradling the ball like a newborn, and with his left hand extended straight out, almost like a human divining rod, his eyes surveying the field, looked like one helluva passer.

His looks weren't deceiving. For Sammy Baugh altered the basic chemistry of the game single-handedly—or single-armedly, if you will—as much as Red Grange had changed it with his running. If not more. Before Baugh came on the scene, the game of football was about as glamorous as an unmade bed, a grinding, smash-mouth game that stood in permanent, suspicious opposition to the passing game. But Baugh would change all that, opening the game up like a flowering rose, filling the air with enough identified flying objects that football would forever bear his imprint.

Baugh, who had learned his trade as a youngster throwing a football through a tire suspended from a tree limb, began his fabled career in the midthirties as a member of Dutch Meyer's "Aerial Circus" at Texas Christian University. With 10 passes a game in those days considered more than somewhat excessive, Baugh made dust out of conventional wisdom by taking to the air lanes 30 to 40 times a game, throwing 599 times over three varsity seasons. Ever calm and serene, the all-American's style was one that caught the attention of all-time great Pudge Heffelfinger, who wrote, "For calm poise, for nonchalance under fire, no college passer has equaled the fabulous Baugh."

It was while Baugh was at TCU that George Preston Marshall, the owner of the Boston-soon-to-be-Washington Redskins, took note of the man now being called Slingin' Sammy, by drafting him second in the 1937 NFL draft. But the thinking amongst the writers was that Baugh's lank frame wasn't suited to the pro game. One of them, the dean of all sportswriters, Grantland Rice, warned Marshall, "Take my advice: If you sign him, insure his right arm for a million dollars. Those big pros will tear it off."

But Marshall never gave Baugh's chances a second thought, one thought covering it all, thank you! Believing that Fate had cut this player out of the herd to lead the Redskins to the championship, Marshall began negotiating with Baugh. However, Baugh had determined upon a career in professional baseball, and had already started negotiations with the St. Louis Cardinals. Marshall upped the ante, offering Baugh a contract for the then unheard-of $8,000 a year and a $500 signing bonus, payable in Roosevelt dollars—this in a day and age when the next-highest NFL salary hovered somewhere in the neighborhood of $2,750.

Baugh stepped off the plane carrying him to Washington's

National Airport for the signing wearing spiked cowboy boots and a ten-gallon hat—all the better, thought Marshall, to start the legend of a colorful Texas cowboy called Slingin' Sammy, although he had never worn boots before, nor could he walk in them without wobbling. However, truth to tell, Baugh's golden right arm was all the paraphernalia he needed for legend status. And two months later, he would crank up that right arm to pass the College All-Stars to their first-ever win in the All-Star Game, beating the NFL champion Green Bay Packers 6–0 on a Baugh-to-Gaynell Tinsley pass.

In Baugh's first workout with the Redskins, head coach Ray Flaherty instructed him to hit end Wayne Millner "right in the eye" on a buttonhook. Baugh, with enough coolness to air-condition the nation's capital, plus some of the surrounding suburbs, is reported to have answered, "Sure, coach, but which eye?" Or so the story goes.

However, it wasn't a story but recorded fact that Baugh began to make a partial repayment on his handsome salary and his greatness to be, in his very first pro game, completing eleven of sixteen passes as the Redskins beat the New York Giants, 13–3. Ten games later the Redskins came to New York to play the same Giants with the division title up for grabs. This time Baugh completed eleven of fifteen as the Redskins demolished their division rivals, 49–14.

All of which was but a table setting for one of Sammy Baugh's greatest games, the 1937 NFL championship game against the Chicago Bears. The Windy City lived up to its advance billing, the field frozen and slippery, the thermometer showing a very low opinion of the temperature, and the ball kept aloft by prankish flurries. And yet, on the very first play from scrimmage, Baugh, passing from his own end zone, slingshotted the ball sidearm to running back Cliff Battles for a 43-yard gain. It was like that all day as Baugh fought both the Bears and the elements, putting the ball in the air thirty-four times and completing seventeen of those passes for 358 yards—more than any *two* teams had gained, combined, in any previous NFL championship game—to lead Washington to a 28–21 victory. The era of the pass had arrived, with interest.

But instead of quietly returning home to his native Sweetwater, Texas, with his first NFL championship and passing championship tucked under his long, lanky arm, Baugh now turned to his preferred sport, baseball. Reporting to the training camp of the St. Louis Cardinals, Baugh's prowess with the glove was noted by Eddie Dyer, then the manager of the Cardinals' Rochester farm club. Dyer, who would later manage the Cardinals to a World Series victory, recalled Baugh: "When he was working out around third base, we had another rookie at shortstop. You could hardly tell 'em apart. They looked like twins in appearance and action. The shortstop was Marty Marion, and anytime anybody looks anything like Marion he must have a lot of ability." (So spoke Dyer of Marion, the shortstop who would anchor the Cardinals' infield for eleven years, lead the league in different fielding categories no fewer than ten times, and play in four World Series.)

After playing down on the farms for both Rochester and Columbus during the '38 season, Baugh decided that his future lay not in baseball, but in football. And for the next fifteen years this supposedly frail and fragile Texan set an endurance record as he filled the air and the record books with his passes. Six seasons he led the league in passing, more times than any other quarterback; seven times in completion percentage; five each in pass completions and lowest interception ratio; and four times in yardage gained. And this in a day and age when short, high-percentage passes were neither the norm nor Baugh's way of doing business. No wonder longtime sportswriter Arthur Daley of the *New York Times* wrote, "The wiry Texan with the whiplash arm was the best passer of them all. This isn't merely an opinion. The record book proves it."

And in one of those little tricks history continually plays on us to see if we are really paying attention, Baugh was—and still is, in a sport where records have all the longevity of a Hollywood bridegroom—the all-time punting leader, his records for lifetime and season averages still the standards to beat. Consider that in the 1940 season he *averaged* 51.4 yards per punt and in the 1942 NFL championship game Baugh averaged an incredible 62.5 yards on six punts, and that with the non-streamlined ball of today!

Add to all of the above the fact that Baugh was the first player to have four interceptions in one game and in 1943 led the NFL in passing, punting, *and* interceptions, and you might have some idea why the man who graced Number 33 for sixteen years, Sammy Baugh, is a "picture perfect" pro who developed into an all-around great.

37

Honus Wagner

1874–1955

Honus Wagner, like the proverbial camel put together by committee, looked like one of nature's irregularities. His legs hardly looked like they could fulfill the obligations they had been sworn to uphold, so bowed were they that one writer noted, "They took off at the ankles in a curving sweep to meet in surprise at his waistline." They were anchored by size-14 violin cases, more familiarly known as feet. Grafted onto his huge barrel chest were two long arms that flowed out of his uniform at odd spots, dangling so low they almost scraped the ground. Lefty Gomez, seeing Wagner for the first time, commented, "He could tie his shoes standing up." And from the end of those long arms hung two hands better described as "shovels" by archrival Johnny Evers, the party of the second part in the famed Cub infield trio.

But when it came to assessing the worth of Wagner, you didn't examine the package's contents, only the package itself. And the value of that package far exceeded its contents.

For while a generation of baseball fans raised on cable TV barely know his name, at best, back when the sports world wafted on print, and word of mouth, John Peter Wagner, known as Hans, a contraction of the German "Johannes," was Ty Cobb's rival as baseball's greatest player, his bat and legs transforming him from a curio piece into a piece of Americana.

Playing for Louisville and then Pittsburgh—back when the town of Pittsburg didn't even have an H to hiss in—this pumpkin-turned-into-a-golden-carriage led the National League in batting eight times, in doubles seven, in RBIs five, in stolen bases four, and in triples three.

At bat, he played the pitcher like a fisherman plays a salmon. Standing as far back in the batter's box as the rules and the end of the chalk line allowed, Wagner stood ready to shift his feet with the pitch, his hands held inches apart and the bat—looking more like a match—awiggle in those massive hands. Then, bending low to the ground, Wagner would get his entire body into the pitch, driving it, like a gunshot, on a line to whichever field he chose. Trying to sneak a ball past Wagner was like trying to mine coal with a nail file—which is a fair metaphor, Wagner having been a coal miner before he became a baseball player. A notorious bad-ball hitter, Wagner was all the more dangerous with men in scoring position, never giving the pitcher a chance to waste a pitch. When young Christy Mathewson asked his catcher what Wagner's weakness was, the catcher barked back, "A base on balls."

Wagner fed on the offerings of the leading pitchers of his day, skewering the ball for a .524 average against Amos Rusie, .352 against Kid Nichols, .343 against Cy Young, and .324 against the aforementioned Mr. Mathewson—Hall of Famers all.

On the base paths, this human caricature with legs going loose at the ends was, incredibly, a speedster. Batting from the right side, the man called the Flying Dutchman could get down the first-base line in sprinter's time, faster than most left-handed batters. And, even with his awkward stride, he was one of the greatest base stealers of all time, scurrying like a hunted rabbit, close to the ground. Then, as he approached the bag, this 190-

pound slab of beef would come in hard and fast, his patented slide taking him far away from the tag.

But it was in the field that Wagner earned his name. And his fame. Bent double, like a carpenter's rule, he covered the left side of the infield like no shortstop before. Or since. For you could get a barrel through Wagner's legs, but not a batted ball, Wagner picked up every ball in the name of challenge, sometimes roaming far back of third to retrieve a ball that had gotten past the third baseman. Then, taking no time for thoughtful exploration of the ball, he would rifle it over to first, together with all the pellets, smithereens, and quidbits of dirt and grass he had picked up in his massive hand. The first baseman would have to pick out the baseball from all the grassy flybys that came his way, almost as if he were in the middle of a threshing machine. And many's the time Wagner, with his great howitzer throw, would throw out the base runner while on one knee or on the seat of his pants.

As soft-bitten as his rival for the title "Greatest Ballplayer," Ty Cobb, was hard-bitten, Wagner got his chance to face Cobb in the 1909 World Series, when the two batting champions faced off for bragging rights. As the story goes, when Cobb reached first base in the second game of the Series, he stood there, cupped his hands to his mouth, and shouted down to Wagner, "Hey, Krauthead, I'm coming down on the next pitch." Wagner, drawing on his fine command of the English language, said nothing. But he waited. And, true to his word, on the first pitch, Cobb took off for second. Ripping into the base with his spikes held high, Cobb found Wagner—and the ball—waiting for him. Wagner, without regard for the spikes, or Cobb for that matter, slapped the ball in Cobb's mouth, tagging out the by-now tamed Tiger and splitting his lip in the process.

Forget the fact it never happened. The "story" was told and retold and became part of the Wagnerian lore. And went to making Honus Wagner one of the most storied figures in the first decade of the twentieth century. Called by managerial legend John McGraw "the greatest player in the twentieth century," and referred to by Ed Barrow, the man who turned Babe Ruth into an outfielder, as "the greatest all-around player," he was elected into Baseball's Hall of Fame in its first pledge class, right behind Ty Cobb. As Honus Wagner stood the day of his induction on that sparsely populated island of greatness, his feet were still size 14, but his feats were even larger.

38

Ben Hogan

b. 1912

Whenhen there are no more stories of great comebacks to write and all of fiction is exhausted, we can call up the story of Ben Hogan, whose comeback was the triumph of Everyman against insurmountable odds. All other candidates can be discharged for lack of evidence.

Ben Hogan's hardscrabble roots were as far removed from the privileged advantages most great golfers enjoy as his birthplace, Dublin, Texas, was from those golf courses in Augusta, Merion, and Oakland where he would later win lasting fame. With no golf courses gracing the outskirts of the tiny burg of twenty-five hundred people nor a golfing father to teach him the game, conventional wisdom would have made Hogan a long shot, at best, to become a golfing great. But Hogan was to make dust out of conventional wisdom by remaking himself into a great golfer with grim, bulldoglike determination.

When Ben's father died, the Hogans moved the thirty miles

northwest to Fort Worth, where young Ben sold newspapers to support his family. And then, at the age of twelve, finding that caddying paid more than hawking papers, the youngster made a career move: He became a caddy at the Glen Garden Country Club.

Almost from the very first day, as the undersized caddy began struggling under the weight of the oversized golf bags, he saw something in the game that fascinated him. And he began to take the game seriously. He would study the motions of those he caddied for, comparing his beginner's swing with theirs and then copying their movements on the course, on his front lawn—"until there was no more lawn left"—and everywhere he went with a conscientious zeal until, one day, he began to take on the appearance of a golfer—even turning his stance around, from his natural left-handed one to right-handed.

But it wasn't enough of an appearance to impress the members of Glen Garden, even when he surprised everyone and tied for first place with another caddie, Byron Nelson, in the annual Christmas Day tournament. Nor was his appearance, at five-foot-six and 135 pounds, calculated to stun the optic nerve, his size reminding one of a golf club with a thyroid problem: almost invisible from the side.

At the ripe old age of nineteen, and despite owning a left hook that would have done justice to Joe Louis, but not to a golfer, Hogan turned pro. His successes on the hit-the-trail campaign were few and far between—like qualifying for the U.S. Open in 1936, but not scoring low enough on his first two rounds to "make the cut"—and far too few with which to scratch out a decent living. Finally, he managed to make the 36-hole cut in the '39 Open, but finished in sixty-second place, a full twenty-four shots off the pace.

A perfectionist doomed forever to be unsatisfied, Hogan spent thousands of hours on the practice tee and in his hotel room working to cure his near-fatal hook. And waiting for the wheel to turn. Determination and constant practice finally began to pay off as victories started to come the way of this comparative newcomer who had taken such a long time in coming. By 1940 he was the leading money winner on the tour.

His tensile strength soon became evident to everyone else on the tour. During a World's Four Ball Championship in '41, Hogan was paired with veteran Gene Sarazen. During a break in the action, Sarazen sought out writer Grantland Rice and said, "Know something? I've just found the game's toughest golfer. I thought Bob Jones, Hagen, and myself belonged in that class. We don't. I'm playing with him today." Sarazen was referring to the fact that although the Hogan-Sarazen twosome had won six of seven holes, Hogan had come over to him and said, "Wake up, Gene. We're loafing. Let's get to work." Sarazen, somewhat puzzled by this outburst, had replied, "We've won six of the seven, haven't we?" And Hogan had said, "Yes, but we halved the other. We can't throw holes away like that!"

Bobby Jones himself seconded the emotion, saying, "I thought I was a hard fighter. I thought Hagen and Sarazen both were. We're not in a class with this fellow Hogan. He's fighting for every inch, every foot, every yard on a golf course."

Writer Herbert Warren Wind believed, "As long as he remains a competitive golfer, he will probably never be so new or so mellow that the chip on his shoulder will entirely disappear. He seems to like it that way."

With a face as unmoving as the faces on Mount Rushmore and the straight-ahead look of someone who didn't wish to be distracted, Hogan became known as the Iceman. His second nickname, Bantam Ben, was a reference to his diminutive size. But there was nothing diminutive about his accomplishments, as he continued to perform like a surgeon, his club now sharpened to a razor's edge by his constant practice. And continued as the leading money winner on the tour for the next two years. By now, the once-impoverished Hogan had so many savings-deposit books he could afford sectional bookcases to house them.

And then, along with every other Johnny, Ben went marching off to war. Entering the Army Air Corps, he served three years during World War II. Mustered out, he picked up right where he had left off, winning his first major, the 1946 PGA. The year 1948 was a banner one for Bantam Ben, as he won the U.S. Open and his second PGA title. The decade looked like it would end the way it had begun, with Hogan on top of the tour.

But after a slow start in 1949, Hogan and his wife, Valerie, headed back home to Fort Worth so he could work on his game. Then disaster struck: On an early foggy morning in February, the Hogans' car collided head-on with a Greyhound bus on a Texas highway, leaving Hogan's frail body entangled in the wreckage, his pelvis fractured, his legs mangled. He was all but crushed to death in the collision, his life saved when he threw himself in front of his wife to save hers.

Ben Hogan now faced the longest and most agonizing battle of his life. Lucky to be alive, with many doubting if he would ever walk again, let alone play golf, Hogan viewed all such great truths as blasphemous, at best. Stiff with the ramrod conviction that comes with determination, Hogan constituted a majority of one who thought he could come back. And that's all it took. Lesser mortals wouldn't have tried it, but Ben Hogan was no mere mortal. Hogan submitted his entry for the 1949 U.S. Open with a note that began: "This may be just a dream, but miracles sometimes happen...."

A year later, at the U.S. Open, that miracle did happen. Facing as severe a test of his technical resources as he ever had, the fire in his legs now a dull ache, Hogan, radiating a hard glow of high purpose, pushed himself through the final-day marathon of thirty-six holes to tie Lloyd Mangrum and George Fazio. The next day this modern descendant of Lazarus won the playoff with a 69, for his second U.S. Open victory.

Conserving his energies, Hogan limited his appearances in '51. Still, the little man with the patented white cap won the Masters and his third U.S. Open title, with his final-round 67 at Oakland Hills still standing as one of the best rounds of golf ever played as he relentlessly stalked the monster course to its knees.

After an off year in 1952, Hogan came back in 1953 to win five of the six tournaments he entered, including the Masters, his fourth U.S. Open, and the British Open. His unprecedented "Triple" was arguably the greatest year any pro golfer ever had, a feat as impressive as Bobby Jones's 1930 Grand Slam—made even greater by the fact that he was unable to win the PGA merely because it had been scheduled at the same time as the British Open.

By the end of his fabled career, Hogan had won sixty-two tournaments and dominated his sport as few before or since. Still, the Ben Hogan story was not the number of tournaments he won, but the man himself. Playing with a reserve that bordered on aloofness and a precision that bordered on complete control—almost to the point where he could control every one of the 336 dimples on the golf ball—Hogan imposed his iron will on opponent and course alike. And on himself as well, willing his own comeback. And greatness.

39

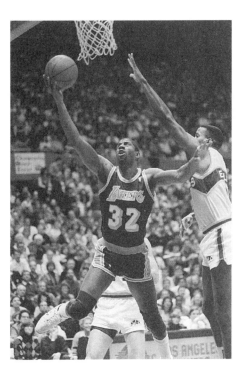

Magic Johnson

b. 1959

When there are no more Christmas carols to write, upbeat fiction has been exhausted, and newspaper and television word and sound bites have all been recycled to sameness, they still will be sitting around sports' smoldering campfires telling tales of one athlete who played sports with a little boy's enthusiasm and abandon that made watching him a pure joy: Earving "Magic" Johnson.

Lighting up the game of basketball just as he lit up his face— with a cheerful kind of smile that lifted his hairline, almost as if he had invented the very act of smiling itself—the man-child known simply as Magic played basketball with all the exuberance and enthusiasm of a truant out on a playground romp.

That playground romp began in Lansing, Michigan, where, as a youngster, Johnson would wake up early and be out before school on the playground, practicing. "People thought I was crazy," he remembered. "Here it was seven-thirty in the morning and they'd be going to work and they'd say, 'There's that crazy June Bug, hoopin'.'"

"June Bug" quickly became "Magic," as Johnson took his frenetic 88-rpm energies to Everett High in Lansing where, in 1976–77, he led his team to the state championship. Then it was on to Michigan State, where he led the Spartans to their first Big Ten championship in nineteen years in his freshman season and then, in his second year, led them to the NCAA finals, where, in a dramatic matchup against Larry Bird and his No. 1-rated Indiana State team, he outscored Bird 24 points to 19 and led Michigan State to the NCAA championship.

It was while at Michigan State that Magic developed his freelance style. With eyes that could summon up the whereabouts of his teammates in a hurry, Johnson would proceed to deal out passes like a waiter would dishes. Some were as planned and concise as Western Union telegrams; others, almost independent of conscious effort, were no-look passes thrown abruptly out of the unknown with the magician's misdirection—lollipops from over the head, balloons from behind the back, and seeing-eye passes between a forest of arms and limbs. All thrown with a pool shark's touch.

Michigan State coach Jud Heathcote encouraged him. "He didn't care how I got the pass to my teammate, as long as I got it there," said Johnson. "Behind the back, over the head—any way. But I had to get it there or I'd be in trouble."

But Magic Johnson not only invented himself at Michigan State, he reinvented his position as well, changing the basic equation of the game and the definition of a point guard. Before he came on the scene, the center was the biggest player on the team, both literally and figuratively. But with the arrival of Magic, the emphasis shifted to the passing game. And, for the first time, the quarterback on the team was a tall man—in Magic's case, six-foot-nine. Johnson, who had started his career as a forward and shifted to guard because the team needed his guard skills—read: passing—was fortunate that he had coaches "who didn't discourage me" from playing point guard. In fact, they encouraged him. And, in so doing, changed the face of basketball—to a face wreathed in smiles, belonging to a man who could pass the hell out of the ball.

The Los Angeles Lakers, with the first pick in that year's NBA draft—courtesy of a trade with the Utah Jazz—chose this part magician, part mechanic, and all player as their first selection, believing that his talents and high-octane energies would make the Lakers a winner.

At the preseason training camp, the Laker veterans watched in amusement as the new kid on the basketball block ran everywhere like a ferret on a double espresso, "nervous and scared because I wanted to do so well." Because his overflowing energies had him dashing around like an excitable deer, they called him Buck, not Magic. But "Magic" or "Buck," it made no difference as Johnson electrified the whole team, pushing the ball upcourt, passing it off, as one writer wrote, "with the unselfishness of an early Christian martyr," and throwing up arrow-straight jump shots, all accompanied by more backslapping and smiles than could be found at a Shriners' convention.

Johnson's "magic" worked, as the Lakers—who had finished the previous year 47–35, then lost in the semifinal round of the playoffs—went on to win the 1979–80 NBA championship with—you guessed it—Magic, who was the straw that stirred them, being named the playoff MVP.

But Johnson brought something more than his great skills to the NBA, something far less tangible but far more important. For, at the time of Magic's entry into the league, the NBA was badly in need of a charisma bypass operation. The achievements of its many stars were far more arresting than their personalities. Their faces were as unmoving as the faces on Mount Rushmore, their words to press and public just about as expressive. And then, along came Magic, luxuriating in the spotlight the others shunned, punctuated with a smile as wide as John Smith's after Pocahontas went his bail. The press loved him.

The public did, too. Especially those at that psychiatric outpatient ward known as the L.A. Forum, where celebrities celebrate celebrities. With every unbelievable pass, every artful dodge, every withering shot, every joyful grin proclaiming it was "Showtime," the Forum fully fell for his charms, adding the name "Magic" to those of other one-name celebrities in LA-LA Land, like Cher, Woody, and Sly, as one of their own.

And, as Johnson took his Magic show on the road, other fans

in other NBA cities joined in the chorus. Enough so that it seemed that almost single-handedly, Magic had stuck his finger in the electronic eye of television and made it blink, made it sit up and take notice. And, in so doing, changed the "City Game" of the sixties and seventies into the ultimate "Cool Game" of the eighties.

For the next eleven years, Magic went his merry, playing with a sheer joy that exuded the crackle of excitement. And the league, in appreciation, pressed upon him every honor within its gift to give—including Most Valuable Player (three times), playoff MVP (three times), all-NBA First Team (nine times), etcetera, etc., etc.—for the player who introduced the phrase "double-triple" to basketball jargon.

And then, suddenly, on November 7, 1991, it was all over. At a press conference called by the Lakers, hundreds of members of the press and almost as many well-wishers sat in the audience holding back tears as Magic let them in on the shocking, almost indigestible fact that he was HIV-positive. "Life is going to go on for me and I'm going to be a happy man," he said, flashing that big, infectious, Magic smile of his.

But even though Magic had retired from the NBA because of his infection with the virus that causes AIDS, his smile and spirit were still there for all to see. It was on exhibition first at the NBA All-Star Game three months later, when he hit a 3-point shot for the game's final points ("It was like I was at my typewriter and it finally hit me: That shot was my ending"), and then at Barcelona, where he appeared as a member of the "Dream Team" and inspired hundreds of athletes of all nations to break ranks during the opening ceremonies just to get a glimpse of this "all-World" legend.

Earving Johnson had lived up to the nickname "Magic" just by playing sports the way they should be played: for the pure joy of playing. Maybe that's what his longtime rival and friend Larry Bird meant when he said, "I'd pay to see Magic play." For no athlete ever had a better "handle" than Magic. Nor more fun in becoming a great one, a fun he communicated to all of us.

40

Ted Williams

b. 1918

In one of his rare unguarded moments, Ted Williams once drew back the curtain and gave the world a brief glimpse of what made Teddy bat, saying, "All I want out of life is that when I walk down the street folks will turn and say: 'There goes the greatest hitter who ever lived.'"

And there were many who believed he was. One of those was Jimmy Dykes, the old A's third baseman, who was often heard to comment about Williams, "Best damned hitter I ever saw!" And that covered a lot of ground, Dykes's career having started back in the late 1910s when Ty Cobb and Joe Jackson were the two greatest hitters in the game and having lasted until 1939, Williams's first year in the Majors.

177

At spring training before the '38 season, eyeing his team-mates-to-be with a defiant pride known only to youngsters, Williams willingly imparted the benefit of his inexperience. When someone tried to put the puppy-youth in his place, telling him, "Just wait 'til you see Jimmie Foxx hit," Williams retorted, "Just wait until Foxx sees me hit!"

Sent back down to the Red Sox's Triple A team in Min-neapolis for more seasoning, Williams, before he packed, boldly predicted that not only would he be back, but he would outhit the combined Red Sox outfield—a tandem that consisted of Ben Chapman, Doc Cramer, and Joe Vosmik, all .300 hitters. Williams would make good on both promises. And many more during his career.

Never one to allow Fate to trample him beneath its iron heel, Williams demonstrated to all and sundry that he belonged back up in the Big Show, redeeming the second part of his round-trip ticket to the minors by leading the American Association in no fewer than six offensive categories. In 1939 he continued his assault on American League pitchers, leading the league in RBIs with 145, the most ever for a rookie; batting .327; finishing second in doubles and third in homers; and accumulating 107 walks, the most ever for a rookie.

In fact, of all his record-breaking statistics, perhaps the most amazing one was his walk total, testimony to his uncanny "eye"— eyes that navy physicians, who examined him before his two tours of duty as a marine aviator, estimated were the eyes of one in a hundred thousand. Dykes, who had seen them all, could only marvel, "If he took a pitch, the umpires called it a ball. They figured he knew the strike zone better than they did."

Bobby Shantz, an outstanding pitcher in his day, remem-bered Williams's forbearance at swinging at pitches that missed by less than the anatomical hair: "Man, I threw him some wicked curveballs that didn't miss by more than a fraction, and he'd just stand there and look at them, and that bat would stay back, not budging an inch."

But whatever it was about the six-foot-three, under-200-pound Williams—his eye, his batting prowess, or his seeming and seamless perfection in the batter's box—after only one year baseball writers and fans alike were using catchall phrases like "superstar" and "great" to describe this smooth-swinging young-ster. And 1940 would only add to his glow, as he raised his average to .344, finished third in slugging average and total bases, and led the league in runs scored.

And then there was 1941.

For all Williams did during that last prewar season was hit .406 (it was the first time an American Leaguer had broken the mythic .400 barrier in eighteen years, and the last time it was breached); lead the league in homers, runs scored, slugging average, and base on balls; and win the All-Star Game with a two-out, bottom-of-the-ninth home run in one of the greatest games ever played. In fact, it was so dramatic that the usually loquacious Red Barber, announcing the game, was struck dumb by Williams's mammoth over-the-roof blast.

How Williams broke the .400 mark is a story unto itself, and an insight into the self-assurance, even cockiness, of this singular-minded great, who, in his own words, "lived to hit." Going into the last day of the season, Williams owned a batting average of .39955, which rounded off to an even .400. His manager, Joe Cronin, advised the young slugger that he had "better sit it out." But Williams, disdaining a cheap record, refused to sit it out and instead opted to play both ends of a doubleheader against the Philadelphia A's. In the first game he had four hits, including a home run, and in the second he laced out two more hits, ending with six hits in eight at-bats and a .406 average.

After leading the league in 1942 with a .356 average and winning the first of his two Triple Crowns, Williams went off to serve his country as a marine pilot for the next three years. And when Teddy came marching home, along with Johnny, he picked up right where he had left off, batting .342 and leading the Red Sox to their first pennant in twenty-eight years.

Over the next decade, the lank and willowy batsman, taking his place in the batter's box and wagging his bat from his left-handed stance as he studied the pitcher like a scientist studies a specimen, continued his assault on the offerings of American League pitchers. Over that ten-year period, Williams led all American Leaguers in overall hitting, batting .344.

And then, in 1957, with the sand beginning to flow to the bottom of his hourglass, Williams led the American League in batting at the advanced age of thirty-nine, with a .388 average, the highest since his own .406 average sixteen years before. And just to prove it was no mistake, he again led the league in hitting the following year, as a senior citizen of forty.

Williams would go on to play for two more years, into 1960, making him one of baseball's curios: the four-decade player. And, in his final at-bat ever, he stroked what might well have been the longest home run he ever hit, the 521st of his grand and glorious career. And then, true to his custom, as he ran around the bases, with the Boston fans making an Aeolian trombone of the stands, he refused to doff his hats to their cheers, disdaining the niceties—and the fans as well.

For Ted Williams, throughout his career, had shown a commendable independence. That wonderful eyesight of his was so sharp he could read between the lines of every baseball writer's story and could read into the fans' cheers their ability to boo him when the mood moved them. A maverick who spent his entire career different-drumming, Williams stood head and shoulders, literally, above the crowd—and the crowds as well. Some could call him "the Kid," "the Splendid Splinter" or "the Splendid Spitter," others "Teddy Ballgame" or "the Thumper." But to almost all—including Joe DiMaggio, who said, "I can truthfully say I've never seen a better hitter than Ted Williams"—he was simply "the Greatest Hitter Who Ever Lived."

41

Bobby Hull

b. 1939

Bobby Hull had the looks of an athlete, one made of sunshine, blood-red tissue, and clear weather. And the build of the proverbial brick outhouse.

This well-put-together block of chiseled muscle possessed shoulders as wide as a door, arms as hard as diamonds, the dense body of an expandable filing cabinet—prompting Gordie Howe to say, "And he gets bigger as he takes off his clothes"—thighs like ship masts, and mountainous bicep, chest, and neck muscles that dwarfed those of Sonny Liston or any other modern heavyweight champion. All of which was outlined by a golden grass plot that rimmed his ruggedly handsome features—which included the obligatory broken nose that curled upward ever so slightly—making him look like the embodiment of a lower-cased Greek god.

One of those who thought so was a Chicago society-page columnist who gushed that he was a "statue come alive from the Golden Age of Greece, incredibly handsome even without his front teeth." Indeed, he was hockey's Golden Boy, its Golden Jet.

But Hull's five-foot-ten, 195-pound, bull-like physique and the strength it generated were hardly the largest components of his athletic genius. For Bobby Hull was lightning on skates, the fastest skater in the National Hockey League, once timed at 28.3 mph with the puck and 29.7 mph without it.

But if his lightning was impressive, it was his thunder that was awesome. For with the puck, Hull was at his best—maybe the best ever. Shooting from the left side, Hull frescoed, tattoo'd, bruised, laced (or whatever other concussive verb you might wish to insert here) the puck at 120 mph—nearly 35 mph faster than the average hockey player. It's no surprise, then, that he put it into the net with alarming frequency, averaging 40 goals a season and turning the hat trick a record twenty-eight times.

Players who got in front of Hull's Mach-speed shots were hockey's equivalent of those who defuse bombs for a living. One who did, and lived to tell about it, could only say, in amazement, "When Hull winds up and lets fly, that puck comes at you like a small town." Another, who had stopped one of Hull's patented sixty-foot slap shots, could only marvel, "It felt like I had been seared by a branding iron. His shot once paralyzed my arm for five minutes. It's unbelievable!" Others just got out of the puck's way faster than you can get an Elks meeting to pass a motion to adjourn. Or suffered the consequences.

This bundle of strength, speed, and sheer power first skated onto the NHL ice for the opening game of the 1957–58 season, a fuzzy-cheeked lad of eighteen. But Bobby Hull had been playing hockey for most of his life, almost from the time his father had laced up a pair of skates on his size-4 feet. He learned the basic rudiments of the sport playing on the pond on his father's farm in a wide spot in the road known by mapmakers as Point Anne, Ontario, and then graduated into organized hockey, playing first in the Pee Wees and then the Juniors. It was while he was playing in the Juniors that his golden attributes were first noticed, by coach Rudy Pilous, who cut him out of the herd and recommended the youngster to the Chicago Black Hawks organization. Brought to their training camp in the fall of 1957, Hull showed his potential by scoring two goals in his first exhibition game against the New York Rangers and, as a result, became the youngest player ever to be signed by the Black Hawks. It was a move they—and their fans—would never regret.

Playing center for the Black Hawks, Hull scored 31 goals in his first two seasons. Then, in the 1959 playoffs, when one of the Black Hawk left wingers was injured, Pilous, by now the Hawk coach, switched Hull over from center to fill his place. Hull liked the change of scenery right from the start. "I felt right at home, because I didn't have to do so much checking. I had something left when I went to the goal."

Freed of his figurative foot bindings, Hull now turned his attentions from the sinew-cracking exercises of checking to the far more satisfying chore of gathering great gobs of goals. He was a movable feast to be watched in his new role. Picking up the puck on the face of his stick and then, the blades of his skates a blur in two strides or less, hurtling down the ice in full flight, running his own interference, he'd unleash a left-handed power surge that billowed out the cords of the cage. A minute later he could be seen, his skates clicking on the ice like the ticking of a clock, cradling the puck on the blade of his stick and then, from a distance of sixty feet, letting loose with one of his patented arrow-straight slap shots, shot abruptly from the unknown, for another goal. His cannonball shots, the most feared in the NHL, were described by no less an authority than Montreal's Boom Boom Geoffrion, who knew, as "the hardest I ever saw."

Pretty soon it became a dog-bites-man story that Hull had scored. His 39 goals led the league in 1959–60. In 1961–62, he scored 50, only the third man ever to do so, joining an exclusive catalog of all-time greats numbering only Maurice Richard and Gordie Howe. Four seasons later he scored 54, five seasons later 52, and seven seasons later 58—each time breaking his own record, becoming in the process hockey's version of Babe Ruth.

And he did it all while maneuvering through, around, and over hapless defenders who'd been assigned the awesome task of stopping this man with circus-strongman strength from scoring. But, with strength pouring out of every hollow, he would carry the would-be defender on his broad back like a piano mover while wristing off another slap shot for yet another goal. Trying to stop

Hull from scoring was akin to trying to stop a runaway freight train. And just about as effective.

Finally, after fifteen years and 604 goals, the man who had once admitted, "I just enjoy scoring goals. That's what I play hockey for...to score," decided even that wasn't enough. With the fire that had once been in his legs now a dull ache, and tired of his contractual battles with the Black Hawks, Hull decided to pick up his hockey sticks and go home.

However, a funny thing happened to Hull on his way into retirement. At least it seemed funny to the established National Hockey League at the time. It was the formation of a rival league, the World Hockey Association, the idea for which had sprung full-blown from the brow of that packager of instant franchises, Gary Davidson, who'd already given the sports world the likes of the American Basketball Association and the World Football League. But the WHA wiped the smirk from the collective faces of the NHL establishment by offering Hull a $2.75 million package on the strength of his reputation, his goal-scoring abilities, and his drawing power.

And so the Golden Jet traded his golden assets for a sackful of same, turning in his black-and-red Hawks jersey to become the player-coach for the WHA's newly minted Winnipeg franchise—appropriately named the Jets. Hull benefited from his second installment of scenery, slashing, smashing, and just plain ol' bashing his way to 508 more goals before calling it quits—but not before becoming hockey's second most prolific scorer of all time.

When he finally retired after twenty-two years on the ice, his stick worn thin with goals, Bobby Hull had firmly established himself as one of the superstars of hockey—its most feared scorer, its hardest shooter, its most colorful performer, and its strongest box-office attraction. It is on the strength of these golden attributes that hockey's strongman will be remembered as one of its all-time greats.

42

Julius Erving

b. 1950

It was one of those moments that could be described expansively, but never plausibly. A moment that will be told and retold by those who witnessed it with disbelieving eyes until someone ups and labels them as hallucinators. Or worse. Many, less than anxious to be so labeled, have merely maintained a polite fiction of its nonexistence and let it go at that.

But happen it did, at an extraordinary council of war called the annual NBA-ABA All-Star Game, the second—and last—of those little get-togethers between the stars of the established National Basketball Association and those of the upstart American Basketball Association, held at New York's Nassau Coliseum for the benefit of the New York press. And for that of the stars themselves, who used it more as a showcase than for bragging rights.

And none showcased his range of talents more than Julius Erving, the New York Net known to those who followed the game as Doctor J. Caught in the high beam of attention, Erving reduced both the press and the assorted group of onlookers to a state of disability with his range of aerial artistry. For here he could be seen flinging himself into the air like a balloon with its string suddenly removed to haul down a rebound; there propelling the ball downcourt, looking as if his feet never touched the ground; and everywhere, amazing and astounding all with his air-defying jams.

But one moment more than any other began the legend of Doctor J. That magic moment came when Erving cleared the defensive boards of an errant Connie Hawkins shot, dribbled the entire length of the court, coast-to-coast, as they say, in a fluid dash to the basket, and then, at the top of the key, took off and soared up and over Hawkins, the original owner of the copyright for such moves, and, cradling the ball in his massive hand, snapped off a flying dunk before finally succumbing to gravity. It was less a get-out-of-my-face than a get-out-of-my-airspace move. And it left those who saw it with powers barely those of respiration.

Erving had been flying high on his magic carpet ride for several years by this time, using the hardwood less as a court than as a launch pad. Trouble was, his talents had always been hidden, first at the University of Massachusetts and later under the red-white-and-blue bushel basket of the ABA.

A late bloomer, young Julius, then called Junior, started his career at Roosevelt High in Hempstead, Long Island, where, despite his ability, he got little playing time 'til his senior year, when, as a skinny six-foot-three forward, he made the all-Long Island team. Not highly recruited, he chose the University of Massachusetts "because," as he said, "if I was going to develop athletically, I would be given the time." And develop he did, not only growing three and a half inches in college, but also averaging 26 points and 20 rebounds a game.

He also developed something else at UMass: a nickname. A classmate of Erving's, one Leon Saunders, hung the moniker on him. Seems that Saunders, while not as talented as Erving, had his own special talent, that of arguing. Playing in pickup games, without the benefit of referees, Saunders would spot fouls and call them, immediately launching into an argument to support his contention. And usually winning that argument. "I used to call him Professor," Erving would recall many years later, "because he always wanted to argue. In return, he always called me Doctor. We went to college together and he'd call me Doctor around the dorm and it stuck."

Erving liked the name so much that in the summer following his junior year at UMass he brought it with him to the famed Rucker Tournament in Harlem. When his windmill dunks and gravity-defying moves inspired the public-address announcer to begin calling him everything from Houdini to the Black Moses, Erving walked over to the PA announcer and quietly said, "I already have a nickname....Just call me Doctor." And so "Doctor," as in "Doctor J.," it became from that time forth—and forevermore.

Something else happened at the Rucker Tournament as well. For his awe-inspiring exploits not only captured the attention of the public-address announcer, they also captured the imagination of the new pro league, the American Basketball Association, which offered him a four-year, $500,000 contract to play with the Virginia Squires.

For two seasons, playing before few fans and even fewer members of the press, Erving's many skills were sacrificed on the altar of anonymity. Finally the Squires, sinking in a sea of red ink even Moses couldn't have parted, had to sell their franchise player—and the league's leading scorer—to the New York Nets to stay alive.

From that point on, he shone like the star with the bushy Afro he always was, his above-the-rim artistry finally getting the attention it deserved as the New York press trotted out its storehouse of adjectives to describe him. As the man now known as Doctor J. performed his crimes against the senses, every one of them a highlight clip, he began to take on epic proportions and to be described in terms like "magical" and "breathtaking."

And then, after his third season with the Nets, the NBA and the ABA ended their bidding and basketball war as the NBA merged four ABA teams into its league for the 1976–77 season. Many believed the reason for the sudden peace had less to do with the four teams than with one man: Julius Erving.

But even before the Nets, one of the four teams taken into

the NBA, had played their first game in the established circuit, Julius Erving was gone, the result of an impasse in the renegotiation of his contract.

Philadelphia 76ers general manager Pat Williams remembers hearing of Erving's availability and calling the owner of the Sixers. "I've got great news," he said. "We've got a chance to sign Julius Erving." "That's great," said the owner. "But who's Julius Erving?" Williams, never given to using small letters when caps would do, answered, "He's the Babe Ruth of basketball, that's who he is."

And, in his own way, he was. For Julius Erving was every bit as much an entertainer as Ruth had been, crowds coming out just to witness his theatrics in the hope that they could see him do something remarkable, create that one unforgettable moment they could press in their book of memories for a lifetime.

Erving didn't disappoint, turning every game into entertainment. And often high drama. Continually pushing the window of physical improbability, he could lull Newton's Law of Gravity into a brief enough suspension to perform his skywalk; or, believing one good turn deserved another, be able to contradict his flight in midair, almost as if he'd hit an air pocket and had veered off his appointed route; or sweep down the court in full flight as if propelled by some potent supernatural force. Watching him, you always had the idea that this instinctive artist had so many moves he could follow you into a revolving door and come out first.

For eleven seasons Doctor J. continued to perform his electrifying routines for hundreds of thousands of fans who wouldn't have believed man could fly unless they'd witnessed it with their own eyes. And when he finally retired—after the '89 season as the third-leading scorer in basketball history and the most exciting player of his generation—the soft-bitten man with the deep baritone voice and a whimsical manner of expressing himself could only explain his flamboyant style with: "It's easy, once you learn how to fly."

43

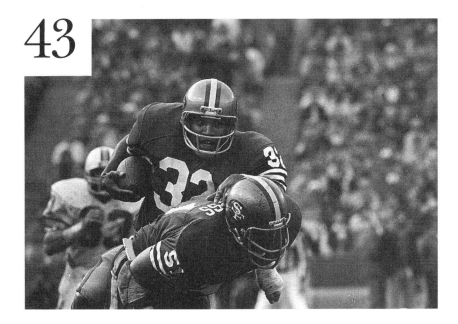

O. J. Simpson

b. 1947

The language of poetry comes in many different forms, appearing, as it does, in the poetry of eccentricity of little e. e. cummings, the poetry of the dramatic of giant T. S. Eliot, and the poetry of motion of the multidimensional O. J. Simpson.

For Orenthal James Simpson—whose name was scissored to just plain ol' O.J. by claustrophobic headline writers—possessed a style as unique as any ever expressed by other creative geniuses, whether that style was expressed on paper or on an athletic field. It was a style that seemed independent of conscious effort; one of elegance and eloquence. It could be seen in his one-man power surges, snapping off directions like an electric light, leaving would-be tacklers caught in the switches. Or in his fluid runs, where he could be seen zigzagging across the field as if he were building bridges for his retreating enemies. Or even in his attacking opposing lines with gusto, the way Dempsey would an

189

opponent. But no matter what form they took, all of O.J.'s runs had a certain now-you-see-him, now-you-don't quality to them.

The career of Orenthal James started unceremoniously as a five-foot-ten, 160-pound tackle at San Francisco's Galileo High School with legs so thin he was called "pencil pins," the result of a childhood bout with rickets. By the time he became a senior, this growing talent was an all-City running back. However, if his performances on the gridiron were sterling, his classroom performances were decidedly less so, and no four-year college would—or could—take this D-ficient student. So, with no major college open to him, Simpson enrolled at City College of San Francisco, where, in his first year, he became the most sensational junior college player in the country, scoring 26 TDs and averaging 9.9 yards a carry.

Simpson now wanted to go to the University of Southern California, there to compete against the records of former Heisman Trophy winner Mike Garrett. Unfortunately, USC didn't want him; at least, the registrar's office at USC didn't. That is, until he had earned some more transferable credits. And so, after rejecting offers for his services tendered by Arizona State, Fresno State, and Utah, Simpson returned for another year at City College, this time to score 28 touchdowns.

Soon, with bids from the University of California and USC ringing on his phone and in his ears, just scant days before the start of the spring 1967 semester Simpson finally chose USC because, as he told one reporter, "It's the thing I've really wanted to do all along."

The man they now called O.J. didn't come to USC to be a star; he brought that with him. But even so, it would take a little time for that star to shine—at least on the football field. For Simpson missed most of spring football practice, opting instead to compete in his second love, track and field—where he ran a 9.4 hundred and helped the USC team break the world record in the 440-yard relay.

That fall O.J. continued his record-breaking running for Southern Cal, this time carrying the ball instead of the baton. From the very first time he came in contact with the football—a 15-yard run with a swing pass against Washington State— through his two-touchdown performance in the 1968 Rose Bowl, the legend of O.J. continued to enlarge itself in breadth and range as he turned every run into high drama.

But even if he made dazzling broken-field runs a vocation in and of themselves, one he made in his first year in a Trojan uniform best defined the genius of O.J. And fully credentialed him as the greatest collegiate broken-field runner since Red Grange. That one came, fittingly enough, against crosstown and Pacific Coast Conference rival UCLA for both the conference championship and a trip to the Rose Bowl—not to mention the mythical national championship as well. Before 90,772 fans and a national television audience, with the score 20–14, UCLA, O.J. took the ball at his own 36-yard line and, in one stride, bolted through the hole at left tackle. Then, with a move that could hang in the Museum of Modern Art, he cut back sharply across the sidelines and, contradicting his direction in midflight, once again swerved back across the field, leaving a trail of UCLA tacklers snaking out behind him, looking as bereft of motion as sails without wind as they chased the quickly disappearing Number 32. One writer was moved to write of "the Run": "The thrill of it will live to the last day of the last man alive who saw it."

That one run won not only the game for USC, 21–20, but also the conference and national championships as well. And had there been an investiture, should have also won the Heisman for O.J. But the Heisman voters, in their infinite nonwisdom and citing some palaver or other about O.J. being a junior and "being able to win it next year," discounted his talents and accomplishments at less than face value and voted instead for Gary Beban of UCLA, based on his three-year record.

Rolling up his sleeves of determination, Simpson put on an even better performance in his senior year. Operating as the tailback in USC's I formation, the durable Simpson carried the ball thirty or forty times a game. "And why not?" his coach, John McKay, breezily asked. "He doesn't belong to a union. And the ball isn't very heavy, anyway." Indeed, it seemed that nothing could weigh down Simpson, as this Trojan workhorse carried the ball around, over, and through opposing tacklers for an NCAA-record 1,709 yards and 23 touchdowns. This time the Heisman voters acknowledged by the largest margin in history what everyone already knew: O.J. Simpson was the greatest collegiate player in the country. And, almost as if to make up for arrearages in recognizing his genius, he was also voted college football's greatest player of the decade.

In a field given to fashioning nimbuses, O.J. came out of

college heralded by pro scouts as the second coming of a combination of Gale Sayers and Jim Brown. And when they graded him and crunched into one of their giant computers his nine measurable qualities—quickness of reflexes, mental alertness, toughness, blocking, tackling, receiving, speed, personal character, and judgment—his rating came out an 0.5, the highest rating ever accorded a potential draftee. And so it came as no surprise that the Buffalo Bills, professional football's most woebegone and threadbare franchise, selecting first, made O.J. their top draft choice.

But even though the Bills were such a lackluster team that thousands of Buffalonians showed their appreciation for their home team by coming out to root for them disguised as empty seats, and even though they had just signed O.J. to the most lucrative professional football contract ever for a rookie, Simpson was merely a role player during his first three years as Buffalo's head coach John Rauch, incredibly, built his attack—such as it was—around the passing game.

Despite playing for a team described by writer Pete Axthelm as "a floundering, leaderless team that lacked both confidence and ability," Simpson continued to give out-of-the-ordinary performances in ordinary games. His freewheeling style and almost instinctive genius brought the fans out, first to dilapidated War Memorial Stadium and then to new Rich Stadium, called, appropriately enough, "the House that O.J. Built."

Finally, after watching the Bills win just eight games over three years and O.J. carry the ball just fourteen times a game, owner Ralph Wilson decided enough was enough. He fired Rauch, bringing in Lou Saban to attempt to make chicken salad out of the chicken droppings that were then the Bills. In his first year at the helm, 1972, Saban went to Simpson twice as often as he had been used in his first three years, and O.J. responded, leading the league in rushing with 1,251 yards.

The 1973 season was to belong to O.J. It was to be one of the greatest years in the history of professional football—if not the whole of sports. In Week One he opened the season with a record 250-yard performance. His numbers kept building, game after game: 103 yards, 123, 171, 166, 55, 157, 79, 99, 120, 124, 137, and 219. Finally, after thirteen games, and only sixty yards shy of Jim Brown's single-season record, it all came down to the final game of the season against the New York Jets. With the thermometer registering a low opinion of the weather and snowflakes swirling around Shea Stadium, the Juice raced, leaped, and dashed for 34 carries and 200 yards, breaking Brown's record by 140.

After the game a news conference was scheduled for the New York media to spotlight O.J. and his singular achievement. But even those in the writing dodge, who count every cheery word thrown their way by sports figures as misers do their treasures, weren't prepared for what happened next. For the hopelessly polite Simpson, knowing full well that his achievement wasn't "singular" and that the lot of the NFL offensive lineman is to be so invisible he could be taken to the Missing Persons Bureau for identification, brought along "the cats that made it poss-ible"—his front line, better known as the Electric Company—and introduced them to the press. By doing so, Simpson also set an NFL mark that afternoon for thoughtfulness and selflessness.

Simpson would go on to play another six years and gain another 6,055 yards before retiring in 1979 to enter a new career in entertainment and broadcasting—gaining millions of new fans as the man who hurdled suitcases in airports with the ease he had once hurdled tacklers on the gridiron.

However, performing as a national icon is a transitory act, subject to abrupt discontinuation. Notice was posted in June 1994, when the legend of O.J. collided hard with the shocking, almost indigestible indictment of this beloved superstar for the murder of his wife. As the trial of O.J. unfolded, the polish and grace of his public life were peeled away for all to see the private man. The lyric poetry of the gridiron turned instead into the tragic poetry of real life.

44

Rafer Johnson

b. 1935

To many, the enduring symbol of the Olympics is the Olympic flame, which in inspiring tradition goes back, in myth and mystery, to those days sometime before Zip B.C. in ancient Greece when the Olympics were held to honor the great god Zeus. In modern times that symbol, representing as it does the continuity between the ancient and modern games, is carried from its site near the Temple of Zeus at Olympia by a relay of runners, some three thousand in all, each lighting one magnesium torch from another, to the ceremonial fire-font, where the flame burns brightly during the quadrennial enactment of the ancient games.

And nobody, but nobody, ever carried that Olympic torch higher or more proudly than Rafer Johnson, who completed the relay as the final torchbearer at the 1984 Los Angeles Games. Johnson, who had approached his being the final caretaker of the flame as if it were "the eleventh event in the decathlon," waited on the track until the torch had been passed to him by the next-to-last torchbearer, Gina Hemphill, the granddaughter of Olympic great Jesse Owens, then ascended the stairway that climbed to the farthest reaches of Los Angeles Coliseum. "It was like a piece of artwork; it was so beautiful with the sun hitting it, like a painting," Rafer remembered thinking of the rising stairway as he raced to the top, the torch carried high above his head. Reaching the top, he turned, ever so slowly, then held the torch aloft to salute the crowd before igniting the huge gas jets, sending the flame toward the Olympic rings and, finally, to the Coliseum torch, perched high atop the Coliseum.

Going back to the 1960 Olympics, Rafer Johnson had first shown the world his hard glow of high purpose by picking up his own sputtering torch to barely win what many called the most two-sided decathlon in Olympic history. For the story of Rafer Johnson is the story of competitive spirit, of an athlete capable of lifting his performance to unassailable heights in the cauldron of competition.

But the story of Rafer Johnson didn't begin at the 1960 Olympics. Instead, it began some fifteen years earlier, when the Johnson family moved from Hillsboro, Texas, to Kingsburg, California, and made their home in a railroad boxcar near a cannery. Young Rafer attended nearby Kingsburg High, where he starred as an all-around athlete—averaging 9 yards a carry as a football halfback, hitting over .400 in baseball, and scoring 17 points a game in basketball. And he was even better, if that were possible, in track.

During his junior year at Kingsburg, Rafer's track coach drove the sixteen-year-old twenty-five miles southeast to the town of Tulare, there to witness the reigning Olympic decathlon champion, Bob Mathias, in action. Young Rafer was impressed by Mathias. "But on the way back, it struck me: I could have beaten most of the guys in the meet. That's when I decided to become a decathlon man."

And so, with the seed planted, this by-now six-foot-three, 200-pound steel etching with a Y-shaped body that triangulated from a 35-inch waist to a 46-inch chest turned his attentions to the decathlon. And to his already substantial talents grafted on the additional talents necessary to compete in the grueling ten-event contest. So well did the graft take that he won two state meets and earned a scholarship to UCLA.

By the age of nineteen, competing in the National AAU Championship, in what amounted to a passing of the torch, he broke Mathias's world record. After winning the gold at the 1955 Pan-American Games, he was acknowledged by all as the successor to Mathias and installed as the gold medal favorite for the '56 Melbourne Olympics. However, an injured knee and torn stomach muscles compromised his many talents at Melbourne, and he finished second to teammate Milt Campbell.

During the four years between the Melbourne and Rome Olympics, Johnson, Russia's Vassily Kuznyetsov, and Formosa's C. K. Yang rewrote the record books, shuttlecocking the world record between them. First it was Kuznyetsov who set a world record, in May of '58. Then Johnson regained both his world-class status and the world record by defeating Kuznyetsov 8,302 to 7,892 the same year. In 1959, Johnson suffered injuries in an automobile accident that sidelined him for the season. During his absence from the circuit, Kuznyetsov recaptured the world record. Showing supernatural recuperative powers, Johnson returned to the decathlon wars in 1960, winning the combined Amateur Athletic Union and U.S. Olympic trials with a world record of 8,683, in a meet that saw Yang also eclipse Kuznyetsov's world mark.

All of which served as a scene setting for the 1960 Rome Olympics. And a showdown between Johnson, UCLA teammate Yang, and Kuznyetsov.

But not before the three had taken part in an interesting aside in both international and personal relations—a snapshot of their relationship, if you will. As the trio went through their warm-ups for the upcoming decathlon, Kuznyetsov came up to Johnson and asked him to take a picture with him. "Sure," said Rafer, "you and me and Yang." This posed a sensitive problem for Kuznyetsov, whose country did not recognize the Chinese Nationalist government. But Rafer was persistent. Finally, Kuznyetsov relented, but as he did he turned to Yang, grinned, and said, "Okay, but remember, I don't know you." And so they posed for the picture, three friends and the three best decathletes in the world, with Rafer, the peacemaker, in the middle. One coach, watching all of this, could only say, "Rafer can do anything asked of him." And indeed he could, as he would prove shortly.

The wearying two-day decathlon began at 9 A.M. on the Monday before the close of the games. Sometime after the three had finished the 100-meter dash, the broad jump, and the shot put—and as they were in the middle of their fourth event, the high jump—the heavy clouds hovering above Stadio Olimpico unloaded their burden. Or, as John Kiernan wrote, "J. Pluvius, still waiting for the forgotten sacrificial lamb, lashed out in fury." Whatever, the waters of heaven went on an unlimited run, turning the Olympic stadium into a giant waterway, the track and field afloat, the starting blocks washed away. As lightning bolts crackled and thunder boomed, the now-navigable stream once known as Stadio Olimpico was drained and competition was suspended. Finally, after eighty minutes, the decathlon was resumed, not to end until 11 P.M. that night, fourteen hours after its start. After five events, Johnson led Yang by the slimmest of margins, just 55 points, 4,647 to 4,592.

The competition resumed ten hours later, at 9 A.M. the next morning, with the first event the 110-meter hurdles, one of Johnson's specialties. However, the by-now exhausted Johnson hit the first hurdle poorly and took 15.3 seconds to reach the finish line, far slower than his best time of 13.9, while Yang crossed the line in 14.6. As the point totals continued to mount like international debt figures, Johnson made up for the points he lost in the hurdles with a personal best in the pole vault of 13′ 5½″, then added to his totals by outthrowing Yang in the javelin.

With nine events down and but one to go, Yang had outscored Johnson in all six of the running and jumping events. But Johnson, a throwing decathlete, had so dominated the three throwing events that he still managed to lead by 67 points. Now all that remained was the final, deciding 1,500-meter race, as severe a test of Johnson's physical resources and gifts as he'd ever had to face. All of which prompted him to say: "The whole decathlon is ridiculous, but the 1,500 is insanity."

Referring to higher mathematics, Johnson figured he had a working margin of ten seconds in the final long-distance running event. Translated, this meant that Johnson, whose best time in the 1,500 had been the 4:54.2 he recorded in the '56 Olympics, had to finish within ten seconds of Yang, whose best time was 4:36.0, to win the gold. And so he formulated a plan as careful and concise as a Western Union telegram, one of "staying with Yang...not to let him get away."

In the dank chill of the Roman night, the two tired rivals began their final run for the gold, with Yang in the lead and Johnson dogging his every step, two yards behind, sticking to him like a shipwreck survivor. Racing against time and each other, the two ran as if in lockstep, the space between them no bigger than that of little kid's hands being held wide to receive his grandmother's knitting. As the stands first gasped at Johnson's strategy, then grasped it, a roar began to make itself known. But Johnson, his eyes those of a meditative fish, fastened on the nape of Yang's neck, and did not hear it. All he heard was the clock in his head as he ran step for step with Yang. Yang tried mightily to shake him off, but couldn't, as Johnson, running with a relentless pride, plodded doggedly on in the shadow of his rival, his granite jaw set to the task at hand—and foot.

Coming into the last lap, Yang tried desperately to pull away, to increase his lead beyond the ten-second window. But Johnson, running as if his legs had a mind of their own, moved with him. Again, coming off the turn into the last straightaway, Yang tried one final kick, but Johnson, running with every fiber of his being, hung on grimly, never letting Yang get more than four or five yards ahead. Both men were now wobbling, barely able to keep their legs under them in their last killing strides down the gold medal road. As they neared the finish line, Yang looked despairingly over his shoulder, but Johnson was still there in his rearview mirror, the flame that had once burned so brightly now but a flicker, but there nevertheless. And he was there at the finish, just one-plus tick of the second hand behind Yang, having run the 1,500 six seconds faster than he had ever run it before.

Both Johnson and Yang had broken Milt Campbell's Olympic record, but, in the end, the gold medal belonged to Rafer by 58 points, 8,392 to 8,334.

Afterward, as Johnson sat in the dressing room, so exhausted his words were barely audible. "All I could think of in that 1,500 meters was, 'This is the last race I'll ever run in my life.' I wanted that one real bad. But I never want to go through that again...never." And so, one of the greatest athletes of all time retired, a winner.

Rafer Johnson's flame will be remembered by all as one of

the greatest ever to light up the Olympics. Former decathlete and Iowa State coach Bob Lawson spoke for many when he said, "In my mind, for basic talent and the symbol of competitive spirit, Rafer was the world's all-time great athlete." And one who lit up the Olympic spirit like the torch he would carry twenty-four years later.

45

Kareem Abdul-Jabbar

b. 1947

There's an old-world proverb which holds that each child carries his own blessing into the world. For Lew Alcindor, that blessing was one of size. From his birth, as a 22½-inch-long baby, young Lew grew...and grew...and grew some more, so much so that by the age of six he already towered more than a foot above his first-grade classmates. On the opening day of school his teacher, spotting the long, lanky figure in the back of the classroom, cried out above the normal opening-day turmoil, "You, there, please sit down!" To which the youngster, in the soft voice that would become his trademark in later life, answered, "But I *am* sitting down."

Growing like a cedar, and just as slender, young Alcindor soon began to pass heights heretofore reserved only for high-jump bars and balloon ascensions. By the time he was ten, he stood six feet; by 12, he was six-foot-three; and by the time he was ready to go to high school, he was somewhere up in that rarefied ozone layer that starts at the seven-foot mark, give or take an inch or two.

Singled out because he was the biggest baby in the hospital and the tallest kid in the class, Alcindor would now be singled out for something else: his basketball skills. But they hadn't come easily. For he was, by his own admission, "the clumsy kid in the neighborhood." To conquer his awkwardness, he turned to sports: weight lifting, rope jumping, tennis, track—and, of course, basketball, where he began, in his own words, "doing things that other people couldn't do."

As Alcindor continued to grow, so did his reputation. So much so that his towering achievements also gained for him the admiration of three New York City high schools. After a sort of intramural tug-of-war between the three Christian Brothers schools for his services, Alcindor finally decided upon Power Memorial Academy, there to begin one of the most fabled prep school careers in the history of athletics.

His legend now grew even faster than he had, as this one-man team scored 2,067 points, garnered 2,002 rebounds, and led Power to a 95–6 record and three New York City championships. And, in the process, caught the eye of almost every inmate of the registry of college scouts as they all took turns, like people holding numbers at a meat market, at recruiting this prize. With his coach, John Donohue, and his father screening all offers, the catalog of petitioners was narrowed to but four: far-far UCLA, far-near Michigan, and near-nears St. John's and NYU.

Finally, after listening to the blandishments of all four (and receiving visitations from famed alumni, like Jackie Robinson and Ralph Bunche of UCLA), young Alcindor elected to break his East Coast umbilicus and head to the Left Coast, with its implied promises of wide-open spaces and freedom—not to mention the chance to play for coach John Wooden and his dynasty-in-the-making at UCLA, one he would help to build in the four years to come.

Alcindor came with all the tools, as advertised, and acquitted his immense buildup the very first time he stepped onto the court at UCLA's Pauley Pavilion, where he led the freshman team to a 15-point win over the varsity Bruins—not incidentally, the defending NCAA champions. With Alcindor dominating the court, and his opponents as well, the rest of his freshman season was a repeat performance as the "Brubabes" went undefeated. The Lew Alcindor Era had begun.

On December 3, 1966, he made his varsity debut. And did what every rival coach had feared he would: reduced his opponents to a state of disability, scoring with ridiculous ease and effortless grace. For when the smoke had cleared and the box score was tallied, Alcindor had made 23 of 32 field goal attempts—most of them turnaround jumpers, with one spectacular slam dunk thrown in for good measure—10 of 14 foul shots, swept the boards of 21 rebounds, and, overall, imposed his will on crosstown rival USC.

Coach Wooden, watching his colossus, could only shake his head and say, "There's nobody around who can handle him alone." And then Wooden, uncharacteristically, added, "Sometimes he even frightens me." Teams desperately, but imaginatively, tried to contain him. Washington State's coach had his reserves hold up tennis rackets in practice to simulate Alcindor's outstretched arms. The result: The rustle of Cougar hands became a sigh as Alcindor blocked several Washington State shots and scored 61 himself. Others sighed and tried anything and everything: Southern Cal a stall; Purdue a free-floating defense. The results were always the same, as Alcindor led a team made up of four sophomores and one junior to a perfect 30–0 record and a 15-point thrashing of Dayton in the NCAA finals.

Watching Alcindor become the litter bearer of their team's chances, other coaches echoed Wooden's sentiments. Johnny Dee of Notre Dame volunteered, "The only way to beat Alcindor is to hope for the three F's—Foreign Court, Friendly Officials, and Foul Out Alcindor." Steve Belko of Oregon offered up, sarcastically, "I think they ought to lower the basket to five feet and give everybody an equal chance." And Marv Harshman of Washington State said of his tormentor: "He can hold you off with one hand and stuff the ball in the basket with the other." And then, throwing his own hands in the air, he asked, "How are you going to stop him?"

Those Abominable No-Men who sat on the college rules committee took heed of the pleas by Belko, Harshman, and others by passing a new rule after Alcindor's sophomore year reading "No More Dunking." It was the ultimate compliment, albeit a backhanded one, similar to equalizing the skills of Wilt Chamberlain and Bill Russell by widening foul lanes and outlawing goaltending—which, translated, means that if one player is too big for a game, then just make it a level playing field for all by paring him down to size.

But try as they might, the rules committee could not legislate the number of ways Alcindor could dominate the court, whether by his shooting, his rebounding, his defense, or just his presence. For his size obscured a true appreciation of his talents. He was too big, too agile, too fast, and too good a shot to be whittled down to size by some rule change. Combined within this one player was the grace of an Elgin Baylor, the size of a Wilt Chamberlain, the finesse of a Jerry West, and the presence of a Bill Russell. Put them all together and this oversized package of talent—listed at 7'2", but rumored to be anywhere up to, and including, 7'4"—averaged 29 points and 15.5 rebounds a game in his sophomore year, his shooting percentage from the floor an amazing 66.7, a major-college record.

The next two seasons were more of the same, so much so you could have written "ditto, ditto" for both as Alcindor and UCLA fed on their opponents, going 29–1 both years and winning the NCAA titles in each. The only two times they were proven to be vincible in otherwise all-winning seasons came in an early-season 71–69 loss to Houston and their "Big E," Elvin Hayes, in 1968, and another loss to Southern Cal and their perfectly executed stall in '69. But the Houston game was one with a Roger Maris–type asterisk attached, coming as it did one week after Alcindor sustained an eye injury that left him with double vision in his left eye, accounting for his poor 4-for-18 shooting from the floor. However, Houston and Hayes had to face UCLA and Alcindor one more time during the '68 season. That came in the NCAA semifinals, where Alcindor more than gained his revenge by holding Hayes to just 10 points as the Bruins blew out Houston 101–69.

Having scored a total of 2,325 points during his three-year career—an average of 26.4 points and 15.5 rebounds per game and a shooting percentage of 63.9—the greatest player in college basketball history now found himself smooth of coin, negotiable in any arena. And the newly minted Milwaukee Bucks, having won a coin toss with the Phoenix Suns for the draft rights to Alcindor, rewarded him with valuable coin of their own, giving him a five-year contract worth more than $1.4 million—roughly $200,000 a foot.

It would be nice to say that Alcindor's professional career took root and flourished from Day One. Such, however, was not the case. For instead of welcoming him to their ranks with open arms, opposing centers took to welcoming him with closed fists, sharp elbows, and other adjuncts of power. Finally, tiring of dragging around a pile of assorted millstones and of hearing charges that he was "not aggressive," Alcindor's usually polite and scrupulously civil manner took on a more belligerent cast. Within a few months his "rap sheet" included one broken jaw, one knockout, and one foiled attack, as he gave the lie to the slander that he was "not aggressive."

His off-the-court demeanor was also undergoing a change. Having described himself as "more or less a mystic," he had always possessed the concentration and intensity of one, his steel-etched countenance proof against emotion. Protective of his isolation, his privacy, his space, he always had the ability to divorce himself from all around him with the cool detachment of a mystic—or of a jazz player, his father having been a musician—when that privacy was threatened. Now, with "a lot of things in my mind," he emerged from that world of detachment to express himself. The press and public, unsure of how to deal with this sudden change of persona, described him as "moody." And worse.

He underwent another change as well: a change of name. Adopting the Muslim faith and abandoning his Christian name, he became Kareem Abdul-Jabbar—a name which meant "Generous," as in Kareem, and "the Most Powerful," as in Abdul-Jabbar. In an area that prided itself on sameness and conformity, again the press and public were at a loss as to how to deal with this change, branding him a revolutionary, even a subversive. One who was able to handle the new handle was Philadelphia 76er public-address announcer Dave Zinkoff, who greeted his name change with a twist of his own, calling him "the Kareem of the Krop."

There was, however, one constant: He continued to be a winner. During that first NBA season he transformed the Bucks from a cellar-dwelling expansion team into an instant title contender, his personal stats including 28.8 points and 14.5 rebounds a game, the second- and third-best figures in the league. In 1971, his second season, he returned to the top of the basketball mountain, leading the league in scoring and powering the Bucks to the NBA championship.

At about the same time he also added two other elements to his growing basketball resumé. One was the donning of a pair of oversized glasses, almost goggles, to protect his eyes from probing fingers, giving him the look of a man peering out from behind a mask. (His later adoption of a clean-shaven head gave him, along with the goggles, an otherworldly look.)

The other new element was something called the Skyhook, a cloud-buster of a shot delivered with a flick of the wrist which traced a perfect arc to the basket before succumbing to gravity and entering the yawning hole, unmolested by human hands. Abdul-Jabbar described the shot in terms of higher mathematics, calling it "a matter of triangulation…the three corners of the triangle [being] your eyes, the ball, and the rim." Whatever, it was a signature shot that he rode to unimaginable heights, first in Milwaukee and then in Los Angeles, becoming professional basketball's most dominant player, its all-time scoring leader, and the longest-running show in its history.

That long-running show finally came to an end after twenty years. But not before Kareem Abdul-Jabbar, at the age of thirty-eight, led the Lakers to the 1985 NBA championship and won the award as the Most Valuable Player in the finals—fourteen years after he had won his first finals MVP trophy as Lew Alcindor.

Together, Kareem Abdul-Jabbar and Lew Alcindor had combined to write and rewrite the record books—in very big type, of course.

46

Gale Sayers

b. 1943

Gale Sayers was football's version of the three-card monte player: Now you see him, now you don't. No runner, with the possible exception of Red Grange, was such a movable feast. Sayers's smorgasbord of moves included running in a now-you-see-him-now-you-don't manner, leaving would-be tacklers with empty arms; circumscribing the gridiron in a giant Z, cutting and recutting across the field like a hare doubling back away from the hounds. All accompanied by lightning speed and a tinge of specialized intelligence.

Sayers had first put his style on display at the University of Kansas, where, during a three-year collegiate career, he rushed for 2,675 yards, or 6.5 per carry, including an incredible 7.1 per-carry average in his junior year. His accomplishments were rewarded with two all-American selections. But besides football Sayers had also starred in track and field, running the high hurdles and the 100-yard dash and jumping 26 feet in the long jump.

George Halas, who'd been one of the first to see the genius of Red Grange when he played for the Bears some four decades before, now sought to capture this lightning in a bottle by selecting Sayers on the first round of the 1965 NFL draft.

Almost from the very first moment he trotted out onto the field, Sayers was a star. Running in his they-went-thataway manner, his runs, receptions, and returns of punts and kickoffs in his rookie year totaled 2,272 yards, or 9.8 yards every time he touched the ball. His moves not only left tacklers grasping at air, but words as well. One of those who had reached for him with all the delicious expectation of a clerk grabbing for his weekly pay envelope, then come up empty, was George Donnelly, San Francisco's defensive back, who could only shake his head and say, "He doesn't look any different coming at you, but when he gets there, he's gone."

Halas, who had seen them all, seconded Donnelly, saying "He detects daylight. The average back, when he sees a hole, will try to bull his way through. But Gale, if the hole is even partly clogged, instinctively takes off in the right direction. And he does it so swiftly and surely that the defense is usually frozen."

But the day that went most to the proving of his potency was the next-to-last game of his rookie season, December 12, 1965, against the 49ers. The weather that day was a typical wintry Chicago day, with gelid rain coming down in a steady drizzle. The rain was such that Halas, believing the weather more suited to web-footed amphibians than to cleated athletes, ordered his equipment manager to change the Bears' cleats from the regular rubber ones to nylon, a quarter-inch longer, all the better to get traction. Whether it was the cleats, Sayers, or a combination of the two is impossible to tell. But what can be told is that it was a moment that still echoes down football's long corridors. For all Sayers did that afternoon, supplying the lightning amid the rain, was swim upstream for six touchdowns to equal the existing NFL one-game record. The TDs came in all manner and forms: one on an 80-yard reception, four on runs of 1, 7, 21, and 48 yards, and one on an 85-yard punt return. In the process he gained 336 yards in total offense and set the all-time rookie record for most touchdowns scored in a season, with 22.

For the next two seasons Sayers continued to give opposing tacklers more looks than they could find at an Easter parade as he left them and their collective athletic supporters strewn all over the field. Then, in the ninth game of the '68 season, with Sayers well on his way to his greatest season, that dread moment feared by every player ended his year—and almost his career as well. Aiming at Sayers's blockers, Kermit Alexander of the 49ers missed and instead took out Sayers. Sayers fell to the ground with a ruptured cartilage and two torn ligaments in his right knee.

Mere mortals would have hung up their cleats. But Gale Sayers was no mere mortal. Miraculously, he came back in 1969 to lead the league in rushing for a second time. But 1970 saw a leavening of his skills, and by 1971 he was playing out the string, his knees possessing all the consistency of Swiss cheese.

Sadly, after only seven years, this all-time great called it a day. But what a day it had been. Red Smith, the poet laureate of his day, said it best when he wrote, "His days at the top of his game were numbered, but there was a magic about him that still sets him apart from the other great running backs in pro football. He wasn't a bruiser like Jimmy Brown, but he could slice through the middle like a warm knife through butter, and when he took a pitchout and peeled around the corner, he was the most exciting thing in pro football." Amen.

47

Stan Musial

b. 1920

Take one part of a corkscrew, two parts of a carpenter's rule bent double, and add a pinch of what Hall of Fame pitcher Ted Lyons called "the look of a little boy peeking around the corner of a door," and you have the makings of Stan Musial's batting stance, less that of a classicist than a contortionist.

Despite looking like one of nature's irregularities at the plate, Musial could wield his bat like a matchstick. Enos Slaughter got his first real look at Musial when he came up to the Cardinals at the end of the 1941 season, and his first impression reflected that held by many: "I don't think anybody knew what a great hitter he was going to be because of that odd batting stance he had."

But that "odd batting stance" was about as harmless as a powder magazine built over a matchstick factory. Bucky Walters, the National League's leading pitcher in 1939 and '40, recalled the first time he faced Musial: "He stepped into the batter's box with that funny little stance he had—remember it? I said to myself, 'Well, here I go. Might as well find out something right now.' I put one inside. I thought I'd got it in there pretty good and tight. Boy, he hit a screaming line drive down the right-field line. I'll bet he put blisters on that ball."

Some seven years—and 1,200 blistering hits later—that same Bucky Walters, by now managing the Reds, watched as his ace, Ewell "the Whip" Blackwell, carefully pitched to Musial. Blackwell threw one of his patented sidearm sizzlers by Musial for a third strike. Unfortunately, he also threw it past catcher Dixie Howell as well, allowing Musial to go all the way to second on the strikeout. In the Reds' dugout, Walters could be seen slamming his cap to the ground and could be heard, amongst other muttered maledictions, groaning, "That guy Musial is so good that even when he fans you're lucky to hold him to two bases."

But Musial's path to greatness was far more circuitous than the route from home to second. Signed by the St. Louis Cardinals at the age of eighteen as a left-handed pitcher, Musial began his career with the Williamson Red Birds in the Class D Mountain State League in 1938, where, in twenty games, he overwhelmed six teams and underwhelmed an equal number for a .500 pitching record. The next year, again playing with Williamson, Musial started twelve times and improved his won-lost record to 9–2. But Harrison Wickel, the Williamson manager, saw something in Musial beyond his growing pitching talents, and began using him as a pinch hitter. The 1940 season saw Musial moving up in the famed Cardinal farm system to Daytona Beach in the Florida State League, where he performed double duty, playing in the outfield between pitching starts. It was while stationed in the outfield one day that Musial, reaching for a dropping ball with all the expectation of a tot on Christmas morning reaching for his presents, fell toes over teakettle, coming down heavily on the point of his left shoulder.

By all rights—and lefts—with a shoulder now up for adoption, that should have been the end of his career. But here Fate, in the person of manager Dickie Kerr—the same Dickie Kerr who won two games for the White Sox in the infamous 1919 World Series—stepped in and tapped Musial on his sore shoulder. Just when it was thought that both Musial's arm and his chances for stardom were deader than the proverbial doornail, Kerr reinvented Musial's future by converting him into a full-time outfielder. Musial repaid Kerr's faith in him by batting .311. The next year, after a look-see by the Cardinals at their minor-league training camp, Musial was consigned to another year of second-class citizenry, with Springfield of the Western Association. In eighty-seven games, he piled up 132 hits, 26 home runs, and 94 RBIs, and was promoted to the Rochester Red Wings of the International League, where he continued on his batting tear, hitting .326 over fifty-four games.

Now, dear readers, jump-shift with us back up to the Major Leagues, the National League in particular, where the Brooklyn Dodgers and the St. Louis Cardinals are in a dogfight for the catbird seat. Just about every time the Cardinals put together a winning streak the size of a tablecloth to make a run at the front-running Dodgers, something or other seemed to happen—such as third baseman Jimmy Brown breaking his nose, outfielder Terry Moore getting beaned, or outfielder Enos Slaughter falling and breaking his collarbone.

With a sufficient number of Cardinals at home studying the undersides of their bed blankets and the games dwindling down, Cardinal general manager Branch Rickey began combing the list of those available to him in the bushes to fill in the missing parts. Rather than rounding up the usual suspects from Rochester, Columbus, and all points north, east, south, and west, Rickey put out a call for three of his best minor leaguers to join the Cards for the last month of the '41 season: Erv Dusak, Whitey Kurowski, and the hero-designate of our story, Stan Musial.

But, for once, Rickey's timing was peccable. He had waited too long, and there wasn't enough time for Musial to pick up the Cardinals' sputtering torch before the Dodgers shut the door. Though it wasn't for want of trying, as the twenty-one-year-old with the strange stance skewered opposing pitchers to the tune of 20 hits in 47 times at bat for a .426 average. One afternoon in particular served as a sign of things to come: the Cardinals' final Sunday at home, playing a doubleheader against the Chicago Cubs. For all the rookie did that day was make two great catches, throw out a man at the plate, hit two singles and two doubles, steal a base, and score the winning run. And that was just the *first* game. In the second game he continued on his merry, making two more great catches—one an acrobatic, double-somersault stab—and adding two more singles to cap a six-hit day. Afterward, Jimmie Wilson, the manager of the Cubs, was heard to say: "Nobody can be that good."

Ah, but he was. For that last month of '41 was to serve merely as an appetizer for what was to come: a steady diet of hits. In 1942 he picked up right where he had left off, and by the end of his rookie year he had 147 hits and a .315 batting average. And had gone, as he said, from "a dead-armed left-handed pitcher in the minors to a wide-eyed outfielder in the Majors."

In 1943 Musial led the National League in hits, doubles, triples, and batting average with .357, won the Most Valuable Player award, and served notice on all of his future greatness. After a slight leavening of his numbers in 1944—to "just" .347— and a year in the navy, he returned in 1946 to once again lead the National League in batting, as well as almost every other offensive category. And thereafter, if you were keeping score, it was almost as if you could have written "ditto" next to his name, at least as far as hits and batting average were concerned.

Baseball archaeologists can't quite pinpoint the exact date, but it was somewhere in this period that Musial first became known as "the Man," as in "Stan the Man." Seems that Musial, who always enjoyed the friendly confines of Brooklyn's right-field foul line, which measured just 297 feet from home plate, practiced unspeakable acts of destruction off the offerings of Dodger pitchers, batting over .500 in Ebbets Field for two straight years. During this period, one of the inmates who ran the asylum, watching in horror tinged with just a little bit of awe as Musial once again advanced to the plate, trotted out the moan, and the phrase as well, "Here comes that man...that man..." Those in the press box picked up the cry, almost a keening, and Musial became, from that day forward, "Stan the Man."

The man called "the Man" continued to deliver great gobs of hits for the rest of his career, and by the time he retired at the end of the 1963 season, he had 3,630 of them, then the second-most in the history of baseball. The rest of his records would fill a Manhattan telephone directory. One of those who faced him— perhaps more than he wanted to—was Warren Spahn, who said, upon Musial's retirement: "1964 will be different from all the others I've spent in the big leagues: Stan Musial will no longer be there. Once Musial timed your fastball, your infielders were in jeopardy." And so, too, of course, were the pitchers who faced him, most of whom had to be removed in caskets made by Hillerich and Bradsby.

Upon his retirement, the grateful citizens of St. Louis erected a statue of their hero—one with a man wearing Number 6 and in a corkscrew stance that defied description—proving that time does not relinquish its hold over men or monuments. And Stan "the Man" was both.

48

Arnold Palmer

b. 1929

Television, that magic lantern which, throughout the fifties, transported more people to fantasyland than Aladdin's wish-giver dreamed of, was poised by 1960 to train the glare of its cameras on the world of sports. For that was the year TV "found" the Olympics, with CBS paying all of $50,000 for the rights to televise the 1960 Winter Olympics from Squaw Valley and another $660,000 for the Rome Summer Olympics. That was also the year ABC won the rights to NCAA football and acquired the rights to the new American Football League's games. And that was the year that television discovered golf, bringing its newest star, Arnold Palmer, into our living rooms. And into our consciousness as well. It was to be a perfect marriage.

But it hadn't always been thus. As late as 1955, when golf was suggested to him, Tom Gallery, then head of NBC Sports, had said, "Golf isn't a spectator sport." But stimulated by the front-page treatment golf was getting in the Eisenhower years, thousands were turning to it in a variation of that old game of "follow the leader." And, all of a sudden, golf was seen on more and more networks as broadcast executives finally got the big picture.

Gone were the days when a golfer could turn to a cameraman on the eighteenth hole and mutter, along with other imprecations, "The next time you take my picture when I'm putting you're going to get a putter in your mouth." Or some other anatomical opening. Golfers now managed to sublimate their old prejudice against cameras and cameramen breaking into the funereal silence that surrounded golf, where any sound—be it a sneeze, a whisper, or a camera—could distract them. Now they only heard the sound of money. And the louder it talked, the better.

But it would take the personality and charisma of Palmer to turn golf into a TV show. For here was a swashbuckling star, bold, daring, and strong, complete with a red-blooded, 100 percent all-American face topped by a tousled grassplot, who was capable of weaving sand castles in the air with his clubs and daring the Fates. Palmer's exploits were followed on the course by a great human fringe of humanity that stampeded, whooped, and eddied around him like herds of sheep, grubbing the scenery, a fusion of souls known as Arnie's Army that was as much a spectacle as the match itself. It made for great television.

Palmer first appeared on the golfing landscape in 1954, when he won the U.S. Amateur. The next year he turned pro, and by 1957 he was the fifth-leading money winner. In the '58 Masters he finished a stroke ahead and sweated out his first majors victory for an hour. And when defending champion Doug Ford couldn't catch him, he helped the youngest Masters winner ever put on his new green jacket. The Palmer legend was taking form.

It all began with the 1960 Masters. Ken Venturi was already in the clubhouse with a one-stroke lead, being measured for the traditional green jacket. But Palmer was still prowling the course, his breath so alive it could becloud a mirror. Reaching the seventeenth green, Palmer took aim at the hole some twenty-seven feet away and confidently stroked the ball. The ball followed every contour, circumference, and concavity of the green—not to mention every mean elevation, angle, and slope—until it fell into the yawning hole for a birdie. The noise that greeted his heroics from his newly formed Arnie's Army was like that created by a thousand trucks going over a wooden bridge.

Par on the 420-yard eighteenth would force a playoff. Palmer decided to go for broke. After a good drive, he hit a six-iron that took off straight into the wind, stayed low, and came to rest five feet from the pin, five feet from another birdie, and five feet from victory. Palmer stood there but a brief second and then, after surveying the green, taking another drag on his cigarette, and hitching his trousers, confidently sank the putt. The Army exploded with more backslapping and noise than could be found at a Shriners' convention. Their hero had won.

Bobby Jones, who had written the book on golf, was prompted by Palmer's putting display to remark, "If I ever had to have one putt to win a title for me, I'd rather have Arnold Palmer hit it for me than anybody I ever saw. I have never seen a fellow in a whole career who is able to sink as many important putts as Palmer."

But Jones—and the golfing world—hadn't seen anything yet. For that summer, in one of golf's most memorable moments, Palmer put on an all-or-nothing charge that gave new meaning to the word *comeback*. Going into the final round of the U.S. Open, Palmer found himself seven strokes back of the leader, "no more in contention," wrote one reporter, "than the man operating the hot dog concession." As he sat in the tent before his final-round tee-off, Palmer asked another reporter, "What would happen if I shot a 65?" The writer, who, like everyone else, had come to view Palmer's presence only as a rumor, could only shake his head and answer, "Nothing. You're out of it!"

With no unconditional surrender to undeniable facts, Palmer went out to impose his will on the Cherry Hill course. Throwing every round of ammunition in his arsenal into his attack on the course, Palmer sank six birdies on the first seven holes and was away to a 30 on his outward nine, thus preserving his negotiability.

Now a strong current running, Arnie continued his go-for-broke assault on the back nine, his loyalists greeting his every swing with the exultant cry of a rallying army as they sang out, in unison, "Charge!" One of the enlistees in that riotous assembly recalled his historic charge: "He's one down on the fifteenth and needs a birdie to tie. So instead of playing it safe from the green, he misses, chips past the hole, and he's down in par. Well, he comes up to the sixteenth, and he's in the same spot again. And damned if he doesn't try the same shot, again. Knocks the ball in the cup this time, and went on to win the match."

Palmer had once again stuffed the toothpaste back into the tube, finishing with a 65 and a winning score of 280 and, in the process, turning his seven-stroke deficit into a coach plus six.

The Palmer legend was made. No golfer, before or since, has ever captivated the public's fancy, in person and on TV, as had the man *Sports Illustrated* described as "combining the boldness of a Brink's bandit with the fearless confidence of a man on a flying trapeze. He doesn't play a golf course, he assaults it."

49

Hank Aaron

b. 1934

As we deal in that multitude of memories that comprise the whole of sports, there are very few moments that stay with us. But there is one. It was an instance when time was separated and unified at the same time, when the record book and the flickering image on the 23-inch magic lantern in our living rooms became as one: Hank Aaron had just broken the most revered record in all of baseball—Babe Ruth's lifetime mark of 714 home runs.

It was 9:07 P.M., April 8, 1974, when Aaron smote one of Al Downing's fastballs over the fence into the bullpen with his first swing of the nationally televised game. As scoreboard lights flashed in six-foot numerals the now-magic number "715" over and over again and 53,775 fans stood in riotous assembly, millions more were told by ABC announcer Curt Gowdy, "He did it! He did it!" Thus ended Aaron's long climb up the baseball Everest that had stood for thirty-nine years since Babe Ruth had hit his 714th and last career homer. And it was only fitting that the record had been broken thirty-nine years after Ruth had established it, Aaron being thirty-nine years younger than Ruth, less a day.

But Hank Aaron's first years in professional baseball, while giving promise of a great career, hardly gave promise of one whose career statistics would be generously dotted with home runs. Starting as an eighteen-year-old shortstop for Eau Claire in the Northern League in 1952, Aaron batted .336 with but 32 extra-base hits—and only 9 of those homers. The next year, at Jacksonville, he led the league in batting and had 22 home runs—good, but scarcely the stuff that would cause concern to the keepers of the Ruthian flame.

Coming up to the 1954 Milwaukee Braves—then only a year removed from Boston—Aaron joined a young team, on the ascendancy. The Braves infield was made up of equal parts talent and youth, with Eddie Mathews, Johnny Logan, Danny O'Connell, and Joe Adcock all holding down their positions. All very well, thank you. With no room at the infield inn, Aaron was moved to the outfield to take the place of the injured Bobby Thomson. But Aaron's start was somewhat less than spectacular. In fact "underwhelming" might better describe it. "A typical rookie start" was the way Aaron himself remembered it, going "0-for-4 or 0-for-5, I forget which." By the end of his rookie year he had managed 131 hits and a .280 batting average, along with 13 homers, the first olives out of the home run jar.

His sophomore year saw him hit .314 and, with his smooth, economical swing, smite 27 homers. Remarkably consistent, he had 26 homers in his third year, along with a league-leading .328 batting average. And in his fourth year he climbed to the top of the home run mountain, hitting 44 to lead the league and match his uniform number. It was the first of four times he would hit exactly 44 home runs in a season, three of those seasons leading the league.

Baseball slowly "discovered" Hank Aaron as he continued to drive ball after ball out of Milwaukee County Stadium—not the parabolic cloud-busters of the Ruthian variety, mind you, but straight-as-a-rope line drives. Aaron's sweet-swinging bat would make him the most consistent home run hitter in the Majors over the next eight years.

Then, in 1966, the Braves, which had been the first franchise ever to relocate, hopscotched again, moving lock, stock, and franchise to Atlanta. Almost undetected in the switch was the fact that Aaron was now playing in Atlanta Stadium, with its more inviting left-field wall, an area that would soon become known as Home Run Alley. Aaron, who had hit 398 in his first thirteen years, would begin hitting more homers at home than on the road. As Aaron's reputation grew amongst his peers—Curt Simmons saying of him, "Throwing a fastball by Aaron is like trying to sneak the sun past a rooster"—so did his home run total.

Without any of those recognizable landmarks like a 50-homer season that the minds of the fans and the press could wrap themselves around, Aaron had quietly snuck up on Ruth's record. In the process, he was laying claim to more records than an Alaskan claim-jumper in the areas of runs batted in, total bases, hits, and extra-base hits.

Unconcerned with the brouhaha his attack on baseball's most legendary record was generating, Aaron went on about his task in his usual workmanlike manner—44 here, 38 there, another 47 there, here a 34, and another 40 there.

Finally, going into the 1974 season, Aaron stood on the threshold of history with 713 round trippers. Chasing the ghost of Ruth, he hit the record-tying number 714 on opening day against Cincinnati's Jack Billingham and then, with the first swing of his 34 3/4-ounce bat, sent Al Downing's fastball over the fence in Atlanta Stadium. On the fourth day of the week in the fourth month of the year 1974, forty-year-old Number 44, batting fourth, hit the home run that was in the air and in the record books at one and the same time.

Hank Aaron was now not only the first name in the *Baseball Encyclopedia*, but the first name in baseball itself, as the game's all-time home run leader.

50

Jimmy Connors

b. 1952

In days of old, the upper-class game of tennis was a chivalrous sport, one where good manners reigned and the words "nice shot!" rang out with almost every passing volley. It was a time when the game itself was far more important than winning. In the 1940 Forest Hills finals, Don McNeill defeated Bobby Riggs in five sets even after "throwing"—or surrendering—points when he thought Riggs had received a bad call.

The world of sports manners and etiquette lost its virginity some years ago, replaced by a "win at any cost" mentality—except for the naive few who haven't yet discovered that Father Adam had been displaced by apple salesmen. The exact date when good manners went out of vogue is a little hard to pinpoint, but its beginnings can be traced back to 1947, the year Stephen Potter authored a little tract entitled, *The Theory and Practice of Gamesmanship or The Art of Winning Games Without Actually Cheating*. Amongst the many textbook maxims on gamesmanship and one-upmanship advanced by Potter was one which read: "Make the other man feel that something has gone wrong, however slightly." Another held: "A good general rule is to state that the bouquet is better than the taste. And vice versa."

Perhaps the greatest practitioner of gamesmanship and one-upmanship was Jimmy Connors, a street fighter in tennis shorts who perfected his own code, one more of convenience than of conduct.

Connors's curriculum on the court was a wide one, everything, like skywriting, writ large. One minute, the pouter-pigeon proud Connors, breezily nonchalent, would be joking with the crowd. The next, with manners hardly overcharged with courtesy, he would act like a youngster with green-apple colic, growling and sounding like he had just swallowed something or other. And in the next, he'd be jumping up and down like Rumpelstiltskin, hurling an acrid torrent of words in the direction of some poor linesman.

While his on-the-court loudishness and loutishness were calculated to win him games, it was behavior hardly calculated to win him friends and influence people—most of those on the tennis circuit viewing Connors as the kind of person who subscribed to the theory that to know Connors was to loathe him included Tom Okker, who called him a child; the normally mild-mannered Rod Laver, who sneered, "He probably thinks he's the next best thing to 7-Up"; and Stan Smith, who voiced his disesteem by saying, "He does things that annoy a lot of guys."

But if Connors was one part gamesman and one part boor, he was all player, his straightforward game offering a striking contrast to his underhanded manipulation of conventions—or his "working of gamesmanship," as Arthur Ashe called it. Possessing a straight-back forehand and an equally straight-back double-fisted backhand, both delivered without excess motion, Connors played, in his own words, "a more compact game" than his rivals.

He also possessed something else: unlimited energy. Ashe, describing his game, summed it up by saying, "Connors certainly has the guts. He will chase down everything, exerting himself to the fullest." With an all-out game, the greyhound-lean and wolfpack-mean Connors could hit the ball on the run with slashing, punishing strokes; or fly at the ball, his feet strangers to the ground, to return seemingly unreturnable shots; or charge the net, after handling his opponents' serves, to jump all over their returns; or work his opponents into a state of numbness with his high-velocity and unrelenting shots. "Playing him is like fighting Joe Frazier," said TV commentator Dick Stockton. "The guy is always coming at you. He never lets up."

Connors learned his tigerish qualities at the knees of his mother and maternal grandmother. Literally. Introduced to the game by the twosome when he was barely old enough to hold a racket, young Jimmy took to the game "as if it were part of him," recalled his mother, Gloria Thompson Connors, a former tournament player who had ranked as high as thirteenth nationally among juniors. She also instilled in him some of those qualities that were to make him such a tough, no-holds-barred competitor. "When he was young, if I had a shot I could hit down his throat, I did," she remembered. "And then I'd say, 'See, Jimmy, even your mother will do that to you.'"

Jimmy remembered: "There was a practice court in our backyard, and I was always drilling with one of them. They went to tournaments with me always, and when I went to high school, they used to pick me up, right after school, for practice."

By the time Jimmy was sixteen his mother had come to the realization that she had reached her limit in teaching her prodigy, and began casting around for someone else to take him to the next level. It was at this point that she contacted her old friend Pancho Segura, a tournament veteran then teaching at the Beverly Hills Tennis Club, and persuaded him to take on Jimmy as a student.

It has long been held by those on the Right Coast, and elsewhere, that the only reason to go to L.A. is to improve one's backhand. That's exactly what Jimmy did, as Segura, one of the first to use the two-handed backhand, grafted one more important dimension onto the youth's hustling, overwhelming game: his patented two-fisted backhand, a shot so rich and good-looking it reminded observers of something with mushrooms on the side.

Jimmy stayed on the Left Coast to attend UCLA. But after one year, during which he won the NCAA singles championship, he decided, like Paul, to look for the proceeds of the gold-brick road, and dropped out of college to go the pro route.

He signed up with Bill Riordan, a maverick tour promoter who told him, "If you want to be number two in one of the World Championship Tennis groups, you'll be a nonentity. But if you want to be the best-known tennis player in the world, come with me." Jimmy turned pro in '72 and won his first two tournaments. Under Riordan's management, Connors finished his first year with seventy-five victories, the highest number amongst male American pros, and $90,000, the second-highest figure in prize money.

The following year he won the U.S. pro championship and shared the No. 1 ranking in the USLTA rankings with Stan Smith, a shared billing the outspoken Riordan attacked as an "immoral, unethical fraud."

By 1974, playing "the best tennis I've ever played in my life," Connors stood all alone atop the ratings mountain. That was the year he won three of the four tournaments in the so-called Grand Slam of tennis—winning the Australian Open, Wimbledon, and Forest Hills—but was denied an opportunity to join Don Budge and Rod Laver as the only men to win the Grand Slam when the International Tennis Federation barred him from entering the fourth, the French Open, because he had played World Team Tennis. It was to be the beginning of his long running gunfight with "the Establishment," one which saw him continually give them the verbal finger. But battles on the courts and in the courts notwithstanding, by the end of the year he had given his signature victory gesture, a clenched-fist punch in the air, 99 times in the 103 matches he had played. And had begun looking for other mountains to scale.

Those other mountains came in the form of "Winner-take-all" challenge matches. And because of the crafty plotting of Bill Riordan. After Connors had disposed of Ken Rosewall at Forest Hills in the '74 finals, 6–1, 6–1, 6–4, Connors was reputed to have hollered, "Now get me Laver." However, according to one writer, Mike Lupica, it ain't necessarily so. Lupica, who happened to be eavesdropping at the time, recounted that as Connors came off the court, Riordan approached him and said, "Junior, when you get to the press conference, somebody's going to ask you who's next now that you've won Wimbledon and the Open." Connors, again according to Lupica, canted his head and replied, incredulously, "How do you know?" "Trust me," Riordan grinned. "Somebody'll ask. And when they do, you say, 'Get me Laver.' And I'll take care of the rest." And so was born one of tennis's all-time circus acts, the supposed "Winner-take-all" challenge round which turned out to be, on closer inspection, merely "Winner-take-most." Still, it made Connors $100,000 richer and reinforced his credentials as the best tennis player in the world.

Fast-forward, dear reader, from 1974, when the mop-haired, apple-cheeked, and cheeky youngster was all-winning, to 1991, when his image and game had both softened somewhat and Connors, not yet ready to pack his career in lavender or moth-balls, took center court at Forest Hills again at the age of thirty-nine, a fully credentialed member of the Geritol Generation. No longer tennis's "Bad Boy"—having lost that title to John McEnroe—he was now just plain ol' "Jimbo." And the fans, drawn more by the force of his reputation than by his declining skills, flocked back to see him, just as the pigeons flock back in circles to the West Side Tennis Club in the off-season.

Connors more than repaid their interest, reinventing what someone called the Jimmy Wheel. Finding himself No. 936 on the computer, but No. 1 in the hearts of his fans, Connors, exuding that essential oil of competitiveness he had once owned in abundance, went on a one-man run. Dealing out equal servings of hard smashes and cold calculations, he fought his way, against all odds, into the semifinals. For one glorious moment, he was the Jimbo of old, recycling his greatness.

Some claimed he had, as he said in the Nuprin commercial, just "Nuped It." But others, remembering Jimmy Connors in his salad days, when his moves had been as light as cucumber salad and his motivations as hard-boiled as a Freud egg, swore he had done it on "gamesmanship," a skill he had mastered better than anyone else ever to play the game of tennis. Or any other game, for that matter.

51

Lou Gehrig

1903–1941

T he story of Lou Gehrig inspires the reflection that life is made up of equal parts smiles, satisfactions, and sniffles—with sniffles predominating.

It was a story that was well documented, both in record books and on film, of an athlete who rolled up his sleeves, spat on his hands, and went to work, giving an honest laboring man's effort, each and every time. For 2,130 consecutive times. And yet, that most famous of baseball records—and the nickname he was given because of his superhuman feat, "the Iron Man"—tended to obscure a true appreciation of the skills of this tremendously talented ballplayer.

But, then again, it seemed as if the Fates had always conspired to hide this man and his exploits under a bushel basket.

From the very first day Gehrig broke into the New York Yankee lineup—courtesy of the most famous headache in sports history, the one suffered by Wally Pipp that allowed Gehrig to take his place at first—Gehrig was destined to play in the rather ample shadow of the man he called the Big Guy, Babe Ruth. For the next ten years he was to bat fourth behind Ruth's third in the Yankee batting order. And for most of those ten years he was to stand behind the Babe both statistically and in the hearts of the fans.

But Gehrig accepted his position on the team with the dignity demanded, saying, "I'm not a headline guy. I'm just the guy who's in there every day, the fellow who follows Babe in the batting order. When Babe's turn to bat is over, whether he strikes out or belts a home run, the fans are still talking about him when I come up. If I stood on my head at the plate, nobody'd pay attention."

But pay attention they did as the solid-looking Gehrig—by now called Larrupin' Lou—took his place in the batter's box, his open stance and high-held bat only hinting at his intention to smash the ball into smaller smithereens. Unlike Ruth, the balls he smote were not of the cloud-buster variety, but were instead bludgeoned, lined like an arrow, the ball almost screaming in pain as it headed for parts unknown.

By the end of 1927, Gehrig's second full season, he and Ruth had become the heart of the Yankees' famed "Murderers' Row." The year 1927 is remembered by most as the year that Ruth hit his record-setting 60 home runs. It was also the year that Gehrig, in the race until the last month of the season, finished second with 47—the third-leading home run hitter had all of 18! Gehrig also was to finish second in slugging average, hits, and walks, proving that he and Ruth were each a jewel in a separate setting. He also led the league in RBIs with 175—quite a feat considering that Ruth, batting ahead of him, drove in 164 of his own, many times leaving the bases denuded of Yankee base runners before referring the matter to Gehrig. And it was Gehrig, not Ruth, who was named the league's Most Valuable Player.

Even as Ruth continued to dominate the headlines, Gehrig continued as the Yankees' perennial most valuable player. Take the 1928 World Series, for instance, a four-game sweep by the Bronx Bombers. The Series is best remembered as the one in which Ruth hit three home runs in a single game and batted .625. What is not remembered is that Gehrig hit four home runs in that same Series and batted .545—and, characteristically, had nine RBIs (to Ruth's four).

It seemed that Gehrig was forever doomed to be the crown prince to Ruth's sultan, consigned to the same fame as the second man to cross the Atlantic solo.

And when, in fact, after dogging Ruth's mincing footsteps in the home run derby the next two years, he had an opportunity to replace Ruth at the top of the home run mountain, in 1931, Fate again allowed him to get just close enough to touch her hem. And no further. For that was the year that one of Gehrig's frescoed shots went into the stands and ricocheted back into the hands of the center fielder, so hard was it hit. The Yankee base runner, only looking up to see the center fielder catch the ball, assumed it was caught and ran to take his place in the field as Gehrig passed him on the base paths and was called out. The home run would have been his 47th. As it was, he finished with the same number as Ruth, 46, to share the home run crown rather than wear it alone.

The next year, 1932, against the defending champion Philadelphia A's, Gehrig became the first player in the twentieth century to hit four home runs in one game. Unfortunately for Gehrig, that same day John McGraw stepped down as the manager of the New York Giants after thirty-one years in the saddle. Again, Gehrig was deprived of the spotlight.

And then there was the 1932 Series, the one forever remembered as the one in which Ruth hit his "Called Shot." It was marked by passions that recalled the worst excesses of the French Revolution, with the Yankees and their rivals, the Chicago Cubs, using language that would have caused the coarsest billingsgatespouting seaman to blush. The Yankees screamed "cheapskate" at the Cubs for voting their former teammate Mark Koenig only a half-share after he'd sparked them to the National League pennant. The Cubs retaliated, screaming every four-letter word that came to mind, including the hated word "Ruth." Ruth got even for the real and imagined slights in the third game, hitting a three-run homer in the first and his "Called Shot" in the fifth. What wasn't reported by the members of the press, caught up as they were in the drama of the moment, was that Gehrig had homered in the third and then followed Ruth's beau gesture with another homer for the go-ahead run. For the entire Series, Ruth batted .333, hit two homers, and batted in six runs; Gehrig hit

.529, hit three homers, and batted in eight. But, again, it was Ruth's moment.

It was always thus with Gehrig, destined as he was to play second fiddle behind the greatest story in the history of sports, to be the second half of baseball's early-day version of *The Odd Couple*. Gehrig, the consummate team player, understood his role, saying, "The Babe is one fellow...and I'm another, and I could never be exactly like him. I don't try...I just go on as I am in my own right." The fans, identifying with this quiet, unpretentious man who epitomized the hardworking and forgotten man of the Depression, knew that if Babe Ruth was the spirit of the Yankees, Lou Gehrig was its pride.

By 1934, with Ruth on his last legs, literally, Gehrig finally came into his own, leading the league in home runs, RBIs, and batting average for the Triple Crown. And when Ruth left the next year, Gehrig became the team leader. And the embodiment of everything that was the Yankees: class, tradition, and confidence. Rarely, in his role as the team's leader, did he have to cock more than one eye to bring some rowdy into line, or to raise his high-pitched voice in reprimanding some rookie who had shown up in public without a jacket.

With the arrival of Joe DiMaggio in '36, Gehrig became the Yankees' hero emeritus. Still he was their leader, their most valuable player, as he approached every game with the spirit of a college football player—which he had been at Columbia—and continued to inspire through example as his consecutive streak continued through its twelfth season.

And then, just when it seemed as if Lou Gehrig would be the only first baseman the New York Yankees would ever need, that grappling hook known as Fate reached out for him. At first, his stiff-jointed, almost halting walk was thought to be nothing more than advancing age, something he would conquer, as he had every other injury and malady with his superhuman recuperative powers. But then came the shocking, almost indigestible disclosure that Lou Gehrig had been struck down by an illness known as amyotrophic lateral sclerosis—and now more commonly known as Lou Gehrig's disease—a rare disease that destroys the tissues of the spinal cord.

On May 2, 1939, 2,130 games after he had replaced Wally Pipp, Lou Gehrig asked manager Joe McCarthy to excuse him from the lineup for "the good of the team." Two months later, at a

"Day" in his honor, in front of thousands of well-wishers at Yankee Stadium, Lou Gehrig proudly shuffled to the microphones and tearfully proclaimed himself to be "the luckiest man on the face of the earth."

He died two years later, two weeks short of his thirty-eighth birthday. He was survived by his widow, Eleanor, and his achievements, which included the most all-time grand slam home runs, the American League record for most RBIs in a season, 13 straight years of 100 or more RBIs, the fourth-highest batting average of any Hall of Famer, 493 home runs, and 2,130 consecutive games—a record that, until broken 56 years later by Cal Ripkin Jr., was so alive it vibrated in tribute to him. And tended to obscure a true appreciation of his tremendous talents.

52

Diego Maradona

b. 1960

The most noteworthy aspect of Diego Maradona's career was the dazzling inconsistency of it. On the soccer field, always the center of attraction, he was so elusive opponents couldn't get close enough to hit him in the hide with a handful of buckshot; off the field, ever the center of controversy, he was unable to hide his Hyde. Inevitably, one subtracted from the other.

It was ever thus for this undisciplined product of a Buenos Aires shantytown. A prey to curious sensations throughout his career, his life was, in reality, a tour map reading less as an atlas of his achievements than a record of his antics, with as many appearances on police blotters and front pages as on sports pages.

The starting point on that map was a place called Villa Florita, Argentina, a pretty-sounding but hard-looking place on the outskirts of the Argentine capital. As local legend would have it, at the age of three little Dieguito was given a soccer ball by his father. And from that point on, it became a part of him, almost as if they were joined by an umbilicus, as the boy kicked it by day and slept with it by night, never letting his constant companion leave his side. The inseparable twosome put on TV variety-show performances at soccer game intermissions, as Dieguito entertained the crowd by juggling the weightless ball off his head, shoulders, chest, knees, ankles, feet, and any other anatomical appurtenance that came into play, never once letting it touch the ground during the entire intermission. When the two teams returned to the field to resume play, the crowd would express their appreciation for Dieguito and his magic ball by shouting, "Stay! Stay!"

At the age of nine this prodigy-cum-magician was recruited to play for the famous Argentine children's soccer team, Los Cebollitos—the Little Onions. Wearing Number 10, the number worn by the great Pelé and traditionally given to the leading scorer on the team, Dieguito did with the ball what magicians do with colored silks. "He wouldn't stop bouncing the ball," said one of those who witnessed him that first day he trotted out in his Number 10 jersey. "He was already a phenomenon, born that way."

For five years and 140 straight victories, spectators oohed and aahed his every move, which were many. One of his early fans recalled: "People who weren't even interested in soccer came to see him as a spectacle, as a show, like going to the opera."

By fourteen, he had quit school to play soccer full-time; by fifteen, he had signed his first professional contract, joining the Argentinos Juniors; and by his sixteenth birthday he had played his first professional game. Devotees crowded into the tiny Argentinos Juniors stadium, there to worship at his shrine and greet his smorgasbord of moves with choruses of *"Y ya lo ve, y ya lo ve / Es Maradona y su ballet."* ("You can see it here, you can see it here / Maradona and his ballet.")

Elegant and eloquent, this stocky "Señor Five-by-Five" with the body of a tank could maneuver through a picket of defenders by giving off misdirections of small, almost hypnotic movements and then, while everyone was speculating about their meaning, move around his dazed rivals with a tango step here and a stutter step there; or bounce the ball off his knees or any other part of his body close at hand four, even five times as he ran past them in full flight; or scurry around them with his low-to-the-ground, crablike moves, making it all but impossible to knock him off the ball. And then, with the smell of the goal in his nostrils, he'd clip the ball in the middle of his "running" stride with the "wrong" foot, his left, as they all stood stock-still in the manner patented by Lot's wife.

It was a style that made great demands on his defenders, a style of impromptu vamping born of the same roots as Maradona. As Cesar Luis Menotti, the coach of the Argentine national team, explained it: "He came from a poor background, and he somehow transferred to soccer the inventiveness that a street kid uses to survive."

But street inventiveness or no, Maradona didn't survive the last cut by Menotti before the 1978 World Cup, the seventeen-year-old being viewed as too green for the blue-and-white squad. "I told him he would be great, very great," remembered Menotti. "But he could not bear the blow. He cried like a child."

Denied a place to showcase that potential greatness on Argentina's World Cup championship team of '78, Maradona would have to wait until the next year. For that was the year he went to Japan as a member of the under-21 Argentine side that won the Junior World Cup tournament and was voted South American Player of the Year. Finally made a member of the full Argentine national team, Maradona led the team on a triumphal tour of Europe.

Rarely had the world of European soccer seen an executant as skillful as the heavy-shouldered, thick-chested, massive-thighed youngster with the mane of tight, black curls whose every move was a highlight film. Foot soldiers were left to grasp at air and fans to gasp in amazement as he practiced unspeakable acts with the ball. Even the staid London press waxed ecstatic about this artful dodger, the *London Sunday Times* devoting an entire page in its main section to Maradona. "About once in twenty years, a footballer of genius emerges," the newspaper wrote. "The last one was Pelé, the great Brazilian player. Now there is another—Diego Maradona of Argentina."

Latin American soccer gods do not have two names, any more than a Zeus or an Apollo did. They are simply Pelé or

Maradona. Anything more is unnecessary. Now called the New Pelé, or just Maradona, the new king of soccer returned home to Argentina to a royal welcome. And a proverbial king's ransom, offers coming in from all over the world for his services.

But in Argentina, where soccer is Everyman's religion and obsession, rumors of Maradona's impending offshore sale were met with everything from outright denials ("Maradona is not transferable") to pious pronouncements ("Dieguito is a little angel God has sent down to bestow happiness on Argentine soccer"). Still, Maradona found the profit system to be more compelling than the prophet system, and soon signed a six-year contract with Barcelona of the Spanish League for the ungodly sum of $12 million. Reaction was immediate. Faced with the unthinkable knowledge that they were losing one of their prized natural assets, Argentine soccer fans exhausted their vocabulary of tearful indignation. And the Argentine Football Association announced that Maradona would not be permitted to join his new team until after the 1982 World Cup competition.

Ironically, the '82 World Cup finals were held in Barcelona. Expected to lead his country to a second Cup title, Maradona, plagued by a "marker" who less defended him than showed a gift for grab, constantly fouling him, gave a subpar performance as Argentina was eliminated in the second round. The local media, taking note of the player who would soon be representing their city, ridiculed his performance, one paper even going so far as to call him *Mini Doña*, or Little Lady.

It was to be the beginning of a two-year hate-hate relationship between Barcelona and Maradona. Despite being starved for success—a success Maradona fed them in his very first year, as he led them to the Spanish League title, scoring twenty-two times in thirty-six games—the citizenry of Barcelona soon came to the realization that this dark, uncouth outsider was not quite the dish they had ordered. Incurably hard to deal with, this brash product of the barrio clashed with Barcelona's high standards of gentility. Particularly galling were his participation in an on-the-field brawl during a game attended by King Juan Carlos and his rumored sniffing of everything, including the soccer fields' white end lines. Whatever. After two years, the management of the Barcelona team threw up their hands and washed them of Maradona by selling his contract to Naples of the Italian League for $10.8 million.

Napoli had gone eighty years without a championship—that is, until the arrival of Maradona, who turned a perennial loser from one of Italy's poorest regions into a dynasty, winners of five Italian and European tournaments. His presence also helped turn around the local economy, most notably the unofficial betting system that profited everyone from sellers to bettors. The Napoli general manager, assessing Maradona's worth, said, "Maradona has meant twenty billion dollars for the club."

Maradona was to prove his worth to his home country in the '86 World Cup. On the pitch of Mexico City's huge Azteca Stadium, his talents were without boundaries, almost limitless: Here, he could be seen heading for the ball like a hart streaking toward a cooling stream; there, delivering the most sumptuous of crosses to the head of a teammate; and everywhere, practicing that devilish dribbling of his, dancing past defenders and destroying the opposition. The spoils might have belonged to Argentina, which won the World Cup for the second time in eight years, but the glory belonged to Maradona, who scored five goals in six games, was selected the tournament's Most Valuable Player, and was hailed as the best soccer player in the world.

But while he had become the world's best-known athlete, he had become its most controversial as well, his extracurricular antics turning the on-the-field *olés* into off-the-field *oy vays!* His every move was analyzed and writ large in headlines, the bill of particulars including everything from cocaine abuse to horrendous alcohol consumption to frequent dalliances that led to a spate of paternity suits. Suspended by the soccer powers-that-be for "grave offenses," the career of Diego Maradona was apparently at an end, the only thing that seemingly could improve him at this point was embalming fluid.

But life deals in wrought ironies, none more so than the one it now dealt to Maradona. For while he was in Seville, Spain, failing in a comeback attempt, his body gone to flab, his career to pot, Argentina, which had won thirty-three straight games without him, including two South American championships, was suffering a humiliating 5–0 defeat at the feet of Colombia that left the country on the brink of elimination from World Cup '94.

Despite all his troubles and travails, the Argentine soccer fans had stayed loyal to their idol through hell and high jinx. Now, in response to their pleas, Argentine president Carlos Menem called Maradona back to try to restore his country's

crumbling hopes. In only his third game in four months following his troubled eleven-year stay in Europe, a new-look Maradona, slim and almost gaunt after a physical transformation at a
health farm, led his countrymen into a one-game eliminator
against Australia for the last place in the twenty-four-nation
lineup.

Wearing the Number 10 shirt he had worn leading his
country to the 1986 World Cup, Maradona showed flashes of his
old brilliance as Aussie defenders, as so many before them,
discovered that guarding Maradona had about as much effect on
his play as a fig leaf at a nudists' convention. The Maradona-led
team won, 2–1.

But the on-again, off-again career of Diego Maradona,
which had long hissed and sparked like a loose electric wire, once
again went out, this time short-circuited by his making too much
of a bad thing. He was suspended by the Argentine soccer team
for drug use and sent a-packing, a sad end to a once-brilliant
career.

53

Roberto Clemente

1934–1972

To some, Roberto Clemente was a moody Hamlet in Pittsburgh Pirate black-and-gold, a lifetime .317 hitter and a .400 kvetcher, assailed by sore distractions, both bodily and mentally. To others, he was the personification of the honor-bound man, possessing pride in his bearing, like the immortal Casey. Either way, Roberto Clemente heard a different drummer, one with a salsa beat, and marched accordingly, his moral compass set on its own peculiar course.

On the field Clemente played, to use his own words, "mad all the time." Off the field he showed more sides than a Rubik's Cube, by turns intelligent, petulant, intense, sensitive, outspoken, and antagonistic—almost as if he carried his bat on one shoulder and his proud ancestry on the other, like a chip.

The young Roberto, obsessed with his dream of becoming a baseball player, grew up in a modest wood house located in San Anton Carolina, Puerto Rico, where he honed his skills by hitting bottle caps with a broomstick and throwing tennis balls against the walls of his house. At the age of eighteen he attended a local tryout camp cosponsored by Dodger scout Al Campanis (yes—*that* Al Campanis). The scout watched, his mouth opening and closing like a fresh-caught fish, as the youngster "threw the hell out of the ball. Then we had timed races—sixty yards. Everybody's running about 7.2, 7.3, which is average major-league time. Then Clemente came and ran a 6.4-plus—that's a track man's time. And in a baseball uniform. I asked him to run again, and he was even faster. He could fly! I said, 'If the son of a gun can hold a bat in his hands, I'm gonna sign this guy.' He got up to the plate and he was hitting nothing but ropes. Line drives. He was the best free-agent athlete I have ever seen."

Despite his obvious credentials, Campanis couldn't sign the underaged Clemente, who signed, instead, with the Santurce club in the Puerto Rican winter league, where he spent the next two seasons playing alongside Willie Mays in the outfield, batting .288. In February of 1954 Clemente finally signed with the Brooklyn Dodgers, for a $5,000 salary plus a $10,000 signing bonus, and was sent to the Dodgers' farm club in Montreal—the same minor-league Ellis Island where another Dodger great, Jackie Robinson, had made his entry into organized ball eight years before.

But even though Clemente was destined to become as idolized by Puerto Ricans and all Latin Americans as Jackie Robinson had been by blacks, he was not destined to become so in a Dodger uniform. For the baseball rules at the time were held together with little more than a bit of mustard seed, and held that a player who had been signed for a bonus of more than $4,000 and not kept on a major-league roster was eligible to be drafted by another team. Ironically, the man who had seen the potential in Robinson, Branch Rickey, was now the general manager of the Pittsburgh Pirates and saw the potential in Clemente too, grabbing him posthaste in the postseason draft.

Clemente was later to confess, "I didn't even know where Pittsburgh was." But he could easily have found out—not by looking in the pages of Rand McNally, but instead by looking on the sports pages, where Pittsburgh was easy to find if you read the National League standings, starting from the bottom. For the Pirates were then the most god-awful team in baseball, a woebegone team that had lost 100 games the previous three seasons. How bad were they? These "Bums of Summer" were so bad that manager Billy Meyer, addressing a group that included Bobby Del Greco, Catfish Metkovich, and a host of others whose names have thankfully escaped memory, had once lamented: "You clowns could go on *What's My Line* in full uniforms and stump the panel."

The twenty-year-old youngster stepped right into the Pirates' starting lineup—right into right field. And from the very first day he stepped onto Forbes Field, anyone with any baseball sense could sense the makings of a future superstar. In the field, Clemente could be seen racing to catch a fly ball and then throwing the ball on a line, cutting down an enemy base runner trying to advance. A mental crayon picture of him in the batter's box would show a hitter standing so far back he would have had to take a taxi to reach the front chalk mark, one foot in the proverbial bucket, feet spread wide, bat held high, rolling his neck and stretching his back; then reaching across the plate to lay the business end of his bat on a curve to the outside and, with a mere snap of the wrists, driving it deep into right-center. And, on the base paths, the mind's eye could catch a glimpse of this beautifully tooled machine racing like a strong current, his helmet flying off, as he stretched a routine single into a double. But however one saw him, he was 100-watt excitement, lighting up the field as few before him.

But while most fans appreciated the sparkling genius of his play for what it was and accepted him, others, especially members of the press, didn't—or maybe, because of the language barrier, couldn't. One early story, written by some dishonest ventriloquist posing as a reporter, had him supposedly spouting gibberish: "I like run all the time. I go 100 meters eleven seconds. Goot? I wance run 400 meters fifty-two seconds. Better? One theeng I like Merica—new autos. I buy myself new auto. Whee!" Embarrassed because of such heavy-handed attempts to burlesque him, the sensitive Clemente crawled into his shell, distrustful of the press.

And then there were his injuries. Over the years Clemente's injuries and illnesses would include everything from malaria to bone chips to food poisoning to insomnia to tension headaches to floating disks, not to mention injuries to arms, shoulders, elbows, hands, back, ankles, thighs, etc., etc. But whereas players in the past—such as Luke Appling, who had lovingly been called Old Aches and Pains for his many complaints—had their complaints accepted at face value, Clemente was unfairly labeled a malingerer.

Clemente, who wore his feelings in open view on his black-and-gold Pirate sleeve, felt misunderstood and underappreciated. And felt that charges of his being a malingerer were further evidence of cultural bias. "When Mickey Mantle says his leg is hurt, it is okay," he complained to a reporter. "If a Latin or a black is sick, they say it is in his head." To a *Sport* magazine interviewer he went into further depth, complaining of baseball's caste system that consigned him to second-class citizenry: "Latin-American Negro ballplayers are treated today much like all Negroes were treated in baseball in the early days of the broken color barrier. They are subjected to prejudices and stamped with generalizations. Because they speak Spanish among themselves, they are set off as a minority within a minority, and they bear the brunt of the sport's remaining racial prejudices."

But instead of brooding, Clemente took bat in hand and proceeded to prove himself. By 1960, the thunder that had taken so long to erupt finally came as Clemente hit .314, led all outfielders in assists, and played a vital role in leading the once-pathetic Pirates to the National League pennant and—in the most two-sided Series of all time, against the Yankees—to a World Series win in seven games, in which he hit safely in all seven games and led the Pirates in total hits.

During the off-season his smoldering pride was further affronted by what he perceived as second-class superstardom when the Baseball Writers selected his teammate, shortstop Dick Groat, as the National League MVP, relegating him to eighth place, with nary a first-place vote in the balloting. Not used to practicing the usual servilities, Clemente complained, "I never say Groat should not win it. I feel I should not be close to tenth." And forever after he refused to wear his 1960 championship ring, preferring instead to wear his 1961 All-Star ring.

For 1961 was indeed the year that Roberto Clemente came into his own as a superstar. Playing as if in his own crucible, he led the National League in batting with an average of .351.

But not only did the year 1961 belong to him, so did the entire decade. Just as Ty Cobb had spread-eagled the decade of the teens and Rogers Hornsby the decade of the twenties, the decade of the sixties was Roberto Clemente's, as he led the Majors in total hits and had the highest batting average over that ten-year period. He won four batting championships, the first right-handed batter since Hornsby to do so, and also won, at last, recognition from the Baseball Writers, who voted him the National League's Most Valuable Player in 1966—although truth to tell, they could have given it to him for the entire ten-year period.

That Most Valuable Player award was more than a personal Everest—it was Clemente's crusade for all Latino players. Clemente had now become their paterfamilias, their leader. He would take them under his wing, as he did with Matty Alou, teaching him to punch the ball to left, a move that enabled Alou to win the National League batting championship. And he would stand up for the rights of all of them. He was, in the words of Orlando Cepeda, "a leader to all Latin Americans." And, to Minnie Minoso, "an inspiration."

But his bat and leadership were only part of the picture. For Roberto Clemente was a complete player, one whose feats of arm were legendary as he cut down player after player tempting the fates—and Clemente—by trying for another base. One who remembered his arm was Cepeda, who told of Clemente throwing him out with an arrow-straight throw that was particularly striking to the optic nerve. "I was on second," remembered Cepeda, "and running on the pitch. Tim McCarver hit a line drive to right field. I rounded third and when I looked up, the catcher was waiting for me with the ball. I couldn't believe it! It was impossible! The very next inning, he did the same thing to Lou Brock." Cepeda and Brock were but a couple of the 266 the rifle arm of Clemente cut down during his eighteen-year career.

To shoplift a line from Jim Murray: "Roberto Clemente might have been as good a player as ever played the game." And Roger Angell, baseball's poet laureate, after watching Clemente in the 1971 World Series, wrote that Clemente played "a kind of baseball that none of us had ever seen before—throwing and running and hitting at something close to the level of perfection."

But Clemente was more than a ballplayer—he was also a caring individual. That showed when, after doubling for his 3,000th hit in his last regular-season at-bat, he dedicated the hit "to the fans of Pittsburgh and to the people of Puerto Rico." And his caring further showed when, on the morning of December 31, 1972, he lost his life going down with an overloaded cargo plane he was taking down to Nicaragua to help the victims of an earthquake.

Roberto Clemente was indeed a great athlete. But he was more, much more, one with many sides to him—all of them great.

54

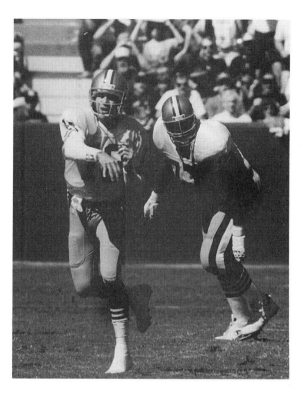

Joe Montana

b. 1956

With the possible exception of the fictional Phineas Fogg, nobody, but nobody, has ever defied time and gotten away with it better than Joe Montana. A human time machine, Montana made the clock his ally in last-second comebacks so late they could be asterisked like delayed flights on an airport departures board.

Montana's pedigree was impressive, coming as he did from that western section of Pennsylvania where they mine lodes of coal and quarterbacks—including the likes of Johnny Lujack, Arnie Galiffa, George Blanda, Joe Namath, and Jim Kelly, to name but a few. Not only was Montana an outstanding addition to this tradition of excellence, but his feats were such that he could take his place in their company and not have to stand in the back row for the group photo. Instead, based on his eleventh-hour heroics, he could take his place front and center.

Those last-second heroics began, fittingly enough, at Notre Dame, where such miraculous occurrences seemed to happen almost as if they were foreordained—going all the way back to the Irish's come-from-behind win over Ohio State in 1935 just as the clock was set to strike twelve. But before the slipper was fit to his foot, Montana would spend his freshman year performing as what he called Practice-Dummy Montana in those sinew-cracking exercises known as team practices. By his sophomore year, the youth with a faceful of politeness and manners to match would prove that although soft of manner, he could be hard as nails when the situation dictated. As North Carolina, the first of many parties of the second part, would find out.

With Carolina leading, 14–6, late in the fourth quarter, Notre Dame coach Dan Devine brought in Montana from the bench to rejuvenate the sputtering Irish offense. First, running the team effectively and the clock efficiently, Montana took the Irish seventy-three yards in just five plays and then added a 2-point conversion on a pass to tie the score at 14-all. Then, with just 1:15 to go and the ball on Notre Dame's 20-yard line, he threw an 80-yard completion for the winning TD. In the postgame locker room, athletic director Moose Krause told the team, in concert assembled, "I've been around since the days of Knute Rockne, and I'm telling you this was the greatest comeback by a Notre Dame team I've ever seen."

But in the immortal words of Al Jolson, Notre Dame fans and Joe Montana fans-to-be "ain't seen nothin' yet." There was a comeback against Air Force after the Irish were down 30–7 at the half; a comeback against Purdue after his team trailed 24–14 with less than two minutes left in the third quarter; and that Mother of All College Comebacks, the 1979 Cotton Bowl against Houston.

It was an utterly improbable scenario. The game, Montana's last in a Notre Dame uniform, was played in conditions more suitable for alpine skiing than football, with sleet and winds turning the Cotton Bowl field into an unnavigable ice floe. To add to the story line, Montana had come down with a case of the flu the week before the game. Come the third period, with the score 34–12, Houston, our hero-designate had been consigned to the bench, as weak as a vegetarian dog, his body temperature registering just 96 degrees and racked with a bad case of "the shakes" that registered about 5.5 on the Richter scale. All of which sounded like a complication of disorders even a miracle would fail to correct. But after being fed a modern miracle drug known as chicken noodle soup, Montana reentered the game late in the third quarter. And would soon prove that holding a lead against a Montana-led team is merely a transitory act, one subject to discontinuation on a second's notice—or, in this case, a quarter's notice.

The normal fan wouldn't have given the chances of a Montana comeback enough thought to cause a headache equal to the one Montana himself was suffering. But, in the fourth quarter, with the hurricane-like winds at his back and going into that end of the field where all 46 points had been scored, Montana began to do that voodoo he did so well. First, Notre Dame scored with 7:37 left and Montana added the 2 points on a pass to Vegas Ferguson. 34–20, Houston. Then, after taking over on the Irish 39-yard line with 5:40 to go, Montana engineered a six-play drive in just one minute and twenty-two seconds, going in for the score himself on a 2-yard run. Another 2-point conversion followed. 34–28, Houston.

But then Montana apparently fumbled away Notre Dame's last chance when the ball was stripped from his hand while he was running at the Houston 20. However, Houston, trying mightily to accommodate the Fates, which are abnormally partial to come-backs, gave the ball back to the Irish with twenty-eight seconds left on the clock. With ice water in his veins to match the sleet coming down, Montana worked the ball down to the Houston 8-yard line with just six seconds left in the game. Montana now called an "out" pattern to Kris Haines. But his pass was low and away, incomplete. Two seconds now remained.

At this point Coach Devine called Montana over to the sidelines to confer with him on the next—and final—play. Contrary to popular belief—a belief best captured by a wonder-ful Gallagher cartoon that ran in *True* magazine back in 1969 showing a large, robe-clad hand coming out of lightning-laden clouds with a piece of paper extended toward huddled ball-players and an announcer, up in the press box, intoning, "Here's a play coming in for Notre Dame!"—this play would be called by Devine and Montana, not some Higher Divine Authority. "Joe, one shot—what do you think?" asked Devine. There must have been some argument against it, but unable to marshal any facts, Montana answered, "I like the same play again." "Okay, run it again," said Devine, sending Montana back out on the field, back to the well. And, Montana threw the same low pass to a space the size of half a napkin and Haines dived, catching the ball in the right corner of the end zone before rolling out. 34–34. The extra point, with no time left, gave Notre Dame the win, 35–34. And the greatest comeback in collegiate history.

Montana next took his pocketful of miracles to the San Francisco 49ers, which drafted him in the '79 draft on the third round, the eighty-second pick overall. The 49ers were, at best, a threadbare and lackluster team, their biggest star O. J. Simpson, then on his last legs, literally. San Francisco fans were easily identifiable by their hunched shoulders and looks of shellshock, many of them having started rooting, like writer Peter King, "for the 49ers when the team's only marquee player was a kickoff returner named Abe Woodson." And then, as an afterthought, King added, "Now think about that. Only on a truly bad team does the poor guy who runs back kicks after opponents score emerge as a star." And the current edition was *that* bad, as attested to by the team's 2–14 record in '78.

Under new 49er head coach Bill Walsh, there was an immediate changing of the guard—and tackle and running back as well. But not quarterback. And so Montana spent his rookie season wearing down the seat of his new uniform behind starting QB Steve DeBerg—who threw an NFL-record 578 times— getting in to throw only 23 passes, one of those a TD, a 16-yarder in the twelfth week of another of San Francisco's fourteen losses as it again went 2–14.

The 1980 season began where '79 had left off, with DeBerg as the starting QB and Montana the backup. But by Week Seven, Walsh decided to alternate his quarterbacking currencies, and Montana responded by giving the team a much-needed electric charge with his mobility and intelligent play. In Week Fourteen he gave another hint of what was to come as he brought the 49ers back from a 35–7 deficit, rallying to beat the Saints on a 71-yard bomb to Dwight Clark, a 14-yard scoring pass to Freddie Solomon, and a 1-yard TD plunge of his own for a 38–35 win. Overall, he completed 176 of his 273 passes for a league-leading .645 completion percentage. And, not incidentally, the 49ers went to 6–10.

The 1981 season was to be something else altogether as Walsh, deciding that Montana was his quarterback of the future, traded DeBerg and gave the ball to Joe. Montana proved that the future was now as he led the 49ers to a 13–3 record and their first NFC Western Conference championship since 1972, using the running game only to set up an all-out passing attack. Completing 311 of his 488 attempts for a .637 completion average, Montana ranked No. 1 among quarterbacks. And, in the process, engineered three come-from-behind victories, including one over the Rams as the clock expired.

But even though Montana would compile comeback after comeback, he would hang his helmet on just one: the 1982 NFC title game against the Dallas Cowboys, a game known forevermore in San Francisco lore for "the Catch." With 4:19 left in the game and the 49ers down 27–21, Montana, maintaining a polite fiction of the clock's nonexistence, moved the team inexorably downfield. Then, with the clock down to just fifty-eight seconds, and counting, and the ball on Dallas's 6-yard line, Montana dropped back, pressured by three members of the Dallas Doomsday II defense, who were bearing down on him like avenging angels of death. Just before he was buried, Montana got the ball off, throwing it high to the back of the end zone, where Dwight Clark, running across from left to right, leaped to the full extent of his six feet four inches to pull it down.

Two weeks later Montana would lead San Francisco to a Super Bowl win over the Cincinnati Bengals, completing 14 of 22 passes and winning MVP honors. Three more times "Mr. January" would lead 49er teams to Super Bowl wins, including a come-from-behind win in Super Bowl XXIII over the same Bengals when he engineered the greatest drive in Super Bowl history, a 92-yard effort that saw Montana direct a hurry-up offense against man-to-man coverage, completing one short pass after another to first Jerry Rice, then John Taylor, then Rice again, until, with just thirty-four seconds left, he hit Taylor for a 10-yard TD to give San Francisco an unbelievable 20–16 win.

It was during that same Super Bowl game, just before the start of the 92-yard drive, that Montana showed why he had won the handle "Joe Cool." According to guard Randy Cross, as the other 49ers bent over in the huddle, tensed in anticipation of his first call on the soon-to-be eleven-play drive, "He was looking over toward the Bengals' sideline and he had a funny look on his face. He said, 'Hey, isn't that John Candy over there? Yeah, I guess it is.'" Ten plays later, Candy or no Candy, Montana fired a bonbon to Taylor for the come-from-behind win.

Throughout his storied career, Montana has always seemed to be operating with the assurance of a riverboat gambler, less passing the ball than pulling winning cards out of his sleeve. Twenty-nine times he has rallied his troops back from the brink of defeat by coming to life like a clockwork toy when the scoreboard clock's hands have pointed to the final minute of play.

With injuries compromising his greatness and the flame that had once ignited into being at his every command now but a dull ache and a flicker, he was able to make it flicker one more time as he pulled off still another comeback, this time in 1993 with the Kansas City Chiefs, as he took them to their first AFC Western Division championship since 1971—and then, unbelievably, brought them back in two divisional playoff games with two more patented come-from-behind wins, the twenty-eighth and twenty-ninth of his NFL career.

For Joe Montana always played as if the faint of heart never won so much as a scrap of paper. And, in doing so, this Cinderella in cleats staged more comebacks than Frank Sinatra and Sarah Bernhardt combined.

55

Larry Bird

b. 1956

If, the first time you ever laid eyes on Larry Bird, someone had told you he was a future basketball superstar, you might have thought yourself a prime candidate for believing anything. The hero of *White Men Can't Jump*, maybe; a superstar, never, his physical credentials unable to stand up to even the vaguest sort of examination. For starters, he couldn't run, his movements almost slo-mo as he waddled more than ran on ducklike legs that were strangers to each other. Then there was his shot, an anything-but-eloquent one-hander which began with his cradling the ball behind his ear and ended with his launching it basketward like a fly-cast off his shoulder, within seemingly easy reach of the probing and prying hands of any and all defenders. And, finally, there was his inability to jump, a shortcoming called White Man's Disease in NBA locker rooms and one which he joked about, saying "a piece of paper couldn't be slid under my sneakers when I jump."

How could a player with so many athletic strikes against him become one of the all-time greats? Maybe it had to do with those indefinable somethings called intangibles which made the complete package called Larry Bird one which far exceeded the sum of its parts. "Basketball was never a recreation for me. It was something I fell in love with. I just played basketball and always tried to do everything possible to win," he said in trying to explain what made Larry run, shoot, jump—and win.

Bird's improbable rise to superstardom began in the equally improbable town of French Lick, Indiana, a town so small drivers passing through thought its name was "Resume Speed." There he sought refuge in his "love," using it as a means of escape from his hardscrabble, small-town Indiana background, much as his inner-city counterparts sought an escape from their dire circumstances by playing "the City Game." As a tall, gawky teenager with a head of cotton-candy hair and an obstinate I-can-do-it jaw, the young Bird averaged 31 points, 21 rebounds, and 9 assists in his senior year at small Springs Valley High School, becoming, in the process, all-State.

College coaches, however, were underwhelmed by his skills, convinced there was less to his play than met the eye. Coach Joe B. Hall of Kentucky, after giving him a look-see, determined that Bird was too slow to fit into the Wildcats' fast-break style of basketball. Indiana's Bobby Knight, after watching the gangly youngster in action, could only shake his head and say, "The kid must learn to shoot a jump shot." Still, Knight offered him a scholarship to IU. But the seventeen-year-old Bird, library-quiet and small-townish, felt intimidated by the sprawling Bloomington campus and, after only six weeks, packed his bags and returned to French Lick. He next enrolled in a little local junior college, Northwood Institute, but dropped out of there too when he learned he would have to stay two years before applying to a four-year college. Returning once again to French Lick, Bird got a job driving a municipal garbage truck to help support his mother and played a little AAU basketball on the side, his dreams of a college career apparently at a dead end.

At this point the basketball gods in the sky stepped in to give one of those soon-to-be-numbered-in-their-pantheon-of-greats an off-ramp, a way out, by offering up a scholarship from out of the proverbial azure blue to Indiana State University. And so it was that Bird enrolled in the little-known school, nestled, as balladeers are wont to sing, "on the banks of the Wabash" in Terre Haute, there to play for the aptly named Sycamores.

After serving as a member in good sitting by sitting out his first year as a transfer student, Bird suited up for the 1976–77 season and scored 32.8 points while pulling down 13.3 rebounds a game as he led the Sycamores to their best-ever record, 25–3. His junior season was more of the same, as the Bird-led Sycamores reached the NIT quarterfinals and Bird finished second in the nation in scoring with a 30.0 average. Still, both Indiana State and Larry Bird remained submerged in anonymity, their accomplishments world-famous only in that part of the world located on the banks of the Wabash.

The 1978–79 season was to change all that. For that was the season Bird truly soared high, finishing second in the nation in scoring and fourth in rebounding and being named College Player of the Year. It was also the season he single-handedly carried some of the most unrecognizable names this side of the Riga telephone book from the obscure college in Terre Haute to the No. 1 position in the national rankings, a position they held all year until the final game of the season, when they lost to Magic Johnson's Michigan State team in the NCAA championship game. It would be the first time Bird's and Magic's names would be linked. But hardly the last.

From the time they entered the NBA together in 1979, Larry Bird and Magic Johnson would form a bicoastal rivalry, one which would light up the sport. But while one craved the spotlight, the other was reserved and quiet in the face of public glare. That became evident on the night of April 6, 1979, when the big kid from the small Indiana town with the odd name first set foot in the big city with the odd accents, Boston.

Celtic president Red Auerbach remembers taking one look at the face that looked like it came right off the side of a barn, next to the Red Man chewing tobacco sign, and thinking, "He looks like a country bumpkin." But country bumpkin or no, Auerbach knew Larry Bird was the future of a franchise that was in the process of going 29–53 and had nowhere to go but up. And

so, on this night, after Auerbach had signed Bird to his first
Celtic contract, he trotted him out to the Boston Garden, there to
introduce him to the fans, most of whom were there to see him,
not the Celts, who predictably lost again. And to the press, which,
trying to pry something, anything, out of the newest Celt on the
block, were reduced to counting each and every word he tossed
their way, his verbal recitations coming in sentences so short they
made a grade-school primer seem as long as a legal brief.

After the game, Bird, tired of being on display, meandered
off on his own in search of local flora and fauna. Sometime
around 1 A.M., assistant general manager Jeff Cohen got a frantic
call at home to come and fetch the newest member of the Celtics,
who had somehow, some way, found a watering hole in one of the
toughest neighborhoods in downtown Boston. Arriving at the
appointed spot posthaste, Cohen raced in, and what to his
wondering eyes should appear but a scene with "Bird up against
the bar with these guys, wearing his Mack cap and his overalls
and having a great time. He was fitting in with them beautifully.
He was making fans."

The player who would refer to himself in time as the "Hick
from French Lick" also fit in beautifully with his new teammates,
alchemistically changing them into immediate winners. In his
first year the Celtics became the league's winningest team and
Bird was named NBA Rookie of the Year for his part in the team's
turnaround. For an encore he led the Celts to the NBA championship in his second season. And, from that point on, the
player the press called Larry Legend would continue to rewrite
that legend each and every year, so much so that in 1986, after
only seven years in the NBA, a Dallas newspaper poll of sixty
leading basketball authorities selected him as the greatest forward ever to play the game.

An overall picture of Larry Bird would be next to impossible
to paint in words. But there are a few scenes culled from the many
that bear retelling, etched more than painted in the memory of
those who saw him.

Xavier McDaniel, X of the Supersonics, remembers the
Seattle-Boston game when, with time-out called and scant seconds remaining in a tie game, Bird hollered at him, "When I
come back I'm going to throw up a shot from right here!"
pointing to a spot on the parquet floor halfway to Providence—
and then fulfilled his promise when play resumed by squeezing

off a delicate swisher to win the game. Admitting that "like a gymnast, I'm into degree of difficulty," Bird would let shots go up with either hand—he writes and eats with his left hand—and sometimes call out "Left hand!" to opponents while releasing a southpaw shot to claim a mental dividend when the ball went in, which it most often did. Writer Fred Kerber remembers one All-Star Game workout when Bird set up shop shooting "his" shot, the one from twenty-three feet nine inches out that made him, in the words of *Sports Illustrated*, "the king of the three-point shot." And incredibly, throwing up brick after brick. Muttering to himself, Bird looked over to a little knot of reporters standing around and said something or other about needing an incentive. One of the ink-stained wretches, only too happy to oblige, offered up a $10 wager on Bird's next shot. Bird "thought over" the proposition for less time than it takes to read this, then turned and threw up a well-aimed shaft that touched nothing but net. And then, the two horizontal slits he used for eyes suddenly lighting up as he laughed, the smile filling his face, he said, "There's one born every minute."

His passing was such that astronomer Carl Sagan could only say: "Larry Bird threads a precise, no-looks pass." Teammate Dennis Johnson, who credited Bird and Magic with having changed pro basketball from a scoring game to a team game, remembers a few Celtics "moving the ball and telling the other guys, 'If you move, we'll get the ball to you. Larry will see you.'" And writer Steve Jacobson remembers the time Bird was seemingly trapped by two defenders, pinned down at the baseline, back to basket, facing the right corner and without an escape route. The teammate, open by virtue of the double-teaming on Bird, came down the right side of the court looking for the ball, but Bird, caught in a momentary cul-de-sac, had no way of getting the ball to him. Or so it seemed. But Bird, working both his hands and his rabbit foot successfully, merely punched the ball off his right hand with his left fist through the dense thicket of arms surrounding him—directly into the hands of his teammate for an easy basket.

And then there was "the STEAL!"—an act so big it would forever be written in capital letters in baskektball lore. It happened in the 1987 playoffs when Bird, with the touch of a pickpocket, agilely stepped in front of an Isaiah Thomas inbounds pass and fed to a cutting Dennis Johnson for the game-winning shot as Boston defeated Detroit in Game 5 of the Eastern Conference finals. The theft picked Isaiah clean, taking everything but his wallet—even pride. Left to open and close his mouth like a fish out of water, when he opened it next all his frustration at being burgled and humiliated poured out and, in a statement eloquent in its anger, said, "If Bird were a black guy, he'd just be another player." Thomas's statement was so patently ridiculous that, according to writer Jim Murray, "even his teammates hooted at him," the players having referred to Bird for years as "Our brother from another planet."

Thomas's statement had also missed the quintessential Larry Bird. For, like the man he came into the league with and would, ironically, leave at the same time with—Magic—Bird was part athletic ability, part hard work, and all player. To allocate those offensive hot-buttons, "athleticism" and "natural talent" to one and "hard work" to the other would insult both the words and the players.

For Larry Bird transcended all such labels. Single-handedly, this rare Bird had made dust out of conventional wisdom: that rural whites cannot play the black inner-city game, and that you must possess certain basic skills to play the game well. For even though he was not cut from the normal pattern, Larry Bird had cut and restitched his skills to fit his own hard-hat game, an overwhelming game which combined touch, toughness, and a killer instinct. And with those qualities, the man who couldn't jump had risen to epic heights.

56

Eddie Arcaro

b. 1916

Great athletes come in all sizes, but few smaller than Eddie Arcaro, whose shadow measured no more than five feet two inches. But what a shadow he cast, inseparable as it was from the 1,200 pounds of horseflesh under his control, as he booted, hand-rode, elbowed, and kicked some 4,779 winners across the finish line in his three decades in the saddle.

To most bettors, Arcaro's very presence in the saddle was the same as getting money from home without writing, as the man they affectionately called Banana Nose, for obvious reasons, finished in the money on more than half the twenty-four thousand horses he rode. Heeding the time-honored adage of horse trainer Sunny Jim Fitzsimmons that a good jock "does not impede the animal," Arcaro fit his mounts like a well-suited saddle. And handled them with the sensitive touch of a piano player, earning him the label "the Master" amongst the jockey brotherhood.

However, at the beginning of his career Arcaro looked like anything but a "master." In fact, he barely looked like a "mister." And the odds against him becoming either were prohibitive, at best.

Quitting the Cincinnati public school system at the age of thirteen, Eddie got a job at nearby Latonia Race Track galloping horses at 50 cents a romp, mostly on credit. After months and months of wageless and thankless service, and more than a few taunts from trainers that he would never become a rider, the youngster took off for California, where a gypsy trainer named Clarence Davison gave him his first chance.

But his first win was unforthcoming. In fact, in stories lengthening like Pinocchio's nose—which is only fair considering the size of Arcaro's—his first 45 or 100 or 250 starts were unforthcoming.

Arcaro entered the winner's circle for the first time on January 14, 1932, aboard a plater named Eagle Bird. With a fire in his soul and a style that saw him treating the rules in a cavalier manner, as gladiatorial as a hornet, Arcaro grew into a scrapping rider.

He was soon marked as a rough and dangerous rider, always riding like he was an accident on its way to happening. One Washington Park official described him as "a kid who either had to be awfully lucky or get killed."

One extraordinary council of war at Arlington Park best illustrated Arcaro's hard-bitten style. Finding himself on the rail, all but hidden from the judges, Arcaro expertly slid a foot out and held the leg of a rival jockey all the way to the finish line. When the stewards inquired of Arcaro whether he had interfered with the ride of his rival, Arcaro's answer was, "Not so's you'd notice it." For that he was set down for the rest of the meet.

Another time, at Aqueduct, the hot-tempered Arcaro, sure that another jockey had deliberately interfered with him, tried to drive him into the rail and knock him off his horse. When called upon by the stewards to explain his actions, Arcaro, growling and sounding like he had just swallowed something or other, told the authorities that he was only sorry he hadn't thrown his tormentor into the infield. For that infraction Arcaro's license was revoked for a year.

But still, through it all, Arcaro was a proven winner, one who desired only what he could accomplish. And he could accomplish much, as attested to by his 132 winners in 1933 and his continued streak the next year, a streak that caught the attention of Warren Wright, then putting together his formidable Calumet Farm stable. Wright bought Arcaro's contract, and with that Arcaro went from riding nags and bags that were just one step short of pulling milk carts to riding some of the finest thoroughbreds in the game.

Two years later, despite a contract that in essence read "'til obituary notices do we part," Arcaro again moved, this time jumping from Calumet to Mrs. Payne Whitney's prestigious Greentree Stable. It was while at Greentree that Arcaro got his first big break. With Greentree having no entry in the 1938 Kentucky Derby, Arcaro was offered a chance to ride Lawrin by "Plain Ben" Jones, Lawrin's trainer. It was a chance he grabbed, and never regretted. Jones told Arcaro that Lawrin would give him an eighth of a mile in eleven seconds whenever he decided to make his move, and the timing was up to Arcaro. Arcaro rated his horse for three-quarters of a mile, holding him back without punishing him. Then, at the mile, he referred the matter to his boot and booted Lawrin home for the jockey's first smell of the roses. Netting $4,705 as his share of the purse, Arcaro had reached the top of his profession on that Grade-A May Day in Louisville.

From that point on, Arcaro rode with the fire but not the fury of his earlier days, his rough-and-tumble style replaced by one that encompassed intelligence and sensitivity. So much so that that other great authority on horseflesh, Willie Shoemaker, was moved to say, "Eddie Arcaro was the greatest rider I ever saw. He could do everything. The way he rides, he looks like part of the horse."

The tandem of Arcaro and the horse he came in on finished ahead of the field in 554 stakes races—including a record seventeen Triple Crown races aboard the likes of Crown winners Whirlaway and Citation—making him "the King of the Stakes Riders." He was, if not the greatest jock in all racing history, a man whose shadow had grown so large by the end of his illustrious career that *Sports Illustrated* called him "the most famous man to ride a horse since Paul Revere."

57

Henry Armstrong

b. 1912–1988

Henry Armstrong was a physical loan shark, a fighter who adopted General Clausewitz's theory that the winning general is the one who can impose his will upon the enemy. One hundred and forty-five times, Armstrong imposed his will on his opponents, suffocating them in his swarming style, firing off his punches, and then running over them.

But the perpetual-motion machine might have been a mere footnote to boxing history, more a curio than a contributor, had it not been for the fact that one of the members of his managerial brain trust was entertainer Al Jolson. And that Armstrong's greatest year, 1937, was also the year of Joe Louis.

Until 1934, Henry Armstrong had been a struggling feather-weight, fighting in and around Los Angeles with mixed results against opponents who will remain almost as unknown as the soldier under the tombstone in Arlington National Cemetery. During one of the weekly Hollywood Legion fights, in front of a star-studded crowd, Armstrong distinguished himself, scoring a sensational knockout. Two of the stars in attendance, Al Jolson and wife Ruby Keeler, took a liking to the human hurricane and underwrote the purchase of his contract for their friend, Eddie Meade. All of a sudden, Armstrong's fortunes improved. And so did the caliber of his opponents.

By 1937, betting on Armstrong was more bankable than Shirley Temple's *Little Miss Marker*. He fought an incredible twenty-seven times that year and won all but one of those bouts by knockout. Together, Armstrong and his manager didn't care what his opponents weighed or what their credentials were. They took on anybody and everybody, regardless of race, creed, or weight, fighting featherweights, a few lightweights, and a sprinkling of welterweights as well.

But because Joe Louis had just won the heavyweight championship and because Armstrong never shared Louis's celebrity, they determined a course of action that would make them more money. And, not incidentally, make ring history at the same time.

Armstrong remembered the meeting between Meade, himself, Jolson, and George Raft, another financial backer: "Joe Louis was going to take all the popularity, everything, away from me, from all the fighters, because everyone was saving their money to see Joe Louis fight." That's when someone hit upon the idea that would rival all the ideas that spilled out of the Hollywood "Dream Factories" in those golden days of pictures, all spelled "colossal," "stupendous," and "bigger-than-life." The idea, simply stated, was to embark on a course that would win Armstrong three titles. Simultaneously.

Meade started moving Armstrong along in the boxing world willfully, their collective eye on the three brass rings. Armstrong took the first olive out of the jar in October 1937: the feather-weight title, beating Petey Sarron in six rounds. With the 126-pound title stashed away, Armstrong turned toward heavier foes and more lucrative bouts. Fourteen more fights and fourteen more wins followed, and then Armstrong was matched to fight welterweight champion Barney Ross. The perpetual-motion machine took the fight to Ross and the crown away from the gallant warrior, halting his whirlwind attack only long enough to carry Ross through the last five rounds.

With the welterweight title now added to his growing list of crowns, the man who sought more titles than Charlemagne dropped down to the lightweight limit to wrest the lightweight crown from Lou Ambers, playing the part of the original rubber man, in a brutal fight that had Armstrong swallowing his own blood for the last six rounds in fear that the bout would be stopped.

Three titles in a little more than nine months—a hat trick that was indeed something "stupendous," "colossal," and "bigger-than-life."

No one who ever saw the fighter known as Hammerin' Hank or Homicide Hank or Hurricane Hank will ever forget him: a nonstop punching machine, his style more rhythmic than head-long, his matchstick legs akimbo, his arms crossed in front of his face, racing the clock with each punch and each punch punctuated by a grunt. And each bout, it sometimes seemed, punctuated with a crown.

58

Mickey Mantle

1931–1995

Someone or other once opined that the door to greatness rarely needs a picked lock, only the right combination to open it. And so it was with Mickey Charles Mantle, who, after ten years of flashing his brilliance on and off, like a loose electrical connection, finally found the right combination.

Mantle's potential for greatness was first displayed in the winter of 1951. Just two years out of high school and with two years of organized ball behind him, the youngster had so impressed the Yankee powers-that-be that they invited him to their Phoenix training facility. There he exhibited his talents, batting the ball into the stands some five hundred feet away and running the base paths in 3.1 seconds, faster than anyone then on the team.

The Yankee brass, salivating as they watched the switch-hitting phenomenon disassemble the ball, decided then and there that this perfect specimen of a man with boyish, tousled good looks would be the replacement for a fading Joe DiMaggio.

From that moment on, Mantle's glass slipper was measured for greatness. The Yankee publicity department began trumpeting the arrival of the next superstar in the Yankee dynasty, making him baseball's biggest story. Depending upon which inspired press release one read, he could (A) outrun rabbits and Rolls-Royces; (B) strike the ball with the sound of an explosion capable of killing three or four innocent bystanders; (C) throw with the might of a howitzer; or (D) all of the above.

But in New York, such claims are viewed with cynicism. And even though Mantle brought with him a veritable smorgasbord of talents, the largest being his strength—coming from his size-17½ neck and a set of shoulders you could serve a sit-down dinner for six on—the quiet country boy who could hit the ball a proverbial country mile couldn't quite justify his massive buildup. The fans, feeling their faith in Gibraltar had been misplaced, began taking out their frustrations on the youngster, even to the point of jeering him. He began to show the signs of strain, and sulked. And so, to relieve the pressure on him, the Yankees sent him back down to the minors.

Down at Kansas City the young Mantle continued to struggle, both at the plate and with his own self-doubts. With only one hit in his first twenty-two at-bats—and that a bunt single—a depressed Mantle told his father, "I'm not good enough to play in the Majors and I'm not good enough to play here. I'll never make it." His father, who had named his son after his own boyhood baseball idol, Mickey Cochrane, could only shake his head and say, "Well, Mick, if that's all the guts you have, I think you better quit." It was a psychological crossroads for the youngster, and he chose the right path, as he batted .410 for the rest of the season. The Yankees reconfirmed their faith in their future by calling him up before the end of the '51 season, just in time for the World Series.

Mantle started the Series in right field. But in the fifth inning of the second game, racing across Yankee Stadium's "Death Valley" with manifest gusto toward a long drive by Willie Mays—which would be caught by DiMaggio in right-center—he stepped into a drainage ditch and wrenched his right knee. It was to be but the first in a long list of injuries that would greatly compromise his greatness.

By 1952, DiMaggio was gone and Mantle had taken his place in center—but not in the hearts of those fans in that psychiatric chamber known as Yankee Stadium. Freighted with the baggage and expectations of promised greatness, the heir-assumptive to DiMag's mantle was struggling, alternating between driving balls into the wild blue yonder and striking out like an immense sail going limp in a change of wind. One time, almost tearful in indignation after striking out for one of the 111 times he would do so that season, Mantle took out his frustration on a water cooler in the dugout. "That water cooler ain't striking you out, son," gravel-voiced Casey Stengel, the Yankees' manager, offered. But Mantle continued kicking it anyway.

For the next two years, between taking time off to watch his bones mend, the remantled Mantle continued to deliver prodigious blast after prodigious blast—one of which became known as a "tape-measure job," going some 565 feet—as he finally began striding toward the greatness that had been forecast for him. Then, in 1955, as the Yankees once again reigned supreme, he became their biggest rainmaker, for the first time walking more than striking out, and leading the league in home runs. But the best was yet to come.

In 1956, Mantle—whose highest batting average heretofore had been .311 (an average twice bettered by crosstown rival Willie Mays) and whose highest home run total had been 37 (three times bettered by another crosstown rival, Duke Snider)—was suddenly an overnight sensation, even if it had taken him five years to become one. During the 1956 season, Stan Musial, the six-time batting champion, told writer Roger Kahn "The kid looked different in the spring. He always struck out a lot, but now he was letting bad pitches go. If he hits sixty homers and bats .400 now, I can't say I'll be surprised."

And there were others. Lou Boudreau said "Ted Williams could never hit as hard as Mantle." And Al Lopez, the courtly manager of the Cleveland Indians, who had been in baseball since 1928, added, "Mantle has more power than Babe Ruth." But perhaps the most telling endorsement came from Bill Dickey, the Yankee batting coach who had played with both Ruth and Lou Gehrig: "I thought when I was playing with Ruth and Gehrig, I was seeing all I was ever gonna see," said Dickey. "But this kid...Ruth and Gehrig had power, but I've seen Mickey hit seven balls, seven, so far...and I've never seen nothing like it."

In 1956, the hero-designate became a hero in fact as he bashed, mashed, and slashed the ball from both sides of the plate to lead the league in runs batted in, home runs, and batting average for the Triple Crown—and the Most Valuable Player award as well.

But the year that finally and firmly solidified Mantle's place in the public esteem was 1961. That was the year that both Mantle and the new Yankee on the block, Roger Maris, took off in quest of baseball's version of the Holy Grail: Babe Ruth's seemingly insurmountable record of 60 home runs in a season. As the season progressed and Mantle & Maris continued to keep pace with the home run Everest, the fans began to pull for Mantle, and almost *against* Maris. But as the days dwindled down, Mantle had to remove himself from the chase, his struggle against Ruth's record losing out to his struggle against pain and injury. And Maris was left to go it alone, taking the slings and arrows of the press and the fans that had once been aimed at Mantle.

All of a sudden Mantle was being toasted and coffeed as a worthy successor to the great Yankees of yesteryear: Ruth, Gehrig, and DiMaggio. He was now "The Mick."

Once accepted merely for his power surges and now accepted for his stellar brightness, the once-surly Mantle mellowed, befitting a legend. For the next seven years Number 7 enjoyed his celebrity, until, in 1968, his knees so dead you could wrap crepe around them, he was forced to retire. But not before he had walked through that door marked "Greatness."

59

Sebastian Coe

b. 1956

Going all the way back to antiquity, the number of father-and-son tandems that have proven successful can be entered on the head of a pin, with more than enough room left over for the Lord's Prayer. Oh, sure, there have been some success stories, like the proverbial carpenter's or piper's son of folklore who went on to become the pride of their fathers; but most, like the biblical Absalom, became instead the calamity of their fathers.

One father-and-son tandem which succeeded as a fusion rather than fail as a fission was that of Peter and Sebastian Coe. And therein hangs our tale of the greatest middle-distance runner of all time.

Born in London, where people in all walks of life prefer to ride, Sebastian—a name abbreviated to "Seb"—preferred to run. Everywhere. "It seems that from the time I could walk, I preferred to run," he would later remember. "It just seemed natural. I would regularly run two miles or so into town and back again on errands for my mother, never using a bicycle, preferring the feeling of running. I never walked anywhere, it seems."

Father Peter, watching his son run the way a beagle chases a rabbit—instinctively—worked at harnessing that natural ability. Finding that he had the rare youngster who would allow himself to be pushed, the self-taught coach-trainer pushed his son into doing thousands of sprint repetitions and almost as many rigorous uphill runs, all the better to develop Seb's wind and leg strength—leg strength that would later carry him to the lofty heights from which he would ultimately look down on the rest of the track world.

Young Seb joined a club called the Hallanshire Harriers at the age of twelve, and it began to look like the watering of last year's crops as he won race after race, almost in a stop-me-if-you've-heard-this-one-before manner. But while Seb won several junior events, he was far from all-winning. And his times paled in comparison to those of another, more promising junior, Steve Ovett. Still, Father Peter, sensing that his son had all the paraphernalia of a great, began to train his son for speed. And from that point on, the only thing that mattered to Coe & Son was "speed, speed, speed..."

By the age of twenty, the five-foot nine-inch runner with the frame of a coat rack and no other physical dimensions to speak of was regarded as a good prospect, but still not of the class of Ovett. However, he was to change that during the 1977 season by first winning the Emsley Carr Mile in 3:57.67 for his first important victory and than bettering Ovett's United Kingdom 800 record with a 1:44.76.

Unfettered by normal metes and bounds, Seb, more as an explorer than a glutton, tried a veritable smorgasbord of distances to enhance his speed.

The speed training paid off, handsomely, during the '78 season, as Seb won a 400-meter race in 48-flat, ran a relay leg in 47.3, and lowered the UK record in the 800 to 1:44.25, less than a second from Alberto Juantorena's world record.

All of which served merely as the parsley on Seb's platter.

The real meat and potatoes of the '78 season was the mile at the European Championships at Prague and his matchup with Ovett, the first time the two had raced head-to-head—or foot-to-foot, as may be the case.

Going into the matchup, Seb was hardly hale and hearty; damaged merchandise might be more like it. For not only had he stepped into a posthole earlier that spring, rupturing his ankle tendons, but now he was suffering the ravages of a severe stomach bug. The never-robust Seb was now down to 112 pounds and looking, at best, frail as they lined up for the start of the mile race.

Common wisdom would have had it that in his weakened condition Coe would have hung back and used his patented power surge at the end. But then again, common wisdom has always been an underdog and Coe wasn't. And so it was that Seb spurted right to the front, setting a blistering pace of 49.3. He held the lead down the last backstretch and around the curve, but the fire that had once been in his legs was now but a dull ache, and he was tiring. And Ovett was right behind him. So, too, was a third runner, Olaf Beyer of East Germany. Going into the stretch, Seb struggled to hold both his speed and the lead, but first Ovett fought past him and then, surprise of surprises, so too did Beyer, who rushed by to win the fifth-fastest mile ever, with Ovett finishing second and Coe third.

Having lost his matchup to Ovett as well as his UK record, Coe came back to regain his prized 800 mark from Ovett later that season as the two began passing records back and forth like a Christmas tie nobody wanted.

After taking time off to finish his degree, Coe returned to the track wars in July of 1979, running in the 800 at the Bislett Games in Oslo. Running behind a rabbit, Seb ran the first 200 meters in 24.6, then, fearing burnout, cautiously slowed down to 26 seconds for the second 200. Far in front and feeling amazingly fresh, he passed 600 meters in 1:15.4, faster than any man had ever run before. With shouted encouragement from the other competitors, who had been left to stare at his heels with a dull resignation to their fates, Seb, now feeling as if he were running on autopilot, flashed by the finish lines in 1:42.33—breaking the world record by 1.11 seconds.

Twelve days later he returned to Oslo for the Golden Dubai Mile, which attracted every top miler. And another record win, over a field that included world record holder John Walker, indoor record holder Eamon Coglan, European record holder Thomas Wessinghage, Commonwealth champion Dave Moorcroft, and American Steve Scott. Seb won in 3:48.95, in what would be called "the greatest mile ever run"—each of the first ten finishers recording the fastest time ever for their place.

Less than a month later, Coe set another record in the 1,500, in Zurich's famed Weltklasse Invitational Meet, in 3:32.03, his third world record in forty-one days. He was ranked as the world's best in both the 800 and 1500, and named Athlete of the Year for 1979 by *Track & Field*.

Preparing for the 1980 Moscow Olympics, Coe stopped just long enough in Oslo to graft on another world record, his fourth, running the 1,000 meters in 2:13.40. But holding a record is a transitory act, subject to discontinuation without notice, and one hour later Ovett broke Seb's mile record with a 3:48.8. And then, nine days before the heats of the Olympic 800, Ovett equaled Seb's 1,500 record.

And so it was that the Muhammad Ali and Joe Frazier of middle-distance running, both of whom had preferred to fuel their rivalry by running against the record book rather than against one another, were finally to meet, *mano a mano*, for the first time since 1978, in the '80 Olympic Games.

Many thought that Coe, who had run the 800 faster than anyone in history, would win the 800, but that Ovett, running like a streak on a streak of forty-one consecutive 1,500 and mile wins, would win the Olympic metric mile, the 1,500 meters.

Circumstances had so arranged themselves that the 800 was first. And Coe, apparently undone by nerves, ran the race as if he were communing with nature, wasting time in outside lanes and unsure of what tactics to follow. Ovett won the race and Coe, with a finishing kick, won the silver, good enough for most, but for Seb a symbol of failure. At the postrace press conference, Seb, keeping his lip stiff and upper, admitted, "I chose this day of all days to run the worst race of my life. I must have compounded more cardinal sins of middle-distance running in one and a half minutes than I've done in a lifetime. What a race to choose." Father Peter, stripping his statement of any fig leaf, told his son, "You ran like an idiot."

Six days later the two would meet again in the 1,500, Ovett's best distance. But Coe, with the words "I must win it" as his battle cry, and tortured by visions of finishing second in the 800, ran with a fierce determination. Hell-bent on avoiding the tactical mistakes he had made in the 800, he stayed near the front of the pack and then, coming into the final curve, shifted into second gear to take the lead. A hundred meters from the end he put on a finishing kick that saw him running the final 100 in 12.1 and winning the gold. Immediately after crossing the finish line, Coe dropped to his knees and, touching his forehead to the ground, broke into sobs.

In 1981, Coe continued to reshape the legend, with a world indoor 800 record, his sixth world record in the 1000, in 2:12.18, and then, two days after Ovett broke his mile record, set a new world record of 3:47.33. Undefeated in the season, he again earned *Track & Field*'s Athlete of the Year award.

Time, like taffy, stretches out, and over the next three years it would for Coe, as he encountered a series of maladies, starting with a simple sore ankle and culminating in a severe case of glandular toxoplasmosis, requiring the removal of a lymph node. His career, it seemed, was all but over.

He had been written off like the national debt, but Coe constituted a majority of one who thought he could successfully run in the 1984 Los Angeles Olympics. And that's all it took. After finishing a disappointing second in the 800 meters for the second straight Olympics—and confirming the suspicions of the press that he was all but through—running with every fiber of his being, he outkicked fellow countryman Steve Cram to repeat as the Olympic 1,500-meter champion, the only man to win two Olympic 1,500s. Crossing the finish line with his arms held high in exultation, Coe shouted at the doubters and naysayers, "*Now* believe in me!"

It was the final burnishing of a legend—a legend that became not only a man for all distances, but the greatest middle-distance runner in the history of track.

60

Jack Dempsey

1895–1983

William Harrison "Jack" Dempsey was, purely and simply, the first great sports box-office attraction and boxing's all-time fistic attraction. And one helluva fighter to boot.

Any Dempsey opponent who could walk away from a fight considered it a success. Some sixty foes, including those he met in exhibitions, never walked away from the first round, so great was his punch.

Dempsey was the perfect picture of the ring warrior. Approaching his opponent with his teeth bared, bobbing and weaving in a metronomic sway, the better to make his swarthy head with the perpetual five-o'clock shadow harder to hit, his black eyes flashing and his blue-black hair flying, Dempsey took on the look of an avenging angel of death.

His amazing hand speed and lethal left hook, combined with an anything-goes mentality bred of necessity in the mining camps of his youth, made every bout a war with no survivors. He used every possible means at his disposal to win—hitting low, after the bell, behind the head, while a man was on the way down, and even when he was on the way up. "Hell," he'd say, "it's a case of protecting yourself at all times."

But Dempsey never had to; his opponents did. After having spent several years outboxing the local sheriffs, Dempsey came out of the West with a fearful record; a nickname, the Manassa Mauler; and a manager named Doc Kearns who was to play Svengali to Dempsey's dazzling Trilby. With an animal instinct, an inner fury, and a lust for battle never before seen, Dempsey blazed a searing path through the heavyweight division. Dispatching contender Fred Fulton in just eighteen seconds in July of 1918, Dempsey proved he was no one-fight phenomenon as he followed that up with a fourteen-second knockout of former "White Hope" contender Carl Morris. Now all that stood between the Manassa Mauler and the heavyweight crown was a small mountain of a man named Jess Willard, the six-foot-six conqueror of Jack Johnson some four years earlier. But after one puerile jab-cum-slap with his left Dempsey whipped out his meal ticket, his left hook, and left a dazed Willard on the floor, his jaw shattered in seven places, along with his dreams of retaining his title.

Jack Dempsey's place on the sports landscape cannot be measured by statistics. What Dempsey had, perhaps more than anyone else, was the ability to capture the imagination of the American sporting public. He alone spawned the Golden Age of Sports, becoming the first of the five great sports heroes of the 1920s, the others being Babe Ruth, Red Grange, Bobby Jones, and Bill Tilden. In the process he became the greatest gate attraction of all time, without exception, catnip for the masses who paid millions in Harding and Coolidge dollars for the privilege of witnessing this legendary great in action.

61

Jerry West

b. 1938

Most of those so-called experts in the world of sports, when called upon to give you the makings of a great athlete, start with one part talent, one part records, one part performance, and one part dominance. To that concoction of heady ingredients, they then add one last item, that intangible garnish known as dynamic self-confidence—as in a Babe Ruth supposedly "pointing," a Joe Namath "guaranteeing," a Muhammad Ali "predicting."

However, no such formula for greatness would even come close to explaining the greatness of Jerry West. For Jerry West lacked one of the essential elements in the above mix, that of self-confidence. Self-effacing and freighted with more self-doubts than anyone this side of a psychiatrist's couch, West instead added his own garnish to the formula: the desire to excel.

That desire first took root when West was but a small boy back in West Virginia—Chelyan, to be exact, a proverbial one-horse town next to the one-word town of Cabincreek. As West remembered it, "There wasn't much to do except sports." And so, when one of the neighbors tacked up a basket on a garage wall, the youngster naturally gravitated toward the only game in town.

At first that participation took the form of "just watching." But the magnetlike attraction of the basket had drawn the youngster in, and soon he found himself taking part, even though he was "unable to shoot the ball overhand, so I had to shoot underhand." However, with that exuberance that is so often lost on the young, he continued everlastingly at it until he was throwing the ball up every which way, every waking hour, morning, noon, and eve. "I had a tremendous desire to play. Summer and winter, when there was snow on the ground...I played all the time, constantly. It was something I really loved."

But even though he was getting older, he wasn't getting any bigger. And even with an unquenchable "desire to play on some level," that desire was severely compromised by his lack of size. Unable to make the junior high school team in the seventh grade because of that size, he finally made it in the ninth, but, by his own admission, "I wasn't very good. I was small and not growing very much." Come high school and he finally made the junior varsity squad, but was still, by his own account, "very small." Then, like Tom Hanks in the movie *Big*, one morning between his junior and senior years, he was prey to curious sensations: "I just woke up one day...and all of a sudden, I grew, almost to six-feet-two."

Still adolescent-awkward, the young West continued to practice, his workload such as it would have glutted the cap of a steam shovel. By his senior year, he had developed his skills to the point where he not only played and starred on the East Bank High School team, but, now called Tarantula for his ability to throw up a web around the man he was guarding, paced the school to the championship in the state tournament.

Besieged now by every college worthy of a scholarship offer West chose to stay and play at home, at the state university at Morgantown. There, from 1956 through the 1959–60 season,

West would pilot West Virginia to three Southern Conference titles, average 24.8 points per game—including 29.3 his senior season—make the all-American team twice and, in 1959, take the Mountaineers to the NCAA finals, where they lost to California by one point despite his game-high 28, winning for him the tournament's Most Outstanding Player award.

The governor of West Virginia acknowledged his contributions by tendering him an invitation to visit the governor's mansion in Charleston. Presenting himself to the receptionist, West, in his quiet, singsong Mountaineer voice, introduced himself by saying, "I'm Jerry West. I have an appointment with the governor." The receptionist took one look at the young man and said, "You don't have to tell me who you are. You're better known than the governor."

It was always thus in the state of West Virginia. However, on the world stage, beginning with the 1960 Rome Olympics, where, with Oscar Robertson, he served as cocaptain of the triumphant U.S. basketball team, West would become the second-most-well-known player of the class of '60—behind Robertson. For most of their fourteen years in the pros, inevitable comparisons would be made. And, most times, West would come out second best.

The two heroes turned pro after being drafted in the 1960 NBA draft—Robertson the first choice, and West the second. The self-effacing West said, "I didn't think I was good enough to play in the NBA."

Robertson would score at a 30.5 clip, third best in the league, lead the league in assists with 11.4 per game, and make the first-team all-League squad. West's figures were hardly as sterling, as he scored "only" 1,389 points for the Lakers, for a 17.6 average. West was far from satisfied. "I was awkward, I had little confidence," he would say. He was able to pinpoint one of his problems: "I wasn't moving to my left, so the defense 'cheated' on me, playing me one step to my right." With the determination that was to become his trademark, West, a natural righthander, built up his drives to the left. He also worked on looking for his shot. And by his second year, he had become an integral part of the Los Angeles Laker attack, his shooting, ballhandling, and competitive drive giving the Lakers an unmatched inside-outside scoring punch in West and the incomparable Elgin Baylor.

With his high hard dribble, West became one of the most dangerous jump shooters in the league, as attested to by his 30.8

average that second year, the exact same average as Robertson. Together, they were selected as the two all-League guards on the NBA All-Star team, the first of six straight years the two would hold those positions.

Throughout the ensuing years, as his scoring average continued to hover around the 30-points-per-game mark, he also combined that deadly shooting touch with speed, quickness, and wraparound vision, allowing him not only, as Jim Murray said, "to see his ears," but also open teammates as well.

West brought something else to the table as well, something called "dedication" by one observer, "foolhardiness" by another. For despite giving away as many as sixty-five pounds and looking like an emaciated strip of gristle compared to the rather large slabs of meat populating the NBA hardwood, West demonstrated an infinite capacity for taking hurt, driving in where angels would fear to tread and flinging himself headlong at right angles for a gypsy ball, as witnessed by his roamin' nose, broken nine times, a league record. But he played better brittle than most everyone else played whole and hale.

Red Auerbach, the Boston Celtics coach, having tried everything but snipers to stop West, said in frustration, "You really can't stop West. You can try a number of ways—play him close, loose, keep him away from the ball. He'll still find a way to get his twenty-five to thirty points."

But despite his greatness, Jerry West was tortured by visions of being something less than the best. "I had self-doubt because we lost against teams that I couldn't believe we could lose to. It weighed heavily. All the times we played in the playoffs and came so close so many times to winning, yet we couldn't, I'd say, 'Are we jinxed? Do we choke?'"

But finally, in 1972, after they'd reached the finals in seven of the previous ten seasons with no championship jewelry to show for it, it all came together for West and the Lakers, as they won thirty-three consecutive games during the season and then capped their 69–13 season by racing through the playoffs to win the league championships in five games.

Jerry West had it all now, including the appreciation of those who had played against him. As Bill Russell said on Jerry West Night, "The greatest honor a man can have is the respect and friendship of his peers." Russell told West in front of the crowd at the L.A. Forum on this night of nights, "You have that more than any man I know. If I could have one wish granted, it would be that you would always be happy."

Whether it was being appreciated by others or being immortalized on the NBA logo—which is a silhouette of him dribbling the ball—Jerry West had to be happy finally knowing he had made it on his own terms, that "Mr. Clutch," by mixing his own desire to excel and unconquerability had formed his own definition of greatness. Beyond any doubt.

62

Christy Mathewson

1880–1925

The America of the early 1900s was confident and cocksure, certain of its place in history, but casting around for an identity. It found that identity in its heroes: Teddy Roosevelt in politics, Jack London in literature, and Christy Mathewson in sports.

Baseball had other celebrities, to be sure, men like Honus Wagner and Ty Cobb, to name but a few. But in an age when baseball had a reputation for rough-and-tumble players—or, as Jimmy Powers was to characterize them in later years, "tobacco-chewing, beer-guzzling bums"—Christy Mathewson was an idol, a Frank Merriwell character, one who seemed to be made of sunshine, bloodred tissue, and clear weather. In a field devoted to fashioning halos for its performers, Matty wore a special nimbus.

Under the blond grassplot he wore on his head, Matty's face was as clearly chiseled as a Roman emperor's on an old coin, giving him the overall look of a sun god. Six-foot-one, quiet as a deacon, and dangerous as a six-shooter, the man they called Big Six—after the famed New York City fire engine of the same name—was treated with such reverence by fans that if they had worn hats, they would have doffed them at the very mention of his name.

Mathewson's reputation was built upon his famed "fade-away"—a reverse curve released with his hand turned over until the palm faced the ground instead of upward toward the sky, twisting off his thumb with a peculiar snap of the wrist and twisting away from the batter as well, a sort of in-curve to right-handed batters that fell in across their shoetops—and on his uncanny control. Elegantly moving the ball in and out, Matty would alternate his "freak pitch" with his fastball and curve, all the while picking his spots with the precision of a barber shaving a mustachioed patron. Giving up but one and a half walks per game, Matty's control prompted sportswriter Ring Lardner to rhapsodize, "Nobody else in the world can stick a ball as near where they want to stick it as he can." In fact, Matty's control was such that he owns the record for consecutive innings without a walk—68, over a thirty-day span in 1913.

The cornerstone of Mathewson's fame, however, did not lie in his control or his fadeaway, but in his three shutout wins over the Philadelphia Athletics in the 1905 World Series, three hills from which he would forever look down on the baseball world. And its record books as well.

It was a performance, as one biographer would later write, "as matchless as Bobby Jones's Grand Slam in golf." Pitching three complete games within a period of six days, Mathewson reduced the bats of the mighty A's to matchwood, holding them to just fourteen hits in those three games, walking just one, and turning in the greatest display of pitching power ever witnessed—in a Series or otherwise. The manager of the Athletics, the immortal Connie Mack, would later say, begrudgingly, "Mathewson was the greatest pitcher who ever lived. He had knowledge, judgment, perfect control, and form. It was wonderful to watch him pitch— when he wasn't pitching against you."

Over the first fifteen years of the twentieth century, Mathewson's growing stature on the mound extended far beyond his six-foot-one frame. For not only did he average almost 22 wins a season during his seventeen years on the mound, but in the very same year the A's went 0-for-the-Series against him, Matty won pitching's version of the Triple Crown, leading the National League in wins, ERA, and strikeouts, and winning thirty games for the third consecutive year. His precision and concision were such that it was always a pleasure to watch him, even when his opposition was, at best, commonplace. Two teams in particular, the Cardinals and the Reds, probed at his offerings with a dull resignation to their fates, losing 23 and 22 in a row, respectively and respectfully, to Mathewson. It got to the point where all Mathewson had to do was throw his glove on the mound to win; as writer Damon Runyon noted, leading off his story: "Mathewson pitched against Cincinnati yesterday. Another way of putting it is that Cincinnati lost a game of baseball. The first statement means the same as the second."

A great athlete who has starred as a runner and a drop-kicker for Bucknell and later played pro football, Matty had heard the siren call of baseball and dropped out of school to pursue his dream. He was never to look back, winning 20 games thirteen times during his career, ending with 373 wins, a National League record which still stands.

One of the first five members elected to the Hall of Fame, this gentleman-hero was, according to John McGraw, "the greatest pitcher who ever lived." But he was more. Much more. Christy Mathewson was also, as sportswriter W. O. McGeehan wrote, "the best loved of all ballplayers and the most popular athlete of all time."

63

Bob Mathias

b. 1930

Iff sports is a metaphor for a metaphor, as someone once suggested, then the year 1948 was the year when the sports stage was crowded to overflowing with more aspirations—past, present, and future—than at any other time in its long history. On center stage, refusing to exit, were several performers whose careers had been extended by World War II, now less sports figures than father figures. Add to their ranks several stars whose careers had been put on hold by the war and who had now returned for one final curtain call. And waiting in the wings for their cue to come front and center were several future stars. One of those was a seventeen-year-old schoolboy from Tulare, California, named Bob Mathias.

Mathias, a powerfully built, six-foot-two, 175-pound young-ster with matinee-idol good looks, had given notice of his potential in both basketball and football. But it was in the world of track that he excelled, setting more than twenty high school records in the shot put, discus throw, high hurdles, and high jump. In the spring of '48 his coach suggested that his all-star performer take up the decathlon.

But what Mathias and his coach knew about the decathlon could be written on the head of a pin, with more than enough room left over for a full choir of angels. As Mathias remembered it, the coach had come "and suggested I try the decathlon, and I asked him what a decathlon was," and all the coach knew was that "it was ten events, but he didn't know which ones."

It was at this point in the story that Fate stamped Mathias's library card: his coach wrote for a book describing the decathlon. Upon receipt of the $3.95 volume, they looked up under the letter D what information was offered, and found listed such events as the pole vault, the broad jump, the javelin throw, and the 400- and 1,500-meter races, events Mathias had never before competed in.

With but three weeks to practice before the upcoming Southern Pacific AAU Games, Mathias became a one-man labo-ratory, devoting every fiber of his being to conquering the ten obstacles to his greatness. He took naturally to each and every one of the events—with the notable exception of the pole vault, which the future champion found almost insurmountable as he failed, time and again, to clear at a height of eight feet, his style about as glamorous as an unmade bed. Not accepting the situation as unalterable, Mathias continued to practice until the pole vault, too, was easily within his reach.

Unencumbered by reputation or expectancy, Mathias won the regional decathlon, qualifying him for the National AAU Championships and Olympic trials two weeks later. In but his second decathlon, Mathias defeated three-time national cham-pion Irv Mondschein of New York University and Floyd Sim-mons, North Carolina's strong man, to become, at the age of seventeen years, eight months, and three weeks, the youngest American ever to qualify for an Olympic track team. And a national celebrity.

The 1948 London Games, the first Olympics to be held in twelve years, caught the attention of the world. And no athlete captured the attention of the press more than the seventeen-year-old caretaker of America's flame. But before he could legitimize his buildup, the youngster had to face the largest contingent in decathlon history—twenty-seven decathletes from nineteen other countries, a field so large it had to be divided into two parts. Mathias drew the short straw, the second grouping, a disadvantage since that section of athletes would finish last, late into the evening.

The late afternoon of August 5 was a struggle for Mathias, both against his competitors and the rain. Mathias's few high-water marks that first day could bear quick investigation, his inexperience cost him valuable points, and almost his chance at the gold.

Still, by the end of the first day, Mathias's 3,848 points put him in third place behind France's Ignace Heinrich and Argentina's Enrique Kistenmacher.

With rain pelting Wembley Stadium and turning the seventy thousand spectators and twenty-eight participants into poor imitations of speckled trout, the second day's competition began at ten in the morning. And dragged on into the darkness of night in total confusion.

The struggle against the elements—no gentle rain from heaven this—began with Mathias suffering through a bad start and doing less well than expected in the hurdles. Next came the discus, his specialty. Mathias threw the discus some 145 feet, but because somehow, some way, someone had knocked over the marker, Mathias was given a lesser score after his discus had been unearthed in the sea of muck that had once been the field. Nevertheless, the official reading of 144 feet 4 inches was still good enough to put him in first place. The javelin throw took place under especially trying conditions, officials reduced to holding flashlights so that Mathias could see the takeoff line. Still, on his second try, the youngster overcame the elements and made a winning throw of 165 feet 1 inch, all but slamming the door shut. Now all he had to do was finish the 1,500 meters in good time to clinch victory. With no outcaving of the knees from exhaustion, Mathias, buffeted against the wind and rain with his collarbone, staggered across the finish line with 49 seconds to spare.

The decathlon, having lasted some twelve hours and thirty-five minutes, had been a survivor sport in and of itself. But, in the end, the man who had become the youngest American ever to qualify for the Olympic track team had also become the youngest ever to win a gold medal, exceeding Jim Thorpe's 1912 record in all but the 100-yard dash and the 1,500-meter run. Allison Danzig wrote in the *New York Times*: "In rain, on a track covered with water...in fading light, and finally, under floodlights, it was an amazing achievement." A newspaper reporter asked what he planned to do now. Mathias replied, "Start shaving."

But if his performance in the 1948 Olympic Games was an "amazing achievement," his performance four years later at Helsinki was even more so. For Mathias, despite the aches and pains of a pulled thigh muscle, became the first repeat decathlon winner, breaking his own world record and winning by the largest margin in Olympic history. His heroic struggle against pain and injury was such that Brutus Hamilton, the coach of the '52 team, was moved to extol his performance by calling him "not only the greatest athlete in the world, but also the greatest competitor."

And with that, Bob Mathias retired undefeated, closing the book on one of the most amazing stories in the annals of track and field—and indeed, in all of sports.

64

Bob Cousy

b. 1928

With Bob Cousy, it was always a case of who you were going to believe: the storytellers or your own eyes. For his many accomplishments on the basketball court were particularly striking to the optic nerve, whether he was throwing seeing-eye passes that could thread a needle's eye, dribbling behind his back in a now-you-see-it-now-you-don't fashion, or performing sleight of hand that made spectators' and opponents' eyeballs rotate in their sockets.

Called the Houdini of the Hardwood, Cousy was what you could call a medium tall man of average smallness, standing just 6'1½", short by basketball standards. But what he could do with those seventy-three and a half inches defied description.

The man whose name was abbreviated to just plain ol' Couz played the game of basketball like a harp of a thousand strings with more variations on a theme than Mussorgsky ever thought of. At one moment you would swear he could leave one button unbuttoned in the back of his waistcoat and still be able to fasten it while dribbling the ball with his free hand. The next, throwing passes from behind his back, out of his ear, wherever. And at others maneuver in a melange of moves toward the basket, leaving his opponents to stand stock-still like members of Madame Tussaud's waxworks. Cousy credited his talents—which he described as "speed, quickness, peripheral vision, etc."—for his success. But, truth to tell, Dame Fortune should be credited with an assist.

Graduating from New York's Andrew Jackson High School in 1946 as an all-City performer, Cousy was, in his own words, "deluged by all of two college offers." He chose Holy Cross, a small Jesuit school in Worcester, Massachusetts, where over the next four years the skinny youngster with the extraterrestrial peripheral powers took to building his own better mousetrap. Excelling in the mechanics of the game, he also created some of his own moves, including a behind-the-back dribble, a reverse dribble, and a behind-the-back pass. Selected as an all-American in 1948, '49, and '50, Cousy graduated with little thought of playing for the newly formed National Basketball Association. "I was going to play only if Boston drafted me," he remembered saying to himself at the time.

But the Celtics—and several other teams as well—passed over the local star before he was selected by Tri-Cities. Even before Cousy could ask, "Where, in the name of Rand McNally, are the Tri-Cities?" he began to be passed around like a parcel post package nobody wanted postage on. First the Tri-City Blackhawks traded him, sight unseen, to the Chicago Stags for guard Frankie Brian. Then, in one of those convulsions that constantly afflict new leagues, the Chicago franchise folded and its stock was dispersed to the other teams in the league. The names of three of their guards—Max Zaslofsky, Andy Phillip, and Cousy—went into a player pot, with the names to be drawn out of a hat by New York, Philadelphia, and Boston, in that order.

Red Auerbach, then as now the head thumbscrew of the Celtic company store, wanted the two other guards rather than Cousy, whom he figured to be an unlikely pro prospect. However, when the Knicks, selecting first from amongst the duty-free merchandise, selected Zaslofsky, seemingly the prize of the three, and the Warriors picked Phillip, a great playmaker, the Celtics were stuck with Cousy.

But Auerbach, pulling last, had pulled to an inside straight. For Cousy would not only blossom into a perennial flower in Boston Garden, he would immediately turn the Celtics into a winning franchise. And make dust out of the conventional wisdom that bigger is better.

Playing with enough electricity to branch out and light up Boston's many suburbs, Cousy gave the static game a crackle of excitement. With his instinctive playmaking ability, impromptu vamping, and capability of rising above any crisis through the sheer wizardry of his passing and dribbling, Cousy did everything but sell nostrums from the back of a wagon to the unsuspecting rubes who tried to contain him. In the process, he became the linchpin of the greatest dynasty in sports history.

Cousy would begin paying dividends to his reluctant employers in that very first year. Not only did he average 15.6 points a game—as compared to Zaslofsky's 14.1 and Phillip's 11.2—but he added 4.9 assists a game. Most important, the Celtics, which B.C.—Before Cousy—had never had a winning season, were transformed into an instant winner by this one-man power surge.

By his second year Cousy's heroics were such that every game became a clinic. Playing with the equanimity of a veteran, he was capable of turning every game into high drama.

In one game against New York, with the Knicks leading by 4 points with just thirty seconds to go, Cousy picked New York clean, taking everything but their wallets, as he stole the ball twice and forced the game into overtime, then scored 12 of the Celts' 20 OT points for the win. Another time he resorted to his own form of filibustering, dribbling out the clock, which he did in a scampering solo for the last twenty-three seconds of the game for another Celtic win. Afterward, Jimmy Cannon was to write, "If Cousy never put the ball in the basket, he'd still be the most respected man in the league."

But Cousy *could* put the ball in the basket when forced to stand and deliver, as witnessed by a game in the 1953 playoffs versus the Syracuse Nationals. First he tied the game up in the final seconds to send it into OT and then, in a wild four-overtime game, he scored 17 of the Celtics' last 21 points to end up with

50—20 of them on his patented one-handed set shots, plus an incredible 30 on 32 foul shots—in an 111–105 win.

By the 1956–57 season, circumstances had so arranged themselves that the Celtics were crowded to overflowing with talent. Bill Russell, Bill Sharman, Tommy Heinsohn, Frank Ramsey, and Jim Loscutoff had joined Cousy, who was to act as their quarterback. With his passes air-conditioning the court and his sparkling play proving to be the spark plug that propelled the Celtics, he drove them to the first of many championships.

Five more times Cousy was to serve as the quarterback, the cupbearer, and dispenser of the champagne for championship Celtic teams. But perhaps his greatest contribution was, in the words of Bill Russell, the fact that "the image of the Celtics is the image of Bob Cousy."

When he finally retired after the 1962–63 season, Cousy had claimed a slew of records, including eight straight seasons of leading the league in assists, the all-time record for most minutes played, and the NBA record for most lifetime assists, as well as being second in total games played and fourth in most points scored.

Here's what Red Auerbach, the man who hadn't wanted him in the first place, had to say on the occasion of Cousy's retirement: "What can you say when you know you're going to lose the greatest backcourt man who ever lived? Nobody will ever take his place. There's only one Cousy." But you had to see him to appreciate this spectacular performer. As Joe Lapchick, who was around for almost as long as the game itself, said, "He could do more with a basketball—shoot, pass, dribble, anything—than anyone else I ever saw." Or anyone else for that matter. For Bob Cousy was more than a passing fancy.

65

Wilma Rudolph

1940–1994

If you're old enough to remember that oversized piece of talking furniture that sat on the floor of your living room—for the benefit of you younger readers, something called a radio console—you're old enough to remember sitting on the floor in front of it, sticking sharpened pencils into the metallic mesh covering the speakers and listening to a program that came through those same speakers on Friday nights called *The Bill Stern Show*. From the moment it first came on, introduced with a little ditty that announced, in breathless tones, that "Bill Stern, the Colgate Shave Cream Man, is on the air," and for the next fifteen minutes, you were treated to improbable stories of some sports figure or other having been dealt a bad hand by Fate and having overcome it. Never mind that most of the stories were pure blarney, or that they all seemed to sound like "…And that man with no head, no arms, and no legs is today…second base at Yankee Stadium," they were all entertaining. And all uplifting.

However, not even Bill Stern and his staff of fantasy-weavers could have scripted the improbable saga of Wilma Rudolph.

For the story of Wilma Rudolph is the story of one person's triumph over overwhelming odds. The twentieth of twenty-two children born to a tobacco plant worker in rural St. Bethlehem, hard by the Tennessee town of Clarksville, where getting through life was enough of a survivor sport without complications, Wilma was also afflicted by a complication of disorders that included childhood bouts of pneumonia and scarlet fever that left her crippled at the age of four, her left leg paralyzed.

But for extreme illnesses there are extreme treatments, in this case a family's love, dispensed in extra-heaping dosages. Not accepting her daughter's condition as unalterable, Wilma's mother sought help, and was told that daily therapeutic massages might restore to life the useless leg. Upon such shallow water can the bark of hope remain afloat. And so her mother and the rest of the Rudolph family took turns massaging the little girl's impaired leg, four times daily. By the age of six Wilma was back on her feet, with the help of a leg brace. Soon thereafter, she graduated from a leg brace to an orthopedic high-top shoe and was able to hop around on one leg. Able now to attend school, she also began her own form of rehabilitation, which took the form of coming home after classes to shoot baskets at a peach basket her brothers had mounted in the backyard. One day when Wilma was eleven, her mother returned home to find her daughter playing basketball barefoot, her corrective shoes lying nearby. From that day on, Wilma Rudolph was able to refer all matters to her feet.

With her legs now back in circulation, Wilma went out for the basketball team at Burt High in Clarksville. Her coach, Clinton Gray, took one look at the thirteen-year-old mosquito flitting around the court—almost as if she were trying to make up for the time she had been unable to use her legs—and could only shake his head and say, "You're just like a 'skeeter.' You're little, you're fast, and you always get in my way." But again Wilma's indomitable spirit was not to be denied, and by the age of fifteen the young lady known as Skeeter had become all-State, scoring 803 points in twenty-five games, including a single-game record of 49 points.

At the suggestion of Ed Temple, the women's track coach at Tennessee A&I, Gray established a women's track team at Burt High to showcase Wilma's abilities. Wilma paid off the interest in her as, feet and records a-flying, she went undefeated over three years of competition.

Even more miraculously, after less than a year of high school competition—and just five years after she was first able to walk without support—she qualified for the U.S. Olympic team. And even though she was eliminated in the first round of the 200 meters at Melbourne, the sixteen-year-old phenomenon left her calling card by winning a bronze medal running the third leg of the 4x100-meter relay for the United States.

Within the year Wilma, by now 5-foot-11 and with the legs of a gazelle, had enrolled at Tennessee A&I, where she was running full-time for the "Tigerbelles" under the watchful, even stern, eye of Ed Temple, who had built the best women's track program in the country based on two principles: hard competition and unbending training habits. His training theories were best summed up by one rule: Come late to practice and you run an extra lap for every minute of training you've missed. Wilma once showed up for practice thirty minutes late and had to run thirty extra laps. She was never late again. As for the competitive part of his program, Temple explained it—and what made Wilma, and the rest of the Tigerbelles, run—by saying, "Her teammates are the next three fastest girls in the country. Rudolph runs fast because she is pressed so hard in practice. Without it she wouldn't be nearly as good as she is." The proof of Temple's program came in 1960, when the entire 400-meter women's Olympic relay team was chosen from his Tennessee A&I squad.

But before she would go to the 1960 Olympics, Wilma had to face another series of debilitating illnesses and injuries. In 1958 she was smote by an illness that caused her to miss the entire season; in '59 she pulled a thigh muscle; and in 1960 she suffered serious complications from a tonsil operation. Wilma, however, was not going to miss the Olympics. For even though she had a bad case of the flu during the Olympic trials, she knew that "if I didn't run, I couldn't make the team." So she did, and she did, setting a world record of 22.9 seconds for the 200 meters, winning the 100 and 200, and anchoring the winning Tennessee A&I relay team.

Arriving in Rome as the favorite to succeed Australia's Betty

Cuthbert as the world's fastest woman, Wilma gave notice of her intention in the very first race, the 100-meter dash, dominating it from the beginning. Aroused from a nap to run the semifinal heat, she swept to a three-yard victory, equaling the world record time of 11.3 seconds without, as *New York Times* writer Arthur Daley wrote, "pressing the accelerator to the floor." Then, in the final, with an easy motion that looked like she was just stretching her long, willowy legs, she fairly flew down the track, running away from the field in world-record time of 11.0. However, it was later disallowed because the cranky wind gauge had shown a wisp of a breeze that was barely above the acceptable limit.

The 200-meters was next. And again Wilma dominated, setting an Olympic record in her opening heat and then racing to her second gold medal in a time of 24.0, this time *against* a strong wind.

Now came the women's 4x100 relay. Joining Wilma were three other Tigerbelles, Martha Hudson, Lucinda Williams, and Barbara Jones. Together the foursome had set a world record of 44.4 in the semifinals, and they looked to duplicate it in the finals. But with one lap to go, it wasn't a world record they were seeking so much as a baton. For just as Wilma, running in the anchor position, prepared to take the final baton pass from Barbara Jones with a two-yard lead over the German team, something went awry and both the baton and the lead were momentarily lost in a poor pass. Somehow, some way, Wilma managed to get a handle on the baton and then, running as if propelled by some potent force, the long-striding Wilma moved to the front. Coming down the straightaway she increased her lead with each long, graceful step, crossing the finish line three full yards ahead of the Germans.

As she crossed the line with her third gold medal, someone asked a French photographer standing near the finish line, "Who won?" "*La Gazelle, naturellement*," he said. "*La Chattanooga Choo Choo.*"

She was "*La Chattanooga Choo Choo*," "*La Gazzèlla Nera*," "the Female Jesse Owens," and the darling of the multitudes, who took to this tall, graceful beauty with a face saturated in good-naturedness and with, as one English writer wrote, "the carriage a queen should have." Barbara Heilman captured the phenomenon, writing, "She can command a look of mingled graciousness and hauteur that suggests a duchess, but in a crowd that is one part 'Skeeter' and five thousand parts people, young men and babies will come to her in thirty seconds."

Hailed around the world by fans and dignitaries alike, she was America's goodwill ambassador, as Dick Schapp wrote, "without portfolio and without equal."

Wilma Rudolph's story was without equal as well. For no more valiant hero ever fought back from such adversity for the right to sit in the pantheon of sports greats. As they used to say in radio "Bill Stern, please copy!"

66

Rogers Hornsby

1896–1963

So great was he that both Rogers Hornsby's name and deeds were written in the plural. But in that Era of Wonderful Nonsense known more familiarly as the twenties, he was a singular force from the right side of home plate.

Hornsby crept virtually unnoticed upon baseball's big stage in 1915 as an anemic 135-pound, nineteen-year-old shortstop for the lowly St. Louis Cardinals. His manager, Miller Huggins, himself a hardly robust 140 pounds, took a liking to this equally diminutive infielder. Hornsby hardly looked like he was destined for baseball greatness when, in his first major-league game, he struck out the first two times he came to bat and compounded his first day nonheroics by muffing his very first fielding opportunity. Huggins took the youngster aside and told him, "You don't have the strength to get the bat around. Try choking up on it." Hornsby did, and managed a first-year average of .246 in eighteen games. Still, Huggins felt he hadn't taken Hornsby lightly enough, and by the end of the year farmed him out, sending him back to the Texas League from whence he had come. Hornsby, misunderstanding the phrase "farmed out," thought it had something to do with his conditioning, and spent the off-season working on a farm, fleshing out his scrawny frame.

By the next grass, the now-heavier Hornsby came back to make the club, as a third baseman. And abandoned his batting stance of choking up and crouching as if he had caught his uniform shirt in the zipper of his pants, to adopt the stance he was to make famous: Standing as far back in the batter's box as the rules and lines would allow, feet close together, Hornsby would step into the ball with a tremendous stride, meeting it with a picture-perfect swing and driving the ball, on a line, to all fields. Add to this his sharp eyesight, one that would almost allow him to read the signature on the ball as it came toward him—and you have the makings of the greatest right-handed batter in the history of baseball.

Through 1919, Hornsby, alternating between short and third, became known for his fielding greatness more than his bat, his long, loose arms, sure hands, and strong throws making him one of the league's premier infielders. His bat was not quiet, his average for his first four-plus years a respectable .310, but hardly the stuff of which greats are made.

Then, in 1920, Hornsby began hitting driving, lining—and other concussive verbs inserted here—the ball to all fields, imposing his will on National League pitchers. Whether Hornsby's arrival was due to the advent of the so-called lively ball or his transfer to second base by the new St. Louis manager, Branch Rickey, is not known. But what is known is that, starting in 1920, Hornsby began his batting reign of terror. That year he led the league in batting for the first time, with a .370 average. Over the next five years he led the league in batting five more times, three times batting in the rarefied atmosphere of .400 and averaging .402 over those five years. No gentle despoiler he, Hornsby also led the league in doubles four times, RBIs three, home runs twice, and twice won the Triple Crown as he outdistanced the runner-up batsman over his six-in-a-row streak by an average of 32 percentage points.

As reverence earned by his feats increased, Hornsby became known as the Rajah, a billing inspired not only by his sitting atop baseball's batting throne but by his regal, almost mysterious, bearing. Pitcher Ferdie Schupp, who had been Hornsby's teammate for three years, was once asked what manner of man Hornsby was. "Nobody knows," Schupp answered. "He never talks to anybody. He just goes out and plays second base and when the game is over he comes into the clubhouse, takes off his uniform, takes a shower, and gets dressed without saying a word. Then he leaves the clubhouse and nobody knows where he goes."

And yet, in mid-1925 this loner who was known for hoarding his words like a miser his treasure was called upon to talk to twenty-four other men, entrusted as he was with the managerial reins of the St. Louis Cardinals. Under his administration, the Cards rose to fourth place. Then, in 1926, aided by the midseason acquisition of pitching great Grover Cleveland Alexander, found by Hornsby leaning against a help-wanted column of a sports newspaper, Hornsby brought the Cardinals their very first pennant, then capped it off with a World Series win over the New York Yankees of Ruth, Gehrig & Co., managed by Hornsby's old mentor, Miller Huggins.

Nonetheless, this man whose personal comings and goings were always clouded in mystery was gone by the next season, told by Cardinal management never to darken their towels again and sent off to the New York Giants. One year later manager John McGraw decided he had had enough of the difficult Hornsby, and once again he was mysteriously sent packing, this time to the lowly Boston Braves. There he showed both his brilliant bat and his blunt belligerency, leading the league in batting once again with a .387 average and constantly jousting with players and press. In one interview, a reporter asked Hornsby if the Braves had a chance for the first division that year. Hornsby incredulously answered him, "These humpty-dumpties? The first division? With what?" Hornsby would become manager of "these humpty-dumpties" midway through the season and, fittingly, guide them to a seventh-place finish.

By 1929, for the fourth time in four years, baseball's version of rolling stock was with a new team, this time taking his different-drumming to that toddlin' town of Chicago, where he batted .380 and helped lead the Cubs to their first pennant in eleven years. By 1930 he would become their manager, and by '32, predictably, he would be fired.

Hornsby would continue to manage clubs for another seven years, with what might be called underwhelming success. But it was not as a manager that he will be remembered. It was as a hitter whose bat, flashing in that fluid swing of his from far back in the box, frescoed the ball with amazing regularity.

His legend as a batter was such that years later, when a frustrated member of the Boston Braves complained to his manager, Casey Stengel, that it was impossible to hit at windswept Braves Field, Stengel, who knew his baseball flesh, quietly replied to his carping player, "All I know is that Hornsby played here one whole season and batted .387." That was Rogers Hornsby who, like the mailman, could deliver regularly through all manner of weather and conditions, to the point where he was the greatest right-handed batter in the history of baseball.

67

Maurice Richard

b. 1921

The eyes. That's the first thing you saw as Maurice Richard came rocketing down the ice. The eyes. Burning calculation beaming from one and divine fire from the other, his teeth bared in an unwelcoming smile, Richard looked like an evil face which had suddenly appeared on the window of a house.

One goalie who remained tortured by such visions long after he retired was Glenn Hall. "What I remember most about Rocket was his eyes," recalled Hall. "When he came flying toward you with the puck on his stick, his eyes were all lit up, flashing and gleaming like a pinball machine. It was terrifying." Another goalie, Don Simmons, said, "His eyes flash like the headlights of a big truck."

Other goalies, equally terrified by the presence of the fiercest man on ice, would stay awake nights rather than conjure images of this one-man gang with coal-black eyes and hair to match coming at them with flames shooting out both eyes.

And it wasn't just puck-drunk goalies who stood in fear of Richard; so did opposing defensemen and just about everyone else who crossed his path as he thundered-and-lightning'd his way down ice. For Maurice Richard, long on talent and short on temper, was the most explosive player ever to play the game.

But if, at the beginning of Richard's career, one had calculated his chances of becoming the most electrifying skater ever to play hockey, the odds would have been longer than the time between New York Ranger Stanley Cups. For, in the third period of his very first minor-league game, playing in the Quebec Senior Hockey League, Richard was checked heavily, fell, and snapped his left ankle, putting him out for the rest of the season. The next year, skating with reckless disregard for his underpinnings in a mad dash for the goal, he slammed into the boards and broke his left wrist, missing most of that season. By this time Richard had begun to ask himself "whether this was worth all the pain and frustration."

Still, he looked so good in fall training at the start of the 1942–43 campaign that he was offered a contract by the Montreal Canadiens. But, after just fifteen games, playing against the Boston Bruins, he was checked hard by Jack Crawford. Richard's skate tip lodged in a flaw on the ice and he fell awkwardly, snapping his right ankle.

The Canadien management, concerned that Richard's "brittleness" jeopardized any chance he had of playing the "man's game" of hockey, discounted his talents and advised him to quit. But Richard pleaded with coach Tommy Gorman to give him one last chance. Gorman relented, and invited him back for the 1943–44 season.

With the Sword of Suspended Judgment still hanging over his head, Richard took the ice for his first game. Here Dame Fortune stepped in, changing Richard from a limb-breaker to a record-breaker.

Playing against the Boston Bruins, Richard picked defenseman Dit Clapper as his designated hittee, carelessly parting his hair with his stick. More than somewhat angered by what he considered to be the impertinence of a brash rookie, Clapper lay in wait for his chance at revenge. It came scant seconds later, when Richard came rocketing into Bruin territory, there to be met with a bone-rattling check from Clapper, knocking him base over apex into the expensive seats. "Keep your head up, kid," hollered Clapper at the fallen form, "or I'll do it again." Sure enough, before the large hand on the clock had moved twice, here came Richard down the ice again, his eyes glued on the puck that had just been passed his way. Wham! Clapper caught him again, making him at one with the ice, a limp pile of red-and-black laundry. Skating over to the fallen form, Clapper screamed, "Keep your head up!" Somehow, some way, the words sank in, and from that point on, Richard set his gaze straight ahead, on the goal, not on the puck—much to the chagrin of the rest of the league.

Now, playing with a fire in his soul that matched the fire in his eyes, Richard became part of an attacking line that Montreal coach Dick Irvin had assembled. It included Elmer Lach, who spoke only English, at center; Toe Blake, fluent in both French and English, on left wing; and young Richard, the darling of the French-Canadian fans, who pronounced his name "Ree-chard," on the right side. Called the Punch Line, they produced 82 goals, 32 of them by the fiery Richard as the Canadiens raced through their schedule, losing only five games and winning the regular-season championship by 25 points over second-place Detroit.

The thunder that had taken so long to erupt finally came in the opening round of the '44 Stanley Cup playoffs. In a close-checking game, with Toronto defenseman Bob Davidson shadowing Richard's every move, the Maple Leafs had played the Flying Frenchmen to a scoreless standoff in the first period. But, in the second, Richard broke loose, putting on a little one-act drama. Within the first two minutes and five seconds, he had scored two goals, and would add yet another later in the period for a single-period hat trick—despite having been sent to the sin-bin twice for two-minute penalties. And even though the competitive phase of the game was finished, Richard wasn't. Twice more you could write "ditto" next to his name as he beat Leaf goalie Paul Bibeault to make the final score: Richard 5, Toronto 1.

And then, as was the custom at the Montreal Forum, the top stars of the game were honored. Normally, when the stars selected in one-two-three order are announced, the accompanying roar rises for each name and falls almost as if a choirmaster were waving it off. On this night of nights, stars number one, two, and three were the same: Maurice Richard. And the fans rent the air with their hosannas for the entire time it took the announcer to pronounce the name of the man they called "the Rocket."

Now, unbound like Prometheus, Richard continued his one-man assault on the record books the next season, exploding at an incredible goal-a-game pace. Richard's eyes would fire first, then his stick, as he bruised, blasted, and battered the puck into the net fifty times in a fifty-game season. During one nine-game stretch he had fifteen goals, and ten times during the season he scored two or more goals in a single game. Today the half-century goal season has become commonplace, but, truth to tell, these Maurice-come-latelies do it in eighty games, and merely merit Roger Maris-like asterisks, while Richard can rightfully lay claim to the original copyright.

The other part of Richard's terrifying mien was his temper, so fiery, rumor had it, that seven gendarmes were needed to hold his hat. Richard would brook no quarrel, no matter how small, and was as handy with his fists as he was with his stick, able to wield both weapons from both sides with equal ease and equal damage.

Three fights in particular received more ink than Louis-Schmeling. Interestingly, all involved the Detroit Red Wings, the Canadiens' archrival for dominance of the NHL during the forties and fifties. In one, Richard was decked by his rival for greatest right wing of the two decades, Gordie Howe. On this night, Richard got up to look for the fast-flying Howe, only to have Sid Abel taunt him. Unable to find Howe, Richard took out his revenge on Abel, teeing off and breaking his nose with one punch. Another time, he helped win a Stanley Cup for Montreal by coldcocking Detroit's Ted Lindsay with a solid right to the jaw.

But the most celebrated fight came in the closing days of the 1954–55 season, a season that wound down with Montreal holding a slight lead in the standings over Detroit and Richard holding an equally slight advantage in his quest to win his first scoring title. On the last Sunday of the season, playing against the Bruins in Boston, Richard took a just-getting-acquainted swipe with his stick at Bruin Hal Laycoe and, in the ensuing brawl, took a punch or two at linesman Cliff Thompson. League president Clarence Campbell, outraged at Richard's behavior, suspended the star for the final three games of the regular season, as well as the entire playoffs.

The Rocket took his punishment sitting down, but his fans didn't. And when Campbell showed up at the Forum—a place too big for an insane asylum and too small for a nation—to watch Les Habitants play the Red Wings, he was greeted by an ugly scene reminiscent of the French Revolution, as fans, rocking with the din and roar of patriotism, threw imprecations, programs, peanuts, popcorn, tear gas, and finally fists his way. Soon the scene tumbled out onto Montreal's main drag, Ste. Catherine Street, as the angry mob broke windows and looted stores. Only Richard's going on radio and pleading, in French, "I will take my punishment and come back next year to help the club and the younger players to win the Stanley Cup," finally quieted the unruly crowd.

For five more years Richard continued to lay waste to the landscape, much as his fans had done in his name, laying down layer after layer of his masterpiece. Finally, after the 1959–60 season, and with a then-record 544 goals, the Rocket retired. Apparently forgiven his transgressions, he was hurried into the Hockey Hall of Fame after only nine months, a proper gestation period for a great but far shorter than the normal waiting period of five years required of mere mortals.

But then again, maybe the eyes of those beholders known as electors were as unclouded in their search for greatness as Maurice Richard's had been as he'd searched for goals.

Walter Johnson

1887–1946

Walter Johnson may have looked like one of nature's irregularities, a gangly six-foot-and-change pitcher with long, stringy arms which flowed out of his uniform at odd angles. But when he threw his fastball in a whiplike fashion, coming sidearm by way of third base, he was one of nature's wonders.

From the very first day the nineteen-year-old with the behind-the-plow gait came to the Washington Senators, F.O.B. Weiser, Idaho, he had the ability to throw a well-aimed shaft that could deprive even the best of batsmen of their breath. His first start was against the biggest bats in the American League, the

Detroit Tigers, that fearsome crew of Ty Cobb, Sam Crawford & Co. For three innings the rawboned rookie, working easily and effortlessly, if gracelessly, kept the Tigers from fattening their league-leading batting averages. Finally, convinced of the futility of taking their regular cuts against the young phenom, the Tigers took to bunting their way on base, beating Johnson on just six hits, three of which were bunts.

Johnson would win his next game, the first of 416 career victories. He had already begun to make an impression even before he made his mark. Sam Crawford, who faced Johnson in that first game, said that the young pitcher "reminded me of one of those compressed-air machines...comes in so fast when it goes by it swooshes. You hardly see the ball at all. But you hear it...swoosh..."

Johnson continued to swoosh his pitches past batters, pitches that begot two whistles, one by the ball coming in and the other by the appreciative batter as he admired it. It was this pitch with the sound of a train's yowl that inspired Grantland Rice to call him the Big Train. And then to ask, "How do you know what Johnson's got? Nobody's seen it yet."

Johnson swooshed his way to 82 wins in his first five years, always ranking amongst the pitching leaders in complete games, strikeouts, and ERA—and this for a team that never vacated the depths of the second division.

By 1912 Johnson had established his credentials, his molten fastball moving the *New York Times* to call him "the greatest pitcher of modern days, undoubtedly the greatest the game has ever produced." That was the year Johnson won 32 games—16 of them in a row to set the American League record—and led the league in strikeouts and ERA. In 1913 Johnson had perhaps the greatest year any pitcher has ever had: He won 36 games, most in the league; led the league in winning percentage, complete games, innings pitched, strikeouts, and shutouts; and gave up only 38 bases on balls in 346 innings, less than one a game.

Yankee pitcher George Pipgras once took two blurred streaks and threw away his bat, telling catcher Muddy Ruel, "Muddy, I never saw those pitches." Ruel, grinning through the bars of his mask, answered: "Don't let it worry you. He's thrown a few Cobb and Speaker are still looking for."

As the twenties dawned, the premier pitcher in all of baseball, with ten straight 20-game seasons behind him, was still far from his dream of a World Series win. With time running out—his 1920 won-lost record had been his worst since his rookie season, an 8–10, sore-armed season punctuated by his only no-hitter—it seemed he might never see that dream come true. For his team, the Washington Senators, continued to finish in the second division with monotonous regularity.

But then, in 1924, the Lord, in His heaven, began to look upon Johnson beneficently, and all came right again after years of frustration, as both Washington and Johnson were to rise to the top of baseball's mountain in one of the greatest games ever, the seventh game of the 1924 World Series. After losing two of the first five games, Johnson finally got his chance in the ninth inning of the final game. And then, for four innings, Johnson held the New York Giants in check, until a ball hit a pebble in front of the Giants' third baseman and bounced over his head, bringing home the winning run in the twelfth inning for Walter Johnson's—and Washington's—first World Series win ever.

After the game, losing pitcher Jack Bentley summed up everybody's feelings when he told his crestfallen teammates: "Cheer up, fellers... I guess the Good Lord couldn't stand seeing Walter Johnson lose again."

Walter Johnson won far more than he lost, setting records wholesale: most strikeouts, most innings pitched, most shutouts, most complete games, most consecutive scoreless innings, etc., etc., etc. And though most of his records have fallen, the black type in baseball's record book could never fully capture the greatness and power of the Big Train.

69

Jean-Claude Killy

b. 1943

To many, skiing is the ultimate man-versus-nature competition. And to almost all, the greatest name in the sport was parted in the middle with a dash that rivaled his dash as he parted a mountainside: Jean-Claude Killy.

Killy, who carried a proud hyphen in the middle of his first name, also hyphenated his last, at least in terms of pronunciation, giving it a Gallic sound that came out "Kee-LEE," as in Robert E. And with the dark, swashbuckling good looks of a matinee idol, right down to the scar cutting across his left cheek and lip, he was as big a folk hero in his own country as the aforementioned general was in his. So much so, in fact, that one wag was to say of his popularity: "When Killy has a sore throat, all of France gargles."

According to his father, who gave little Jean-Claude his first pair of skis at the age of three, the youngster was "born to ski." And the boy, who "loved them as some babies love teddy bears," would promptly disappear for hours into the hills surrounding the little French Alp village of Val d'Isère to play with his new toys.

By six he had won a ski-jump competition. By eight he was skiing better, and faster, than his instructors. And by sixteen he had quit school to join the French ski team and devote himself full-time to his one consuming passion.

But even as Killy was making his name as a skier, he was gaining another reputation as well. For he attacked life in the same way he attacked a slope—always in the name of what the French called "letting the good times roll."

At one ski-jump competition in Switzerland, Killy caused a sensation by dropping his ski pants during takeoff and finishing the jump in his long johns. Always in search of the social ramble, the après-ski party, and the genial bonhomie of *les femmes*, Killy was named in a paternity suit in Austria and contracted a case of *mal de sex* in Sun Valley.

Over the next few years Killy would put together a long list of maladies and ailments, making him almost a one-man outpatient ward—including the usual injuries from jumping to contusions, such as broken legs and ankles, plus a few unusual ones, like infected lungs and even amebic parasitosis, a souvenir of his service with the French army in Algeria.

But through it all, Killy maintained his self-confidence. "I have never known physical fear," he said. "There's no apprehension. When there's a bad accident, I think, 'Well, that's someone else, not me.' When I hurt myself, I look for the mistake I made."

By twenty-one, Killy, freshly mustered out of the army, had the requisite experience to qualify for the 1964 French Olympic team. But at Innsbruck, Austria, he only placed fifth in the giant slalom—behind the gold medal winner, fellow countryman Francois Bonlieu—and failed to finish both the downhill and the slalom.

But Jean-Claude Killy's compass was set on a particular course, one which would soon see him become king of the mountains, both literally and figuratively. Killy won the European championship in 1965, two world titles in '66, twelve of the sixteen World Cup meets during the 1966–67 season, and then—

after taking time off to do something only a man very sure of himself could do: enter, and win, a sports car race in Sicily in 1967—the World Cup championship again in 1968.

Killy had become a national treasure, France's glamour boy. And with France hosting the 1968 Winter Olympics in Grenoble, the man they now called *le superman* would carry the tricolors into the Alpine trievents—in addition to the hopes of all Frenchmen.

Although each of the three alpine events was a jewel in a separate setting, the opening event, the downhill—the most grueling of the three, demanding everything a skier had to give—had by far the greatest luster. In the words of Killy's teammate, Guy Perillat: "The downhill does not leave room for compromise. You're either in front or you perish." And so saying, Perillat, the first skier down the treacherous two-mile course, crossed the finish line in 1:59.93, becoming the man to beat.

Taking his place in the starting gate after a dozen other hopefuls had failed to break the two-minute mark, Killy, the fourteenth contestant, stood ready to stalk the course to its knees, to beat Perillat's time. At the signal he hurtled out of the gates, his skis cutting through the white meringue of the Grenoble mountainside with a hiss, straight downhill, so fast he fairly flew out of his Jacques-strap. Exhorted on by the din and roar of his countrymen, who called out his name in smoke signals, Kee-LEE, Kee-LEE, and his nickname, *Casse-cou,* (or "breakneck"), he thundered down the hillside, flashing past the finish line in 1:59.85, eight-hundredths of a second faster than Perillat, roughly the margin of a ski tip.

The second leg of Killy's quest for an alpine triple was the giant slalom, a race between a series of blue- and red-flagged double poles that looked like they had been laid out by a group of somewhat tipsy football first-down crews. Torquing, pirouetting, and shuttlecocking his way through the poles at a high rpm, almost as if he were flying, Killy turned in the fastest time on his first run. The next day he extended his winning margin on his second run to win his second gold by the comfortable margin of two-plus seconds.

Now all that stood between Killy and the coveted triple was the slalom, a shorter version of the giant slalom where one good turn, as in the giant slalom, deserved another. But whether all the turns made by the competitors had in fact been good ones was somewhat lost in a fog of interpretation, much as the mountainsides at Grenoble were lost in the icy fog that rolled in just before the race. For the race, which started in fog so dense that the skiers pleaded with officials to cancel it, would end under an equally dense cloud and controversy—one of the greatest in Olympic history.

After the officials, in their collective nonwisdom, waved away the skiers' complaint, explaining that while the fog might present some difficulties, the conditions would be the same for all, the slalom began with skiers and officials alike shadowy, barely discernible images, even at short range. Somehow, some way, the sun miraculously broke through the only time that afternoon to shine on Killy, who, taking advantage of the momentary clearing, darted and swiveled his way through the sixty-nine gates with controlled abandon to take the first-round lead.

With the slope so shrouded in fog it could have doubled as the movie set for the *Casablanca* airport scene, Killy took his place at the top, standing as stock-still as a granite cliff above a canyon, the first skier of the second heat. With his seeing-eye skis propelling him gate to gate, he threaded through them like a proverbial needle, recording a combined time of 99.73 seconds. And was now forced to wait anxiously with all his fans in the saucepan while others competed.

The first to take aim at his time was Haakon Mjoen of Norway, who came down in a faster combined time for his two runs, but was disqualified for having missed two gates. Now it was the turn of Karl Schranz of Austria, the biggest threat to Killy's triple crown. Schranz, who had been third after the first heat, pulled up short just before the tenth gate, a mysterious intruder in the mist crossing the course and causing him to skid to a halt. With three witnesses in tow, Schranz sidestepped his way back up to the top to ask the officials for a rerun. Permission was granted, and Schranz once more flashed down the course, this time in a near-perfect run to finish with a combined time of 99.22 seconds, a full half second faster than Killy.

The parishioners, who just minutes before had been cheering their hero, now fell into a deathly silence. For a second it looked like Killy's third gold would be unforthcoming.

But just as Dame Fortune was about to hang a funeral blanket over Killy's chances for an alpine triple, she had a change of heart and wrapped him up in the folds of her skirt. Or, more correctly and prosaically, the judges had a change of heart. For even as Schranz was attending a postrace press conference as the unofficial winner, the judges were huddling in an extraordinary debating society to consider a report that he had missed a gate before the interference on Gate 10. Finally, after two hours, the judges issued a bulletin which held that since Schranz had gone through somewhat less than the union scale of gates, he was disqualified. And the gold medal was awarded to Killy, touching off the most riotous scene since the storming of the Bastille.

With three mountains from which to look down upon the rest of the sports world, Killy decided that "an athlete should retire from sports at the climax of his career." And retired, the better to coin money from his mint performance. However, five years later he emerged from retirement to win the world professional title, declaring, "My clients would rather see me on a mountain than in a department store in Detroit." Jean-Claude Killy would return one more time, in 1988, when, as the copresident of the Albertville organizing committee, he saw his dream come true: the XVI Winter Games were awarded to France in his honor.

Which was only fitting for the man who had made the entire sports world into skiing fans. Maybe Dan Jenkins said it best when he wrote: "Years from now, when the sport is better understood and more popular, Killy's record may be regarded with all the misty-eyed reverence accorded a Babe Ruth summer."

70

Chris Evert

b. 1954

To some, watching Chris Evert play tennis ranked right up there in the thrills department with watching trees form their annual rings; it was just as inevitable, and just as exciting. To others, especially those admirers of her style and her apple-cheeked, girl-next-door looks, who made her their darling, watching her was pure excitement. It was a division of opinion best captured in a *New York Times* write-up of the 1975 U.S. Open finals between Evert and Evonne Goolagong when, after what the newspaper described as "a final [that] had a pattycake placidness at times," it eavesdropped on a conversation between two Forest Hills parishioners with different views from different pews on Evert's style of play. " 'Is this exciting or boring?' a man asked a woman friend. 'It's exciting,' the woman answered. 'It's great.' 'I think it's terrible,' he said." But whatever the perception of Chris Evert and her style of play, one thing was indisputable: She was a winner.

Chris Evert was defined as much by her style of play as by her wins. Hers was a game of survival, one which made great demands upon both herself and her opponents. Setting up residency on the baseline—almost as if she had paid two months' rent on the backcourt line and intended to use all of the prepaid amount—and rarely, if ever, moving into volleying range, Evert returned everything hit her way like a human backboard. Her opponents would attempt to stay with her, shot for shot, until finally, wearying of the interminable exercise of hitting the ball back against a wall named Evert, they became reduced to a state of disability—or, as one opponent put it, "tennis'd out."

One of the few who knew better than to fall into the trap of playing Evert's game was Billie Jean King, who knew it was akin to trying to take cheese from a set mousetrap to play a shot-for-shot game with her. "The times I've beaten her," said King, "I've been able to put pressure on her without making errors. I try to keep her moving and try to keep her from getting into any sort of baseline rhythm."

Billie Jean to the contrary, most of Evert's more aggressive foes were stalked to their knees by her relentless baseline game, a game she learned at the knee of her father, a teaching pro at Holiday Park in Fort Lauderdale, Florida. A nationally ranked player back in the days before Jack Kramer popularized the big serve-and-volley game in the postwar era, father Jimmy took his little five-year-old daughter out to the Holiday Park clay courts, there to school her in the game he knew best, one of running every ball down and hitting it back. No big serves, no taking chances, merely baseline stroke after baseline stroke after baseline stroke, etc., etc., etc., until her racket was worn thin with returns.

Little Chrissie, barely tall enough to see the stitching atop the net and too small to hold a tennis racket in one hand, learned her lessons, and very well, thank you! She also learned two other important disciplines from her father: a two-handed backhand, a throwback to the days of Pancho Segura, which at first allowed her to hold her racket in both hands and in years to come would give her a backhand that was eloquent in its power; and the most important element in her genius, an infinite capacity for patience.

It was a patience which manifested itself in an ice-cold air, one which connoted a quiet but conscious reserve force, enabling her to shut out all around her in order to concentrate on the only thing that really mattered: her game. Not surprisingly, she became known on the tour as the Ice Princess of the Court—and in England as the Ice Lolly, the latter the British word for a Popsicle.

One rival, Julie Heldman, believed Evert's coolness was calculated. "She created a good deal of her image," Heldman said in trying to explain her rival's cold persona. Evert agreed that she ofttimes showed all the impassivity of one of the members of Madame Tussaud's waxworks, but explained it by saying, "I don't show emotion, but it's there, believe me. If I smile and laugh out there, I'll lose concentration."

And even though growing up she had shown the normal adolescent emotions—throwing temper tantrums, rackets, and even a rare expletive deleted with equal abandon—by the time she made her debut on the circuit at the 1971 U.S. Open at Forest Hills, she had outgrown these emotional outbursts and adopted her unemotional mask. That was also the year America adopted as its sweetheart this pert, poised, ponytailed sixteen-year-old with the youthful face, clearly molded and calm with beauty's unchallenged confidence. Writer Grace Lichtenstein, noting the emergence of tennis's new darling, wrote, "Men thought her adorable, little girls worshipped her, middle-aged mothers came up to her at tournaments and told her she had restored their faith in youth. She was Miss American Pie."

Not incidentally, she could play tennis, too, becoming, three months and ten days short of her seventeenth birthday, the youngest semifinalist in the history of the women's national championship. In 1972 she won the U.S. clay-court championship; in '73 she won eleven tournaments and reached the Wimbledon and French finals; and, in '74, at the age of nineteen, she finally arrived at the top of the tennis mountain, winning a then-record 55 consecutive matches and the Wimbledon, French, and Italian titles.

At first it had been assumed that Evert's main competition for queen of the hill would be the ebullient Australian, Evonne Goolagong, whom she had first faced at Wimbledon in 1971 when Chrissie was just sixteen. In that first face-off, the ballerina-like Goolagong had beaten the machine-like Evert. But by the '75 U.S. Open Evert had not only turned the tables in winning her first Forest Hills title, but had done it in typical Evert fashion.

Down two games to one in the third and final set after a service break by Goolagong, Evert, with an obvious disinclination to be second, took matters in hand and became more aggressive, her lengthy baseline rallies grinding down Goolagong as surely and as monotonously as water a rock. First Goolagong's concentration began slipping, then her game, as Evert's style suffocated her, Evert winning the last five games—giving up a total of only three points over the last three. Afterward Goolagong would confess, "She was getting too much back, and I'm not patient enough to play that type of game and keep going....Getting everything back isn't my type of game."

"Getting everything back" wasn't many players' game, almost all eventually suffering loss of concentration—or, as Evert called it, "walkabouts"—in the face of Evert's overwhelming efficiency. Evert's wins were becoming routine—the U.S. Open victory was her eighty-fourth straight on clay over two and a half years—prompting one observer, leaving Forest Hills after the Goolagong match, to say, "What a surprise! Chris Evert won."

As Goolagong faded from the tennis landscape, Evert's real competition came from a new arrival, both on the scene and in the country: Martina Navratilova. Together they would stage the most two-sided rivalry in modern tennis. At first Chris's "tough as nails" mentality gave her a decided edge in the series, as she won fourteen of the first sixteen meetings between the two. But Martina, finally shaking off a bad case of nerves, began to overpower her. Still, Chris was able to impose her will on Martina in the 1985 and '86 French Opens, two matches which Evert would point to as the high points in her career: "In both matches I had to come from behind, and Martina was considered by many people to be in better shape, not to mention she was ranked number one and I was number two. It meant even more winning in the latter part of my career over Martina, who was then dominating the pro circuit."

By the time she finally decided to hang up her tennis racket after playing in the 1989 U.S. Open—appropriately enough, the place she had started nineteen years before—Chris Evert could look back on a career that proved patience was more than a virtue, it was its own reward. For over the course of that nineteen-year career, she had become the first to win a thousand singles matches—including 125 straight wins on her native surface, clay, an unmatched feat—and had become the first woman to win $1 million in prize money overall. All of which is another way of saying that tennis brought Chris Evert many happy returns—and vice versa.

71

Don Hutson

b. 1913

Just as a great martini is the correct mating of gin and vermouth at precisely the right moment—not a second too early or too late—the correct mating of football and the forward pass occurred when a mixture of genius and genuflection named Don Hutson came to pass.

Up to the time of Hutson's arrival, the presence of the pass had only been a rumor, football then a game of three yards and a cloud of dust. But Hutson was to rewrite the playbooks. And the record books as well.

Football, from Day One, had always been a plain-vanilla game, with the run the order of the day and the forward pass thought of merely as a novelty play—when it was thought of at all.

But then, on a cloudy November day in 1913, with the sun playing hide-and-seek with the clouds on the plains of West Point, a prohibitive underdog team from Notre Dame used the passing combination of Gus Dorais and Knute Rockne to pass the Cadets silly, clobbering the highly favored Cadets 35–13.

For the next two decades the game, both college and pro, set like ice on a pond, with only an occasional pass to break the monotony of the running game. Bronko Nagurski of the Bears experimented with the jump pass, throwing the ball as he approached the line of scrimmage—and a horde of opposing tacklers. But still, it remained more a curio than a part of the game.

Part of the reason for the forward pass's low profile was the rulebook, which held that passes could be thrown only from a distance of five yards behind the line of scrimmage. But in 1933, the lords of football passed a rule change opening up the passing game by permitting throws from anywhere behind the line of scrimmage. In an NFL meeting, Potsy Clark of the Portsmouth team grumbled, "Hell, Nagurski will pass from anywhere, so we might as well make it legal." It was a rule change that would ventilate the whole of football.

The very next year college also recognized the potential of the forward pass and redesigned the football, which had re-sembled an oversized goat's bladder, making it slimmer in the middle and easier to throw. Not incidentally, the beneficiary of both changes was already in place, ready to take advantage of them: Don Hutson.

Hutson was the second part of a soon-to-be-famous University of Alabama passing duo, Dixie Howell to Don Hutson, a tandem which led 'Bama to a three-year record of 24–3–1. In his usual understated manner, Hutson explained the success of the first great passing combination thusly: "I just ran like the devil and Dixie Howell got the ball there." And run "like the devil" this Southern Conference sprint champion did, averaging six to eight receptions per game, many of those in traffic. But perhaps the game that cemented his fame was the 1935 Rose Bowl, when the Howell-to-Hutson combination combined for six passes, good for 165 yards and two touchdowns—and a 29–13 upset win over favored Stanford.

Hutson's performance won him kudos, one West Coast sportswriter calling the Alabama Antelope "the world's greatest pass-catching, speed-merchant end." Immediately after the Rose Bowl game Hutson became the object of affection for two pro teams, the Green Bay Packers and the Brooklyn Dodgers, both of which, with the draft one year short of birth, signed him to contracts. The pass-minded coach of the Packers, Curly Lambeau, sought him out and argued his case, telling Hutson, "Look, we are a passing team. Brooklyn relies on power football. You're too small for that type of football. Our attack is built around passing. With us you'll be a star." But, truth to tell, Hutson brought his star with him.

The matter was referred to the desk of NFL Commissioner Joe Carr, who awarded Hutson to the Packers based on the earlier postmark of the envelope containing his contract. And if some labored under a delusion that Hutson couldn't cut it in the pros, they didn't labor long. His very first play in a Packer uniform served notice that a new era of pro football had arrived. After the Chicago Bears' opening exhibition game kickoff, the lank and willowy six-foot-one, 185-pound end split out to his left. With the Bears concentrating on the other end, Johnny Blood, Hutson raced down the field, faked the defending halfback to the outside—and out of his cleats as well—and outran the Bear safetyman down the middle. Packer quarterback Arnie Herber let loose with a perfect pass and Hutson took off after the arrow-straight ball and caught up with it without breaking stride for an 83-yard touchdown.

It was to be the first of many as Hutson continued to run past opposing backs for the next eleven years. Add to his speed and balletic moves his uncanny ability to fake, and you had a receiver of whom Chicago Bears coach George Halas once said, "I concede Hutson two touchdowns a game, and then I hope we can score more."

It was against Halas's Bears that Hutson made what many consider to be the greatest catch ever. With Dante Magnani, the fastest man on the Bears, assigned to him, Hutson, starting from left end in that deceptive, shuffling gait that was his trademark, headed in a diagonal line for the right goalpost. With Magnani matching him stride for stride, Hutson shifted into second gear, heading for the H-shaped post on the goal line. Still Magnani stayed with him. Down that imaginary line Hutson had staked out, he sped until he reached the 10-yard line; then he ran directly at the goalpost with breakneck speed and hooked the upright with his left arm, his momentum spinning him around the post just in time to catch and cradle the pass in his free right arm like a newborn while Magnani raced past the goalpost, through the end zone, and into the wall. Thus was born the post pattern.

For eleven years this frail, easygoing speedster with the choirboy face and moves that bedeviled opposing defensive backs continued to make catch after catch, and set record after record. And even though almost all of his records have been eclipsed in a game which has changed radically since he played, all of those who followed Don Hutson owe him a debt of gratitude for making them possible—for having, one might say, given each of them a pass to future records.

72

Joe Louis

1914–1981

Joe Louis's exploits are accorded no special place of prominence in boxing record books. His sixty-six bouts are sandwiched between the records of James J. Braddock, the man he succeeded as heavyweight champion of the world, and Ezzard Charles, the fighter who succeeded him.

Both Braddock and Charles had more professional engagements than did Louis, as did Jack Johnson, Jack Dempsey, Gene Tunney, Max Schmeling, Primo Carnera, Max Baer, and Jersey Joe Walcott. And there have been heavyweight champions with more knockouts, such as Carnera and Charles; a higher percentage of knockouts, such as Marciano and George Foreman; and even those who fought longer, such as Bob Fitzsimmons, Charles, Walcott, and Muhammad Ali. Tommy Burns and Larry Holmes had more consecutive knockouts in defense of their heavyweight titles than did Louis.

But no heavyweight champion—and probably no sports figure—ever captured the imagination of the public, fan and nonfan alike, as the smooth, deadly puncher with the purposeful advance who, at his peak, represented the epitome of pugilistic efficiency. And no man was ever so admired and revered as this son of an Alabama sharecropper, who carried his crown and himself—along with the hopes of millions of others—with dignity and pride.

But the measure of the uncomplicated man they called the Brown Bomber cannot be taken merely inside the ring. For, in a field devoted to fashioning halos, Joe Louis wore a special nimbus.

Louis dispensed his words as he did his punches, with a commendable economy of effort, saying a surprising number of things and saying them in a way we all wished we had. There was his evaluation of his country's chances in the global confrontation with the Axis powers: "We'll win, 'cause we're on God's side." Dignity. And then there was his enunciation of Billy Conn's chances in their second fight: "He can run, but he can't hide." Honesty.

Still, Joe Louis's place in the pantheon of sports greats doesn't rest on his using words, but on his using his fists and his body—as well as the bodies of his opponents. He drove Max Baer into the canvas like a nail, straightly driven, his body almost flush to the surface. He hit leading contender Eddie Simms so hard with his first punch that the beclouded Simms walked over to the referee scant seconds after the opening bell and asked the ref "to take a little walk around the roof." He sent out one single shot that sifted through the supposedly impenetrable network of elbows and arms covering Paulino Uzcudun's face, knocking out his front teeth and knocking out the "Basque Woodchopper" for the first time ever. He destroyed Primo Carnera, shifting his face like pudding and turning the gargantuan's picket-fence smile into that of a hurt, kicked dog with one first-round punch. He dropped the human butcher block Tony Galento with a left hook in the second round of their title fight that was described by writer Bugs Baer as being "so hard they could have counted him out in the air." And he drove into the Boxing Home for the Bewildered most of his other opponents, who, crediting growing legend, approached the ring as if it were an abattoir.

Reporters believed Joe Louis to be the most dependable story in sports. And the public, too, viewed him as dependable, to the point of invincibility. But Max Schmeling, brought out of near-retirement to be yet another sacrificial lamb, derailed the Louis bandwagon, hitting him with a right hand over a lazy left no fewer than fifty-four times and finally knocking out the myth in the twelfth round.

For most fighters such a defeat would have been devastating, their confidence—the essential property for success—taking an enormous jolt. But Joe Louis would come back within two months to knock out another ex-champion, Jack Sharkey, and then, almost one year to the day after his destruction at the gloves of Schmeling, would win the heavyweight championship of the world from Jim Braddock.

Louis would go on to avenge his loss to Schmeling with a 124-second annihilation that would set back the cause of the "Master Race" and bring joy to millions of Americans, and then would embark on what was charitably called the Bum of the Month Campaign, giving everyone a job as a heavyweight challenger, as if he were boxing's version of a thirties New Deal make-work agency, the WPA.

He was the very model of perseverance, plodding forward, his mien imperious, tracking down his prey, his indefatigable patience waiting for the chance. And then he would pull the trigger with the fastest two hands in the history of the heavyweight division, moving almost as if they had an intelligence of thier own. And when he had finally hooked his opponent, Louis, the greatest finisher in the history of boxing, would never let him get away—ask Billy Conn, his tormentor for twelve rounds, for references as to what happened in the thirteenth.

Louis would retire as undefeated heavyweight champion after running out of competition, and then come back. But he had emotionally packed it in, fighting only for the benefit of the IRS and his fans, many of whom were to leave Madison Square Garden on the night of October 26, 1951, their eyes wet with tears for their hero, who had been beaten by a younger future champion, Rocky Marciano.

However, in boxing's galaxy, Joe Louis was a star for a longer period than most, burning intensely and brilliantly, and lighting the way for so many.

73

Bob Feller

b. 1918

Who was it who said, "Lost time is never found again"? Ben Franklin? Or was it Bob Feller, who lost almost four full seasons of his career to World War II? And who, instead of being known as possibly the greatest pitcher of all time, became known only as the greatest pitcher between the years 1936 and 1952. As well as the young baseball phenomenon of the thirties.

On October 24, 1929, the stock market fell with a resounding crash. The feverish twenties had exploded, to be replaced by the troubled thirties; and the word "unemployed," once a seldom-used adjective, now became an oft-used and ominous noun as every fourth worker lost his job. The American Dream had become a nightmare. And, as it did, breadlines and bonus armies took the place of the boom-and-bust atmosphere of the twenties. People who couldn't fill their bellies with food looked for heroes to fill their souls with hope.

In this emotional vacuum one entertainment business, the movie industry, continued to thrive, providing escapism to millions every week. But if the movies were thriving, its fellow entertainment industry, baseball, was striking out at the box office. Major-league attendance, which had reached a high of more than ten million in 1930, had plummeted to less than six million by the mid-thirties. Several franchises were on the brink of collapse, banks already having repossessed the once-proud franchises in Cincinnati and Brooklyn, and several owners, like Connie Mack, down to their last shoestring, were reduced to selling their stars to make ends meet.

If anything, the future looked even less promising for the Mudville sixteen by 1936. However, that was the year baseball inadvertently stumbled onto the magic formula already discovered by Hollywood, serving up its own version of youth in a seventeen-year-old phenomenon named Bob Feller.

It was one of those happenstancical things, like the sighting of Lana Turner at Schwab's soda fountain. As the time-honored story goes, somewhere in that heartland of America known as Iowa, there was a fifteen-year-old youngster who, possessing all the skills of a pitcher of far greater experience and age, was throwing the ball plateward with such force that opposing batsmen were unable to strike up even a waving acquaintance with it. Now, as the Baseball Fates would have it, one of the scouts who covered the Iowa area was Cy Slapnicka of the Cleveland Indians, who had pitched for the Cubs and Pirates many years before, and who hailed from Cedar Rapids—as in Iowa. Slapnicka had tilled the soil, sowing a crop of contacts throughout the state to tell him of just such "phenoms," as those with potential were then called. Some of those contacts were local American Legion umpires who, like astronomers sighting a new star in the firmament of the heavens, now wore a carload of lead pencils down to stubs writing Slapnicka, c/o the Indians, you've-got-to-see-it-to-believe-it postcards, drawing pictures as well as words could to describe their discovery.

Sometime in 1935 circumstances had so arranged themselves that Slapnicka was able to plan a scouting trip to Des Moines. In those hardscrabble days a nickel went very far indeed, and now Slapnicka found it went far enough to afford him a side trip to the nearby farm town of Van Meter for a look-see at the much-heralded prospect. He got more than a look-see—he got an eyeful. For what to his wondering eyes should appear but a kid with a smoldering fastball and a curve that snapped off like an electric light switch. And so Slapnicka hied himself back to Cleveland to announce to one and sundry, "Gentlemen, I have found the greatest pitcher in history." Or words to like effect.

Chances to sign the "greatest" something or other usually vanish quicker than a Chinese dinner. And so the Indians, fasterthanyoucanreadthis, signed young Bobby Feller to a contract—one calling for $75 a month, plus a signing bonus of $1 and an autographed baseball.

Rather than consign the youngster to that Ellis Island of baseball, the minors, the Indians instead assigned him to the parent club as a non–roster player, allowing him to travel and work out with the club on a daily basis—especially with manager Steve O'Neill, a former major-league catcher. It was while in this unique form of baseball servitude, honing his fastball and refining his curve against teammates who would bat a league-leading .304 for the season, that Feller made the first partial payment on his rumored greatness.

For, as luck and scheduling would have it, during the 1936 All-Star break the Indians had scheduled an exhibition game against the St. Louis Cardinals—the self-same Gashouse Gang which featured the likes of Frankie Frisch, Pepper Martin, Joe Medwick, Leo Durocher, and Dizzy Dean. With little at stake, Slapnicka went to manager O'Neill and pleaded for a chance to let his young prospect pitch. O'Neill, looking at Slapnicka as if he had just contracted some horrible disease, like optimism, could only say, "It's a pretty tough lineup." But Slapnicka, assured that the youngster who threw with all the force of a wrecking ball could more than acquit himself, even against the mighty Gashousers, continued to insert his oar in the most meddlesome manner and answered, "I don't think he'll embarrass himself."

O'Neill finally threw up his hands and placed the ball in Feller's. And so it was that the youngster took the mound to face the fearsome Gashouse nine. Caring nothing for reputations,

Feller set his heavy muscles and granite dimpled jaw to the task and, in the three innings he worked, struck out eight Redbirds. One of those who watched Feller's performance in fascinated horror, tinged with just a little bit of awe, was perennial 20-game winner Dizzy Dean, who, when asked by a photographer after the game if he would pose for a picture with the youngster, is reputed to have laughed and said, "You'd better ask *him* if he'll pose with *me*."

One month later Feller made his major-league debut in an official American League game. This time he faced the other team from St. Louis, the Browns. And his performance was just as awesome. With his fastball passing virtually unmolested and his curveball likewise, a total of fifteen Brownies futilely flailed away in the general direction of Feller's deliveries as the teenager came within one strikeout of the modern American League single-game record and within two of Dizzy Dean's Major League record.

The "stuff" thrown that afternoon by the rawboned young-ster, still four years shy of voting age, dazzled not only the Browns, but also veteran plate umpire Red Ormsby. After the game Ormsby allowed as to how Feller had shown him more speed than any pitcher he had ever seen, including Walter Johnson and Lefty Grove.

It was merely a harbinger of things to come. The next year he struck out 17 in a game, tying Dean's record, and then, in 1938, raised it one by striking out 18 Detroit Tigers in his thirty-ninth and final outing of the year to post a league-leading total of 240 for the season. It was to be the first of seven times Feller would lead the American League in strikeouts.

By 1940, Feller had established homesteading rights to the title of Best Pitcher in Baseball. That was the year he started the season with a no-hitter, the only opening-day no-hitter in history. One of those who faced Feller that afternoon, Chicago White Sox outfielder Mike Kreevich, gave voice to the futility of trying to get the business end of a bat on a Feller pitch when, after a called strike, he turned to the umpire to protest. When the umpire asked him what was wrong with the pitch, Kreevich answered, "It sounded a little high to me."

Others, like Bucky Harris, manager of the woebegone Washington Senators, seeing his players as bereft as Robinson Crusoe without a boat in the face of Feller's offerings, could only tell them, "Go on up there and hit what you see. If you can't see it, come on back."

No less an observer than Satchel Paige, who had pitched against Feller in postseason exhibition games, would say of Feller's superhuman speed: "If anybody threw that ball harder than Rapid Robert, then the human eye couldn't follow it."

But it wasn't just Feller's peerless firepower that made him what he was, it was also one of the biggest, most bewildering curves ever seen, described by one player as "having a terrific spin on it. You could almost hear the seams biting into the wind." Joe DiMaggio, who broke in the same year as Feller, said, "He was awfully fast. But his curveball was the best I've ever seen."

Feller would win 27 games in 1940 and 25 more in 1941. And then, just days after Pearl Harbor, he became one of the first major leaguers to enlist in the service, joining the United States Navy and spending the next four years in the Pacific theater, most of those aboard the battleship *Alabama*. Feller picked up right where he'd left off in '46, his first full season back, piling up a record-setting 348 strikeouts and another 26 wins.

It was estimated that had not the Fates intervened, Feller, having left baseball at the top of his powers and having returned similarly inclined, would have recorded another 93 wins, another 989 strikeouts, and another 1,232 innings pitched, moving him as high as second among modern pitchers in these categories.

As it was, Bob Feller's 3 no-hitters, 12 one-hitters—seven spoiled by never-should-have-been scratch hits—and 1,764 strikeouts were more than enough for him to gain entrance to Cooperstown in 1962, his very first year of eligibility. Youth has indeed been well served by a youth who had served well.

74

Bronko Nagurski

1908–1990

Damon Runyon once wrote, "About 95 percent of all sports tradition is pure fiction. Lies, if you like. But harmless. Who the hell cares if long after a sport event the facts get a little twisted?"

Call them "pure fiction," "lies," or plain old myths, they are the coin of the realm and subject matter for storytellers. And no athlete has ever provided storytellers with a more fertile field than Bronko Nagurski. According to one story, his coach at the University of Minnesota asked him what position he played, and he replied, "All of them." And he did, starring at end, tackle, and fullback and becoming the only man ever named to all-America teams at two different positions, tackle and fullback in the same year.

How he got to the University of Minnesota is yet another story, oft-told at banquets and such. The story has it that the Minnesota coach, Doc Spears, on a recruiting trip, asked road directions from a youth behind a plow. As Spears estimated the youth's muscle, the youngster—Nagurski, of course—picked up the plow and pointed. (The story was to be embroidered years later by Nagurski himself, who, when told the story, asked, "Without horses?")

Whatever the truth, one thing is clear: Bronko Nagurski was a mythic figure. And the stories told about him are half true. The only question is, which half?

This much is known: Nagurski was a towering six-foot-two and weighed 226 pounds. And, as George Halas described him, "It was all—literally all—muscle, skin, and bone. He didn't have an ounce of fat on him. A lot of men have passed in front of me, but none with a build like that."

The personification of power, Nagurski ran with all the agility of a man plowing his crops between twin spavines, his feet far apart, carrying the ball with a "trespassers will be prosecuted" mentality, bowling over tacklers with the force of a wrecking ball.

But while Nagurski ran his own interference, it was as a blocker that his fame was formed. Back in those days of bare-knuckle football, with three yards and a crowd of bodies the norm, Nagurski could clear a path through the forest primeval. One unfortunate opponent, knocked galley west by a Nagurski block, awakened to find his trainer bending over him and asking if he was all right. "I'm all right," he responded. Then, looking up at the Minnesota stands, he asked, "But how did all those people get back up in the stands?"

After starring at Minnesota for three years, Nagurski signed with the Chicago Bears in 1930 for the princely sum of $5,000 a year, in Hoover dollars. His presence as the league's top power runner made an impact on the Bears almost immediately—and on his opponents as well. One of those, Ernie Nevers, described what hitting Nagurski felt like: "Tackling him was like trying to tackle a freight train, going downhill." Another, Benny Friedman, recalled, "I was at safety when he broke through, with only me between him and the goal. It was like ordering a switchman to stop a locomotive with his bare hands." And still another, Steve Owen, said, "Tacklers to Nagurski are like flies on the flank of a horse—a nuisance, but not serious."

In a game against the Portsmouth Spartans in 1933, Nagurski took the ball on a pitchout with bare seconds remaining in the game. Thundering around left end, Nagurski treated the Portsmouth tacklers like so many tenpins, bowling them out of his way as he chugged down the sideline, several tacklers clinging to him. He shook them off with barely a turn of his head and shifted into another gear. By the time he had reached the goal line his momentum was so great he charged right through the end line and rammed into a brick wall. Only that stopped him. When he revived, he supposedly said, "That last guy hit me awful hard."

In '34, he turned into a blocking back, leading the interference for little Beattie Feathers, who became the first NFL back to rush for a thousand yards—"about nine hundred of them running up Nagurski's backside," remembered broadcaster Jack Brickhouse. It was also that year that Dick Richards, owner of the Detroit Lions, who had witnessed Nagurski personally trample his team twice that year on the Bears' way to a perfect 13–0 record, sat down at a dinner table next to Bronko and said, "Nagurski, I'll give you ten thousand dollars to get the hell out of this league. Understand, I'm not trying to buy your contract. I just don't want you ruining any more of my ballplayers."

In 1937 he successfully combined his football playing with a wrestling career. In one span of three weeks he wrestled eight times from Vancouver to Philadelphia and played in five games with the Bears. In 1938, demanding an additional $1,000 from Halas and finding his demands unrewarded, he quit to pursue wrestling, but came back in 1943 to lead the Bears to another NFL championship, starring as a tackle, linebacker, and fullback.

Grantland Rice, noting that many called Nagurski the greatest player of all time, wrote, "He was a star end, a star tackle, and a crushing fullback who could pass. I believe eleven Nagurskis could beat eleven Granges or eleven Thorpes." And that's neither tall tale nor lie.

75

Bob Gibson

b. 1935

In the long history of baseball there have been no more than a handful of baseball pitchers who burned with a fire deep within, scornful and surly, pitching with a take-no-prisoner mentality. Their numbers include the likes of Carl Mays, Burleigh Grimes, Red Ruffing, Lefty Grove, Sal Maglie, and Early Wynn, fiery competitors all.

But in any group picture taken of those murderously competitive pitchers, they would all have to move over to make room for the modern addition to their ranks, Bob Gibson. Front and center.

For where Early Wynn, now moved two spaces over to make room for Gibson in the picture, once acknowledged that he would hit his mother if she were crowding the plate with a bat in her hands, you had the distinct feeling that the hard-boiled Gibson would have plunked his mother, his father, and everyone at his family picnic in the ribs if he'd had to.

To say that Gibson was as hard-boiled as a three-day-old egg at that same family picnic doesn't even begin to describe him. As tall and unmoving as a steel etching, complete with a slab face hardly saturated with mirth and eyes as chilling as two ice-cream cones, Gibson was an imposing figure on the mound, one who raised the art of intimidation to a new level.

During his seventeen-year career, Gibson's relationship with batters was such that it was a sure thing they wouldn't be exchanging cards at Christmastime. To him, batters were Public Enemies One to infinity.

Gibson came by his volcano-like anger quite naturally, having been raised in an Omaha ghetto that passed for a neighborhood and, as a youth, suffering from a catalog of disorders that included recurring bouts with pneumonia, hay fever, rickets, and a rheumatic heart, with asthma attacks thrown in for bad measure. Growing up a little slower and a little frailer than the other kids in the neighborhood, he was still sturdy enough to participate in sports in high school—starring in baseball and basketball and high-jumping on the track team. But "I didn't play football," Gibson would remember. "I was too small growing up for that."

Still, by the time he had graduated from high school the talents of this by-now six-foot-one 180-pounder were large enough so that others took notice: the nearby St. Louis Cardinals in baseball and the nearer-by Creighton University in basketball. Gibson had had his heart set on winning a basketball scholarship to Indiana U., but Indiana had apparently already met its quota of black scholarships: one. And so Creighton it became.

There Gibson starred in basketball, scoring well over 20 points a game and setting all manner of school records, and pitched and played the outfield for the baseball team. One source had his pitching record at 6–2, but Gibson remembered "pitching more than that." However, there was no dispute about his batting record, Gibson batting .340 in his senior year to lead the conference.

By now playing semipro ball during the summers, Gibson

determined that "I could get to the Majors fastest as a pitcher. Outfielders are a dime a dozen, unless you're a Willie Mays." But Gibson wasn't Willie Mays; instead he was, then as later, uniquely Bob Gibson. And that was more than good enough for Omaha, the Cardinals' American Association farm team, which signed him to a contract.

In that first season, Gibson pitched for both Omaha and Columbus, Georgia. But, truth to tell, his performance was was at best compromising, as he won all of six games and posted ERA figures that rivaled the national debt. "All I had then," Gibson said, "was a fastball and a slider. No real curve, and no control." The next year, 1958, Gibson again split his season, this time between Omaha and Rochester, New York. But his ERA and strikeout totals suddenly became respectable. Then, in his third year, he again had a split season, but this time the two clubs were Omaha and the parent club, the St. Louis Cardinals.

There he came under the wing of the boss of the Cardinal employment bureau, manager Solly Hemus. With most of his staff's arms up for adoption, Hemus started Gibson for the first time on July 30. And Gibson responded by pitching a shutout, the first of his career 56. But the rest of the year was somewhat less than sterling, Gibson finishing with a 3–5 record and a 3.32 ERA. That winter Gibson became a two-sport man, as he played for the Harlem Globetrotters.

The 1960 season started with Gibson back in the minors. Midway through the season, with the Cards challenging Pittsburgh and Milwaukee for the league lead, Hemus called up the usual suspects to help out, Gibson included. But Gibson went on to lose a big game against the Cubs and Hemus went on to use him less and less frequently during the season, starting him just six times as Gibson posted an astronomical 5.59 ERA, hardly the stuff of which legends are made.

Convinced by now that Hemus "didn't like me," Gibson was overjoyed when, just past the halfway mark of the '61 season, the Cardinals fired Hemus and brought up Gibson's manager at Omaha, the soft-spoken Johnny Keane. Keane, who had once admonished Gibson "not to pout on the mound," now just as quietly, and effectively, handed the ball to Gibson on the manager's first day on the job and said, "Here, you pitch." And Gibson did, hitting a home run to help himself beat the Dodgers. Now part of the rotation with Ray Sadecki, Larry Jackson, Ernie

Broglio, and Curt Simmons, Gibson pitched a total of 211 innings and won 13 games, struck out 166 batters, the fifth-best figure in the league, and posted an ERA of 3.24, also fifth-best.

For the next five years, Gibson would win more games than he had the year before. But the most important of them was his nineteenth win in 1964 when, on the last day of the season, pitching four solid innings in relief, he won the most hotly contested pennant race in National League history for the Cardinals, beating out the Reds and the Phillies, who had led the league by six and a half games just two weeks before.

In the World Series that followed, Gibson left his calling card of greatness by striking out five of the first seven Yankees he faced. Unfortunately, he also left the game after the eighth inning, having given up eight hits and four runs. But four days later he came back to strike out 13 Yankees and win the fifth game on a six-hitter. And then he started Game 7 three days later and won, striking out nine more Yankees, giving him a grand total of 31 strikeouts, more than anyone in history had ever accumulated in one Series—more than Koufax, more than Mathewson, more than Johnson, more than Dean, more than Grove, more than anybody.

For the next three seasons Gibson continued to throw his heat-seeking missiles—now consisting of a fastball from hell, a jagged curve that looked like it fell off a pool table, and a harder-than-hard slider—past batters, who took their places in the batter's box looking like Sunday school teachers fully expecting to be hit in the head by an errant spitball. Scowling and frowning, Gibson would go into his windup and then come at the batter with the weightless ball cupped in his hand as he began his whirling, twisting delivery, leaving them with little chance to find the ball with a divining rod, let alone a bat.

Gibson would conclude his delivery with his signature follow-through, a follow-through that had him falling two steps toward first. But his overall ability, and agility, were such that he could field any ball bunt down the third-base line, pouncing like a cat upon its prey—as he proved in the fifth game of the '64 Series when he made an unbelievable falling throw that just nipped Joe Pepitone at first and saved the game, and the Series, for the Cards.

The 1967 season started out like any other for Gibson. Except more so. In his first start he tied a major-league record for strikeouts at the beginning of a game, striking out the first five Giants he faced. Some 140 strikeouts later, facing the Pittsburgh Pirates, and Roberto Clemente, Gibson rocketed in one of his fastballs and Clemente bruised it back to the pitcher's mound, in the process bruising and breaking Gibson's leg. Gibson went home to watch his bones mend for fifty-six games of the season, but the Cardinals, deep in talent, still won the pennant by ten and a half games. And faced the "Impossible Dream" Red Sox in the World Series.

But Gibson, pitching a six-hitter in Game One, a five-hitter in Game Four, and a three-hitter in Game Seven, made the "Impossible Dream" just that, as the Cards won the Series from the Bosox in seven.

Then along came 1968, when his microscopic ERA of 1.12 was the lowest in the so-called lively-ball era, going back to 1920, and his 13 shutouts were the most in a season since Grover Cleveland Alexander threw 16 in '16. And then there was the World Series. And more records.

In Game One, Gibson was at his overwhelming best, striking out five of the first six Tigers he faced and then, with strikeouts coming in pairs, three-of-a-kinds, and diamond-straight flushes, bearing down in the ninth to strike out the side for a record 17. When the scoreboard flashed the message that he had just broken Sandy Koufax's World Series record with his sixteenth, striking out Norm Cash for the second out in the ninth inning, Cardinal catcher Tim McCarver stood and pointed toward the scoreboard. Gibson, who had divorced himself from all around him, gave a growl that sounded something like "Gimme the goddamn ball!" And then turned around to see what the hell McCarver was pointing at. And when he did, a small castor-oil smile creased his face. Then he went back to work, threading a needle's eye with his fastball to get Willie Horton on a called third strike for his seventeenth K.

Game Four was more of the same as Gibson continued his one-man reign of terror with a five-hit, ten-strikeout perform-ance. It was beginning to seem that Gibson was almost immune to defeat in World Series games. Before the seventh game, the Tiger dressing room echoed those sentiments, as Norm Cash jokingly said, "I don't know about him not being Superman—he's dressing in a phone booth over there." And for three innings he looked the part, as he retired the first nine Tigers, the ninth being

Mickey Lolich, who took a called third strike for Gibson's thirty-second strikeout in the Series, breaking the previous record, set by Guess Who? For six innings Gibson and Lolich matched each other, throwing goose eggs—except that Gibson's goose egg was better formed, as he'd allowed only one hit, a scratch single. Then, in the seventh, Fate pointed her capricious finger at center fielder Curt Flood, who misplayed a ball hit by Jim Northrup into a triple and two runs. The Tigers went on to win the game and the Series, but not before Gibson had performed miracles and near-miracles.

For seven more years, Bob Gibson would continue to write his legend, pitching with a smoldering fire within. Then he'd hang up his spikes to take his place both in baseball's Hall of Fame and in the front row of the group picture of some of baseball's—and all of sports'—most hard-nosed competitors.

76

Otto Graham

b. 1921

If we are to believe the words of coaching immortal Vince Lombardi that "Winning isn't everything, it's the only thing," then we must consider an athlete's ability to win as one of the standards for greatness. And nobody, but nobody, in the history of team sports was a bigger winner than Otto Graham.

Graham's coach for ten years, Paul Brown, certainly thought so when he said, "The test of a quarterback is where his team finishes. By that standard, Otto Graham was the best of all time."

Paul Brown and Otto Graham were what one of the writers of the day, columnist Walter Winchell, might have called an "item," a twosome who were instrumental in the formation of the Cleveland Browns—both as a franchise and as a winner. For when the Cleveland Rams, winners of the 1945 NFL championship, heeded their hibernational ambitions and followed Horace

Greeley's advice to go west to L.A., abandoning Cleveland, the new football kid on the block, the All-American Football Conference, began casting more than a covetous eye at the City by the Lake. It was more than a case of football, like nature, abhorring a vacuum; it was a case of establishing homesteading rights to one of the most potentially lucrative markets in all of sports. But only with a team that could match the dearly departed Rams in winning the hearts of the loyal parishioners by winning on the field.

Putting together a new franchise from scratch is damnably serious business. And Brown approached it as such. The methodical coach—who had already built his reputation as the architect of great teams at Massillon (Ohio) High, then at Ohio State, and later at the Great Lakes Naval Training Station—now went about the task of building a better mousetrap. Unlike Casey Stengel—who, some fifteen years later, faced a similar challenge in assembling a new franchise called the New York Mets and made his first choice a catcher named Hobie Landrith, "because," as only Casey could put it, "without a catcher you'd have all those passed balls"—Brown, hardly saturated with such mirth, decided rather than empty the mission houses in search of manpower he would pick a man who could lead the new franchise to victory. Immediately. And that choice was a young quarterback out of Northwestern University named Otto Graham.

Graham had first caught Brown's eye in 1941, when he threw two touchdown passes to lead Northwestern to a 14–7 upset win over Ohio State and hand Brown his only defeat in his inaugural season as the Buckeye coach. The next year, as a triple-threat tailback in the Northwestern single-wing attack, he caught the attention of the entire country. For "all" Graham did that year, despite Northwestern's 1–9 record, was set a Big 10 passing record, lead the Big 10 in passing and total offense, and be named the Most Valuable Player in the conference.

But Otto Graham was more, much more, than a triple-threat man on the gridiron. He was a triple-threat man in every sense of the word, having lettered in basketball and baseball as well as football. In fact, in his senior year he was named to the all-American basketball team, one of only three men, along with Bennie Oosterbaan and Wes Fesler, to be an all-American in both football and basketball.

In Graham, Brown had a found a passer who possessed both

a terrific sense of timing and fantastic peripheral vision, one who would be the linchpin in the well-oiled machinery he hoped to field, a team built along the premise once enunciated by e. e. cummings that "precision created movement." Besides, hadn't Graham beaten his teams in two out of three matchups and proven himself a winner?

And so, operating with an if-you-can't-beat-them-at-least-join-them philosophy, Brown went to sign up Graham, then enrolled at Colgate in a program for Navy pilots. Graham, who had been drafted by the Detroit Lions of the established NFL—but had never heard from them—succumbed to Brown's blandishments: an offer of a two-year contract, a signing bonus, and $250 a month for the duration of the war.

With the full understanding that owning a Stradivarius does not make you an Isaac Stern, Brown now went about orchestrating the rest of his masterpiece. With the war over and Johnny, Dante, and Mac all marching home, Brown signed such future stars as Dante Lavelli, Mac Speedie, Marion Motley, Special Delivery Jones, Lou Groza, and other war-hardened ex-GI's to complement the presence of his star performer, Otto Graham.

From their very first game of their inaugural 1946 season, a 44–0 trouncing of the Miami Seahawks, the team, now called the Browns—not named after Paul Brown, as is generally believed, but instead after another champion of the time, the Brown Bomber, Joe Louis—were a dynasty in the making. But, truth to tell, Graham did not start that first game, having reported late to training camp after making a small detour along the way to play pro basketball with the Rochester Royals of the National Basketball League, helping them win the 1945–46 NBL championship.

By the third game of the season Graham had been installed as the T-formation quarterback, and he immediately began filling the glass slipper already measured for him. In that first season the Browns won twelve regular-season games and the league championship, and Graham—by now called Automatic Otto because of his incredible precision—led the league in passing. If you were writing footnotes, the 1947, '48, and '49 seasons all would read *ibid.*, the Browns and Graham both leading the league each and every year.

And yet the Browns, indeed the entire new league, was still overlooked by the football public and the Lords of Football. When anyone would even bother mentioning the AAFC to the commissioner of the established NFL, Elmer Layden, he would merely snort, "Let them go get a football." But footballs and all the necessary trappings were costing both leagues more than they could financially endure. Finally, in 1950, the high price of financial warfare brought a truce as the two leagues merged, with three AAFC teams admitted to the established NFL—including the Browns and Otto Graham.

Now the Browns would get their comeuppance, or so the reasoning went, with their very first game under pro football's big tent, to be played at Philadelphia against the defending NFL champion Eagles. But if the members of the football establishment labored under a delusion, they didn't labor long, as in fascinated horror they watched the Browns beat the Eagles in a 35–10 romp that wasn't as close as the score indicated. Again, Graham led the way, completing 21 passes for a whopping 346 yards and 3 TDs and running for yet another.

By the end of their first year in the NFL the Browns had won ten of twelve regular-season games and beaten the Los Angeles, nee Cleveland, Rams in the championship game. The next year saw Cleveland repeat as conference champs but lose to the Rams in the championship game. The 1952 and 1953 seasons were repeat performances, as both years the Browns were conference champs and both years they lost the championship game, each time to the Detroit Lions. But 1954 saw the Browns once again win their conference title and this time turn the tables on the Lions in the championship game, 56–10, with Graham throwing one arrow-straight pass for a TD and running for three more in what was supposed to be his last game. However, Brown prevailed upon Graham to come back for one last victory lap; and victory lap it was as Graham, in his valedictory, led the Browns to the championship, a satisfying 38–10 win over the Rams as he passed for two touchdowns and ran for two more.

It was a fitting finale for the winningest player in the history of professional team sports, a performer who had more than acquitted himself gloriously, both on the gridiron and on the court. Over his decade-long professional career, between the two sports, Otto Graham played in at least one championship game every year. And his teams won twelve of those fifteen championship games. Few athletes ever achieve that level of success in one sport; none, other than Otto Graham, has ever achieved it in two.

77

Pete Rose

b. 1941

Just when it seemed that the old-time virtues of industry and energy had disappeared completely from the baseball landscape, along came a throwback to yesteryear named Pete Rose who spat on his hands, rolled up his sleeves, and with workmanlike vigor brought the hard-hat ethic back to baseball.

The legend of Pete Rose had its start during spring training, 1963. Normally spring training is a paid vacation. With most players merely going through the motions without the accompanying emotions, a twenty-one-year-old rookie tried to make the Cincinnati Reds' roster by hustling every which way in order to dispose of the unfair advantage most veterans had over him. His perpetual motion raised more than a few eyebrows. And voices.

One of those belonged to Mickey Mantle, who, sitting on the bench during a Yankees-Reds spring training to-do, watched what appeared to him to be one of nature's irregularities almost running out of his uniform hustling down to first on a walk. With a breezy nonchalance, he turned to teammate Whitey Ford and remarked, "Look at Charlie Hustle."

That remark, meant as a derogatory aside, was a classic understatement. For Rose, who took the comment as his Big Red Badge of Courage, continued to hustle, not only to first, but into the Reds' lineup at second and then, from his very first major-league game—when he hit a triple off Bob Friend that saw him belly-thomp into third—all the way to the National League's Rookie of the Year award.

Together with the excitement he created on the base paths, the switch-hitting Rose could step to the plate and make any fan feel "Charlie Hustle" alone was well worth the price of admission. Stepping into the batter's box, his eyes holding his opponent's in a fixed stare, Rose went through a little ritual: He would tap his spikes with his bat, shove his batting helmet back on his head with a vigorous thrust, and then crouch down, his posterior approximately two furlongs behind him. But a ballplayer's record is as expressive as his stance, and by the conclusion of his first decade in the Majors, Rose was but 78 hits shy of the 2,000-hit plateau. Now the man of whom writer Larry Merchant noted "gets hits in the present and lives in the past" began to pass some of the greatest names in baseball history like so many road signs on the way to Cooperstown.

Rose—at age 36 but, as he put it, "going on 21"—became the lucky thirteenth man to pass the 3,000-hit mark on May 5, 1978. And during the rest of the '78 season he not only hit in a National League record–tying 44 consecutive games but raised his hit total to 3,164, passing Cap Anson and Paul Waner in the bargain. By the end of 1979 only 819 hits separated Rose and the all-time hit leader, Ty Cobb.

And so it went, for five more seasons, as Rose continued to play like a man who had discovered the secret of perpetual motion. Here he could be seen belly-flopping in that headlong dive of his, there racing the base paths in a manner that looked like he was answering his mother's last call to dinner, and everywhere playing the game with a defiant pride known only to youngsters.

At the age of forty-four, when most self-respecting ball-players would be well-advised to stay home, Pete Rose was still full of spit and vinegar. And just 127 hits shy of Ty Cobb's record 4,191. Having taken his one-man act from Cincinnati to Phila-delphia, with a one-year stopover in Montreal, he now came home to Cincinnati as a player and manager. And it was there, on September 11, 1985, that Pete Rose, penciling himself in to face San Diego pitcher Eric Show, drove a fastball like a shot out of a howitzer toward left field. And as it fell in front of Padres left fielder Carmelo Martinez, Rose added the final note to his fabulous career by hustling all the way to first.

Pete Rose had just displayed the enthusiasm that had led to the nickname Charlie Hustle. He'd also just taken a bat and dubbed himself the most prolific batsman of all time.

But the virtues that had made him one of baseball's all-time greats on the field were replaced by darker ones off it. The man who had tried mightily to fashion himself into the second coming of Ty Cobb turned instead into the second coming of "Shoeless" Joe Jackson. His financial fandangos earned him a year-plus banishment to a federal prison for income tax evasion, and his betting shenanigans earned him permanent banishment from the halls of baseball. And from the Baseball Hall of Fame as well.

78/79

Doc Blanchard

b. 1924

Glenn Davis

b. 1924

There have been twosomes throughout history as well paired as salt and pepper, in many locales and in every imaginable field: biblical, Cain and Abel; mythological, Damon and Pythias; musical, Gilbert and Sullivan; financial, Dow and Jones; Hollywood, Laurel and Hardy; and political Franklin and Roosevelt. Football is no exception, and its most celebrated pairing of all time is that of Doc Blanchard and Glenn Davis, the Mr. Inside and Mr. Outside of college football. Not since the historic mating of the hare and the tortoise had there been such a mix-and-match pair. Both were West Point, Class of '47, but there the similarities ended.

Davis had originally been in the Class of '46, and in his freshman season of '43, as a triple-threat fullback, he had scored eight touchdowns and finished seventh in the nation in total yardage.

Hailing from Bonita, California—where he had earned thirteen letters, four in baseball and three each in football, basketball, and track—Davis, on the basis of his having scored 236 points in his senior year, an average of better than three TDs a game, had won the Helms Foundation Trophy as the best schoolboy athlete in the area. Recommended to Army coach Red Blaik by a Dartmouth professor of dramatics, Davis was to prove the very first time he stepped onto the Plains of West Point that he was as advertised. Taking a ten-event physical-efficiency test that every entering cadet must pass, Davis scored 962½ out of a possible 1,000, breaking the existing record by 61 points.

Davis was so perfectly coordinated that he vaulted ten feet the first time he ever held a pole in his hand. In his final year, Davis was asked to run against Navy on the same afternoon his team was playing against its archrival on the baseball field. Dressing in a staff car en route to the meet, Davis got to the starting line scant seconds before the 100-yard dash, got to the mark, and tied the West Point record at 9.7. He later ran the 220 and set a new record at 20.9.

On the baseball field he was equally at home, or wherever he bivouacked, which was usually center field. He hit around .400, and in his entire career at the academy was thrown out stealing just once. In one exhibition game against the Montreal Royals, he beat out a bunt, then stole second, third, and home. Branch Rickey, who earlier that year had signed another promising speedster named Jackie Robinson, offered Davis a blank contract after his last game at West Point in 1946, saying, "This is my offer. I'll hand you a Dodger contract tomorrow and you can fill in whatever amount you feel is fair."

But it was on the football field that this all-sport athlete truly excelled. Running with gusto, this whirlwind wearing a boyish-tousled look would break the line of scrimmage and without so much as a by-your-leave turn his toes to pasture, running in a smooth and unbroken line toward the end zone. Many's the time that, hemmed in by would-be tacklers, he would give them a head fake or a move and continue on his way, untouched by human hands.

The party of the second part, Felix "Doc" Blanchard, had come out of Bishopville, South Carolina, and had earned his spurs at the University of North Carolina, where, as a 6′1½″, 210-pound freshman, he was hailed by rival coaches, who came away shaking their heads and proclaiming, "This boy will be the greatest ever." But the winds of war were blowing throughout the country, and every Tom, Dick, and Felix was caught up in the draft. Blanchard first tried to enter the Navy, but was turned down because he was five pounds heavier than the Navy manual said a healthy sailor ought to be. His coach, Jim Tatum, tried to sweat the excess weight off him, but it was not to be. As Tatum explained: "He was all muscle and concrete, and I could only cook off about two pounds."

And so this perfect physical specimen—who put the shot almost 52 feet the first year he tried it and was so fast that he ran 100 yards in ten seconds flat—went to the Point, where he was to team up with Davis to form the greatest duo in football history.

The two complemented each other perfectly, Blanchard's thunder playing to Davis's lightning. In the three years Numbers 35 (Blanchard) and 41 (Davis) were an item—1944, '45, and '46— the Black Knights of the Hudson won with startling variety and dismal monotony. Feeding on their opponents like a hungry diner would on a $20 sirloin, with mushrooms on the side, the touchdown twins carried Army to a three-year record of 27 wins and 1 tie. Overall, their scorched-earth policy led to as many casualties on the playing fields as on the battlefield, as their Army teams rolled up 1,179 points to their opponents' 161—an average of 42 points a game against an average of just 6 for their opponents.

In their first year together, scorekeepers almost qualified for disability from hanging numbers as Army rolled over their first six opponents by a combined score of 395 to 21, with four of those games featuring three-TD performances by Davis. Then came Notre Dame and the worst shellacking the Irish have ever suffered, 59–0. After the game, Notre Dame coach Ed McKeever wired home, "Have just seen Superman in the flesh. He wears Number 35 and goes by the name of Blanchard."

The last game of the year was against Army's traditional rival, Navy, which was equally staffed to the gunwales with talent. But it made no never mind to Blanchard & Davis as they ground down the Middies, 23–7. Afterward, Yale coach Herman Hick-man, commenting on Blanchard, could only say, "This is the only man who runs his own interference." But, truth to tell, Davis and what Blaik called his "unlimited gearshifts" had sunk Navy just as surely.

For it was Davis's year as well. Number 41 was the country's leading scorer, with 20 TDs, and his yards-per-carry average was an unbelievable 12.4. He won the Maxwell Club Trophy, the Walter Camp Award, and the Helms Foundation Award as the outstanding college player of the year. Blanchard's statistics were not too shabby either, with 9 touchdowns and a 7.1-per-carry average.

The 1945 season saw the two-man cakewalk continue apace as Blanchard & Davis led Army to crushing victories over the likes of Duke, Michigan, Pennsylvania, Wake Forest, Navy, and Notre Dame. During the first half of the Notre Dame game, after Blanchard had scored twice and Davis thrice, thus ending the competitive phase of the game right then and there, Coach Blaik compassionately benched his dynamic duo. "Heck, Colonel," protested Davis, heaving his helmet in disgust and retiring now to sample the soap in the dressing room, "I want to play football and you're not giving me a chance."

But despite Davis's heroics, 1945 belonged to Blanchard, at least as far as awards and recognition go. For this 208-pound battering ram, who attacked the line like the first gun of a rallying army, was unmatched in his time as a tackler and blocker—and was also an outstanding defensive back. Add to all of those qualities his duties as Army's punter and kickoff specialist, ofttimes kicking the ball through the end zone. And, of course, the 19 touchdowns he scored during the season. For all of this, Felix "Doc" Blanchard was awarded the Heisman and Maxwell Trophies as well as the Walter Camp Award as the outstanding football player of the year, and also became the first football player to win the AAU's Sullivan Award, given to America's leading amateur athlete.

In 1946, the team of Blanchard & Davis was finally challenged—first by Michigan in a game that went back and forth like a parcel nobody wanted to pay postage on and which Army finally won 20–13 on Davis's 105 yards and his seven completed passes for another 168 yards; then by Notre Dame in a pointless 0–0 tie; and finally, by Navy in a 21–18 cliffhanger that went down to the final gun. Now Fate, trying to balance the ledger, shifted her attentions back to Davis's side, somewhat in ar-

rearages, and presented him with all of football's honors, including the Heisman Trophy.

It was a fitting end to three magnificent years by two
magnificent athletes, two football peas in a pod who had,
between them, scored 89 touchdowns and averaged 8.3 yards
each and every time one of them—much to the chagrin of their
opponents—carried the ball. Together, they cut a path across the
football gridiron—and across football history as well.

80

Bruce Jenner

b. 1949

It's but a very thin line that separates sanity and basketmaking. And the athlete who comes closest to going over that line is the decathlete.

Despite the fact that the decathlete has been described as the most well-rounded, balanced athlete in all of track and field, high jumper Dwight Stones, tongue firmly lodged in cheek, once said, "Don't bet on their being well-balanced. There is enormous discipline required in the ten events of the decathlon. They train alone for so long for each event and then compete in the decathlon only about four times a year. How mentally balanced can they be?"

Bruce Jenner was one of those decathletes who stood guilty

as charged of appearing to cross the line. Or at least according to his then-wife, Chrystie, who got a firsthand look at his eccentricities while he was training for the 1976 Olympics. "At the grocery store or at the bank he's going through the motions of throwing the discus, or he's lifting his legs like he's hurdling," she admitted. "I'm sure people think he's crazy."

But such indulgences are to be allowed in the natural ebullition of decathletes. For theirs is a lonely and all-consuming pursuit of excellence in ten events that make great demands upon their participants, in exchange for the honor of being called "the World's Greatest Athlete."

However, all that said, there was still no reason, back in 1969, to believe that a twenty-year-old named Bruce Jenner would someday become "the World's Greatest Athlete." That was the year he matriculated at tiny Graceland College on a partial football scholarship, with minors in pole vaulting and high jumping. And met the venerable track coach, L. D. Weldon, who had trained decathletes over the years.

By Jenner's sophomore year, Weldon had schooled him well enough to enter him in the 1970 Drake Relays. And despite finishing sixth, Jenner got "such a kick out of it" that he divorced himself from all around him—including reason—to concentrate on the only thing that now mattered to him, the decathlon.

Two years later, still an unknown, Jenner entered the '72 Olympic trials. By the end of the seventh event, and standing only tenth in a field of twenty-one, his presence could be viewed at best as a rumor. As he approached journey's end, the only events left were the pole vault, javelin, and his specialty, the 1,500 meters.

After solid performances in both the pole vault and the javelin, Jenner had moved up to fifth, only two places away from qualifying for a trip to Munich. Now only the 1,500 meters, his strong suit, remained.

With a chance to qualify, Jenner recalled, "I jumped up and yelled, 'I can do it!' I was pumped! A mile high! I went totally crazy! I started to hyperventilate and my heartbeat shot up to about one-eighty. I was sitting on the training table crying, I was so excited. I had completely lost the feeling in my hands. I thought, 'Oh my God, Jenner, you're falling apart.'"

Calming down enough to handicap his chances, Jenner figured he would have to run the 1,500 eighteen seconds faster than Steve Gough, then residing in third place, to qualify. Capable of lifting his efforts to unassailable heights, Jenner ran the 1,500 in 4:16, eight seconds faster than ever before, to qualify with a personal best of 7,846 points.

The story stopped there, momentarily, as Jenner finished tenth at Munich, scoring 7,722 points—732 points behind Nikolai Avilov, who set a world record with 8,454 points.

Now, having left his calling card, Jenner set a 1976 goal for himself of 8,600 points. "I made a slogan," he said. "Eighty-five in '75; eighty-six in '76."

In the three years between Olympiads, Jenner won twelve of the thirteen meets he entered. The only time he failed to win, he failed in a manner that was eloquent in its anger and frustration.

That moment came in the 1975 National AAU meet. It was a moment as unbelievable as Santa Claus suffering vertigo, Captain Bligh getting seasick, or Mary having a little lamb. Leading going into the pole-vault event, Jenner suddenly began to experience problems with his approach to the pit. Unable to get off the ground, he first stared at his pole as if it were personally responsible, then ran through the pit and, cursing as loud as he could, threw his pole as far as he could and kept running. "I ran over and picked up my stuff, ran out of the stadium, ran way out through a field, sat down under a clump of trees, and just cried my eyes out," he was to remember.

One month later, in the U.S.–U.S.S.R.–Poland Team Decathlon Meet, Jenner set a new world record of 8,524 points while the world-record holder pro tem, Nikolai Avilov, could do no better than third with 8,211 points. Jenner had kept the first half of his promise to himself.

The second half would be kept in the 1976 Montreal Olympics. Walking out onto the track, Jenner felt "it was sort of my destiny to win." And by the end of the first day of the two-day ordeal, hoping to be within 200 points of the leaders, he found himself only 35 points behind the leader and just 17 points behind Avilov. He was now so close to the Promised Land he could reach out and touch it.

Jenner knew that "all I had to do was come near my best in each of the five events to win." By the time he had finished his first three events on that last day, he was assured of victory. As he realized his goal was about to be attained, the man they called Prince Valiant With Muscles began to cry.

Going into the final event, the 1,500 meters, Jenner had amassed 7,904 of the 8,600 points he had promised himself in his sloganeering. Going into the backstretch and into the last straightaway, he knew he was close to that magic figure. "I couldn't slow down. I kept driving, driving, driving." As he crossed the finish line, he looked up at the clock. The fastest 1,500 he had ever run gave him a world record. And 8,618 points.

Bruce Jenner had proven to the world—and himself—that he was, indeed, "the World's Greatest Athlete." And proven, in the process, that genius is not without its eccentricities.

81

Sam Snead

b. 1912

Wordsmiths who dabble in language have tended to overuse the adjective *sweet*, applying it to everything and anything from girls in song named Adeline to rivers in poetry flowing gently by like the Afton. But, in the world of sports, the word has been reserved to describe poetry in motion, the sweet swing of one Samuel Jackson Snead.

Snead's "sweet" swing was a rhythmic, fluid one, all in the wrists, moving the leading sportswriter of the time, Grantland Rice, who had an eye for such delicacies, to write: "The tiger contains more grace and less waste motion in one flick of his paw than most of us possess in our entire physical makeup. For pure animal grace, the sight of Sam Snead murdering a tee shot; Babe

Ruth swinging from his heels; and, yes, Jack Dempsey raining savage destruction on a foe—these remain for me the acme of tigerish reflexes in human form."

Snead didn't come by that swing naturally. Some say it was born of a tree limb in the hills of Bath County in western Virginia, hard by the Allegheny Mountains. Others have it that as a high school senior he broke his left hand playing football and, as part of his therapy, started swinging a golf club to keep his hand from stiffening. Whatever, by the time he was twenty-one his game had progressed to the point where he was able to find employment at a local hotel cleaning golf clubs and shoes for the princely sum of $20 a month in Depression dollars. The next year he took a $20 pay cut but was allowed by the hotel to hustle its guests for golf lessons in what he called "pasture pool."

By the time he joined the pro tour in 1936, he was a cocky twenty-four-year-old with a breezy nonchalance and the sweetest swing the sporting press had ever seen. But the press saw something else, too. So used to interviewing stars with all the personality of members of Madame Tussaud's waxworks, they immediately took to the youngster whose face was saturated with mirth and whose feet were strangers to shoes. With a drawl that sounded like warm syrup going over flapjacks, Snead was quickly labeled a hillbilly. But it made no never mind to Snead, who shared his brand of backwoods humor with the press, always punctuated by a vast, substantial smile.

After winning his first tournament, the Oakland Open in '37, someone gave him a copy of the *New York Times* with a write-up of his victory and his picture. Snead is supposed to have said, "How'd they git that picture of me? I ain't never been to New Yawk." Another time, after Snead had won his first PGA championship, a reporter asked him if he did anything different for tournament play. Snead, in one of golf's most memorable fictions, is reputed to have answered, drawl and all, "I never eat on the day of a tou'ment," which came out in the papers, "I never eat on the day of *Atonement*," prompting many golf fans to believe Snead was of the Jewish persuasion.

No one knew if Snead's humor was contrived or natural, or a combination of both. But he made good copy. And as he continued to win tournaments, his legend continued to grow, propped up with reverential anecdotes, cut up and restitched according to the preferences of the storyteller.

But Snead's performances on the tour were as arresting as his personality. Now known by the alliterative nickname Slammin' Sammy—when he wasn't being called the West Virginia Hillbilly—Snead would go on to win the PGA three times, the Masters three times, and the British Open once. In fact, he would win eighty-four tournaments, more than any other golfer in history.

However, his career was defined more by his inability to win the one he called the Big Daddy—the U.S. Open—than by his many victories. Favored to win the very first U.S. Open he entered, in 1937 at Oakland Hills, it was "close, but no cigar," as Snead finished with the second-lowest score in U.S. Open history, only to lose to Ralph Guldahl, who beat him by two shots with a record 281.

Two years later, again the favorite, by the final hole Snead needed only a par five on the eighteenth to win outright. But without a leader board, Snead didn't know this and thought he needed a birdie.

But this time his play would be less classic than catastrophic. He snatched defeat from the jaws of victory and lost by two shots as he three-putted for a triple-bogey eight.

In 1947 Snead once again stood poised to capture his personal Holy Grail, the U.S. Open. Trailing the leader, Lew Worsham, by one stroke on the final hole of regulation play, Snead sank a curling, downhill, 20-foot putt to force an eighteen-hole playoff for the championship. After seventeen playoff holes, the two were still tied. Then, on the eighteenth, Worsham came up short on his third shot, leaving himself with a two-and-a-half-footer. With a chance to win, Snead also came up short. As he began lining up his putt, Fate stepped in with a rather heavy hand, in the form of Worsham, who interrupted Snead to ask who was "away." The balls were measured and Snead's ball was in fact away—30½ inches to Worsham's 29½. His concentration now broken, and affected by a case of what he called "the yips," Snead missed his two-and-a-half-footer and Worsham sank his. Once again the U.S. Open championship had eluded Snead.

Although runner-up to Cary Middlecoff in '49 and to Ben Hogan in '53, Snead would never again come this close to winning a U.S. Open, even though he played in thirty of them and completed seventy-two holes in twenty-seven of them—a figure that still stands as a U.S. Open record. Looking back,

Snead could only reflect, "You know, if I had shot sixty-nine on the last round, I'd won nine of 'em."

Many years later, Slammin' Sammy was still out there on the circuit making the same sweet shots. In 1979, with a skinny-brimmy hat covering his bald, freckled head and his putting stance reduced to a sidesaddle, almost croquet style, Snead astounded the golfing world by shooting his age, 67, and two days later followed that up with a 66 in the Quad Cities Open.

Still, he will be remembered as the greatest golfer never to have won a U.S. Open—sweet swing and all, the greatest tee-to-green player in golf history.

82

Billie Jean King

b. 1943

Many's the athlete whose career has been defined not by his or her overall accomplishments but instead by one event. For references, see Kirk Gibson, Bob Beamon, and, of course, Billie Jean King—who despite winning a record twenty Wimbledon titles, including six women's singles, as well as winning four U.S. championships at Forest Hills, is best remembered for her "Battle of the Sexes" match against Bobby Riggs.

As a youngster, Billie Jean Moffitt had excelled at all sports, especially the sport of baseball. But with one baseball player already in the family—older brother Randy, who would go on to play twelve years at the major-league level—young Billie Jean turned her attentions and energies to the sport of tennis.

Almost from the very beginning of her career, young Billie

Jean found herself on the outside, chosen by Fate to challenge tennis's proud traditions. As a youngster, unable to afford a tennis skirt, she took to the court wearing shorts. Some self-appointed caretakers of tennis's flame included her out of the group picture to be taken of all the junior participants, lest she contribute to the undermining of their country-club values. It was something she never forgot. And from that moment on Billie Jean was at war with the "damned country club" concept of tennis and the lacy, second-class citizenship of women's tennis.

Never believing that all the world was, as announced, a mismatch, Billie Jean sought to right the unfair advantage by rolling up her sleeves of determination and becoming, simply stated, the best. She gave a hint of her potential by almost toppling top-ranked Margaret Smith at Wimbledon in 1963 with a strong volley-and-serve game, almost unknown at the time in women's tennis. By 1966 she sat atop the women's tennis world with her first Wimbledon title. And then the titles and tournaments started coming by the cup and plateful.

But all this was as a prelude to her turning pro in 1968. Soon thereafter, true to tennis's tradition of petty politics, a dispute broke out between Jack Kramer and Billie Jean.

The 1970 Pacific Southwest Championships offered the backdrop for this dispute, one which would alter the face of professional tennis forever. Outraged at Kramer's distribution of prize money—less than one-eighth of that offered the men was offered the women—Billie Jean threatened a boycott of the tournament unless Kramer came up with a more equitable purse arrangement. When he refused, Billie Jean and seven other women pros signed symbolic $1 contracts with Gladys Heldman, the Houston-based publisher of *World Tennis* magazine. It was to be the start of a separate, professional women's tour named after the new Philip Morris cigarette, Virginia Slims.

It was only a short hop from "Women's Lob" to the next promotion, a Thurberesque Battle of the Sexes between Billie Jean King and the Happy Hustler, Bobby Riggs.

For years Riggs had been working the hustling side of the street, hustling everything and everybody. By the age of twenty-one, this son of a preacher man had won Wimbledon, betting on himself and winning $108,000 in the process. With little more to conquer, the man-boy who looked like the winner of the Mickey Rooney look-alike contest had become the quintessential hustler—and the world was his hustle. There were no bounds to Riggs's imaginative ways of winning, only to his opponents' bankrolls. His tennis challenges saw him (A) holding a valise; (B) allowing his opponents two bounces; (C) tethered to a Great Dane; (D) tethered to two Great Danes; (E) holding an umbrella; (F) carrying a rock; (G) allowing his opponents to serve to either service box; (H) wearing galoshes and a slicker; (I) sitting on as many as six chairs; or (J) all of the above.

Witnessing the increase in popularity of women's tennis—and, not incidentally, the amount of purse money Virginia Slims was making available—Riggs hit upon another scheme. Proclaiming himself to the "Jane L. Sullivan of women's tennis," the fifty-five-year-old Riggs turned the "I can beat any man in the house" moth-eaten bluster into a contemporary "I can beat any *person* in the house" challenge.

First he fired off a volley of insulting come-ons: "Women's tennis? I think it stinks. They hit the ball back and forth, have a lot of nice volleys, and you can see some pretty legs. But it's night and day compared to men's tennis." And then he proceeded to add: "Their best player couldn't even beat an old man like me!" So saying, the man who now was suffering through a severe case of Indian summer fired off challenges to the top five players on the Slims circuit. Only one replied: Margaret Smith Court.

Almost from the time Ms. Court accepted Riggs's challenge for what she thought was a "little hit," it became a match which polarized male and female into rival camps. It was Supp-Hose versus panty hose. Women's Lib versus Male Id. It was to sports what garlic is to a salad, something to liven it up. And that it did, becoming what *Advertising Age* called "a SportsQuake."

The date was Sunday, May 12, 1973, Mother's Day. And as Riggs made his way to center court, he came bearing gifts—red roses, ostensibly a Mother's Day gift for Margaret Court. It was merely the first psychological shoe. The psyched-out Ms. Court now awaited the dropping of the second one. She didn't have long to wait. Within fifty-seven minutes, Riggs had given her a wide assortment of Mother's Day gifts—lobs, overspins, undershots, drop shots, and a sound drubbing, to win the best two-out-of-three match, 6–2, 6–1.

Having filled to an inside straight, Riggs now became a magnet for offers of all kinds, from boxers to pool players to golfers. One of them came from Billie Jean King, who, saying

"Margaret opened the door and I intend to close it," defied Riggs to play her in a $10,000 winner-take-all match. Riggs announced, "I want Billie Jean King. I wanted her in the first place!"

Billie Jean, who had publicly stated, "I can't just play for money; I've got to play for a cause," now had both. Her cause was that of feminists everywhere, who were tired of Riggs's outrageous stance that his job was "to keep our women at home, taking care of the babies—where they belong." Her money was to be the same as Riggs's, $150,000, reflecting her belief that because women's tennis provided "an entertainment value as good as men's," they should be paid accordingly—and equally.

On the night of the match, the Houston Astrodome was pure carnival. As the first of the throng of 30,427 began filing into the Astrodome—passing concession stands laden with programs, T-shirts, commemorative racket covers, tennis sweatbands with male and female biological symbols, and all manner of knick-knacks, paddywhacks, and *chatzkas*—many of the $100 courtside patrons were upstairs at a party hosted by Virginia Slims. There, in the very city where the women's tour had been served up three years before, the entire Slims entourage toasted Billie Jean. In the huge domed stadium, many of those in the $50 and $20 seats wore buttons or carried banners showing their preference and their gender. Several men sported piglike hats bearing the legend "Male Chauvinist Pigs for Riggs." "Women-Power" T-shirts as well as those reading "WORMS" (for "World Organization for the Retention of Male Supremacy") were everywhere. One of the many banners hanging over the railings proudly proclaimed: "East West North South, Ms. King's Gonna Close Bobby's Mouth." Others, while hardly as eloquent, screamed out, "Beat Him, Billie Jean" or "Win One for the Bedroom, Bobby."

At the appointed hour, the University of Houston band struck up something out of *Cleopatra* or some such, and six bare-chested men dressed as Nubian slaves came down a red runway bearing a litter with their cargo: Billie Jean King. Then, from the other side, came six girls all wearing red T-shirts reading "Bobby's Bosom Buddies" drawing a rickshaw. There, sucking a huge Sugar Daddy, was the quintessential sugar daddy, Bobby Riggs. Riggs jumped off and handed Billie Jean his Sugar Daddy. She, in turn, practicing her patented version of "one-upwoman-ship," produced a little piglet named Lorimer Hustle, appropriately named after Robert Lorimer Riggs.

After a few more ceremonial offers and an obligatory TV interview or two, the pair forgathered in the forecourt to call the toss of the coin for first serve. Billie Jean was now all business as she stared out, from behind her spectacles, with incurious eyes, almost radiating a don't-screw-with-me-Jack-you-picked-on-the-wrong-patsy-this-time look. There was no quaking-knee factor here, even in the face of Riggs's continued swaggering virility.

Billie Jean won the toss. And the first serve. It was a portent of things to come, as she won the first game with a blazing backhand shot. Riggs, still wearing his by-now unnecessary Sugar Daddy warm-up jacket, served and lost the second game on a double-fault. Unbelievably, the hustler had choked! Removing his jacket, Riggs returned to his chair on the sidelines to have his legs massaged. Momentarily rejuvenated, he went back out to break Billie Jean's service in the third game. It was not only Riggs's first big moment, it was also to be his last, as Billie Jean continued to eat up his soft, inviting lobs with overhand blasts to the far corners, alternating them with bulletlike line shots that had him wrong-footing, looking like he wanted to take the first fire escape going south. Hitting nothing but winners, Billie Jean won the first set going away, 6–4. The second set proved to be more of the same, King winning, 6–3. And when the third went to five games to three, King, with Riggs serving, he double-faulted, then hit a weak backhand return which meekly became enmeshed in the net. It was all over! Billie Jean threw her racket toward the dome of the arena while an obviously tired old man of fifty-five attempted to jump the net to congratulate her, almost impaling himself as he straddled it.

Billie Jean King had also straddled something: two worlds, those of a cause and a sport. The athlete whom Fate had tapped on the shoulder to lead women's tennis to center court had done so. And established herself as one of history's great athletes in the process.

83

A. J. Foyt
b. 1935

Auto racing has been called a true twentieth-century phenomenon, almost an art form, mirroring contemporary society's
fascination and obsession with speed, power, competition, and
destruction in that most modern of all instruments, the automobile. And, by extension, its participants, those who control the
raging machinery produced by modern technology, the racecar
drivers, are today's quintessential athletes.

During the early years of the twentieth century, auto racing
was the preserve of the elite, with "gentlemen drivers" like Willy
Vanderbilt and his Long Island crowd of millionaires importing
fast cars from abroad and driving them themselves over dusty
roads from Port Washington to Brighton Beach. However, the
entrance of Barney Oldfield in that first decade of the century
was to change all that. For Oldfield, a former bicycle rider, was a
hell-bent-for-leather daredevil who drove with a cigar clenched in
his teeth and danger at his elbow. And, in the process, popularized the sport amongst the common folk of America.

Over the next few years the heartland of America was fertilized with races on half-mile, weed-grown dirt tracks, mile dirt ovals, and straightaway roads and at carnivals and country fairs, raising dust and interest in the fledgling sport. And then, in 1911, came the biggest country fair of them all, as the Indianapolis Speedway opened its doors on Memorial Day to a patriotic one-day affair, complete with bunting, banners, and checkered flags, that was pure apple-pie entertainment.

But even though the Indianapolis 500 would grow from a curio piece to a piece of Americana—becoming, as it did, as much a part of the Memorial Day tradition as showing the flag— it would have to wait half a century until it got its first superstar: Anthony Joseph Foyt Jr., better known as just plain ol' A.J.

A.J. was the perfect hero for what might be called soda-fountain America. He was one of them, a good ol' boy from down Houston way possessed of the grit of a John Wayne and good ol' boy looks, from his Popeye I-can-do-it jaw to the crown-fitting crew cut atop his handsome oval face. And the racing crowd adopted him with a passion.

A.J.'s road to Indianapolis was a long, winding one, one that started when he was a little bitty boy of five racing the handmade car he helped construct in his daddy's garage and moving on down the road to dirt tracks racing midget cars, jalopies, modified specials, souped-up stock cars, and even motorcycles. It was a road that would see him drive more miles on more different tracks in more locales with more different types of racing machines than any other man who ever raced. Before or since.

By 1956, that road had reached Indianapolis. However, A.J.'s first start in Indy wasn't at the Speedway, but across the street, where he finished thirteenth in a midget race, winning all of $68. It would be another two years before the twenty-one-year-old, now known as Super Tex and Tough Tony, would debut at the famed raceway.

Foyt's rookie appearance at "the" Indy track came in 1958. But it was less than an auspicious one as he spun out on the 148th lap. The next year he drove all two hundred laps, finishing tenth in the process. In 1960, he was forced to retire after ninety times around the two-and-a-half-mile oval, the result of a clutch problem. But 1961 was to be different, for that was the year he would turn his four-cylinder Offenhauser into a carriage and six white horses.

That '61 500 was one of the most thrilling duels of all time, a two-car race between Foyt and Eddie Sachs. As the laps dwindled down and the two racers ascloseasthis, wheel to wheel and side by side, it seemed as if each had the race won. With but forty miles to go and both having made their third—and final—pit stop, they now referred the matter to their accelerator feet, driving to the full extent of their limits. And their cars' as well.

Then, inexplicably, Foyt pulled into the pits for the fourth time. "The car felt funny; it was too light," said the man with the same sensitive feel for his instrument that a concert pianist has for his. It was that feel that told him what he already knew: "I didn't have the load of fuel I was supposed to have. What happened was that the refueling nozzle had jammed on my third pit stop and I didn't get the full load."

That short, seventeen-second refueling stop was long enough for Sachs to take the lead. With only two laps to go and several seconds for Foyt to make up, it looked like Eddie had the race in the proverbial gunnysack. But being in the lead at Indy is something you can neither bank nor bank on, and Fate now stepped in and pointed her capricious finger at Sachs. Or, more specifically, at his right rear tire, shredding it. Sachs pitted for a quick tire change. But even though his pit stop took only twenty-three seconds, that, added to the time he had already spent on his previous three stops, was seven-plus seconds more than Foyt had spent in the pits on his four stops. And was almost the exact margin of victory for A.J.

That year was also the year Jack Brabham had finished a distant ninth in a rear-engined Cooper Climax Grand Prix–type car, a car which ran on gasoline instead of methanol and could go the entire distance with only one pit stop (the methanol-gulping Offy roadsters required at least three). And although Brabham had only finished ninth, the message was clear: The rear-engine car was the car of the future, the roadster a dinosaur. In '63 one driven by Jimmy Clark came close, finishing second. By 1964 rear-engine cars were the ones to beat.

By 1967, with hair that had once bristled now a little sparser and an air that had once bristled as well now tempered by age and wisdom, Foyt saw the handwriting on the wall and finally subscribed to the inevitable by driving a rear-engine Ford. To victory. But not before employing that specialized brand of instinct that created his racing genius.

It has been said that the union between car and driver is 25 percent driver and 75 percent car. However, with Foyt the driver, the equation was more like 50–50. And '67 showed why. After a one-day rain delay, Foyt found himself in second place behind the pacesetter, Parnelli Jones. Jones was driving Andy Granatelli's legendary turbine-power car, and Foyt was resigned to finishing second. But when a $6 ball bearing malfunctioned, Jones dropped out on the 196th lap, suddenly leaving Foyt in the lead. Now all Foyt had to do was finish to win. But instead of flooring it in an attempt to bring the course to its knees, "something inside" told A.J. to slow down on the last lap. Other than his finely honed instincts, he had no way of knowing that five cars had crashed at the head of the main stretch, virtually blocking the track. Reacting quickly and slowing down from 200 mph+ to a more manageable 170, he wove his way cautiously through the wreckage like a Manhattan taxi driver plying his trade in rush-hour traffic, becoming the only driver to finish the race—and only the fourth man to win three 500s.

Before he was to announce his retirement in 1993 after driving in a record thirty-five consecutive 500s, A.J. had upped the ante by winning his fourth Indy. And had won almost everything else there was to win in the sport, including the Daytona 500, the 24 Hours of LeMans, the Pocono 500, etc., etc., etc. It didn't matter what kind of race it was, A.J. wanted to be dealt in—not for the money, but for the race itself, the roar of the engines always giving a roar to his heart. His obsession with the sport was such that Ken Purdy wrote, "He was known to pass up a $1,500 speaking engagement just to run in an insignificant race in which he could win, at most, $600."

It was a passion that drove him. And flavored his personality and range of moods. No one word could undertake to give a description of his range of moods; only an inventory would suffice. At times he could be irascible, truculent, cantankerous, and tough; at others, he could be a model of charm, the leathery lines around his eyes wrinkling and crinkling when he smiled. And his mercurial mood swings always swung in direct response to his winning. Or losing. "I'll admit it," Foyt acknowledged. "I get moody when I don't win."

But win he did, in all kinds of races, on all surfaces, over all distances, and sixty-seven times in championship races, more than any other driver, becoming the greatest athlete ever to sit behind a wheel.

84

Glenn Cunningham
1910–1988

When the feverish twenties exploded with a crash, to be replaced by the troubled thirties, the American Dream became a nightmare, and people with sagging spirits looked for a tonic in heroes who could lift their hopes. And the most improbable hero of those bleak years known as the Depression was a common man whom all common men could identify with, a man who had overcome adversity to rise to the top of his field: Glenn Cunningham.

The man known, in that awful alliteration beloved in that day, as Galloping Glenn was loved by the sports fans of the era for a flamboyance and courage that made him distance running's version of Babe Ruth.

Cunningham came by his courage the hard way when, as a youngster, his leg was severely burned in a Kansas schoolhouse fire. Rather than spend time consigned to the underside of a large quilt—or worse, face possible amputation—young Glenn turned instead to running as his calling card of hope. With painstaking discipline and exhausting devotion, he strengthened and regained circulation in his limbs—although circulation would remain a problem for the rest of his life. And by the time he burst into the national spotlight by winning the 1932 AAU 1,500-meter championship, it was clear his rehabilitation was a success.

After finishing fourth in the 1932 Olympic 1,500-meter race, Cunningham resumed his winning ways in '33, winning both the AAU 1,500-meter and 800-meter championships—the first athlete since 1919 to pull off the 800/1,500 "double" at the AAUs.

By 1934 the world of sports was in the throes of a depression that mirrored the one then gripping the world, with attendance plummeting and heroes hard to come by. But the world of track and field had its own hero in Glenn Cunningham. Track promoters lined up in an effort to land him for their event. One of those who did was the promoter of Madison Square Garden's Baxter Mile, who matched him against the "Pride of Princeton," Bill Bonthron, in what the press called the Mile of the Century. The event was so ballyhooed that throngs milled around outside the Garden on that cold February 1934 night, forcing New York mounted police to keep the overflow away from the doors lest they break them down.

When Cunningham emerged from the dressing room for his prerace warm-ups—coming out first because of the extra time he needed for limbering-up calisthenics to get the circulation back into his legs—the Garden crowd rose to their feet in such a clamor that the rest of the night's events had to be delayed until the din and roar had subsided. But the noise had hardly died down before the starter's gun had launched the race, and once again cheers rent the air. Both Cunningham and Bonthron hung back for the first six laps of the eleven-lap event, letting a rabbit set the pace. Then they made their move on the seventh lap, with Cunningham moving into the lead with high purpose and powerful strides. As he continued to lead, going into the bell lap, he tried to take Bonthron's finishing kick away from him, but it was not to be as Bonthron caught him on the last bend and breasted the tape mere centimeters ahead of the Kansan, with both in the time of 4:14.0.

Later that spring, in a repeat performance, America's mile kings were rematched in the AAU Indoor Championships at the Garden—in a metric mile, 370 feet shorter than an American mile. This time Cunningham, eschewing the distance runner's stand-up starting stance, got down into the sprinter's stance; and, running with manifest gusto, the endurance runner outlasted the kicker, finishing ahead of Bonthron by a blink of an eye, with both timed at 3:52.2.

In the Princeton Invitational that year, Cunningham was to set a world and American mile record with a 4:06.7.

It was not Cunningham's official record, however, but his "unofficial" record that made him a superstar, even decades before that word was invented. For in an outdoor track meet in Chicago, Cunningham was timed at 3:58 for the mile. But somehow, because the stopwatch was adjudged as faulty and because it was ruled that his 3:58 had been borne on a capricious flurry of wind, the official honors of breaking the four-minute mile were denied him a full twenty years before it was even a glint in the eye of Roger Bannister. Legend has it that his coach told him not to breathe a word about his sub-four mile "'cause nobody'd believe it." But believe it they did, merely because it was Glenn Cunningham.

Glenn Cunningham would go on to win almost every race— and honor—known to distance runningkind, winning more than sixty races in a row, at one point. He would end his career with his fastest 1,500 meters ever, a 3:48.0. That was Glenn Cunningham, a man who had overcome adversity to become America's greatest miler and one of its greatest distance runners ever.

It has been said that great athletes are born, not made. But you couldn't prove that by Glenn Cunningham. Nor his accomplishments.

Nolan Ryan

b. 1947

Nolan Ryan was baseball's version of Ol' Man River. For twenty-seven years he just kept rolling along, washing away records, and the improbability of the calendar as well.

Before Ryan, the standard in balls was three: highballs, mothballs, and snowballs. Now you can add a fourth: Nolan Ryan's fastball. For it seemed that every time Ryan reared back and threw it, he voyaged, Columbus-like, into new worlds. Consider his 7 no-hitters, his 12 one-hitters, his 770 career starts, etc., etc., etc.

And then there were his strikeouts, coming by the heaping plateful: 5,700 lifetime strikeouts; 19 strikeouts in a game, four times; 15 strikeouts in a game twenty-six times; and generous helpings of 10-K games, so routine it became a feat the sports pages yawned at.

Those who couldn't even strike up a waving acquaintance with Ryan's Guinness Record 100-mile-per-hour-plus fastball included many of the usual suspects—like Claudell Washington, who struck out thirty-nine times in his career against Ryan, and Cecil Cooper, who was struck out a major-league record six times in one game by Ryan. And some not so usual ones, like the twenty-one Hall of Famers, forty-four Most Valuable Players, twelve brother combinations, and, in tribute to Ryan's longevity, seven father-son combos, all of whom had their bats reduced to matchwood by Ryan's flamethrower.

No one who saw this eighteen-year-old tall drink of water back in 1965 would have given his chances of becoming one of baseball's all-time greats enough thought to cause a headache. Growing up on his father's cattle ranch just outside Alvin, Texas, the young Lynn Nolan Ryan had developed his speed throwing baseballs against the many barns that spread around the spread. He had attracted local attention as a full-fledged barn burner on the baseball mound at the local high school. But still there were questions, if not about his speed, then about his gangly build. The woebegone New York Mets dispatched one of their scouts, Red Murff, to look at this local high school star. Murff was impressed with the prospect's fastball, less so with his body. But, the scout recalled, "I asked Nolan's daddy how big he was at the same age. He said he was just about like Nolan. That was good enough for me. He was now over two hundred pounds." And so, the Mets selected young Nolan in the eighth round of the 1965 free-agent draft.

After two seasons in the minors—including a season with the Mets' farm club in Greenville, South Carolina, where he led the league in wins and pitching percentage with a 17–2 record and in strikeouts with 272—the ninth-place parent team added him to its expanded roster at the end of the season for a look-see. It was nothing more than the proverbial cup of java. But in the three innings he pitched, the nineteen-year-old impressed with his fastball, striking out six batters—including his first major-league victim, Pat Jarvis of the Atlanta Braves.

There were to be many more strikeout victims, beginning in 1968, when the twenty-one-year-old Ryan took his place in the Mets' starting rotation alongside other young phenoms Tom Seaver and Jerry Koosman. However, a chronic blister problem and one month on the disabled list—the first of fifteen times during his career that he would be placed on the DL—hampered his performance. Still, with an old-fashioned cure for his blistering problems—salve and finger baths in pickle brine ("It toughened the skin, but it made my fingers smell awful")—he was able to come back and strike out 133 batters in 134 innings his rookie season.

But by 1969, there was no room in the starting rotation inn for Ryan on the pitching-rich "Miracle" Mets, and manager Gil Hodges alternated him between starting and relieving roles. In the postseason goings-on, Ryan, appearing as a reliever, won the deciding game of the National League playoff against the Atlanta Braves with seven innings of relief, and then saved Game Three in the World Series against the Baltimore Orioles—in an effort marked as much by his three strikeouts in two and a third innings of relief work as by Tommie Agee's belly-sliding, one-handed catch of Paul Blair's sinking liner into right-center with the bases loaded.

Despite throwing a one-hitter in his first start in 1970 and having a blazing fastball that was dubbed Ryan's Express by an imaginative newspaperman who had seen a similarly titled movie, Ryan's control was a continuing problem, and he struggled for the rest of the season and on into the next. Unable to gain a spot in Hodges's pitching rotation and unhappy with the big-city atmosphere of New York, Ryan requested that he be traded. The Mets obliged, shipping him off to the California Angels along with three other players whose names fortunately escape memory for third baseman Jim Fregosi.

Not only was that the worst trade in New York Mets history, but it was the best thing that could have happened to Ryan. Under the watchful eyes of Angels pitching coach Tom Morgan and veteran catcher Jeff Torborg, Ryan developed both a curve and a change-up that complemented his molten fastball.

This alchemy, along with the American League's so-called high strike, paid immediate dividends as Ryan, given the ball every fourth day, responded with 19 wins and 329 strikeouts—becoming the first right-hander since Bob Feller to strike out 300 batters in a season.

In 1973 the Ryan Express finally arrived, full throttle. For starters, he did something that had been done only four times before in baseball history: throw two no-hitters in one season. In the ninth inning of the second one, Norm Cash of the Detroit

Tigers, who had already accounted for three of seventeen batters Ryan would fan, came to bat brandishing a sawed-off table leg, figuring, "I wasn't gonna hit the guy anyway."

Cash was on the money. For going into his thirty-ninth and last start of the '73 season, Ryan had prevented a total of 367 batters from making contact with the ball—just 15 shy of Sandy Koufax's all-time record. Pitching against the Minnesota Twins in his thirty-ninth start, Ryan alternated his fastball with his curve and his change-up—which, according to many batters, was as fast as most pitchers' fastballs—and by the eighth inning had registered his fifteenth K, striking out Steve Brye to pull even with Koufax. But in so doing he had torn a hamstring in his right thigh. Unable to drive off the mound with his powerful legs, Ryan pitched as if a strikeout could be produced by will alone. And it was, as he blew three consecutive fastballs past Rich Reese for his record-breaking 383rd strikeout—all the more astounding since, in the league using the designated hitter, he never faced a pitcher.

By now Ryan was not only the fastest man in the league, he was also the most feared. Detroit's Dick Sharon summed it up by saying, "He is baseball's exorcist. He scares hell out of me!" Ryan had now added something else to his arsenal: intimidation. Sandy Koufax, the pitcher with whom Ryan was most often compared, said, "Pitching is the art of instilling fear. But if your control is suspect like Ryan's is, and the thought of being hit is in the batter's mind, you'll go a long way." Reggie Jackson added, "Ryan is the only guy who puts fear in me. Not because he can get you out. But because he can kill you."

Armed with his fastball and that fear, Ryan continued to register strikeout after strikeout. And they continued to fly by, like exit ramps off an Interstate: Sal Bando, number 1,000; Sandy Alomar, number 1,500; Ron LeFlore, number 2,000; Buddy Bell, number 2,500. But even as the Texan was establishing homesteading rights to season and career strikeout marks, he was also making his mark in another area as well, no-hitters. Besides his two in 1973, he added a third in '74 and then, in '75, tied the original owner of the copyright, Sandy Koufax, with his fourth. But it would take a change of scenery before Ryan would break either the lifetime strikeout or no-hitter records.

That change of scenery came in 1980 after Ryan's record slipped to 16–14 the previous season and Angels GM Buzzy Bavasi, deciding that Ryan was expendable, said, "I'll just go and sign two 8–7 pitchers." Ryan decided to change scenery again and went to Houston, where he signed baseball's first $1 million contract.

Ryan brought his arm and his ever-growing record book to the Astros, then continued to rewrite it. In his first year he added strikeout victim number 3,000, Cesar Geronimo. In his second, he pitched his record-breaking fifth no-hitter. And then, in 1983, he not only added strikeout victim number 3,500, Andre Dawson, but also number 3,509, breaking Walter Johnson's all-time strikeout record. In 1987, the forty-year-old youngster continued to defy the calendar by registering 270 strikeouts in 212 innings, adding number 4,500, Mike Aldrete, and also becoming the first pitcher to register 2,000 strikeouts in each league. He also won his second ERA title.

And then, just when it looked like there were no more worlds to conquer, Ryan, by now forty-two going on Social Security and so old he had taken to anointing his limbs with Absorbine Sr., signed with the Texas Rangers. In his first year, 1989, he struck out an American League–leading 301 batters, the sixth time he had struck out 300 or more in a season. And, just to prove he could keep rolling along, in 1990 and '91 he added an incredible sixth and seventh no-hitters, breaking, in turn, the records held by none other than Nolan Ryan.

Finally, in 1993, Nolan Ryan decided to end the longest pitching career in major-league history. His farewell tour was nothing like Babe Ruth's more than half a century earlier, where Ruth had been trotted out like the queen's jewels for ceremonial occasions. Instead, Ryan's was a working tour, with the "Ryan Express" the busiest memory in each and every city he hit.

In a day and age when heroes and record holders come and go, leaving not even a whisper of smoke, Nolan Ryan left his smoking fastball pressed between the pages of the record books and time. And while his records and name will go to the Hall of Fame, his arm should be assigned to the Smithsonian Institution as a lasting tribute to a man who just kept rollin' along for what seemed like forever.

86

Willie Shoemaker

b 1931

Jim Murray, the poet laureate of sportswriters, once wrote, "You have to be half-man, half-animal to be a jockey. You have to, in a sense, be able to think like a horse. You have to sense his mood, gauge his courage, cajole him into giving his best." "The Shoe" was a jockey who, in that delicate fusion of horse and jockey, got the most out of his mounts by using a velvet hand, allowing him to play the horse much as a fisherman plays a salmon. Fellow jock great Eddie Arcaro saw this, saying, "His hands...tell him everything about a horse." Writer Jimmy Cannon wrote, "His touch is his secret." And writer Emmett Watson added, "He is the little man who talks to horses through the light, cool touch on the reins."

Moving his horses with little clucks and touches, "the little man" was so skillful it was suggested that while all riders talked to their horses, almost as if it were a scene right out of an old *Mr. Ed* TV show, Shoemaker was the only one they talked back to. But they listened, as he maneuvered his horses home in front a total of 8,833 times with his deft hand.

However, Willie Shoemaker was hardly born on the lead. Just two and a half pounds at birth, he was not expected to survive the night. Shoemaker not only survived the night, but grew up to see the day when he would be proclaimed the greatest jockey for many a day to come.

By the time he took up racing at the age of sixteen, he was a mere wisp of a lad, standing just four-foot-eleven inches tall in his size 1½ boots, so small he would get lost in a crowd of two. And he almost was, as his employer in California told him he'd never make it as a rider and turned him loose, keeping another exercise boy he thought more promising.

Again Shoemaker's survival instincts took over and, not taking his first boss's advice to heart, he instead found another stable where, by the age of seventeen, he was off and running, literally. By eighteen, in his apprentice year, he had ridden 219 winners, second-highest in the nation. By nineteen this painfully shy, almost wordless lad with pointy, batlike ears and equally pointy man-sized buck teeth that were so pronounced he looked like he could eat an ear of corn through a picket fence, had tied for the national championship with 388 winning rides. And by twenty he had led the country in purses won with $1,329,890—and became a big favorite of the improvers of the breed.

That was the year when, after winning the Santa Anita Maturity, Shoemaker was approached by a breathless announcer who thrust a microphone in his face after asking him, "Willie, this is the greatest day in your life. Tell us how you're going to celebrate tonight." Shoemaker, who husbanded each and every word as a miser his treasures, answered only, "Eat, I guess." And with that was gone; probably to eat, as per promise, since, unlike most jockeys, he could eat all day without gaining an ounce over his walking-around weight of 95 pounds.

He was also feasting on a steady diet of winners. In October 1953, he set a record for most wins by a jockey in a single year, 392, going on to win a total of 485 for the year. It might have reached a higher figure except for the fact that with about a month left in the season, Shoemaker decided to push away from the table and take a vacation.

Riding to the full extent of his capabilities, and sometimes beyond them, by 1957, going into his ninth season in the saddle, Shoemaker was an odds-on favorite to break Johnny Longden's then-record of 5,090 winners—a record Longden had amassed over thirty-one seasons and would extend to a lifetime mark of 6,032.

But even as his lofty reputation grew, Shoemaker would become known for a gaffe in that year's Kentucky Derby that would come to define his career as much as all his wins combined.

Common wisdom would have it that after a couple of thousand recitals, an artist develops a sensitivity to his surroundings. But at Churchill Downs during the '57 Kentucky Derby, Shoemaker, aboard Gallant Man, hunched in his mount and, having just inched a nose in front of the front-running Iron Liege, inexplicably stood up in his stirrups and stopped riding about fifteen lengths from the wire. Even though he got Gallant Man moving almost immediately, it was too late, as he lost the race by a nostril to Iron Liege.

Called in by the chief steward to explain his strange behavior, Shoemaker, with unimpeachable courtesy, like a little boy explaining away a bad report card, admitted to suffering a sharp lack of arithmetic and having misjudged the finish line—a finish line different from that most of other tracks, being a sixteenth of a mile from the first turn. But even though he was destined forever to wear that can tied to his tail, Shoemaker, characteristically, took it all in stride. "You can ask a hundred people and ninety of them can tell you who lost that Derby. But they can't tell you who won," he said of his run for the roses in which he harvested not a rose, but a thorn.

Eddie Arcaro, gifted with the class of a true champion himself, recognized it in another and said of Shoemaker, "He's the only one I know who could have suffered that kind of experience in a race like the Derby without going to pieces. That's why the little son of a gun is going to go on and on."

And on and on he would go. From his very first mount, Waxahachie, back in 1949, to his winning ride aboard Dares J in 1970 to break Longden's long-standing record with his 6,033rd win, until he finally hung up his silks after forty-one years in the saddle, and 8,833 wins, Willie Shoemaker was partial to a single orthodoxy: winning. For one of the brightest aspects of his career was the dazzling consistency of it: One out of every five of his rides ended up with a trip to the winner's circle; and almost half the time he rode, he was in the money. In short, Willie Shoemaker was a winner, hands down.

That should be the end of the story, but isn't. Some philosopher or other once opined that a good story is like a bitter pill with the sugar coating on the inside instead of the outside. Willie Shoemaker's story, alas, has the bitter coating on the inside. For, on the morning of April 8, 1991, with Shoemaker at the wheel, his car veered off a southern California highway, jumped a berm, crossed a nine-foot shoulder, and plunged down a forty-foot embankment, leaving the greatest jockey of all time twisted beyond repair, his spine severed below the neck, a quadriplegic. And his hands—those doll-like hands that once coaxed everything there was to be coaxed from a horse—are now lifeless props destined to remain forever on the armrests of a wheelchair that encases his elfin form and which he can operate only by blowing into a tube. Willie Shoemaker, the man who could handle any horse, could not handle a car that, ironically, was named after one: a Ford Bronco.

87

Walter Hagen

1892–1969

The man known as the Haig and Sir Walter was proof positive that golf not only builds character, but characters as well. An authentic American tintype, Hagen different-drummed himself down the fairways and byways of the twenties, outdistancing both the rest of the field and Prohibition by at least five strokes.

The Hagen legend was inexhaustible. And so was the man himself. Believing in life, liberty, and the pursuit of happy hour, the only thing Hagen seemed to fear was sleep itself. Many's the time he would go out in search of genial bonhomie and two-footed wildlife 'til the wee hours of the morn and yet still be able to make it to the tee by eight—in a limousine, of course. Bedecked in silk shirts and riotous clothing—which Grantland Rice once described as "raiment that out-Astored Mrs. Astor's horse"—that were merely window decorations for his enormous skills, Hagen parlayed a go-as-you-please manner and a devil-may-care game of golf into a swashbuckling style that made the Roaring Twenties roar just a little bit louder.

Hagen first swaggered onto the golf landscape as a twenty-one-year-old at the 1913 National Open—the one remembered by graybeards and golf historians for Francis Ouimet's historic victory over British stars Harry Vardon and Ted Ray. Bursting into the locker room at the Brookline Country Club, he proclaimed: "The name is Hagen. I've come down from Rochester to help you fellows stop Vardon and Ray!" Hagen's braggadocio was far from empty, as he proved by finishing fourth behind the aforementioned threesome. And while Ouimet's dramatic victory gave golf its popular appeal, it was Hagen who was to supply it with its human interest and its color from that point on.

In 1914 the twenty-two-year-old "veteran" led the U.S. Open from wire to wire to win by a stroke over Chick Evans. It was to be the first olive out of the jar for Hagen, as he went on to win seventy-five tournaments in all, including the U.S. Open twice, the British Open four times, and the PGA five times—and winning the latter an unprecedented four times in a row, including twenty-nine consecutive head-to-head matches with the greatest golfers in the world. All told, he was to win eleven national and international crowns, then second only to Bobby Jones.

Hagen and Jones met head-to-head only once. It was during the Florida land boom of 1926, and Hagen persuaded his business manager to arrange a challenge match against Jones, then being hailed as the greatest golfer in the world. The arrangements called for the match to be played over seventy-two holes, half on a course picked by Hagen and half over a course of Jones's choosing. Midway through the match, Jones's nerves were shaken when he witnessed Hagen's errant ball disappear into a clump of palmettos and seconds later emerge to land stiff to the pin. "I simply couldn't keep my game going," conceded the Atlanta Boy Wonder. The match ended in a 12 and 11 rout by Hagen, giving him $7,600, the richest purse in golfing history up to that time. The irrepressible Haig promptly went out and spent $800 of it on a set of diamond-and-platinum cuff links for the vanquished Jones.

For Hagen's greatness lay not only in winning golf matches, but in how he won them. It was an exciting game of golf, one which saw him continually recover from the edge of a disaster and scant minutes later be back on the verge of another. And always, when the extremity was direst, his second shot would come to the rescue of his first. He once confided, "I expect to make at least seven mistakes each round. Therefore, when I make a bad shot, I don't worry about it." After making one of his "mistakes," the Haig would simply walk up to his ball confidently, put the business end of his club to it, and make yet another one of his "miracle" recoveries,—many staged to look more difficult than they really were. Tommy Armour, marveling at Hagen's uncanny touch, could only say, "Walter has the touch of a jeweler's scale."

In a game ripe for stratagems and ploys, Hagen was a practitioner pluperfect of the great game of one-upmanship. It was a game lesser mortals could neither play nor understand, many experiencing vapor lock in the face of Hagen's psychological warfare—beginning with his breezy and ballsy cry of "Who's going to be second?" the very minute he entered the clubhouse. In the '26 PGA final, playing against Leo Diegel, Hagen, after conceding six- and eight-foot putts on earlier holes, refused to concede one of Diegel's of about twenty inches on the eighteenth. Diegel, sure that Hagen had seen something he hadn't, began to survey the green for hidden breaks. Truth to tell, there weren't any. But Diegel, fully believing there were and that he had overlooked them, putted oh-so-carefully—and missed. He missed winning the match as well, losing to—you guessed it—Hagen.

Another story that achieved great currency had it that before a match in the 1919 U.S. Open, one well-wisher, finding himself at the same watering hole as Hagen, advised him to retire from the night's social ramble, remarking in a cautionary tone, "Your opponent went to bed hours ago." "I know," replied the confident Hagen, "but he's not asleep." It was ever thus when Hagen was around, none of his opponents daring to go to sleep. For the Hagen legend was worth two to three strokes every round, sometimes more, many of his opponents half-believing that he was invincible.

And yet, for all his many accomplishments, the Haig's greatest contribution to the game might well have been his fight to raise the dignity of golfers—and by so doing, of athletes everywhere. In an age when professional athletes were treated like lepers and accorded accommodations one notch below primitive, Sir Walter faced down some other "Sirs" and challenged the sacred rights of established custom, winning the rights of first-class citizenship for professional golfers.

The defining moment, told and retold around golf's campfires, came when Hagen traveled to England to compete in his first British Open, held at the Royal and Ancient Club of St. Andrews. Nonchalanting his way up to the front door of the club, Hagen found his way blocked by an executive. Said executive, stiff with the ramrod conviction that comes with nobility, said, in a snappish tone, "Sorry, sir, but professionals are not permitted in the clubhouse. If you will be so kind, I will show you to your dressing quarters." And with that, the executive, in his brass-buttoned jacket, marched off in the direction of the pro shop, where he showed Hagen the "dressing quarters," which consisted of a mere peg on the wall. The blood of Hagen rose hastily and mottled the cheek of Walter. Without saying a word, he turned quickly and marched to his waiting limousine. "Drive me up to the front door of the clubhouse," directed Hagen to his chauffeur.

When he reached the front door he sought out the officious executive who had denied him entry to the clubhouse scant seconds before. "I will dress in my car," he said with a so's-your-old-man inflection. And he did, every day of the tournament, pulling the blinds down and changing from tuxedo to golfing attire. Soon thereafter, the blind walls of custom came down as well, and professionals were both allowed and welcomed into the clubhouse.

As Arnold Palmer said at a 1967 testimonial dinner in honor of Hagen, "If it were not for you, this dinner would be downstairs in the pro shop and not in the ballroom."

That was Walter Hagen, a man who always interpreted golf—and life—in an interesting manner. A man who, in the words of his longtime friend, Fred Corcoran, "Broke eleven of the Ten Commandments." And a man who was the first golfer to make a million dollars and spend two—but who also, through his style, color, and overall great play, did for the professional golfer what Babe Ruth did for the professional baseball player. And did it his way, a way he summed up in a sign that hung over his desk: "Don't hurry. Don't worry. You're here only a short time, so be sure to smell the flowers." He did, by the bushelful.

88

Sandy Koufax

b. 1935

In the star-spangled words of Francis Scott Key Fitzgerald, "There are no second acts in America." However, the star-studded career of pitcher S. Koufax is a clear refutation of writer F. Scott Fitzgerald's thesis, Koufax's career as a pitching great clearly beginning with the second act.

Act I began, appropriately enough, on the streets and playgrounds of Brooklyn, New York. There Koufax, far more interested in the sport of basketball than baseball, distinguished himself with a one-handed jump shot and his leaping capability. Possessing that commodity teenagers seem to have in abundance, spare time, Koufax also played a little sandlot ball. His prowess on the court earned him a ticket to the University of Cincinnati on a basketball scholarship. His baseball ability, or lack thereof, at first base earned him a ticket to the pitcher's mound when his sandlot manager suggested he try his hand there.

Arriving on the University of Cincinnati campus in the fall of '53, Koufax immediately took to his first love, the basketball court, where as a six-foot-two forward he averaged ten points a game for the Bearcat five. The next spring, the freshman baseball coach courted him to come out for the team. Koufax proceeded to shoot down 51 batters in 32 innings, 34 of those strikeouts coming in two consecutive games.

That summer Koufax earned a tryout with the New York Giants. But the Giants, after watching Koufax lay waste to the landscape, his pitches in need of a Geiger counter to find the plate, decided that even though he threw aspirin-tablet fastballs, they would use too many of Mr. Bayer's product trying to control the sparkling genius of his left arm, and said, "Thanks, but no thanks."

Other clubs, however, remained interested in the wild lefty with the molten-lead fastball. One of those was his hometown team, the Brooklyn Dodgers. Alerted to his potential by a Brooklyn sportswriter who had seen him in the sandlots some three years earlier and told the front office that the youngster threw as hard as any he had ever seen, the Dodgers had sent one of their scouts to Cincinnati to watch the youngster in action. The scouting report, pruned to its essentials, was that the freshman pitching and playing first for the University of Cincinnati baseball team was a hard-throwing pitcher and weak-hitting first baseman.

With Branch Rickey, by now general manager of the woebegone Pittsburgh Pirates, instructing his scout to top the Dodgers' best offer by $5,000, and the Milwaukee Braves in the hunt as well, ready to outbid the Dodgers, Dodger scout Al Campanis managed to convince the Family Koufax that any true Brooklyn boy would rather stay home and pitch for the local heroes. And so, on December 22, 1954, a week before Sandy's nineteenth birthday, he signed a contract with the Brooklyn Dodgers calling for a $14,000 bonus.

Spring training 1955 found the young pitcher trying to make too much of a bad thing. For the first week Koufax was too nervous and tense to even throw. Then, when he did throw, he tried to make up for arrearages by throwing too hard and coming down with a sore arm, sidelining him for another week. When he finally returned, he was wild. One batter said, "Taking batting practice against him is like playing Russian roulette with five bullets. You don't give yourself much of a chance."

When the Dodgers broke camp and headed north, Koufax went with them. It wasn't a case of this youngster with no more than fifteen, maybe sixteen, games and 100 innings in organized competition under his belt being ready for prime time, nor of his being the best of the young gunslingers the Dodgers had in their training camp—a group which included the likes of Karl Spooner, Roger Craig, Don Bessent, Ed Roebuck, Tom Lasorda, and Don Drysdale. The reason, simply stated, was the bonus rule, which required that any "bonus baby" had to be kept on the roster of the major-league team signing him, not farmed out. And so Koufax trailed along, carrying his bonus as excess baggage—both for himself and the team.

With the Dodgers some fourteen games ahead of the second-place Braves, they decided to take a gamble on their young left-hander and gave him a few starting assignments. In his second start, he pitched a 2-hit, 14-strikeout shutout over Cincinnati. He followed that up with a second shutout, this one of Pittsburgh. But they were to be the highlights of his rookie season, a season in which he pitched in just 12 games, winning 2, losing 2, and striking out 30 but walking almost as many, 28.

Koufax, unhappy with his spot role, went to general manager Buzzy Bavasi to complain. But Bavasi asked Koufax, "How can you pitch when you can't get the side out?" The young pitcher responded by asking his own question: "Who the hell can get the side out sitting in the dugout?" It was a classic case of Catch-22 for the young pitcher.

The much-rumored lightning that had taken so long to strike finally came in his fifth year, after the Dodgers, with hibernational ambitions, had followed Horace Greeley's advice to "Go West" and fled to Los Angeles. Obviously enjoying the change of scenery in L.A., the twenty-three-year-old struck out 16 Phillies in one game. Two months later he saw that total and raised it two against the San Francisco Giants, breaking by one the National League record set by Dizzy Dean and tying the major-league record of Bob Feller. His 173 strikeouts for the '59 season, accomplished in only 153 innings of work, was the third-best total in the league.

The Dodgers, as a team, enjoyed the change of scenery too, and that year won the National League pennant, sending them into the World Series against the Chicago White Sox. Manager

Walt Alston rewarded the efforts of his young left-hander with a start in the fifth game. In front of a record crowd of 92,706, Koufax went seven innings, giving up just five hits and one White Sox run, that scoring on a double play. But it was enough for a 1–0 Chicago win.

Whatever doubts remained about Koufax's potential—a dread word when used to describe someone who hasn't yet arrived—should have been put to rest by his performance during the '59 season. And by something that nearly happened during the off-season: a trade that almost was. For the Dodgers, wheeling and dealing from their position of strength as World Champions, sought to bolster their team by obtaining the services of Elston Howard from the Yankees. To that end, they offered the Yankees a twofer deal: Duke Snider and Johnny Podres for Howard. But when the Yankees counteroffered, inserting the name Koufax for that of Podres, the Dodgers balked, echoing the sentiments of manager Walter Alston, who, explaining why he had never farmed Koufax out, answered, "Because every day I expect him to become a great pitcher."

To many, Koufax included, the Dodgers' faith in him must have seemed misplaced. Especially after 1960, when, as he remembered it, "the roof fell in." His won-lost record went from 8–6 to 8–13, and his self-confidence went just as far south. His problem, according to pitching coach Joe Becker, was that "he'd rush. I tried to get him to shorten his stride and to throw with an easy, natural motion. But he was overanxious." Bavasi called him "a silent temper case" who would "get mad at himself and try to overpower the hitter. His attitude was, 'Here it comes, you dirty so-and-so. Let's see you hit it.' You can get away with that stuff from time to time, but not for a season. You keep defying major-league hitters to hit you and they will." His impatience was such that sportswriter Bob Broeg wrote, "He could throw a grape through a battleship, but he wanted to hear the guns roar."

At this point in his career, Koufax's numbers were, at best, underaverage, even embarrassing. His six-year won-lost record was an unimpressive 36–40, he had finished just 22 of the 103 games he had started, his ERA was up there somewhere in the paint numbers at 4.10, and his strikeout-to-walk ratio was just $3\frac{1}{2}$:2. All in all, it seemed as if this promise unkept had little chance of fulfilling Alston's expectation that he would "become a great pitcher."

However, unbeknownst to all, the curtain to Act I was about to descend, with the curtain to Act II about to go up on one of the greatest pitching careers in all of baseballdom.

It was here that Fate stepped in, in the form of catcher Norm Sherry. Sherry, who was Koufax's roommate, was seated next to him on the team bus one spring day in 1961. Turning to Koufax, Sherry said, "Know what I think, Sandy?" Koufax, who was harder than a clam to open up to conversation, answered only, "No, what do you think, Norm?" With that small opening, Sherry now gave of his advice freely: "Sandy, I think your troubles would be solved if you would just throw easier, throw more change-ups, just try to get the ball over." Koufax mulled over what Sherry had said.

Out of that one-sided discussion a new talent arose and Act II began, as Koufax realized then and there that "there's no need to throw as hard as I can. I found out that if I take it easy and throw naturally, the ball goes just as fast."

And so the man who for six years had just reared back and thrown the twine off the ball now began to alternate a fastball, complete with jet trail, with a curve that circumscribed the letter Q. The result was immediate, as Koufax won six of his first seven starts in '61. One of those who tried to hit the suddenly unhittable lefty with the coal-black hair and eyes to match was Pirates star Willie Stargell, who described the futile exercise as akin to "trying to drink coffee with a fork."

And even though several scouts suggested that he tipped off the coming of his curve, it did batters no good. Jim Davenport, the San Francisco infielder, gave voice to all National League batsmen when, on a postgame wrap-up show after he had won a game with an infrequent hit off Koufax, he was asked: "Jim, with Koufax, do you look for the fastball?" "Oh, shit, yeah," Davenport answered, to the discomfort of the host and the delight of the listening audience. "The curveball you can't hit anyway!"

Koufax was now well-nigh unhittable. And, on four occasions, he was totally unhittable, as he threw four no-hitters in back-to-back-to-back-to-back years, 1962–65—one of those a perfect game.

The press, which had always found his achievements far more arresting than his personality, now began referring to him as the Man with the Golden Arm. But there was little else the gazeteers could unearth about him. For Koufax was a private person who kept his personal feelings far from public scrutiny, behind a scrim of his own making. He rarely fraternized with any of his teammates—and never with opposing players—preferring instead his own company. He once told a biographer, "My personal feelings have always remained private and I would prefer to keep it that way."

One of those personal feelings was his strong conviction about his religion. It was so strong that when the opening game of the 1965 World Series fell on Yom Kippur, the holiest day of the Jewish calendar, Koufax removed himself from the rotation, saying, "The club knows that I don't work that day." Instead, the starting assignment for Game One went to Don Drysdale. Drysdale was treated with somewhat less than loving care by the Minnesota Twins, who greeted him with seven hits and an equal number of runs in just two-plus innings. As manager Walter Alston approached the mound to remove Drysdale and send him to an early rendezvous with the Lifebuoy awaiting him in the shower, "Big D" flipped the ball to Alston and, equally flip, said, "Geez, Skip, bet you wish *I* was Jewish, too." Koufax was to come back into the rotation and pitch shutouts in Games Five and Seven to lead the Dodgers to the World Championship.

But no matter how hard Koufax tried to hide his off-the-field activities, it soon became known that the man who was capable of lifting his game to uncharted heights was having trouble lifting his golden arm, as painful traumatic arthritis in his left elbow threatened his career. Nevertheless, as he turned in successive 26- and 27-win seasons, opponents refused to believe his condition was as serious as it turned out to be, Roberto Clemente saying, "No man with a bad elbow can throw like that."

Finally, after a spectacular 1966 season—underscored by his leading the National League in wins, in ERA for the fifth consecutive season, in complete games for the second straight year, in strikeouts for the fourth time in the last six, and in innings pitched—Sandy Koufax retired, the fire that had once been in his arm now but a dull ache. "I don't regret for one minute the twelve years I've spent in baseball," he said, announcing his retirement. "But I could regret one season too many."

And so, retiring "while I can still brush my teeth," Sandy Koufax personally brought down the curtain on his own second act—the most dramatic second act in the history of sports.

89

Don Budge

b. 1915

In one of those little tricks Dame History always seems to be playing on us to see if we're paying attention, she managed to hide one of sports' greatest moments—and one of its greatest heroes—under a proverbial bushel basket. And damned near got away with it.

The year was 1937, a year sandwiched between the years 1936 and 1938, when two momentous sporting events—the Berlin Olympics and the Louis-Schmeling rematch—were covered like the Creation of the World, Part II. And a year when sportswriters were writing about the other distractions of the moment, such as War Admiral's winning the Triple Crown, Joe Louis's winning the heavyweight championship of the world, and the United States' winning its first Davis Cup since 1926.

And somewhere in there lies our story, the story of what sportswriters, exercising their chroniclers' right, then called, simply, "the Greatest"—no dash, no comma, no apostrophe, no anything, as in the "Greatest Tennis Game Ever Played"—the Davis Cup match between Don Budge and Baron Gottfried von Cramm.

Don Budge had learned to play the game of tennis on the public courts of California, which was equal to having taken all the correspondence courses in all the country. As such, he was the first of thousands of youngsters who would take tennis away from the society bluebloods who had owned the sport for as long as anyone cared to remember. Although only eighteen when he arrived on the tennis scene, full-blown and full-grown, he possessed an overwhelming, smashing game that was heaven-sent and a backhand from hell—plus what those in the game called "the potential of a world champion."

Writers catching their first glimpse of him described this young phenomenon as a "diffident, stringy, surprisingly agile youth." But to most who saw him for the first time, he had the looks of a tallish Andy Hardy, complete with a plot of reddish hair which led most to label him carrot-topped, but which in truth was more the color of a red-brick schoolhouse, and more than enough freckles to keep a census taker busy for a week.

But what caught the attention of most was his backhand, delivered with a heavy rolling stroke and containing power, elegance and flair, and a spin-and-a-half. It was to become the most celebrated stroke in tennis, one which veteran tennis writer Allison Danzig called "probably the most potent backhand the world has ever seen."

Budge was to ride that backhand to a No. 6 ranking in the world by 1935. And a spot on the United States Davis Cup team. The Davis Cup, emblematic of world tennis supremacy and long synonymous with the United States during the reign of Bill Tilden, had become a two-nation cakewalk, with first France and then Great Britain winning it, the U.S. having been without since 1926. The year 1935 was to prove no different, despite the addition of the twenty-year-old youngster from California, who, showing his inexperience, lost two singles matches to Great Britain's best in the challenge round.

But the boyish-looking lad had made tennis history, of sorts, during that challenge round. Stepping onto the court at

Wimbledon for the very first time, Budge, instead of rendering the usual formal bow in the direction of Queen Mary, as dignity demanded, greeted the queen with a cheerful wave of his racket and an equally cheerful smile that filled his features and lifted his red hairline, almost as if he had invented the art of smiling. He received a genial wave in return from both the royal box and the crowd, which embraced him and made him their new favorite.

By 1936 Budge, combining a gentle bonhomie and a hard backhand and smashing service, was ranked No. 3 in the world and No. 1 player in the hearts of most tennis fans. Now called the California Comet, in tribute to his native state and native abilities, Budge took Fred Perry to five sets in the finals of the U.S. Open before losing the final set 10–8, and had beaten Australia's Jack Crawford, then ranked No. 6 in the world, in five sets in the interzone Davis Cup finals, the final set a two-hour deal played in 105-degree heat. Unfortunately, and through no fault of Budge's, America's quest for the Holy Grail failed again, Great Britain repeating as Davis Cup champions for the fourth straight year.

All of which brings us to the year 1937, which is where we came in. The right to be called the best tennis player in the world in 1937 belonged exclusively to Budge and Baron Gottfried von Cramm of Germany; no others needed apply, thank you. Von Cramm, who had finished second to Perry in the previous two Wimbledons, was now poised on the threshold of greatness. The only obstacle standing between him and that pinnacle was the soft-of-face but equally hard-to-face Budge. Between them, they contested the right to be called "the best." First had been the U.S. Open finals, where Budge had beaten his German competitor in five hard-fought sets. Now they would face each other again, this time in a heroic struggle that would echo down tennis's long corridors forever.

Their historic contest, in the deciding match of the '37 Davis Cup interzone finals at Wimbledon, pitted strength against strength, hope against hope, and great player against great player. But something else had been added to the bragging rights for player and country: a phone call to von Cramm from Adolf Hitler exhorting von Cramm to win this match for the Ripper and the Fatherland and all that other pious twaddle about Aryan supremacy, an exhortation Hitler had made in the '36 Olympics and was to make again before the '38 rematch between Max Schmeling and Joe Louis.

Von Cramm came out on the court wearing that dull, leaden, soul-pressing look known as sense of duty, a sense that fell upon his shoulders as a weight and charge against his honor. Playing like a man possessed, von Cramm won the first two sets. But the dust was a long way from settling, and Budge returned the favor by taking the third and fourth sets to force the match into a best-of-one final set.

The fifth, and final, set began at seven-thirty as lights began to spangle the area around Wimbledon like popcorn bursting on the skillet. The two combatants—good word, that—continued. It was Budge's howitzer versus von Cramm's Big Bertha as they rolled out their entire arsenal of shots: devastating ground strokes, fierce overheads, killer placements, and big services. After five games, with both rackets worn thin, von Cramm, playing with the imperative of patriotism ringing in his ears, was up four games to one.

As Budge, down 1–4, went over to take a sip of water after the fifth game, he leaned over and whispered to the American team captain, "Don't worry, Cap. I'll make it." And Budge did, tying the final set at 5 all. Soon the most two-sided match in tennis history match went to 6 all. Budge then held his service in the twelfth game and broke von Cramm's service in the thirteenth, setting up still more heroics.

In the fourteenth game, match point came and went, came and went, etc., etc., no fewer than six times. And each time the win was unforthcoming for Budge, as von Cramm, continually just one shot away from extinction, would fight back, almost as if he were a martyr saving himself from the stake by some potent moral force. "The crowd was so quiet," Budge was to recall, "I am sure they could hear us breathing." On the seventh match point, Budge delivered one of his trademark rocket serves to the German's forehand, but von Cramm, amazingly, returned it, full force. In the ensuing rally, von Cramm got his full weight behind a forehand crosscourt shot which went behind Budge and to his left. In what has been called the shot of the century, Budge lunged in desperation, torquing his body, and, sprawling, got his backhand on the ball. "I realized the ball felt pretty good on the racket. I looked up in time to see von Cramm try to reach it on his right-hand side and miss it." The match of the century was over. It had been as one London newspaper wrote, "not so much a contest as a cumulative spectacle."

Budge would go on to beat Bunny Austin and Charles Hare in singles and team up with Gene Mako to take the doubles as the United States beat Great Britain in the Davis Cup finals to win for the first time since the heyday of Big Bill Tilden and end the European Golden Age of Tennis.

The year 1938 belonged to Budge, as he continued his white-clad mastery of the court and opponents, stayed immune to defeat, and became the first player in history to win the Grand Slam—the championships of Australia, France, England, and the United States. And then, having won everything there was to win, Budge turned professional, dominating the pro tennis landscape just as he had the amateur scene.

Those ancient and honorable romantics who had committed themselves to the notion that Bill Tilden stood alone in the tennis pantheon now had to make room for a second great: Don Budge. For Budge was, in the words of Sidney Wood, "a player with no weakness. When he was in his prime, no player, past or present, could have beaten him."

90

Sonja Henie

1912–1969

The Winter Olympics, conceived by the International Olympic Committee to give competitors from the habitually slighted smaller nations an opportunity to achieve glory on ice and snow, first came of age in 1924 at Chamonix, France. One of the stars of that first Winter Olympics was a little, underage blond doll from Norway with toothsome Viking features who would soon change the face of figure skating.

In a sport then known for its mechanical perfection and

scrupulous plainness, eleven-year-old Sonja Henie, unencumbered by reputation or expectation, looked like a little schoolgirl out on a romp as she took the ice. Wearing skates as white as the proverbial piece of linen and a fur-lined skirt as short and serviceable as modern fashion and modesty would allow, the 75-pound wunderkind, knee-high to a herring at five feet, made everyone sit up and take notice. And although she was to finish eighth and last in the field, one of the judges gave her the highest scores in the free-skating portion of the program.

The press also sat up and took notice of this child prodigy, one scribe writing, "Future aspirants for the world title will have to reckon with Sonja Henie of Norway, already a great performer who has every gift—personality, form, strength, speed, and nerve."

Young Sonja went home to Oslo to devote herself to fulfilling that promise. Working everlastingly at improving her style, she grafted on new skills and lyrical movements until, like a panther, she positively purred as she moved about the ice. One of those stylistic improvements included the adoption of innovative short skirts that swirled above her knees in eye-catching colors, all the better to catch the eyes of the fans and the judges as she executed her breathtaking spins.

The alchemy began to pay dividends in the 1926 World Championships, as Sonja, alternately flashing her brown eyes, blond hair, and variety of colors as she whirled around the ice, finished second. The young skater vowed never to finish anywhere but first from that point on. It was a promise she would keep, but not without another addition to her repertoire.

Before the 1927 World Championships, the still-impressionable young Sonja chanced to see the immortal Anna Pavlova perform. Calling the performance "the greatest influence in my life," Sonja incorporated the ballerina's movements into her figure skating, along with choreographic design. With the "Dying Swan" sequence from *Swan Lake* now part of her repertoire, along with balletlike movements and gravity-defying spins, Sonja won the first of her ten straight World Championships.

By the time the Winter Olympics got around to its second change of scenery—this time St. Moritz—Sonja, by now fifteen years old, had become the darling of the multitudes. Reacting to her girlish charms and veritable smorgasbord of moves—which included difficult double Axel Paulsens, jumps ending in graceful splits, and brilliantly executed spins, twirls, and jumps, as many as nineteen of them—they rent the air with cheers for her every move. The judges, too, reacted to her artistry on ice and, with six of the seven awarding her their first-place votes, she won the first of her gold medals.

Sonja Henie's star had taken on such a stellar brightness by the time the Olympics traveled across the pond to Lake Placid in 1932 that even though the United States was in the throes of the Depression, scalpers were able to ask for, and receive, $50 in hard-earned Roosevelt dollars for a ticket to see the phenomenon with the winning smile. Reporters, too, were overwhelmed by the beautiful five-foot-two, 109-pound youngster they quickly labeled, fittingly, the Pavlova of the Ice. Smitten by her little-girl dimpled good looks and beautiful blond locks, they made her the focal point of story after story. And even though she had difficulty breaking through the language barrier, she still was able to convey the thought that "most always, I win."

And win she did, capturing all seven judges' votes—and her second gold medal.

The young girl-woman—who had been skating for eighteen years and harbored ambitions that included "winning three Olympics and ten World Championships...and then the movies"—now postponed, at least until after the 1936 Winter Olympics and the World Championships, her plans for retirement.

Arriving in the little Bavarian resort of Garmisch-Partenkirchen to defend her gold medal for the last time, Sonja felt the pressure—both from within and without, as the police had to be called out to control the crowds demanding to catch a glimpse of the superstar. Those who did get in to watch her in her practice sessions were astounded to see a possessed whirling dervish going through her practice routines, her skates a blur as she spun around as many as eighty times at speeds that frightened the timid of heart.

Her frayed nerves continued on exhibit as well. And when the first day's compulsory figures, showing Sonja only 3.6 points ahead of her heiress apparent, fifteen-year-old Cecelia Colledge of Great Britain, were posted, she did something unknown to the porcelain world of figure skating: she lost her temper. Doing a slow burn, she ripped the offending notice off the board and tore it to shreds.

The girl who was called "the Iron Butterfly," steel-willed and wily, steeled herself not only to do better, but to win. And win she did, her third Olympic gold.

One week later, as per invoice, she won her tenth consecutive World Championship and hung up her skates—at least her amateur ones—to begin her film career. But not before this picture-perfect skater had won three gold medals, ten consecutive World Championships, and a total of 1,473 medals, cups, and trophies and changed the shape—or the "figure"—of her sport.

91

Willie Pep

b. 1922

The man who scissored his given surname "Papaleo" into the pallindromic "Pep" was boxing's master illusionist: Now you see him, now you don't. His movements, which had the look of tap dancing with gloves on, left his opponents to speculate on their meaning and his fans to listen for the accompanying music.

Willie Pep fought as if he didn't like to get hit, which he didn't, having developed a great respect for his teeth at a very early age. He had the uncanny ability to anticipate an opponent's blows—and then parry them, pick them off, or just plain beat them with his own form of rat-a-tat punches.

Throughout his l-o-n-g career, Pep substituted shiftiness and cunning for a lack of power, most of his knockouts coming not from a malicious blow but merely from his opponents' falling to the ground in utter exhaustion, unable to keep up with the man labeled Willie the Wisp, a name that was soon to be contracted, as his own had been, to Will o' the Wisp.

Many of his opponents, unable to cope with an opponent they couldn't find, let alone hit, likened fighting Pep to battling a man in the Hall of Mirrors. Others compared the experience to chasing moonbeams with a jar, or chasing a mirage or a shadow. And yet another, Kid Campeche, said, after a fight in which Pep had pitched boxing's version of a no-hitter, "Fighting Willie Pep is like trying to stamp out a grass fire."

Pep's greatest virtuoso performance came the night he gave the fans a run for their money, literally, as he won a round without throwing a punch. His opponent on this occasion was Jackie Graves, a southpaw puncher with more than his share of knockouts. Pep had already tipped off a few friendly sportswriters that he would not throw a punch during the third round. Incredulous though they were, they saw an incredible performance: Pep moved; Pep switched to southpaw, mimicking Graves; Pep danced; Pep weaved; Pep spun Graves around and around again; Pep gave head feints, shoulder feints, foot feints, and feint feints—and never threw a punch. In the words of one sportswriter, Dan Riley, "It was an amazing display of defensive boxing skill. So adroit, so cunning, so subtle that the roaring crowd did not notice Pep's tactics were completely without offense. He made Jim Corbett's agility look like a broken-down locomotive. He made even Sugar Ray Robinson's fluidity look like cement hardening. Never has boxing seen such perfection!" Just as incredibly, he won the round on the judges' scorecards.

Willie Pep's long, twenty-two-year career was, in reality, two careers. During his first one, one that spanned seven years, Pep outclassed and outraced 109 of his 111 opponents—fighting one draw and losing only to the clutches of ex-lightweight champ Sammy Angott—and won the featherweight crown at the tender age of twenty years and two months.

Then, on January 8, 1947, Pep suffered near-fatal injuries in an airplane crash. His career, and perhaps his ability ever to walk again, seemed behind him. Miraculously, five months later, rather than staying at home on the underside of a blanket to watch his bones mend, Pep came back—not only to walk, but to fight. And to win.

Pep went on to once again denude the featherweight division of contenders, winning twenty-six more times and defending his title twice more. With his supply of worthy opponents all but exhausted, Pep accepted the challenge of what he called "a thin, weak-looking guy who looks like you could go 'poof' and knock him over." But the "thin, weak-looking guy," who went by the name of Sandy Saddler, knocked Pep over with a vagrant left in the third and a right in the fourth to finish off the soon-to-be-ex-champion and take his place amongst the greats of boxing.

The rematch was the highlight of Willie's career(s). For on the night of February 11, 1949, in the creaky, hallowed old Madison Square Garden, Pep made his dream come true by recapturing the 126-pound crown he had lent to Saddler the year before. Possessing all the nervous courage of a small pup, and the speed, guile, and ability to recognize pain instantly, Pep stayed true to his instincts and gave Saddler nothing to hit. In return, Pep hit Saddler with his best shots, his combinations and lefts—yet seemed to be doing no damage. "But," said Willie, "when I stepped on his toes, he said 'Ouch!' So I stepped on his toes all night." It was more than enough. At the end of fifteen hard-fought rounds, Pep won, going away, the last big fight he was ever to win.

With the sand—as well as the Sandy, who was to beat him in two return goes—beginning to fill the bottom of his hourglass, his long-running career was now coming to a close. But still—an inapt word in any description of Pep—the name Willie Pep will conjure up images of a balletic grace, put to a symphony named "Will o' the Wisp."

92

George Mikan

b. 1924

Sports archeologists can trace both professional basketball's low point and its birth as a major sport to the beginning of the 1947–48 season.

For it was in 1947 that one writer, sitting next to another at the 69th Regiment Armory in New York, watching two professional teams called the New York Knickerbockers and the Providence Steamrollers line up for the opening tip-off, turned and asked, "Think this sport will ever be big-league?" He had good reason to ask the question. Over the previous two decades, the roster of basketball clubs that had taken turns at being members of the two professional leagues had borne so many advertisements on their uniforms that basketball courts had taken on the look of running, dribbling, jumping versions of the Yellow Pages. The improbable names that bedecked the basketball courts had included the likes of the Anderson Duffy Packers, the Chicago Gears, the Akron Firestone Non-Skids, and the Fort Wayne Zollner Pistons. And by the beginning of the '47 season, the two leagues had begun to look more like a dock wallopers' shape-up than basketball leagues, as the roster of teams took on the madcap comings-and-goings of Grand Central Station at rush hour, with franchises entering and leaving on a regularly scheduled basis.

But it was also the beginning of professional basketball as a major-league sport, with the addition to its ranks of its first superstar, a six-foot-ten, 245-pound, bespectacled hulk who looked like the man Jack met at the top of the beanstalk: George Mikan.

Mikan had attended DePaul University, and after head coach Ray Meyer took him in hand and made him "realize his height was something to be admired, not be ashamed of, he was on his way to being great." And great he was. He dominated the collegiate scene as no basketball player had before him, winning all-America recognition three straight years and being named College Player of the Year twice.

After graduating DePaul, Mikan signed on with the Chicago Gears for a record salary of $12,000. Then, when the Gears went the way of most basketball franchises in those days, Mikan picked up his ball and joined the Minneapolis Lakers.

Mikan's style was really no style at all; it was more self-preservation. Stationing himself to the right of the basket, Mikan, drawing two- and sometimes three-man coverage, would spend most of his time fending off the slings and arrows of assorted elbows. Big enough that if he held out his arms he could become a railroad crossing, Mikan retaliated with more than his fair share of flying elbows. Then, when he was free of the entanglement under the basket, he would make one feint left, wheel to the right, and lob in his patented hook shot.

Over the course of his career, Mikan earned a black belt in basketball, breaking his left leg, his right leg, his right foot, the arch of his left foot, his right wrist, his nose, his thumb, and three fingers, and accumulating 166 stitches. Once, after a rival had accused him of playing rough, Mikan ripped off his shirt, revealing an upper body covered with black-and-blue marks, and growled, "What do you think these are? Birthmarks?"

But Mikan was more than a punching bag. Much more. In his first season, he led the Lakers to the National Basketball Association championship, averaging 21.3 points per game and earning the League's Most Valuable Player award. From 1947 to 1956, he led his team to five titles in six years, leading the league in scoring three times and being named all-Pro his first six seasons.

He was also the League's biggest gate attraction. On one of his first trips to New York, his reputation was such that the arched marquee outside the old Madison Square Garden read: "Wed. Basketball Geo. Mikan vs. Knicks." He was *that* big!

And he was also so big that to counter his effectiveness under the basket, where he stood like a monument, the league widened the free-thrown lane from six feet to twelve.

But it didn't matter to Mikan, as he continued to throw in his hook shot, amassing 11,364 points—5,000 more than any other player of that period.

He was to retire after the 1953–54 season "at the peak of his career, while George Mikan is still George Mikan." But not before he had established the benchmark for future generations and made professional basketball a big-league sport.

93

Johnny Weissmuller
1904–1984

George Carlin, the comedian and social commentator joined at the hip, once said of swimming, "It's not a sport, it's a way to keep from drowning." Carlin had apparently never heard of Johnny Weissmuller, the Tarzan of swimming.

Weissmuller's baptism into the world of swimming came at the age of eight, when his mother first took him to Chicago's Fullerton Beach, hard by the shores of Lake Michigan. There he took to swimming like the proverbial fish to water and soon was challenging "the Rocks," a dangerous breakwater of boulders washed over by unpredictable lake waves. "Swimming had come naturally to me," Weissmuller would remember years later, "and like all kids, I had yearned for adventure. Swimming over the Rocks was dangerous, but it was exciting."

But his adventures in the water were hardly matched ashore. For soon after his introduction to swimming, Weissmuller's father died and young Johnny had to go to work to support his family, first as an errand boy and later as a bellhop and elevator operator. It was at this point, as a teenager, that he chanced to run into a childhood friend who introduced him to the swimming coach of the Illinois Athletic Club, "Big Bill" Bachrach.

Bachrach, a 350-pound local mover of dreams, took one look at the form of the six-foot-three youngster with the dense body and barrel chest and saw that even with all the paraphernalia of a potential great, he'd require the proper form. Taking one chomp on the cigar he held clenched between his teeth, Big Bill made young Weissmuller an offer he could, but didn't, refuse: "Work with me a year, do everything I say, to the letter and no questions asked, and I'll take you on. You'll be a slave and you'll hate my guts. But in the end you might break every record there is."

And so, like a juggler who never varies his routine, Weissmuller practiced hour after hour, day after day, under the watchful eye of his coach-cum-drill instructor, who demanded nothing less than that his troops obey his every command, even if it meant stepping out of a window and turning left. It was almost as if the words of Henry James were written on a sampler above the pool: "Life is effort, unremittingly repeated." But there was no need to embroider the fact that after one year of unremitting practice, Weissmuller had become a beautifully tooled machine.

Now Bachrach, fully satisfied that his young charge had absorbed everything there was to be absorbed about the finer points of swimming, matched him against other swimmers in meets. And Weissmuller swept to victory after victory.

In later years, commenting on his achievements, Weissmuller would say, "I was better than Mark Spitz. I never lost a race." And then, with emphasis, he'd add, "Never!"

Weissmuller's growing legend was such that one oft-recycled myth had it that one warm summer day, swimming offshore in Lake Michigan, he cried out to the bathers on Chicago's Lake Shore Drive, "Is this Milwaukee?" "No, it's Chicago!" came back the cry, in unison. Weissmuller, without missing a beat, merely turned around and swam back out to sea.

Whatever, his reputation had grown to such proportions that by the time Bachrach took Weissmuller to Hawaii for a series of exhibitions against the reigning two-time Olympic champion,

Duke Paoa Kahanamoku, Kahanamoku suddenly discovered he had better things to do than face the young heir presumptive, and excused himself from the competition.

The champions present and future would eventually meet. But before their historic matchup, Weissmuller would further establish his credentials as one of the greats by becoming the first person to swim 100 meters in less than one tick of the clock's big hand, then lowering his world record time from 58.6 to 57.4 seconds. And in a sport where records are transitory things subject to discontinuation without further notice, Weissmuller's would last ten years.

Visiting hordes of athletes descended upon Paris for the 1924 Olympics—runners by the brigades, boxers by the battalions, sprinters by the platoons, weight-throwers by the ton, and swimmers in great shoals. But it was two men who held the attention of the crowds: Weissmuller and Kahanamoku.

As the twenty-year-old Weissmuller stood in anticipation of the starting gun for the 100-meter final, he found the thirty-four-year-old defending champion Kahanamoku on one side of him and the Duke's younger brother, Sam, on the other. Concerned that the two Hawaiians planned to swim a team race against him, Weissmuller was relieved to hear the Duke say, "Johnny, good luck. The most important thing in this race is to get the American flag up there three times. Let's do it!"

And do it they did. When the gun sounded, Weissmuller got off to a fast start. Legs kicking and arms flashing, he pulled ahead of the field at seventy-five meters and won going away in the Olympic-record time of 59 seconds flat, with the Duke finishing second and brother Sam third. After his victory, the crowd of seven thousand at the Olympic natatorium stood and cheered for him for three minutes, their hosannas subsiding only after it was announced he would appear again later in the afternoon.

That afternoon he not only reappeared, but won another gold, anchoring the American 800-meter freestyle relay team in the Olympic-record time of 9:53.4, then adding a bronze in water polo. With his earlier victory in the 400-meter freestyle, again in Olympic-record time, Weissmuller went home with three golds and a bronze.

Four years later, at Amsterdam, Weissmuller put on another golden performance. After carrying the Stars and Stripes during the opening ceremonies, he added to his growing total of gold by repeating in the 100 meters. But not before he almost met with catastrophe—and his first loss, ever. Coming out of the midrace turn, Weissmuller got what he described as a "snootful" of water and almost blacked out. Left with powers barely those of respiration, Weissmuller lost two yards. But he didn't lose his head. "I knew enough not to cough. If you don't cough, you can swallow it." Regaining both his composure and his stroke, he went on to win the fourth of his five Olympic gold medals—again in record time, lowering his Olympic mark to 58.6 seconds. He added his final gold by again anchoring the 800-meter relay team to another victory in the Olympic-record time of 9:36.2.

By 1932, circumstances had so arranged themselves that instead of competing in the Los Angeles Olympics Weissmuller took a job for $500 a week advertising swimsuits to keep his head above treacherous financial waters. One of the photos showing Weissmuller in his B.V.D. swimsuit caught the eye of a Hollywood talent scout, who arranged for him to try out for the role of Tarzan in the upcoming movie *Tarzan, the Ape Man*. Weissmuller got the part and traded in his swimming suit for a loincloth, making twelve Tarzan movies over the next sixteen years.

Today, Johnny Weissmuller is best remembered not as a swimming great who set sixty-seven world records, who held every record from fifty yards to half a mile, and who was never beaten, but as Tarzan. It is a fame that drowns out an appreciation of his skills—skills that made him one of the all-time great athletes.

94

Al Oerter

b. 1936

The Olympics is a telling phrase with multiple meanings. It is the Olympic flag, with its five intertwined rings denoting the participating continents. It is the Olympic motto, *Citius, Altius, Fortius*, calling on the athlete to move even faster, soar even higher, and be even stronger in each quadrennial competition. It is the Olympic Village, where athletes from the nations of the world congregate in one heterogeneous community of friendship and understanding. It is the Olympic awards ceremony, with nationalistic anthems and flags attesting to the achievements of the winners. And it is the Olympic pomp and pageantry, from the lighting of the torch at the opening ceremonies to the extinguishing of same at the closing ceremonies.

For many, it also means one of the most enduring figures ever to participate in the Olympics: Al Oerter.

Al Oerter's first appearance on the Olympic stage came in

1956 at Melbourne, when, as a twenty-year-old junior out of the University of Kansas and holder of the national scholastic discus record, he survived the Olympic tryouts. One of three Americans sent halfway around the world to compete in the discus throw, Oerter arrived totally unheralded and largely unnoticed. Many had installed his teammate, world-record holder Fortune Gordien, and Adolfo Consolini of Italy as favorites to win the event.

And when, in a practice toss just before the finals, Gordien sent his two-kilogram (read: 4 pounds 6.55 ounces) platter soaring almost four feet farther than his world record, Oerter, who had a habit of communing with both nature and self, quietly intoned to himself, "Oh, oh, this man is hot. No one's going to beat him for the Olympic gold."

Throwing behind the two favorites, Oerter watched as they made their first-round throws in the finals, outwardly showing no first-time jitters but inwardly "scared to death," as he later admitted. Now it was his turn to stand and deliver. "Keyed up" and "inspired," the 228-pounder with shoulders as wide as a door and arms like a village smithy's took his place in the circle. Beginning his spin off his left foot, Oerter rotated one and a half turns, spinning like a 78-rpm record, and let fly with a soaring toss of 184 feet 11 inches—the longest throw of his life, and four feet farther than the existing Olympic record. When he realized what he had done, Oerter confessed, "My arm tightened up and my nerves were shot to blazes." Still, no one else came within five feet of that first toss.

Later, standing on the victory podium, Oerter, suddenly overwhelmed by the magnitude of his towering achievement, felt himself "go to pieces," his legs buckling. But he would right himself in time to receive his first gold medal.

Oerter would have several more opportunities to practice standing on the victor's rostrum.

Oerter was to survive a near-fatal auto accident in 1957 and a loss at the U.S. Olympic trials to the giant discus thrower Rink Babka before making the 1960 Olympic team. He was once again the underdog at the Rome Olympics, this time to Babka, the coholder of the world record.

Under great pressure, most of it self-generated, Oerter warmed up for the qualifying round by throwing the discus beyond the world-record marker. He then qualified with an Olympic-record toss of 191 feet 8 inches. But on the day of the finals, after Babka had led off the festivities with a throw of 190 feet 4 inches, Oerter, "so tense I could barely throw," could get no closer to Babka than 189 feet 1 inch. His next three throws brought him no closer. With his chances plummeting like Icarus, Oerter prepared for his fifth and final throw. As he did, Babka approached him and told him he was "doing something wrong" with his left arm when he started his throw.

Oerter thanked Babka and began concentrating on his release, studying its component parts. Finally, with an understanding of what he had to do to win, Oerter took his place in the 8'2¼" circle, ready to take his final throw. Spinning, Oerter torqued his body and then let the discus go with everything he had. And more. By the time the weightless plate had finished its fluent arc and fallen to the lap of the earth, it had sailed 194 feet 2 inches—a personal record, and an Olympic record as well. As for Babka, his fifth throw fell short, and he had to settle for a silver to Oerter's second gold medal.

For Oerter to make his souffle rise a third time in the '64 Tokyo Games, he had to overcome more than the normal union number of problems. First of all, the field was one of the strongest ever gathered to contest for the gold, discus-throw version, including the likes of Ludvik Danek of Czechoslovakia, who had won forty-five straight competitions, and Vladimir Trusenyov of Russia, who had, for twenty-seven days, held the world record before Oerter, in a game of record-breaking tag, had reclaimed it. Second, Oerter was suffering from a chronic cervical disk injury that required him to wear a neck harness. And then, as if that weren't enough, his body contorted as he pirouetted during a practice throw less than a week before the official opening of the '60 Olympics, and he tore the cartilage in his rib cage. Doctors advised him that it would take a month to heal—*if* he didn't compete.

With Dame Fortune about to hang a funeral blanket over his chances, she had a change of heart and instead wrapped him up in the folds of her skirt, just as Oerter himself was wrapped in ice packs and bandages. So injured that it seemed the only thing that would improve him at this point was embalming fluid, Oerter nevertheless determined to defend his gold medal. And, despite having to wear a flak jacket, which hampered his throwing ability, his first throw in the preliminary round set an Olympic record of 198 feet 8 inches.

Before the finals, Oerter had said to another athlete, "If I don't do it on the first throw, I won't be able to do it at all." But his first throw went only 189 feet 1 inch, leaving him in third place after four rounds. Now, before his fifth, and final, attempt, Oerter gave himself a pep talk: "This is the Olympic Games, boy," he exhorted himself. "Forget everything else and stretch one." With that, he gave it everything he had, even as it caused him to double over in pain, and "stretched" one. And when the officials had dragged forth the discus they found it had sailed 200 feet 1 inch, giving Oerter his third Olympic record and third gold medal. Not to mention a victory in his heroic struggle against pain and injury. As Oerter later said, "I gutted this one out."

By the time the 1968 Mexico City Olympics rolled around, Oerter was thirty-one years of age and 295 pounds. He wasn't given a chance, especially against world-record holder Jay Silvester, who in one of the qualifying rounds had thrown the discus 207 feet 10 inches, several inches better than the best Oerter had ever done.

But in the finals, Oerter, who was to recall, "Nobody gave me a show except myself," became the show. Going into the third round, and in fourth place, Oerter uncorked a throw of 212 feet 6 inches—five feet farther than he had ever thrown a discus before. He then let Silvester and the others take aim at his mark. Demoralized, none came close to Oerter's new Olympic record. The "Iron Man" of the Olympics had done it again, becoming, in the process, the first athlete ever to win four gold medals in the same event.

The man whose achievements were far more arresting than his quiet personality would later remember thinking, "I guess I'm very jealous. I don't want to give it to anybody else."

And with that, Oerter retired from competition after having thrown the discus some thirty thousand times. But, after missing Munich and Montreal in 1972 and '76, he became restless, and, rather than sit at home twining willow-wreaths for his own tombstone, he began tirelessly training for the Moscow Olympics in 1980. In an AAU meet in Westfield, New Jersey, he threw the discus 219 feet 10 inches, some seven feet farther than his personal best. Now he believed he was ready to challenge Wolfgang Schmidt, the East German world-record holder, and America's Mac Wilkins—even at the age of forty-three. But after he made the U.S. team as an alternate, Fate pulled the rug out from under his aspirations, in the form of the United States boycott of the games.

But Al Oerter wasn't through. Not yet. Contemplating another comeback, he began accelerating his training for the Los Angeles Games in '84. But even if Oerter, at age forty-seven, hadn't had enough, Father Time had. And now drew the final curtain on Al Oerter's fantastic career. But not before this modern Hercules had scaled the Olympian hills, where, wearing four gold medals, he could look down on the rest of the sports world.

Nadia Comaneci

b. 1961

In the eighth decade of the twentieth century, all that the sports world knew about gymnastics could be written on a postcard already crowded with a description of a small foreign village.

And then, at the 1972 Munich Olympics, an elfin, four-foot-ten, 84-pound munchkin from one of those small foreign villages—Grodno, Byelorussia, to be exact—named Olga Korbut changed all that.

Known only by her first name, Olga was not the best woman gymnast in the Olympics, nor even in her native Soviet Union.

That honor belonged to teammate Lyudmila Tourisheva, who captured the all-around championship. But Lyudmila's style was one of a surgical nature, while Olga's was one that saw her ride her horse vaults and her own particular hobbyhorse to her own delight—and that of her audience, both present in Munich and in front of their TV sets around the world.

ABC Sports served as the witting middleman in the making of the legend, as their cameras fell in love with the impish seventeen-year-old with the infectious smile and little-girl pigtails. Ironically, however, it was not her success in becoming the first gymnast ever to perform backward somersaults on the balance beam and uneven parallel bars that made her a media darling, but her failure. Leading after six of the eight events in the team competition, Olga slipped and fell off the uneven bars. As the cameras zoomed in to reveal the youngster's face hidden behind a veil of tears in an up-close-and-personal look, millions of devotees of the life nonstrenuous took her to their hearts.

That little one-act drama merged Marshall McLuhan's so-called global village and the Olympic Village into one, as Olga Korbut became the darling of the games. By the time the Olympics had come to a close, Olga had captured not only gold medals in the balance beam and floor exercises, but the imagination of a worldwide television audience. "Through television," wrote Paul Attner of the *Washington Post*, "the American public saw a fascinating, delicate creature, the little girl down the street who seemed as removed as possible from the unemotional, cold Communist stereotype perpetuated by her teammates. Here was a Russian who actually smiled and laughed and cried and waved to the crowd."

But even though this Russian Barbie doll was flattered, boosted, and covered in the media like the Burning of Rome, Part II, she was, as teammate Nelli Kim said, "not gymnast; Korbut artist." It remained for another gymnast to combine artistry and athleticism. And for another Olympics to put her talents on display.

Four years later, at the 1976 Montreal Olympic Games, a little five-foot-nothing fourteen-year-old Romanian with the melodious Italian-sounding name of Nadia Comaneci—pronounced Coh-man-NEECH by the Forum crowds, in a strangulated rapture—saw the artistry of Olga Korbut and raised it to a higher level. To a perfect 10.

Young Nadia had been discovered by Bela Karolyi, who had seen her as a small girl doing gymnastic exercises during recess in another of those small foreign villages that constantly show up on postcards, this one Gheorghi Gheorghin-Dej. With Karolyi's help, and painstaking effort, Nadia entered the world of gymnastics. In her first meet, at the age of six, she finished thirteenth. Karolyi gave her a doll and told her "it was for good luck. I told her, 'You must never finish thirteenth again.'"

She never would. In fact, over the next seven years she never finished anywhere but first. By 1976 her doll collection had grown to several hundred, and her skills had grown proportionately. In late March, competing in the American Cup, Nadia had done the ungraspable and astonished the gymnastics world by scoring the first perfect 10 in international gymnastics history. Cathy Rigby, the ABC commentator, could only marvel, "In my twenty years in gymnastics, I have never seen such technical perfection and confidence."

Four months later Nadia arrived in Montreal for the XXI Olympiad, and immediately announced her intentions: "I don't come here to smile. I come here to do a job. I leave the smiling to Olga."

But this time around Olga didn't have much to smile about, as that Aladdin's lamp known as TV quickly adopted Nadia as its new darling and left its ex-sweetheart to stand around, like a fly in coffee, attracting attention and comment but hardly enjoying it. For not only did Nadia have Olga's number, she had her own: the number 10.

On the very first night of the team competition, Nadia made Olympic history by receiving a score of 10 on the uneven bars, the first perfect score ever awarded in Olympic gymnastics history. Even the scoreboard wasn't prepared for the phenomenon, as it was unable to record the historic number. But those programming the scoreboard would have several more opportunities to correct their shortsightedness, as Nadia continued to create new standards of excellence, racking up more 10s than could be seen at a Bo Derek film festival.

The following night, sixteen thousand people crammed into the Forum to see the young lady with astonishing gravity-transcending abilities turn in two more flawless performances, on the balance beam and the uneven bars. Before the Olympics were over, Nadia had been awarded seven perfect 10s, winning the gold in the all-around, the balance beam, and the uneven bars, and taking a bronze in the floor exercise.

Her sheer technical prowess and effortless execution had captured the imagination of the world, even its critics. Jim McKay had likened her to "a woman swimming in an ocean of air." And another critic, answering those who thought Nadia's perfect scores had been given away too freely, said, "When Nadia can flawlessly exceed the most hazardous degree of difficulty in the point book, the judges have no choice but to give her a 10."

Asked by one reporter after the Olympics if she planned to retire, the young Nadia answered, "I'm only fourteen." She was to come back to participate in the 1980 Olympics, winning the beam and floor exercise events, to give her a total of five golds, three silvers, and one bronze in Olympic competition.

Nadia Comaneci not only won, she was perfect, as proven by the thirty-one perfect scores of 10 she rang up over her brilliant twelve-year career. And while the glory for putting gymnastics on the map might belong to Olga Korbut, the spoils belonged to an incredible athlete named Nadia Comaneci, who proved that practice makes perfect indeed.

96

Satchel Paige

1906?–1982

To those four commendations of age—old wood to burn, old wine to drink, old friends to trust, and old authors to read—may be added a fifth: the ageless Leroy Robert "Satchel" Paige.

For Paige was ageless, literally, nobody quite knowing his exact age. According to one source, he was born in 1906. To another, his mother, his natal year was 1903. And to Ted "Double Duty" Radcliffe, also Mobile-born, "He was born in 1900."

But if, somehow, his birth was lost to history, the rest of his story is lost to legend, left to storytellers to cut and restitch from cloth to fit their fashion.

It has been said that one legend is worth a thousand facts, and nowhere is this more true than of Satchel Paige, about whom, in the absence of documentation, only a few vagrant facts are ascertainable, including the origin of his unique nickname.

As a gangly six-footer, young Leroy played more hookey than baseball, and as a result of his truancy—plus more than a few gang fights and bouts of shoplifting—was consigned by the state of Alabama to the Industrial School for Negro Children. Like Babe Ruth before him, he honed his skills while a ward of the state, learning, he was to say later, much of his pitching accuracy by throwing rocks through windows, open and shut. Upon his release at the approximate age of sixteen—give or take a guess—he gained employment as a redcap at the Mobile train station, where he ingeniously devised, by means of a pole and some rope, a Rube Goldbergesque apparatus that enabled him to carry ten to twenty bags at the same time, inspiring one of his coworkers to remark, "There goes Leroy, looking like a satchel tree."

It was about at this point that a Pullman porter from Chattanooga saw Paige pitching for the Mobile Tigers, a black semipro team, and recommended him to Alex Herman, owner of the Chattanooga Black Lookouts of the Negro Southern League. Herman signed him for $50 a month, the money to be sent home. Two years later Herman sold Paige's contract to the Birmingham Black Barons of the Negro National League, where his contract called for $275 a month.

Webster McDonald, the great submarine-ball pitcher, remembers his first encounter with the skinny, rubbery, filleted Paige. Pitcher-manager Bill Gatewood brought Paige over to McDonald and said, "Mac, that old boy can throw hard—don't know where he's throwing the ball, though. And he got no kind of move; he can't hold nobody on first base. I told him you got a good move. I want him to watch what you're doin'." McDonald watched Paige and his exaggerated warm-up, and said, "First thing, you can't come all the way around here when you're winding up. You kind of got to watch the target. And if you do this to throw home, you got to do this—the same thing—to throw to first." Paige watched and said, "We didn't do that way in my home." Gatewood cautioned his prodigy, "Now listen, Satchel!" "We didn't do that way," repeated the stubborn Paige. It was, as McDonald said, "always what *he* wanted to do."

And what *he*, meaning Paige, wanted to do was just rear back, kick his left foot high in the air, and throw his fastball with Promethean heat. Or, more accurately, his fastballs, having several variations on the theme. And descriptive nicknames for all of them. His most famous one was his "hesitation pitch." The pitch was delivered sidearm and left batters swinging at the motion of his foot, for his left leg "hesitated" as it fell, stammering almost, before a delayed, out-of-synch follow-through of the arm. (American League president Will Harridge later banned the pitch as "deceitful.") Others he called "the two-hump blooper," for his moving change-up; the "Little Tom," for his medium fastball; the "Long Tom," for his hard fastball; and the "looper," the "nothing ball," the "bat dodger," the "hurry-up ball," the "trouble ball," and the "bee ball."

Negro League star Crush Holloway remembered, "Satchel Paige was the toughest pitcher I ever faced. He didn't have nothing but a fastball, but he had such great control. When he turned it loose, it was on you. That ball looked like an aspirin tablet. You *knew* he was going to throw nothing but a fastball, but you couldn't hit it. I tried all sizes of bats to try to hit him—big bats, short bats, light bats—but still couldn't do anything with him. Before you could swing, the ball was by you." Second baseman Newt Allen added, "We had a hard time *bunting* Satchel's throws, much less hitting them. He'd strike out eighteen or nineteen men at three o'clock in the afternoon."

Over two decades the shuffling, easygoing Paige is estimated, in a day and age when Negro League records were not kept in "white men's record books," to have pitched in as many as 125 games a year, pitching as frequently as five to seven times a week, for a total of 2,500 appearances. Pitching in the Negro League for such clubs as the Nashville Elite Giants, the Cleveland Cubs, the Pittsburgh Crawfords, the Kansas City Monarchs, the New York Black Yankees, the Philadelphia Stars, and the Baltimore Black Sox, he is thought to have rolled up 2,000 wins and between 50 and 100 no-hitters.

But even though Paige was, in the words of one of his teammates, "the Babe Ruth of the Negro Leagues," the magnet who drew in the fans, the lasting cornerstone of his fame was built on that peculiar American institution called barnstorming.

Barnstorming was a child of the twenties and thirties, taking its shape and form from those early aeronauts who appeared throughout the country, offering everyone their first look-see at the newfangled "flying machine" for just "five dollars for a five-minute ride." And it took its name from a mutual arrangement of convenience, where on a slow day the pilot landed in a farmer's pasture and offered him a five-minute joyride for a place to temporarily park his biplane. Soon the form and phrase would be adopted by others, as baseball players made the term a part of their own idiom, traveling from town to town "shaking money out of the rubes."

And nobody, but nobody, shook that "money out of the rubes" better than Satchel Paige, who made upward of $40,000 a year during the Depression traveling America's backyards and vineyards with the Satchel Paige All-Stars.

Advertising himself as "the World's Greatest Pitcher—Guaranteed to Strike Out the First Nine Men," Satchel would lead his All-Stars into small-town America, then hungry for baseball, to play against all-star lineups of America's best players, both black and white, such as the Dizzy Dean All-Stars or the Bob Feller All-Stars.

First Paige would warm up the crowd by warming up from the mound while on his knees or hold a pregame exhibition in which he would throw, with exacting precision, the ball through a small knothole in the fence ten out of ten times. Then, taking the mound, he would acquit the buildup and stun the fans into submission by indeed striking out the first nine men, sometimes with an assurance that bordered on effrontery, even going so far as to walk the first three men and then, disposing of the unfair advantage, calling in his outfielders or making his infielders sit down as he struck out the side.

Satchel's barnstorming feats formed an institution, as he struck out the likes of Charlie Gehringer and Jimmie Foxx three times in a game, and the greatest right-handed hitter in baseball history, Rogers Hornsby, five times. Hack Wilson was unable to strike up a waving acquaintance with Satchel's offerings, saying "The ball looked like a pea." And Dizzy Dean, after losing a 1–0, 17-inning game to Satchel the autumn after Dean had gone 30–7, said of his mound foe, in the quaint manner of yesteryear, "I know who's the best pitcher I ever saw, and it's old Satchel Paige, that big, lanky colored boy."

Indeed, such was the reverence due his accomplishments that the New York Yankees, after signing a young phenom named Joe DiMaggio and anxious to try out their thoroughbred, sponsored a game in which he faced Paige. With a pickup team behind him, Paige pitched to the team of major-league All-Stars as if he cared nothing for their reputations, striking out fifteen of them and allowing just two hits through the first nine innings. Then, in the tenth, DiMaggio, who had twice struck out and once fouled out, came to bat with the potential winning run on base and hit a scratch single off Satchel's famed "hesitation pitch." The scouts were ecstatic, sending a telegram back east to Yankee headquarters which read: DIMAGGIO ALL WE HOPED HE'D BE. HIT SATCH ONE FOR FOUR.

But Satchel Paige's many skills were sacrificed on the altar of futility. For even though he could strike out anyone, two he couldn't strike out were Mssrs. Plessy and Ferguson, the two parties whose names were affixed to the 1896 "separate but equal" Supreme Court decision to which baseball paid more than lip service by holding to the color line—and holding out of baseball the man who just possibly might have been its greatest pitcher.

However, all of that changed on July 7, 1948, when the owner of the Cleveland Indians, master showman Bill Veeck, signed Paige to a contract with the pennant-contending Indians. Some of Veeck's critics, of whom he had many, thought signing a man who looked more like a father figure than an athletic figure as the first black pitcher in the American league was just another of his promotional stunts. But Veeck was like an alchemist striving to resolve gold from the elements, and knew there was still a lode in Satch's veins. Paige paid off, handsomely, by working twenty-one games, winning six, two of them shutouts, and posting a 6–1 record with a 2.48 ERA to help the Indians win their first American League pennant in twenty-eight years.

Paige pitched in thirty-one games the next season and then was gone the following, along with Veeck, who sold the Indians. But both surfaced in 1951 with the ragtag St. Louis Browns, where Veeck, with his usual sense of absurdity, installed Satchel in a rocking chair in the bullpen, in keeping with his age and his aura. There Ol' Satch delivered little homilies, ironies, and prickly wisdoms—such as "The social ramble ain't restful" and "Don't look back: Something might be gaining on you"—along with several golden golden-aged pitching performances. Satch went on to lead the American League in relief wins in '52 for the seventh-place Brownies and was named to a legitimate All-Star squad, the American League's.

Paige would pitch one more year, 1953, and then come back in 1965 at the age of fifty-nine going on sixty-five to pitch three shutout innings—allowing only a double to Carl Yastzemki—to become the oldest pitcher in major-league history, whatever his actual age.

But although Satchel Paige's age was indeterminate, his skills weren't. And as long as baseball players are discussed, this pitcher, who was as old as the century itself, will be counted amongst its greats, his feats as ageless as he was.

97

Fanny Blankers-Koen

b. 1918

Legend has it that in days of yore all conflicts between warring city-states were put on hold for the staging of the ancient Olympics. In modern times, while men went out and played their little games called war, the Olympic Games were put on hold for the duration. And so it was that while the Olympic flame was twice stilled—in 1916 and then again in 1940 and '44—the rest of the world went up in flames.

The second time the Olympic flame was doused because a madman named Adolf Hitler tried to impose his hobnail footprint on the sands of time. Ironically, he had hosted the last

Olympics before the war he insanely initiated. And the hero of those Olympics was Jesse Owens. Another participant in the '36 Berlin Olympics was an eighteen-year-old high jumper and member of the Dutch women's relay team named Fanny Koen. She had tied for sixth place in the high jump and was part of the 4x100-meter relay team which had finished fifth. But a big highlight of the Olympics for Fanny Koen had been getting Jesse Owens's autograph. Little did the world know that the pen that had been passed from Owens to Koen was, in reality, a baton, one that passed on his claim to the title "World's Greatest Athlete" to the young Dutch girl.

Twelve years and one war later, the Olympic flame once again flared into being. Fanny was now thirty, married, and the mother of two young children. And generally considered too old to compete against a field made up mostly of those too young to vote. But Fanny Blankers-Koen would use the '48 London Games to wash away all improbabilities, especially those of the calendar.

As a child in Holland, Fanny Koen had been considered an athletic prodigy, excelling in almost every contest known to mankind and womankind alike. Deciding that Holland already possessed many outstanding swimmers, she turned instead to track and field. But even though she would later recall that as a child she "never could walk, just run," she received little in the way of guidance or training. Then, in 1935, a track coach named Jan Blankers—who, not incidentally, would become her husband—saw her run, and win, her first major race, the 800 meters. Realizing that despite the young girl's middle-distance victory she was in fact a born sprinter, he undertook her training, training that enabled her to qualify for the '36 Olympics.

Fanny Koen left the '36 Games determined to become an Olympic champion. Within two years she was Holland's top woman runner, by 1938 winning every major sprinting event in the country. By 1948 she owned four world records and forty of her country's titles. And even though she harbored gold medal dreams, most sportswriters believed that she stood as much chance of winning her coveted gold as a palmist would have of getting business by tucking her card into a passing coffin.

Because, in 1928, the Olympic organizing committee had realized that athletes are all from Adam and Eve descended, they had included women's events in the Olympic Games. But, suffering from a sharp lack of arithmetic skills, they had limited women to just three individual events. By 1948, that number had increased to nine. And so it was that despite being the world-record holder in the long jump and the high jump, Fanny Blankers-Koen decided to compete in the 100-meter dash, the 80-meter hurdles, and the 200-meter dash, as well as running with the Dutch team in the 400-meter relay—in all, four of the nine women's events.

Fanny began her little four-act drama in the 100-meter dash, recording the best time of the opening round and then going on to win the final in the mud, running like a web-footed amphibian and winning by three yards. Her next event was the 80-meter hurdles. Running against the favorite, Maureen Gardner of Great Britain, and running against a drizzle, Fanny had a difficult race. Left on the mark at the start and almost swimming upstream, she caught Gardner at the fifth barrier but hit the hurdle and lurched across the finish line.

The race was too close to call, and so, while participants and spectators all stood awaiting the decision the band struck up "God Save the King." It was not to signal Gardner as the winner, however, but instead to signal the arrival of the British royal family at the stadium. Finally, after what seemed an eternity, the results were flashed on the scoreboard: Winner, Blankers-Koen, Holland, in the Olympic-record time of 11.2 seconds.

Her third chance to smell the roses came in the 200 meters. She took her place at the starting line and won her heat by six yards, establishing an Olympic record of 24.3 seconds. The next day, on the muddy track, she won the finals by seven yards, the largest margin ever recorded.

By now the woman who was being called the Marvelous Mama commanded center stage, the first triple winner in Olympic history. But her greatest moment lay before her—the anchor leg of the 4x100-meter relay. The Dutch team was not accorded much of a chance, and by the time Fanny took the baton her team was in fourth place, far back in the pack. But in a dozen strides, she had closed the gap and was taking dead aim on the leader, Joyce King of Australia. As she passed the teams from Great Britain and Canada, respectively but not respectfully, the only question was whether there was enough time and room left to catch the leader. There was, and she did, winning her fourth gold.

That should have been the end of the Fanny Blankers-Koen story, but it wasn't, for in 1952 at Helsinki, she tried again to reap an Olympic gold medal harvest. However, it was not to be, as a combination of blood poisoning, an upset stomach, and a boil on her leg forced her to withdraw from three events, and in the only event she entered, the 80-meter hurdles, she tripped on the second hurdle and had to stop as the field sped by.

But still, for one Olympics, the 1948 Games, Fanny Blankers-Koen proved that the only flame which had never been snuffed out was her indomitable spirit, a flaming spirit that propelled her to four track-and-field gold medals in one Olympics.

98

Abebe Bikila

1932–1973

Fate has a fickle habit of bestowing its fame upon certain people, then later taking them by the scruff of the neck and hurling them overboard. Abebe Bikila was one of those people, reduced in but a few short years from a graven image to the grave. But therein lies the irony, for Bikila was only following in the tragic footsteps, literally, of Pheidippides, the man who held the original copyright on the event that made Bikila great.

The story of Bikila and the Marathon goes back to the year Zip, and beyond, to 490 B.C. According to ancient storytellers, whose tales are known for being tinged with more than a little white hue, the marathon itself was based on the Battle of

Marathon and the efforts of a messenger, Pheidippides. Seems that the Athenian general Militiades, having just driven the army of King Darius of Persia off the Greek mainland and watching them sail away, was afraid that they might set sail for the city of Athens and that the Athenians, not knowing of the Greek victory, might surrender to the Persians. And so, in those days before telecommunications, he chose his fastest runner, one Pheidippides, to carry news of the victory to the city. Pheidippides had just finished carrying dispatches to Sparta and back. Now, with the news of the Athenian victory, he raced off to the city of Athens from the plains of Marathon, a journey of some twenty-five miles. Reaching the city, Pheidippides, stumbling and exhausted, gasped out, "Rejoice, we conquer!"—and fell lifeless.

Now, dear reader, jump-skip ahead to the year 1896, when the modern Olympics were revived after five hundred years. The moving force behind the revival, one Baron Pierre de Coubertin of France, decided that for the very first games, to be held in Athens, a footrace should be run from the Marathon Bridge to the refurbished Panathenaic Stadium in Athens in honor of the tragic messenger, Pheidippides. And so it was that the marathon, fittingly won in that first running by a Greek shepherd named Spiridon Loues, became one of the most popular events in the Olympics.

The prescribed distance for that first Olympics marathon was twenty-six miles, a distance which was the standard for the first three Olympics. And then, in the 1908 Olympics, held in London, the route, laid out from Windsor Castle to the stadium in Shepherd's Bush, was extended 385 yards, or once around the stadium track, so that the finish line would be directly in front of the royal box. This random distance became the standardized length for all marathon races from that point on.

For the next fifty-two years, or nine games, the marathon was, with minor exceptions, more important than the participants, most of whom were esteemed but often obscure. It became the closing track-and-field event and, for some, one of the more anticipated events of the games. But little else.

All of that was to change at the Rome Olympics in 1960, and the agent of that change was a polite and gracious, skinny, barefooted palace guard in the Ethiopian army of Haile Selassie named Abebe Bikila—who was so little thought of that the Olympic program listed him bass-ackwards as "Bikila Abebe."

Bikila, the son of Ethiopian peasants, had been running since he was a child, chasing pheasant for the family table. Those long-distance lopes in the unusually high altitudes of his native land had increased his lung capacity and endurance, all the better to make a marathon runner. Now, as he lined up for only his third marathon race ever—and his first outside his native Ethiopia—Bikila's very presence was a rumor, so unknown was he. But for particulars on what happened next, we refer you to A. Lincoln's sonnet on "fooling all the people," etc.

The race, the first ever held at night and the first to begin and end outside the Olympic Stadium, started at Campidoglio Square (designed by Michelangelo), skirted the Circus Maximus and the Baths of Caracalla, went along the two-thousand-year-old Appian Way, and ended at the Arch of Constantine. Not incidentally, less than one mile from the finish line, at the Arch, stood the obelisk of Axum, which had been plundered by Italian troops a quarter century before in the invasion of Ethiopia and brought back to Rome as a trophy.

Bikila, running barefoot in those days before big shoe endorsements, turned his bare toes to pasture at eighteen kilometers, keeping pace with the favorite, Rhadi Ben Abdesselem of Morocco, the rest of the field trailing behind them like the inhabitants of Hamelin behind the Pied Piper—or, in this case, the Pied Pipers. Mile after mile, the two ran side by side, with nary an oblique glance at one another, their pace easy, unvarying.

And then, at the sight of the stolen obelisk, about a thousand meters from the finish, Bikila made his move on the slight incline and sprinted to the front, effectively ending the competitive phase of the marathon then and there.

Bikila raced for the finish and had increased his lead to almost two hundred yards by the time he breasted the tape at the Arch of Constantine, winning in an Olympic-record time of fifteen ticks of the long hand over two hours, breaking Emil Zatopek's record.

Four years later—and forty days after an appendectomy—Bikila did something no one had ever done before in the apocrypha of the Olympics—he repeated as the winner of the marathon. This time shoe-clad, Bikila defended his endurance title in the record-breaking time of 2 hours, 12 minutes, and 11 seconds. As he approached the finish line at Tokyo's Olympic Stadium, the fans, catching a glimpse of the easy-striding Ethiopian, exploded, sounding like a thousand trucks rattling over a wooden bridge. After he breasted the tape, Bikila ran to the infield and did a series of calisthenics, which he finished before the second-place finisher had even reached the finish line. It was, in the words of Australian marathoner Ron Clarke, "the greatest performance ever in track and field."

Bikila attempted to three-peat in 1968, but was forced to retire after seventeen kilometers due to a bone fracture in his leg. Returning to his home country, Bikila resumed his life as a member of the Imperial Guard, by now having been promoted by Emperor Haile Selassie to the exalted rank of lieutenant.

But the next year tragedy struck. Driving the Volkswagen given him by the government following his second gold medal, Bikila was seriously injured when the auto overturned. Paralyzed from the neck down and confined to a wheelchair, his feet stilled, his hands provided him with a new calling card of hope as he trained himself to handle a bow and arrow, becoming such a proficient archer that he competed in the Winter Olympics. But sadly, the greatest endurance runner in history didn't have the endurance to withstand the ravages of his paralysis, and passed away on October 25, 1973, as effortlessly as he had run.

99

John L. Sullivan

1858–1918

Back in the days when men were men and women were damn glad of it, the man most men wanted to be was a boxer with a swaggering virility named John Lawrence Sullivan—simply stated, the strongest man in the world. In an age when America was cocksure and confident of its future but in need of a national hero to tie its patriotic kite tail to, the Great John L. provided just such a hero. And more. Much more. He was an institution, a deity, a national obsession. The preoccupation with Sullivan took the form of mythmaking and nicknaming, as he became known as the Boston Strongboy, the Hercules of the Ring, the Prizefighting Caesar, His Fistic Highness, and just plain ol' Sully.

His pride was the pride of a newly emerging nation, and his "I-can-beat-any-sonofabitch-in-the-house" defiance was the rallying cry of a young nation intent upon making itself heard back in those early days of Manifest Destiny. It was a pride that inspired anyone who had ever met Sullivan, with thousands of men holding out their hands to others and proclaiming, "Shake the hand that shook the hand of the great John L."

Sullivan was part real man, part folk legend. The only difficulty was separating the two as he became the first sports hero in the history of America. But whatever he was, he continued to rewrite the legend with his fists, devouring his opponents as easily as he devoured the free food and drink at his neighborhood saloons.

One opponent was to remember nothing of his battle with John L. other than that his awesome right "felt like a telephone pole had been shoved against me endways." Another said his right "felt like the kick of a mule." And all should have known better than to trifle with a man behind in his razoring.

Sullivan drank as he fought—prodigiously, never meeting a saloon he didn't like. And, again, the nation loved him for it. He lived for the din of the brass bands, the raucous cheers of the crowd, and the acceptance of the fans, especially the Irish fans, to whom he became a symbol in those days when the four-letter sign "NINA" adorned many a household's window—meaning "No Irish Need Apply" for vacancies in either rooms or employment.

For almost twelve years Sullivan led the parade himself, usually fighting in secluded spots—one step ahead of the local constabulary in those days when prizefighting was equated with purse-snatching—and always winning. It was said that if the government were toppled and our most precious assets stolen during a John L. Sullivan fight, nobody would much notice, such was the excitement he engendered.

Finally, his high living and lack of training caught up with him. No longer able to punch foe and bottle alike, suffering the vestiges of high living and low women, the Great John L.—with a tumorous belly, sagging skin, eyes that hung low, and sockets to match—was handily beaten by James J. Corbett for the heavyweight championship.

But even then, he became a martyr, less to failure than to booze. And as such, retained his place in the hearts of sports fans everywhere.

The figure of John L. Sullivan cast a hulking shadow over the American sports landscape for over a decade in that curious era when boxing straddled the worlds of bare knuckles and white gloves. Ironically, it was Sullivan himself who would bring together those two worlds, by demanding the use of gloves. And that may have been the Great John L.'s greatest claim to fame.

100

George Gipp
1895–1920

Notre Dame is at once a patch of land and a state of emotion, its hold over men and monuments rarely relinquished. George Gipp was both, the only problem being: Which part of the Gipp legend was the man, and which part the monument to his greatness?

Trying to draw a portrait of Gipp as well as a tattered record book would allow, we run afoul of the romantic legend of Gipp, propped up with reverential anecdotes. Although some couldn't stand up to the vaguest sort of examination, stand up they have, aided and abetted in no small way by a three-handkerchief potboiler put out by the Hollywood dream factories called *Knute Rockne—All American*. The improbable scenario of this 1940 addition to the folklore of football has Gipp, played by Ronald Reagan, making a deathbed request of Coach Rockne, played by Pat O'Brien, supposedly saying, "Sometime, Rock, when the team is up against it, when things are wrong and the breaks are beating the boys, tell them to go in there and win one for the Gipper. I don't know where I'll be then, Rock, but I'll know about it, and I'll be happy."

He "probably never gave the fabled deathbed speech," wrote Kerry Temple, in *Notre Dame* magazine. Still, it became part of the legend of Gipp, a legend that just kept growing. Acknowledging the mythic proportions of Gipp, H. G. Salsinger wrote, "His punts will grow longer through the years, and so will his passes and runs."

But even if those nonromantics who are given to constantly touching the paint to see if it is really wet do not buy into the "Win one for the Gipper" story—or any one of a dozen other such myths—there is still more than enough hard-hewn fact in the forest of fiction to tell the real story of George Gipp. There is no need to embroider; the truth makes all things plain. And the plain truth is that George Gipp was a remarkable athlete, one of almost unlimited talent who may, in the final analysis, have been every bit as great as the mythmakers tried to make him.

Gipp came to Notre Dame in the fall of 1916, an accomplished basketball, baseball, and pool player who harbored ambitions of playing major-league baseball. If a story told around South Bend is to be believed, Rockne, then a chemistry instructor doubling as an assistant football coach, was strolling across the campus one afternoon, lost in thought. It was a train of thought that never reached its final destination, interrupted as it was by a football sailing over his head. Watching the ball approach its journey's end, some sixty yards away, Rockne quickly turned to see who had been the architect of the prodigious dropkick. What he saw was a handsome, dark-haired six-footer clad in street shoes. "Why aren't you out for the football team?" Rockne is reputed to have asked. "Football isn't my game," said the student punter. "Afraid?" asked the coach with the boxing-glove face and the knuckled nose. A good challenge, then as always, stimulated Gipp's reflexes, and the next day he reported to practice.

Just a few weeks later, Gipp began to repay Rockne's interest in him. Playing against Kalamazoo College, Gipp's freshman squad was tied 7–7, with seconds left in the game. Bogged down in its own territory, Notre Dame lined up in punt formation, with Gipp dropping back to kick. At the snap of the ball one of the Notre Dame linemen streaked downfield to cover the punt. But just as he approached the Kalamazoo safetyman, who'd been poised scant seconds before to field the ball, the safetyman turned to face the goalposts. Conscious now of the cheers in the stands, the lineman asked, "What happened?" "That sonofabitch kicked a field goal," snarled the safetyman, indicating Gipp's seeing-eye dropkick, which had traveled sixty-two yards, straight through the goalposts, for a record that still stands.

The curriculum of Notre Dame was a very wide one indeed, and before the 1917 season rolled around, Gipp had enrolled in several activities, including freshman basketball and track on campus, and cards, pool, and other such adult games off-campus. By the summer of 1917 he was missing in action. Rockne, who by now had made his discovery his personal reclamation project, found the vagabound athlete playing baseball for the Simmons Baseball Club in Kenosha, Wisconsin, and retrieved him in time for the 1917 season.

But despite the greatness hinted at in the third game of the season—against Army, in which Gipp played sixty minutes, outplaying the Cadets' all-American halfback, Elmer Oliphant, and leading Notre Dame to a 7–2 win—Gipp's season ended the following week when, after carrying the ball one time for 35 yards, he was tackled out-of-bounds and thrown into an iron post near the sideline, breaking his leg.

The year 1918 was a coming-out party, of sorts, for both Gipp and Rockne—Gipp as a full-fledged star and Rockne as a head coach. Gipp proved his versatility, leading Notre Dame—then known as the Ramblers—in rushing and passing and punting for a 38-yard average. The next season was to be even better, as Notre Dame won all nine of its games, and the mythic Western Championship, and Gipp, again leading the team in pushing and passing, was named to the all-Western team. His all-around performance was such that Ring Lardner wrote that the Notre Dame team seemed to have one formation: "Line up, pass the ball to Gipp, and let him use his own judgment."

But if Gipp's judgment on the gridiron could be trusted, his judgment off it left something to be desired. With the all-enveloping hand of Prohibition now lying heavy on the land, somehow Gipp had slipped through its fingers and was spending more time at the "speaks" and pool halls than in the classrooms. So much so, in fact, that Notre Dame saw fit to suspend him for absences far above and beyond the call of duty. Rockne, however, petitioned the priests to give Gipp an examination to make up for the previous year's missed classwork. Somehow, some way, Gipp passed, and was readmitted in time for the 1920 season.

The year 1920 was to be Gipp's greatest on the gridiron. And his final one on earth. In his first game, only four days after having been readmitted to school, Gipp gave an indication of both, running for 183 yards, passing for 46, and scoring a touchdown. And suffering an attack of nausea. The attacks were to occur every game from then on through the end of the season. Something else was occurring every game, too: Gipp was betting, and betting heavily, on Notre Dame to win. For the first four games of the season, Notre Dame and Gipp won; its opponents and the bookmakers lost. Then came the heralded matchup against Army.

The game, played at West Point, drew the national press, even the hard-boiled eastern sportswriters who believed that the only brand of football worth watching or writing about was displayed on Ivy League playing fields. In one game, Gipp opened their eyes and changed their minds. Making the most out of his opportunity to impress the incredulous eastern press, Gipp started out with an appetizer: an impromptu pregame dropkick exhibition. After besting the Army point-after-touchdown man, who dropped out after forty yards, Gipp walked to the midfield stripe and called for four footballs. He drop-kicked two of them through one goalpost and then, turning around, sent the other two, on an arrow-straight line, through the opposite goalpost. And if the writers still weren't paying attention, Gipp then put on one of the greatest exhibitions ever seen by eastern sportswriters—or anyone, for that matter—running for 150 yards, passing for 123 more, and returning punts and kickoffs for another 207 as he led Notre Dame to a 27–17 victory that wasn't as close as the final score indicated. The only thing Gipp failed to do was cover a bet he had made that he would outscore the entire Army team.

The scales fell from the sportswriters' eyes as they fell over their typewriters to bang out paeans for the legend they had just seen in action. Some called him a "wonder man." The *New York American* hailed him as "simply amazing. He did everything. He was a host of great backs in himself." And the *New York Herald* echoed the sentiment, saying, "If anything can be done on a football field which Gipp did not do yesterday, it is not discernible to the naked eye."

What also was not discernible to the naked eye was the streptoccus infection that had spread throughout his body. Playing his last game of the season, against Northwestern, Gipp, too weak to play the first half, shined his seat on the bench. Rockne put him in for the second half and Gipp passed six times, completing five for 157 yards and two touchdowns. The day of Notre Dame's final game of the season, against the Michigan Aggies in East Lansing, George Gipp's name was on the critical list at South Bend's St. Joseph's Hospital. Two weeks later, on the day he was selected as the year's outstanding college player in America, George Gipp passed away.

Whether Gipp, on his deathbed, ever said, "Win one for the Gipper...." is still open to question. But it really doesn't matter, for as Frank Leahy, a latter-day Notre Dame coach, once said, "He is still one of us, a very real part of our winning tradition. No, the Gipper didn't die." Nor will his legend, which will live forever.

101s

Reducing the long laundry list of potential candidates for a book entitled *The 100 Greatest Athletes of All Time* was a task tantamount to writing the Lord's Prayer on the head of a pin. Each potential name was studied the way a scientist studies a specimen—probing them, holding them up to the light and analyzing them. Arbitrarily adopting a code, if not of honor them at least of convenience, I finally arrived at the select list, leaving off several who could easily have been worthy of inclusion. Here are the names.

A

Harold Abrahams
Harry Agganis
Tenley Albright
Grover Cleveland
   Alexander
Vasily Alexeyev
Lance Alworth
Mario Andretti
Paul Anderson
Earl Anthony
Arthur Ashe
Evelyn Ashford
Ted Atkinson

B

Hobey Baker
Ernie Banks
Roger Bannister
Charles Barkley
Rick Barry
Frankie Baumholtz
Bob Beamon
Franz Beckenbauer
Chuck Bednarik
Jean Beliveau

Cool Papa Bell
Johnny Bench
Patty Berg
Yogi Berra
George Best
Matt Biondi
George Blanda
Johnny Blood
Albie Booth
Bjorn Borg
Mike Bossy
Ian Botham
Frank Boucher
Lou Boudreau
Donald Bradman
Terry Bradshaw
Valerie Brisco-
   Hooks
Lou Brock
John Brodie
Valery Brumel
Sergei Bubka
Dick Butkus
Dick Button

C

Chris Cagle

Roy Campanella
Malcom Campbell
Milt Campbell
Vera Caslavska
Giorgio Chinaglia
Barney Cipriani
King Clancy
Dutch Clark
Jimmy Clark
Glenna Collett
Lionel Conacher
Maureen Connolly
Eamonn Coughlan
Yvan Cournoyer
Margaret Smith
   Court
Ted Coy
Bustger Crabbe
Steve Cram
Randall
   Cunningham

D

Dave DeBusschere
Eric Dickerson
Harrison Dillard
Marcel Dionne

435

Ollie Matson
Randy Matson
Joe Medwick
Mark Messier
Debbie Meyer
Ann Meyers
Stan Mikita
Rod Milburn
Del Miller
Earl Monroe
Helen Wills Moody
Archie Moore
Howie Morenz
Glenn Morris
Stirling Moss
Marion Motley

N

Joe Namath
Byron Nelson
John Newcombe
Ray Nitschke

O

Parry O'Brien
Sadaharu Oh
Hakeem Olajuwon
Benny Oosterbaan
Steve Ovett

P

Charlie Paddock
Ace Parker
Bob Pettit
Richard Petty
Lester Piggot
Jacques Plante
Gary Player

R

Willis Reed
Mary Lou Retton
Jerry Rice

Bob Richards
Sir Gordon Richards
Bobby Riggs
Cal Ripken Jr.
Paul Robeson
Brooks Robinson
Frank Robinson
Mauri Rose
Ken Rosewall
Jim Ryun

S

Toni Sailer
Alberto Salazar
Earl Sande
Deion Sanders
Gene Sarazen
Mike Schmidt
Milt Schmidt
Don Schollander
Bob Seagren
Monica Seles
Ayrton Senna
Bill Sharman
Wilbur Shaw
Eddie Shore
George Sisler
Tod Sloan
Emmitt Smith
Tommie Smith
Garfield Sobers
Warren Spahn
Tris Speaker
Mark Spitz
Bart Starr
Roger Staubach
Riggs Stephenson
Jackie Stewart
Lynn Swann

T

Fran Tarkenton
Lawrence Taylor
Theogenes

Isiah Thomas
Eric Tipton
Alberto Tomba
Bill Toomey
Jack Torrance
Lee Trevino
Bryan Trottier
Gene Tunney
Wyomia Tyus

U

Al Unser Sr.
Bobby Unser

V

Andy Varipapa
Ellsworth Vines
Lasse Viren

W

Herschel Walker
John Walker
Stella Walsh
Bill Walton
Charlie Ward
Bob Waterfield
Cornelius
  Warmerdam
Tom Watson
Dick Weber
Greta Weitz
Byron "Whizzer"
  White
Mal Whitfield
Dave Winfield
Mickey Wright

Y

C. K. Yang
Cy Young

PICTURE ACKNOWLEDGMENTS

All photographs not otherwise credited below are reprinted with permission of AP/Wide World Photos. The author thanks the following for permission to reprint:

UPI/Bettman: Paavo Nurmi, p. 59; Ty Cobb, p. 77; Bill Tilden, p. 89; Walter Payton, p. 106

The following photographs are from the author's collection:

Jim Thorpe, p. 3; Muhammad Ali, p. 68; Red Grange, p. 80; Sugar Ray Robinson, p. 110; Bill Russell, p. 156; Ben Hogan, p. 169; John L. Sullivan, p. 428.

438

INDEX

439

Ford, Whitey, 340
Foreman, George, 69, 70, 318
Foxx, Jimmie, 178, 417
Foyt, A. J., 360–63
Franklin, Ben, 321
Fraser, Neale, 141
Frazee, Harry, 26
Frazier, Joe, 70, 223, 268
Fregosi, Jim, 369
Friedman, Benny, 327
Friend, Bob, 340
Frisch, Frankie, 323
Fullmer, Gene, 112
Fulton, Fred, 271
Furillo, Carl, 64

Gainford, George, 110
Galento, Tony, 319
Galifa, Arnie, 243
Gallery, Tom, 215
Gamesmanship, 222
Gardner, Bob, 117
Gardner, Maureen, 422
Garrett, Mike, 190
Gatewood, Bill, 415
Gehrig, Lou, 43, 226–30, 263, 264,
    295
Gehringer, Charlie, 417
Geoffrion, Boom Boom, 183
Geronimo, Cesar, 371
Gibson, Bob, 329–34
Gibson, Kirk, 355
Gillman, Sid, 153
Gimeno, Andres, 143
Gipp, George, 430–34
Gola, Tom, 121
Gomez, Lefty, 166
Gonzales, Pancho, 142, 143
Goolagong, Evonne, 310, 312–13
Gordien, Fortune, 406
Gorgeous George, 69
Gorman, Tommy, 298
Gorno, Reinaldo, 128
Gough, Steve, 349
Gowdy, Curt, 219
Graddy, Sam, 52
Graham, Frank, 71
Graham, Otto, 5, 151, 335–38

Grange, Red, 80–83, 91, 106, 163,
    191, 206, 207, 271, 328
Graves, Jackie, 396
Gray, Clinton, 289–90
Grayson, Harry, 33
Green, Sihugo, 159
Grenbenyuk, Aleksandr, 147
Gretzky, Wayne, 129–33
Grimes, Burleigh, 329
Groat, Dick, 240
Grove, Lefty, 324, 329, 332
Groza, Lou, 337
Guillemot, Joseph, 60
Guldahl, Ralph, 353
Gustav V, 12, 144

Hagan, Cliff, 159, 160
Hagen, Walter, 16, 171, 376–79
Haines, Kris, 245, 246
Halas, George, 43, 83, 106, 207,
    316, 327, 328
Hall, Glenn, 297
Hall, Joe B., 250
Hamilton, Brutus, 283
Hare, Charles, 390
Harridge, Will, 416
Harris, Bucky, 324–25
Harris, Danny, 136, 137–38
Harshman, Marv, 202
Haughton, Percy, 10
Hawkins, Connie, 186
Hayes, Elvin, 203
Hearn, Chuck, 124
Heathcote, Jud, 174
Heffelfinger, Pudge, 163
Heilman, Barbara, 291–92
Heinrich, Ignace, 282
Heinsohn, Tommy, 287
Heldman, Gladys, 356
Heldman, Julie, 312
Hemingway, Ernest, 111
Hemphill, Gina, 195
Hemus, Solly, 331
Henie, Sonja, 391–94
Herber, Arnie, 316
Herman, Alex, 415
Heyman, Art, 87
Hickman, Herman, 344–45